teens
@ the library
series

A Core Collection for Young Adults

Patrick Jones
Patricia Taylor
Kirsten Edwards

Neal-Schuman Publishers, Inc.
New York   London

Published by Neal-Schuman Publishers, Inc.
100 Varick Street
New York, NY 10013

Printed and bound in the United States of America.

The paper used in this publication meets the minimum requirements of American
National Standard for Information Sciences–Permanence of Paper for Printed
Library Materials, ANSI Z39.48–1992 ⊚

Library of Congress Cataloging-in-Publication Data

Jones, Patrick, 1961–
    A core collection for young adults/Patrick Jones, Patricia Taylor, Kirsten Edwards.
      p. cm.—(Teens @ the library series)
    Includes bibliographical references and indexes.
    ISBN 1-55570-458-1 (alk. paper)
      1. Teenagers—Books and reading—United States. 2. Preteens—Books and read-
ing—United States. 3. Young adults' libraries—United States—Book lists. 4. Young
adult literature—Bibliography. I. Taylor, Patricia, 1952– II. Edwards, Kirsten, 1965–
III. Title. IV. Series.

Z1037.J66 2003
011.62—dc21

                                       2002045237

DEDICATIONS

From Patrick
To the soon-to-be Dr. Erica Klein.

From Kirsten
To Mr. Dean Edwards, for everything.

From Patricia
*Ballyhoo and gratitude to Mary Earle Popham,
who has made everything happen for me.*

CONTENTS

Don't Miss the Companion Web Site!

Although sites change daily, no core collection today would be complete without easy access to Web sites and other electronic resources. A core collection of electronic resources for young adults is available at *www.connectingya/com/core*

As a special feature to readers of this book, a series of links to "core" YA Web sites and links to information about subscription databases is provided. You can locate its "hidden" location at http://www.connectingya.com/core.htm

SERIES EDITOR'S FOREWORD

Looking over this core collection I recalled an old advertising campaign. Trying to remake their image and sell cars to baby boomers, a memorable ad proclaimed: "This is NOT your father's Oldsmobile!" My guess is the biggest change was the ad campaign and not the car. Unlike the Oldsmobile campaign, I can certainly say: "This is NOT your traditional core collection." It is the culmination of years of research and it is truly the core collection of the teens we serve. Could it become yours?

First, here's a bit of history. During my first ALA conference nearly fifteen years ago, I met Patrick Jones at the YALSA membership reception. He worked in a public library and I worked in a school library, but as we talked we quickly found we had common interests. Prime among these was working with teens, focusing on how teens are served by libraries and librarians. The ideas behind today's *A Core Collection for Young Adults* were percolating even back then.

Patrick soon became a member of the Quick Picks committee whose charge was to select a list of books for reluctant (think typical male) teen readers. I knew he was an innovative voice in the field when he told me with a laugh, "You know, the best thing about being on Quick Picks is that if you read ten pages and hate the book, you just put it down." What a revolutionary concept! Although shocking to me, I knew he was right. As a member of the Best Books for Young Adults committee I was more of a traditional climb-every-mountain/finish-every-book type of reading fiend. Patrick read non-traditionally, eclectically, including lots of nonfiction. His knowledge of the traditional YA canon focused as much on his knowledge of reviews and recommended lists as on the books themselves. Patrick was a forerunner in redefining "teen reading" to mean more than reading novels. He read to pursue particular interests, such as professional wrestling. This meant he regularly read magazines, books that would never make the professional organizations' "best" lists, as well as fan sites on the Web, TV fanzines, and other nontraditional sources. The result? Patrick's lens is exceptional. It tilts toward challenging accepted practices: toward serving the real needs of real teens, not simply some theoretical or idealized teen. And, as Patrick has become recognized as an authority in the field, his slant is consistently and correctly focused on a vision of service that says, "We are not in the business of checking out books to teens. We are in the business of making teens good people."

A Core Collection for Young Adults applies this lens to the development of the YA collection. If I had the opportunity to create a teen collection from scratch, I'd use this book as a starting point. Since I already have a collection in my library that works well now, I'm going to use this book to improve it while considering the needs of my teen customers, my teacher colleagues, and the greater community we serve. In addition to hundreds of annotated titles in fiction and nonfiction, this book includes graphic novels, an area of intense interest with teen boys, as one of the three core collections. Patrick's co-authors, Patricia Taylor and Kirsten Edwards, bring a broad range of experience and intelligence to the task. I'm certain many readers will find the wit and variety of insights they bring to the annotations appealing reading in itself.

The three major areas of coverage are nonfiction, fiction, and graphic format. Within each area you'll find hundreds of titles annotated and ready for you to order to enhance your YA collection. The Sources and Tips section provides additional suggestions to improve and maintain your collection based on published lists, contributions from other librarians and authors, and the authors' personal experience. Indexes by author and title make it easy to find what you're looking for if you want to check for a particular holding.

The introductory chapters describe the methodology and criteria used to select the more than 1,200 titles annotated in this book. As you read the annotations, you'll see that the focus is on what works—the proven books, the perennial high interest subjects, and the real world printed matter that teens read. Teens will check these books out and come back looking for more, and that's a good thing. But the real goal is not just to increase circulation—it is always to create better teens. And these materials will help achieve that important mission.

Joel Shoemaker
teens @ the library Series Editor

PREFACE

WHAT IS A
CORE COLLECTION?

Let's start with what this core collection is not. This is not a Hall of Fame to honor books. There are many important books in the canon of young adult literature that don't show up here because as important as they may have been to the history of the field, the development of an author, or readers of their time, they are books that contemporary readers just won't want to read. This is also not a catalog; it is a very selective list trying to pull out the best of the best. The selected titles have strong reputations, will remain relevant, and are readable and accessible. These are books that teens should find on the shelves of school and public libraries serving young adults today.

HOW DOES A BOOK MAKE
THIS CORE COLLECTION?

This is a core collection for young adults, not a core collection of young adult books. It is not just a matter of semantics. It's a shift in thinking about who drives collection development and the role, in particular in a public library, of the young adult librarian. It's essential to remember that we serve young adult customers, not young adult collections. In many cases, the call to include a title was a "gut" decision based on a book's author, subject, style, or graphic appeal. That stated, our selections are backed-up by the opinions of others in the field. They are also based on observation and conversation with both teenagers and the librarians that serve them. A large part of the selection criteria arose from this totally unscientific test: was the title a book we could visualize a teen holding in her hands and describing as *cool*? Just as important is the knowledge that in young adult sections of most libraries, teenagers are not likely to find a particular book.

SO, THIS IS NOT A CORE
YOUNG ADULT COLLECTION?

This book recommends a core collection of books for young adults; maybe they are in a library's young adult area, maybe they are not. Novels like *Fight Club*, graphic novels like *The Sandman*, or nonfiction works like *The Hot Zone* were not marketed or even written with the teen audience in mind. You can say the same about almost everything by Stephen King, Dean Koontz, or Orson Scott Card. But you cannot deny that teens read and love these books. This is a core collection that is truly customer-focused: it does not matter that much to the teen where in the library the book is located, just that the library owns it. If you are a young adult librarian, your goal can't be just to develop a young adult collection—it is also to make sure that adult and children's collections contain those items teens actually read. We have noted books that are aimed at mature readers (a loose term to describe any book with more than its fair share of four letter slang, sex, and/or graphic violence). For every title, we've provided the suggested grade levels.

OKAY, BUT *THE ONION*?
PSYCHO? ARE SOME OF THESE
SELECTIONS A BIT PSYCHO?

Many titles we considered challenged us to think about that age-old "censorship versus selection" question. Many older teens, especially the "hip and well-read," want edgy stuff with adult themes or humor books that are beyond Garfield. That is going to make a lot of folks very nervous. *The Onion* is funny in a very mean, dark, and often dirty way: their version of Neil Armstrong's first words when walking on the moon are "Jesus Fucking Christ, Houston. We're on the fucking moon!" Does that belong in your young adult collection? Does it belong in your middle school or high school library? That is your call based on your community, but if it is included here, it is our experience that teens do (or do want to) read titles like these, and it is our belief that the titles have worth beyond pure popularity. The core collection we present here is compiled of good books that young adults read; it is your role to determine if they are the best for the young adults you serve—or want to serve.

YOU DID CONSULT THOSE
OTHER BEST LISTS, DIDN'T YOU?

We utilized just about every "best books" list available in print or online (see "Reference Points" section on page 325). We also looked at genre lists, subject lists, and lists produced by teenagers. We culled every issue of *VOYA* since 1992 for titles that got positive reviews, and looked through *Booklist* for starred reviewed books.

WHAT CRITERIA DID YOU USE?

We initially selected titles from reference books, lists, and Web sites. Once found, we asked seven questions about each title. We evaluated in the following large areas: *honors, attraction, approval, originality, quality, pertinence,* and *availability.* If we found we could answer "yes" to most of the following questions, the book was included:

1. *Honors.* Has the book won awards and/or been included on other best lists, in particular those compiled by the Young Adult Library Services Association?
2. *Attraction.* Does the book primarily appeal to teens for use not related to school?
3. *Approval.* Have teens recommended or praised the book with a review on Amazon or other sources recording teen reader response?
4. *Originality.* Is the book significant or groundbreaking? Does it have "cult appeal"?
5. *Quality.* Does the book represent a quality reading experience?
6. *Pertinence.* Is the book relevant to the experience of 21st Century teens?
7. *Availablity.* Is the book in print (as of the publication of this book, of course)?

We can't say that every selected book hits seven for seven from the floor, but most do, and those that are not included fail to live up to one or more of these criteria.

HOW DID THE THREE AUTHORS
DECIDE ON SELECTIONS?

For the most part, Patrick selected the books for inclusion, with Patricia and Kirsten making additional suggestions for inclusion. (For a complete story of this project, read the introduction "A Brief History of the Core Collection" on page xix.)

HOW MANY TITLES WERE ELIMINATED?

Although this collection ended up with more than 1,200 titles, the first rough draft list was twice as long! We dropped many titles because as we started looking at reader reviews, we realized that they were not books young adults recommended to one another. We learned that many good titles, maybe even great titles, were not necessarily core titles. Also, we dropped a lot of books simply because they were out of print.

WHY DOES IT MATTER IF IT IS IN PRINT?

We want this to be a practical volume for developing a collection, so there is no sense in listing lots of great books (like *Crosses* by Shelly Stoehr) that are out of print. A book's in-print status also says something about the reputation of that title. While there are exceptions, core titles should be titles that are in steady demand from librarians, teachers, and teens. Thus, that a book from the 1980s remains in print (and in stock) demonstrates there is still a demand for it. By the time you are reading this, many titles may have dropped out of print, in particular nonfiction self-help titles. In nonfiction while we believe the titles we have selected are strong, even more important are the topics, the areas of the collection which they represent.

WHO IS THE AUDIENCE FOR THIS BOOK?

A Core Collection for Young Adults is for any librarian in a school or public library that works with teens. Parents and teachers might also be interested. Of course, teens might find this book of great interest to guide their reading, as might education/library school students studying young adult reading.

WHY IS THIS BOOK NEEDED?

While many public library systems are increasing their commitment to serving young adults, they often are unable to back up collections with staff: thus, untrained staff need guidance on what to purchase for teens. Likewise, middle, junior, and senior high school library media specialists are actively seeking to expand their collections to better serve today's young adults. Also, lists of materials are what everyone needs at confer-ences ("do you have any handouts with these titles?"). While there is more information than ever about books, given how busy everyone is with technology, they might not be keeping up on building book collections.

How is *A Core Collection for Young Adults* Unique?

This is the first core collection for young adults. Wilson publishes catalogs for fiction, public library, high school, and junior high schools. Bowker does something similar in its best book series, but those titles are purely curriculum-related. The National Council of Teachers of English publishes the *Books for You* series. This series is good; they use a thematic arrangement which means there are perhaps some titles that we would not consider "core" but fit into a slot. Also, since it is a continuing series, new editions focus on new books: for example, *Ender's Game* isn't included in the latest edition. There are lots of really good thematic bibliographies, like *Hearing All Voices*, but the specialized focus means lots of titles are excluded just by the design of the book. Our goal is to create a comprehensive list.

This book is not the same as sources such as *Wilson's Junior High Catalog* or *Senior High Catalog* (for which Patrick consulted), aimed just at one setting, but a core collection which is looking primarily at titles not tied to, or purchased in support of, a school curriculum. Instead, this core collection might be used as an "opening day" collection for a public library with a new young adult area or a secondary school library desiring to increase the amount of recreational reading. Finally, while the Wilson and NCTE sources have editors and most of the annotations are, by nature, primarily descriptive, we are more prescriptive.

Where are the nonfiction series books?

While teen readers were not directly involved in creating this book, we like to think that we are building a true customer-driven connection based on what young adults would want to find to read for pleasure or for personal information, not to complete an assignment. Thus, we decided not to include most nonfiction series books, principally the books published by the "big" names in the library field (such as Chelsea House, Rosen, Watts, etc.) primarily aimed at curriculum support. These books fulfill a function of providing information in a very functional (and rarely fun) way. They are reviewed in the major journals (*Booklist, School Library Journal*, and *Voice of Youth Advocates*), and almost every librarian receives a catalog in the mail from these publishers. Our intent here however, in particular with nonfiction, is to include books which have escaped, for a variety of reasons, the radar screens of many of those working with teens. They are much more likely to be found on the shelves of Borders or Barnes and Noble than most public libraries. They are books which will provide a teenager with a quality reading experience based on personal interests rather than school assignments or curricular topics. We would like to think that most of the books included here might also be included in a teenager's own lists of favorite books that they own or check out frequently. While it is possible that some teens might include series nonfiction titles among their favorites, that would be more the exception than the rule.

WHAT ELSE WERE YOU UNABLE TO INCLUDE?

Non-book library materials such as audio or video selections are not covered here. Also, while you will find fantasy trilogies or books that happen to have inspired sequels, the numbered series aimed at younger young adults are not included. They should be in a core collection, but they change so rapidly that chances are many listed at this writing would be out of print or unavailable by the time you are reading this. Some of the big fantasy sagas with infinite numbers of "episodes" are missing here, and authors like Margaret Weis, Robert Feist, and Mercedes Lackey. While we didn't have a "budgeted" number of titles, some books just didn't make the cut. If we included titles by every author that might have an audience among young adults, we would have a catalog, not a core collection.

There are no books on the events of 9–11 listed here. While there were some fine books to emerge soon after, in particular the graphic format collections, it is unclear, at this time, which titles really belong in the collection.

WHO WERE YOU UNABLE TO INCLUDE?

There is the final and most important exclusion: your customer. This is not necessarily a complete core collection for the Hennepin County Library, the King County Library, the Houston Public Library, St. Agnes Academy High School Media Center, or the Flint Public Library. This is a collection of materials of interest generally to young adults; what belongs in your collection depends on what the young adults you serve need and want. For example, while we have included only English-language books, if your community serves teens who speak other languages, you'll need books in that language.

HOW MANY BOOKS ARE INCLUDED?

There are about 1,200 titles listed. The breakdown is 60% fiction, 30% nonfiction, and 10% graphic formats. This roughly mirrors the results of the reading interest surveys we looked at which asked a question regarding favorite reading formats. It is a big collection, but it is still just a small subset of all the possible books of interest to teens when we expand beyond just young adult literature.

ISN'T THAT QUITE A LOT FOR A CORE COLLECTION?

Yes and no. When you consider that the audience is teen readers with their wide range of interests, that we are not limiting ourselves just to young adult literature, and that we are including graphic formats, this is actually a manageable number. While we don't grade or rank every book, from the other lists included in the book it should be obvious which are the core of the core.

I STILL THINK YOU'RE MISSING A GREAT BOOK. WON'T YOU RECONSIDER INCLUDING (INSERT YOUR FAVORITE BOOK HERE) IN THE NEXT EDITION?

We hope in this preface that we've explained *what* we included, *why* we included, *who* made the decision, and *how* the selection process took place. If you have question or concerns, feel free to e-mail us at ya_core@yahoo.com

DO YOU CONSIDER THIS CORE COLLECTION ALL "GREAT BOOKS"?

A 1999 survey of teens related to reading interests found that most teens said they would read more if they had more time, while anecdotal evidence suggests that teens might read more if they could find the good books. These are the good books. These are the best of the best, but not *only* in terms of literary quality. In fact, this intersection of quality and potential quantity of circulation (popularity) is the main interest of this collection. The primary selection criterion was *the quality of the reading experience.* By that we mean titles which were not merely easily and quickly readable, but also ones that would strike a chord because of a level of quality, interest, or often experimentation. We figured all those aspects into a working definition of "great book."

DO YOU CONSIDER THE
COMPREHENSIVE NATURE OF
THIS BOOK A STRENGTH?

The core collection does illustrate the wide range of the young adult reading experience. There are works here by authors as diverse as Dr. Seuss, Orson Scott Card, Chris Crutcher, and Cynthia Voigt. The titles reflect the sweeping interests of all the young people you encounter and serve. There are books that appeal to 6th graders and those that might appeal to 12th graders. We think that the strength of this book is that instead of focusing only on young adult literature aimed at 6th graders, we look at a wider spectrum of books to connect young adults and libraries. We hope you like the results; we're confident your teen readers will.

ACKNOWLEDGMENTS

FROM PATRICK

Thanks to Ken "The Slack" Rasak for his invaluable help in preparing the manuscript and also to Lisa Isgett for her assistance. Thanks to the usual suspects of Betty Jones, Brent Chartier, and Erica Klein for their support on a personal level, and to the good folks at Book Wholesalers for their support of this project.

FROM KIRSTEN

Thanks to Perry Plush of Zanadu Comics for supporting public libraries above and beyond the call of duty and to the King County Library System's enlightened collection policy, which has made (and kept) a diverse and fascinating body of graphic novels available to its patrons.

FROM PATRICIA

Thanks to every librarian from my childhood on for understanding my need to live in their libraries. Personal thanks to Sandra Shroyer, Susan Begeman, Anabel Woodmansee, Tina Wong, Linda Goldenstern, Kathy Stearman, Gracelyn Brown, and Jani Fuller: Wild Women every one. I love you all.

A BRIEF HISTORY OF THE CORE COLLECTION

The process that went into creating *A Core Collection for Young Adults* reminds me of the catchphrase used to tout an old Hollywood blockbuster, "This movie was ten years in the making!" The first notion for this collection actually began more than a decade ago. It grew out of the first edition of my Neal-Schuman How-To-Do-It Manual *Connecting Young Adults and Libraries*. Readers responded enthusiastically to one appendix called a "core paperback collection." It became one of the most popular and practical sections of that first edition.[1]

That first try at a core collection was helpful but limited. Ten years ago, there was not a great deal of nonfiction in paperback so it focused primarily on young adult paperback fiction. Back then most librarians were interested in young adult books as opposed to books written for adults but of interest to young adults. In the early 1990s, graphic novels were just appearing on the scene and most librarians, myself included, were mystified about what to do with them. We were also clueless about the appeal that traditional graphic formats, such as picture books and comics collections, held for teens.

This initial attempt at creating a core collection for young adults certainly proved an interesting learning experience. Beside the gaps in information, the good-natured scrutiny of colleagues surfaced quickly. Lots of people asked why a certain book was not included – always making a good case for their favorite. It was tempting to please the crowds and include everyone's suggestions, but I had to resist. Including every title would only create a catalog. The challenge was on! Could a genuine core collection for young adults be created? How?

As the challenge germinated, the second edition of *Connecting Young Adults and Libraries* appeared in 1998.[2] In this edition, I removed the single core collection of titles and replaced them with lists (bib squibs) scattered throughout the section on collection development. My intent was not to limit collections to only titles, as much as to examine thoroughly all the general areas of interest to teens. Shifting thinking toward the actual interests of young adults did offer a much larger choice of titles. The drawback? The additional titles teens read only worked if the titles "fit" into one of the categories. This "widened horizon" approach added a key, new perspective on the best way to create a definitive core collection. Over the next few years my interest in a definitive "core collection" grew. I experimented with creating very small lists for my Web site (available at *www.connectingya.com*), as well as publishing several bibliographies in the professional literature.

By the turn of our new century, I challenged myself with the goal of looking over the entire history of the literature for the best books of the previous decade.[3] It was a stimulating time of growth and excellence for the books aimed at young adults as I tried to perfect my core collection lists. The 1990s developed into an exhilarating period introducing a harder edge in YA fiction. Exciting, original voices emerged (such as Michael Cadnum, Rob Thomas, Joan Bauer, and Jacqueline Woodson) while established authors (like Walter Dean Myers and Stephen Chbosky writing for both teens and college students) improved their games. New explosions of fresh interest in adult books for teens, new formats like graphic novels emerging as mainstream, and an increase in quality nonfiction filled our bookshelves and our imaginations.

All of these groundbreaking books made a difference. Many attained cult status and broke open old barriers. Interestingly, I noticed that some were honored with awards or inclusion on year-end "best lists," while others were ignored. My suspicion years earlier was becoming increasingly true. Any core collection selection would necessarily be subjective. In response, I wrote "Overlooked Books of the 1990s" for *Booklist* with Jennifer Hubert. This was our entirely subjective list, for the most part disregarding the opinions of others, to advocate certain books that we felt had never received their due.

I also recognized that any truly authentic core collection for young adults would need a panoply of smart and wide-ranging opinions. There were certainly lots of other interesting opinions about remarkable books for young adults to consider, often appearing as reviews in professional journals. The best of these review journals is *Voice of Youth Advocates* (*VOYA*) because it uses front-line young adult librarians as reviewers. It also draws on a broad scope of books — looking not only at the manuscripts published by the young adult houses but also at anything of interest to teen readers. *VOYA* also employs a unique rating system. That system assigns numerical values to the quality (Q) and perceived popularity (P) of the book. The very best books earned a 5 Q ("hard to imagine it being better written") and 5 P ("every YA who reads was dying to read it yesterday") rating. I dubbed these titles "perfect tens" since their total review score is 10 (5Q + 5P) and published an article with the top forty books reviewed in the years 1996 – 2000 (dates of review, not of publication) which meet that criterion.[4] This was a perfect list to consider for a book on a core collection.

Another building block was put in place around this time when I discovered that not all of the Printz Award honor books received perfect tens from *VOYA* upon their publication. The Michael L. Printz Award was created by the Young Adult Library Services Association (YALSA) as "an award for a book that exemplifies literary excellence in young adult literature." (It is named in honor of a Topeka, Kansas, school librarian who was a long-time active member of YALSA and a passionate advocate for teens reading "best books.") The first award was handed out in January 2000 to honor books published in 1999. I wondered about all those great books published before the establishment of the award. Which of those books would have won the Printz had it been around at the time of their publication?

Sarah Cornish and I developed the "Retro Mock Printz" project with a goal of naming, for the *VOYA* years (since 1978), the best young adult book for each year.[5] The goal of the project was to name the best young adult book, aka a Mock Printz, retrospectively from 1978–1999. Our vision was to create a process involving others who would have both the interest and ability to make these choices. We put together a final ballot with what we felt were the top ten books in each of those years and then asked a select group of young adult literature experts to choose one "Mock Printz" winner for each year. The voters were selected for their knowledge of young adult literature and represented a large cross section in terms of geography and professional affiliation. They voted and thus provided a list of the single best book for each year since 1978.

Another keystone built into this core collection has been my experience training librarians to serve young adults in school and public libraries. At these training sessions, I offer librarians ideas for thinking about building, then promoting, their collections. They learn how to create active young adult spaces, merchandise, and market materials, organize teen advisory groups, perform booktalks, and develop programs. Yet, it is obvious that despite all the training about the context, development, and promotion of a collection, what people really want and need are *titles* for their collections.

They want the titles to create an excellent core collection or enhance an existing one—a collection that encompasses not just the best young adult novels, but the vast range of teenagers' reading interests. In many training sessions, I conduct an attention-grabbing exercise called "the big one" where librarians identify the most important books any library should have for young adults. Essentially, *A Core Collections for Young Adults* is the ultimate list of the "big ones."

My first core collection in 1992 was based largely on my personal reading at the time. Today, I no longer work full time as a young adult librarian and some of the actual reading I was able to enjoy in that guise has been unavoidably curtailed. In my new role as a library and young adult consultant and researcher, the ability to actually read the materials for the age group has changed. The upside? While I have not read as many of the books, I have read a great deal more *about* the books.

The last decade of expansion in the market also mirrors the explosive increase in the Internet. This tandem growth between books and the Web helped make a vast amount of information available. That fact made compiling this core collection easier than ever to research and assemble. So in addition to surveying a large number of print sources, the infinite possibilities of the Internet allowed me to gather lots and lots of lists. (Both paper and electronic resources are listed in Source 1, "Reference Points.")

I happily explored the plentiful number of lists. I used ones from Amazon, including those put together by teens. In addition I checked records compiled on listservs such as PUBYAC and YALSA-BK. They have provided real insight into not only what books librarians and teens read but also why they enjoy reading them. Via the Internet, I could also easily find the greatly expanded "best" lists put out by YALSA: the Alex list for best adult books for young adults, scores of popular paperbacks lists, and, of course, the new Printz Award winners list.

As you can see, many "resource building bricks" have led to the "selective structure" of books in *A Core Collection for Young Adults*. Perhaps the greatest element added to the research has been the remarkable human element. My teamwork with my co-authors Patricia Taylor and Kirsten Edwards (you can read more about them in the "Introduction") has greatly added to the selection and the soul of the book. We three, in turn, have had the great opportunity to communicate and collaborate with other professionals passionately interested in teens and reading. The occasion to work directly with a great number of teenagers has also made the project as fun as it is real. The products, the process, and the people have come together to create a guide we designed to be as inspiring and interesting as it is useful.

Patrick Jones

NOTES

1. Jones, Patrick. *Connecting Young Adults and Libraries: A How To Do It Manual.* 2nd revised and expanded edition. New York: Neal-Schuman, 1998.

2. Jones, Patrick. *Connecting Young Adults and Libraries: A How To Do It Manual.* New York: Neal-Schuman, 1992.

3. Hubert, Jennifer and Patrick Jones. "Overlooked Books of the 1990s." Booklist v. 97 no. 21 (July 2001). 1998–9.

4. Jones, Patrick. "The Perfect Tens: The Top Forty Books Reviewed in

Voice of Youth Advocates 1996–2000." *Voice of Youth Advocates* v. 24 no. 2 (June 2001). 94–9.

5. Cornish, Sarah and Patrick Jones. "Retro Mock-Printz: The Best of the Best of the Best of Young Adult Literature." *Voice of Youth Advocates* v. 25 no. 4 (scheduled for December 2002 issue).

GENERAL GUIDELINES

A Core Collection for Young Adults is divided into a small number of basic parts. Each part of the reference tool may be used independently, but a front-to-back review is recommended. These guidelines provide a map to the guide. Also covered in this section is "How To Use the 'Collection Checker' CD-ROM" explaining the accompanying title-checker disk. (This information is repeated on the last page, opposite the disk on the inside back cover.)

Next comes the great bulk of the book – more than 1,200 fully annotated titles that make up the actual Core Collection. Chapter 1 is "Nonfiction," Chapter 2 is "Fiction," and the third chapter is "Graphic Formats."

Following that primary part of the book comes a variety of resources and useful support material. "Sources and Tips" includes:

- A guide to more than 100 "Best Books" lists
- Top 10 tips for maintaining a core collection
- Completely subjective choices of selections for a "Core Bookshelf" from leading librarians and authors
- A consensus "Core Bookshelf" list
- Selection tips for major YA genres

The book ends with two useful indices to effectively cross-reference the core collection. One is an author index: the other a title index.

ADVICE AND EXPLANATIONS

Arrangement of the Core Collection:

- The Core Collection is divided into three parts: Nonfiction, Fiction, and Graphic Formats.
- Nonfiction is arranged first by Dewey classification number and then within each section alphabetically by author. Fiction and Graphic Formats are arranged alphabetically by author.

- Each entry contains the following bibliographic information:
  - Author
  - Title, in italics, boldfaced
  - Number of pages
  - Publishing Information: Publisher; date of publication; paper, library, or trade designation; ISBN number; and price
  - Annotation of contents
  - Suggested grade level, boldfaced
  - Reviewers initials, boldfaced

A Word About Bibliographic Format:

- With few exceptions, core collection titles were in print at the time of this book's publication.
- We tried to list all in-print formats (paper, library, and trade cloth).
- The grades are based on both suggestions from the Book Wholesaler's database and our knowledge. Generally, grade 6 is the lowest, grade 12 is the highest. An item with a suggested range of 6 – 12 means it might be of interest and appropriate for all young adult readers. Generally, materials are suggested as being either for grades 6–9 or grades 10–12.
- The page numbers and call numbers are based primarily on catalog records from the Hennepin County (Minnesota) Library.
- Our bibliographic information is designed as an accurate guide rather than an absolute catalog record. We suggest that you consult your vendor's database before ordering items.

About Genres:

- For the most part, we have included full bibliographic information on only the first book in a series or trilogy. That is just a matter of space. For example, in the Shannara series by Terry Brooks, we've only fully annotated and "bibbed" the first book, but within the annotation noted that all books in the series are part of a core collection. Likewise, for graphic formats like collected comics by Gary Larson, Bill Watterson, and Matt Groening, we've listed just one title but noted that all of the works by these authors should be considered.
- For the most part, *short story collections* are included here only if they are the collected works of one author or if the editor is well known.
- *Biographies* present the normal challenges. For the most part, we have opted to put biographies in the subject area rather than at 921.

- In addition to graphic novels, we have included all other graphic formats, including picture books, comic collections, and books of photographs, nonfiction cartoon books, Japanese anime/magna, and illustrated short stories. In addition, there are a few books about graphic formats listed that would certainly be of great interest to teen readers and seemed to "fit" better here than with nonfiction. We've put Shel Silverstein here although one could certainly make a case for his books to go into poetry, but because the illustrations really drive Silverstein's popularity among teen readers, we opted for inclusion here.

Key to abbreviations:

- (Annotation by guest annotator; see full list in Source 3)
- **HIPPLE** = Have You Read selection
- **KE** = annotation by Kirsten Edwards
- **LOST** = Lost Books of the 1990s.
- **(Mature)** Contains mature subject matter, themes, and/or language
- **MOCK** = Mock Retro Printz Winner
- **PJ** = annotation by Patrick Jones
- **PRINTZ** = Printz Winner/Honor book
- **PT** = annotation by Patricia Taylor
- **TEN** = VOYA Perfect Ten
- **YALSA** = Best of the Best 2001

Notes on "Sources and Tips":

- Source 1 is a mixed list of electronic and paper resources of the more than 100 "Best" lists consulted. They are arranged alphabetically. Bibliographic information is cited for paper, URLs are provided for Internet resources.
- Source 2 is a simple "top ten" list of tips for maintaining a collection.
- Source 3 is a list of more than 35 ideal "Core Collection" lists provided by leading librarians and authors. Each complete list is arranged alphabetically by the person who created it. Professional information for each creator is listed. The actual list of books they selected is arranged alphabetically by author.
- Source 4 is a consensus list of the top 30 books in Source 3. Each of these books appeared on at least five of the dream lists.
- Source 5 is three essays, one by each of the authors, on approaches to selection by genres.

Notes on Indexes:

- The author index provides a matching title. It cross-references all of the core collection and is arranged alphabetically by author.
- The title index matches to author. It cross-references all of the core collection and is arranged alphabetically by title.

HOW TO USE THE
"COLLECTION CHECKER" CD-ROM:

- The book you're holding includes a companion CD-ROM component located on the inside back cover.
- The CD-ROM contains several files, each of which holds basic bibliographic information for each title in the recommended core collection for young adults.
- The different file types present the core collection in a variety of ways different librarians will find useful for different purposes. Note: You can use the Excel files to create a database in Access.

The represented formats are:

1. Four **Excel (.xls)** files arranged author, title, call number, and publisher
2. Four **Word (.doc)** files arranged author, title, call number, and publisher
3. Four **Text (.txt)** files arranged author, title, call number, and publisher
4. One **Database Four (.dbf)** arranged by author
5. One **Comma Delimited Format (.csv)** arranged by author
6. One **Rich Text Format (.rtf)** arranged by author
7. One **MS-DOS** with layout (**.asc**) arranged by author
8. One **Works4 (.wk4)** arranged by author
9. One **Data Interchange Format (.dif)** arranged by author

You can use these electronic files to facilitate:

- collection maintenance,
- selection decisions,
- acquisitions, and
- reading guidance and promotion.

For example, you could:

- Send one of the files to your online catalog provider and ask them to run it against your collection to identify core collections titles your library doesn't own;

- Use the file arranged by call number to check your nonfiction holdings in a particular Dewey class or range;
- See which fiction titles we recommend as "core" by a particular YA author or authors;
- Cut-and-paste information from the disk to generate ordering lists for your book jobber or even "wish lists" for your school's PTA group or your library's foundation or Friends group.

To access the files:

1. Insert the CD-ROM in your drive.
2. Open your software program (Word, Excel, Access, Dbase, program, or your text compatible word processing program).
3. Click the "Open File" command (make sure you've selected the proper drive and file format, if applicable).
4. Open the "Core Collection Disk" folder.
5. Click on the file you want.
6. All the files are "read only" from the Disk. To use them, simply save them to your computer.

Or PC users may prefer to simply:

1. Open the sliding disc drawer on your computer.
2. Place the CD-ROM in the drive and close the door.
3. Click on the "My Computer" icon on your desktop.
4. Click the "Core Collection" folder to open.
5. Click the file you want to open.

We hope you'll find the array of file formats and arrangement to be a time-saving device. If you have difficulty accessing these formats, contact Patrick Jones (*Patrick@connectingya.com*).

A FINAL NOTE:

No core collection today would be complete without Web sites and other electronic resources. But they change daily. A core electronic collection for young adults is available at: *www.connectingya/com/core.*

As a special feature to readers of this book, my Web site will feature a series of links to "core" YA Web sites and links to information about subscription databases.

THE CORE COLLECTION

CHAPTER 1

NONFICTION

001 Coleman, Loren. ***Cryptozoology A to Z: The Encyclopedia of Loch Monsters, Sasquatch, Chupacabras, and Other Authentic Mysteries.*** 270 pages.

Fireside 1999 Paper 0684856026 $14.00

An encyclopedia with nearly 200 entries and plenty of illustrations about creatures walking the believe-it-or-not line. **Grades 6—12. PJ**

001 Lemonick, Michael D. ***Other Worlds: The Search for Life in the Universe.*** 272 pages.

Simon & Schuster 1998 Trade 0684832941 $24.50

Lemonick, a writer for *Time*, takes more of a *People* approach, and with great success. In an attempt to explain the variety of hard-core research taking place to determine the possibility of life beyond earth, Lemonick focuses on three scientists and their work. Thus, while the book is a survey, it is also a great narrative about three individuals attempting to reach a goal. What the book demonstrates is that the search for alien life is not just the stuff of parapsychology; real science organizations (such as NASA) are developing technology to find out if the truth is really out there. Accessible, entertaining, and thought provoking, the success of the book is that it really isn't about science at all, but about the search for what truth lies behind speculative fiction. **Grades 9—12. PJ**

Reviews: *Booklist* 4/1/1998

001 Marrs, Jim. ***Alien Agenda.*** 434 pages.

HarperCollins 1998 Paper 0061096865 $6.99
HarperPerennial 2000 Paper 0060955368 $15.00

Jim Marrs is a classic conspiracy buff; his books are always looking for the truth behind the big lie. Here, the lie is that UFOs and aliens don't exist; Marrs, of course, thinks otherwise. But his beliefs are based on facts he has discovered from eyewitnesses, his own investigations, and information from "highly classified CIA reports."

The book is proof of an alien agenda, using 50-plus years of evidence. It's all here: from crop circles to *Chariots of the Gods* to alien abductions to Roswell. The conclusion is the premise—we are not alone. Even worse, Marrs argues that the "Smoking Man" is real and that people at the highest level of government know the truth but keep it from us. Fascinating stuff for those who believe, maybe even for those who want convincing. **Grades 10–12. PJ**

---

004 Hafner, Katie. ***Where Wizards Stay Up Late.*** 434 pages.

Touchstone 1998 Paper 0684832674 $14.00

A readable account of how www and @ became part of daily life. Using both secondary sources and interviews with participants, the authors trace the Internet from its military beginning through the days of hackers and e-entrepreneurs. While Al Gore is not mentioned, the vital role that the federal government played in sponsoring the scientists who created the basic foundation for a wired world is the dominant theme. **Grades 10–12. PJ**

---

004 Katz, Jon. ***Geeks: How Two Lost Boys Rode the Internet out of Idaho.*** 304 pages.

Broadway Books 2001 Paper 0767906993 $12.95

Since the Internet is taking over the social life of teenagers, this book shows how two young guys found a social life and career without a college degree. The additional comments from teenagers explain how the Internet is a place where all can and should be accepted no matter what they look like or what their interests are. **Grades 9–12. AP**

---

031 Adams, Cecil. ***The Straight Dope.*** 301 pages.

Ballantine 1998 Paper 0345422910 $12.00
Ballantine 1986 Paper 0345333152 $6.99

Cecil Adams, no doubt a pen name, is the sharp-tongued age of irony answer to Mr. Science. The Straight Dope column by Adams appears in the *Chicago Reader* and is syndicated across the country. Readers ask, Adams answers, but it is all about attitude. The questions tend toward the scatological, while Adams' retorts are half good research and half insult humor. The irreverence of Adams' pen matches nicely the bizarre drawings of artists Slug Signorino (sure, that's a real name too). Later volumes contain information from the Straight Dope Web site/AOL home as Adams tackles the vital questions of the universe such as "Where is Podunk?" and "Why is it called missionary position?" Lots of sequels, but this is the real deal. **Grades 10–12 (mature). PJ**

---

031 **The Guinness Book of World Records.** (annual publication).

Some teens may have already heard about this book. The small paperback edition is fine, but the oversized, heavily illustrated hardback version is spectacular. **Grades 6–12. PJ**

031 Panati, Charles. **Panati's Extraordinary Origins of Everyday Things.** 463 pages.

HarperCollins 1989 Paper 0060964197 $16.00

For lovers of facts, students of popular culture, history buffs, and science enthusiasts, here are the fascinating stories behind 500 everyday items, expressions, and customs —from Kleenex to steak sauce, Barbie Dolls to honeymoons. **Grades 9–12. PJ**

031 Zacks, Richard. **Underground Education: The Unauthorized and Outrageous Supplement to Everything You Thought You Knew about Art, Sex, Business, Crime, Science, Medicine, and Other Human Knowledge.** 417 pages.

Ballantine 1999 Paper 0385483767 $16.95

A big title for a big book that provides lots of info, plus photographs, on stuff you never learned in school, such as research on decapitated heads. With a penchant for the gross-out, Zacks' twisted view of history and human knowledge is informative and entertaining. **Grades 10–12 (mature). PJ <LOST>**

070 Block, Francesca Lia. **Zine Scene: Do It Yourself Guide to Zines.** 120 pages.

Girl Press 1998 Paper 0965975436 $14.95

Despite the easy availability of publishing on the Internet, zine culture still thrives in many communities as teens cut, paste, and photocopy as a vehicle for self-expression. Block and Carlip gathered the best of zines as examples and offer advice on the ins and outs of zine life. **Grades 7–12. PJ <LOST>**

Reviews: *VOYA* 8/1/1999

100 Irwin, William. **The Simpsons and Philosophy: The D'oh! Of Homer.** 303 pages.

Open Court 2001 Paper 0812694333 $17.95

A collection of essays that looks "beyond the yellow" of the Simpsons television family in search for deeper meaning. And finds it. The purpose of the book is not so much to analyze the comedy of Groening and company as to let readers understand great philosophers by using characters from the long-running hit show. For example, one essay uses Bart to examine the ideas of Nietzsche. A book as good as floor pie. Mmmm, floor pie. **Grades 10–12. PJ**

Reviews: *Booklist* 4/15/2001

---

100 Weate, Jeremy. *A Young Person's Guide to Philosophy.* 64 pages.

Dorling Kindersley 1998 Paper 0789430746 $16.95

The book asks the big questions, such as "Why are we here?" and "Is there such a thing as evil?" and then lets some of the great thinkers in history attempt to answer the questions. The usual great DK mix of text and graphics creates an easy-to-read book about hard ideas. **Grades 6–9. PJ**

Reviews: *SLJ* 1/1/1999, *Booklist* 12/15/1998

---

133 Crawford, Soffi. *The Power of Birthdays, Stars, and Numbers.* 831 pages.

Ballantine 1998 Trade 0345418190 $24.95

Astrology meets numerology in this pseudo-science self-help book. There are profiles for every birthday that provide readers with everything they need to know about themselves in order to succeed in life and in love. **Grades 8 –12. PJ**

Reviews: *SLJ* 4/1/1999

---

133 Gravelle, Karen. *5 Ways to Know About You.* 159 pages.

Walker 2001 Paper 0802775861 $10.95
Walker 2001 Trade 0802787495 $16.95

If the teen years are about a search for identity, then it is not surprising that the junk-science shortcuts that seem to have all the answers are wildly popular among many young adults. Five of the most popular personality pointers—astrology, palm reading, numerology, Chinese horoscopes, and handwriting analysis—are explored in this book. Each chapter provides basic information about one of the topics, but there are also charts, graphics, and cartoon drawings to illustrate various points. **Grades 6–9. PJ**

Reviews: *SLJ* 1/1/2002, *VOYA* 12/1/2001

---

133 Ravenwolf, Silver. *Teen Witch: Wicca for a New Generation.* 251 pages.

Llewellyn 1998 Paper 1567187250 $12.95

A guidebook to the Wicca way of life that doubles as a self-help guide. The book lays out both the facts and fiction about Wicca, while at the same time offering teens advice on a wide variety of issues, such as the relationships in their lives. Like any religion, Wicca has its rules and rituals, which are discussed in detail. While there are many in the community, including parents of teen occult dabblers, who might object to this volume, it is a best seller that speaks to the needs of many teens searching for spiritual answers. **Grades 7–12. PJ**

---

133   Reid, Lori. ***The Art of Hand Reading.*** 120 pages.

Dorling Kindersley 1999 Paper 0789448378 $13.95
Dorling Kindersley 1996 Trade 0789410605 $24.95

Does one ever get tired of writing "another great DK package"? Mixing easy-to-read text with hundreds of illustrations, this volume is loaded with everything anyone could need to know about palmistry. There are photos, illustrations, charts, diagrams, and illustrations that provide not only illumination but also practical how-to advice for teens on how to read their minds by reading their palms.
Grades 7–12. PJ

Reviews: *Booklist* 10/15/1996, *SLJ* 3/1/1997, *VOYA* 8/1/1997

133   Starwoman, Athena. ***How to Turn Your Ex-Boyfriend into a Toad and Other Spells: For Love, Wealth, Beauty and Revenge.*** 121 pages.

HarperCollins 1996 Paper 0732257093 $11.00

Starwoman has written the *Vogue* magazine horoscope for years and began regular astrological columns for the *Star* in 1994. In this collection of spells, she provides mystic and Wicca teen girls with a handbook for getting their way. The book is not aimed directly at teens; however, they will be interested in the love spells in particular, while others will turn right to the "naughty spells for naughty girls" section.
Grades 10–12. KE

153   Barrett, Susan. ***It's All in Your Head: A Guide to Understanding Your Brain and Boosting Your Brain Power.*** 151 pages.

Free Spirit 1992 Paper 0915793458 $10.95

An easy-to-read guide that introduces teens to the basics of psychology and brain development. There's plenty of info on neurons and the like, but also on subjects such as dreams, memory, and intelligence. **Grades 6–9. PJ**

Reviews: *Booklist* 2/15/1993, *VOYA* 1/1/1995

153   Jung, Carl G. ***Man and His Symbols.*** 320 pages.

Laurel-Leaf 1997 Paper 0440351839 $7.99

Jung's last book before his death in 1961, this may be the philosopher's most important work for the layman public. Here is his lifework in psychotherapy presented in terms the nonprofessional can understand, emphasizing that the human imagination must be a study of serious undertaking because it is the most important component of the human being. With illustrations and a full index, this volume is nothing less than a must-have. **Grades 10–12. PT**

154   Parker, Julia. ***Parker's Complete Book of Dreams.*** 208 pages.

Dorling Kindersley 1955 Trade 1564588556 $24.95

From DK comes one of the better dream books available, thanks to the illustrations that accompany the fairly standard text, which hits all the right notes. **Grades 7—12. PJ**

Reviews: *Booklist* 8/1/1997, *SLJ* 8/1/1995

---

154   Shaw, Tucker. ***Dreams: Explore the You That You Can't Control.*** 160 pages.

Penguin Putnam 2000 Paper 0141309202 $5.99

A perpetual teen favorite subject nicely handled in another alloy.com book. After some basic information on sleep and dreams, Shaw looks at specific patterns or themes within dreams. Again, lots of illustrations, sidebars, quotes, and poll results create a reader-friendly presentation. **Grades 7—12. PJ**

Reviews: *VOYA* 2/1/2001

---

155   Galbraith, Judy. ***The Gifted Kids' Survival Guide: A Teen Handbook.*** 295 pages.

Free Spirit 1996 Paper 1575420031 $15.95

A guide for kids at the top of the class. Filled with quotes, teen voices, tips, tools, and techniques, this book allows gifted teens to understand their gifts, accept them, and make use of them. This is meant for gifted teens and the adults who interact with them. **Grades 6—12. PJ**

Reviews: *Booklist* 8/1/1997, *SLJ* 2/1/1997

---

158   Adderholdt-Elliot, Miriam. ***Perfectionism.*** 129 pages.

Free Spirit 1999 Paper 1575420627 $12.95

A perfect title for many of the teens found lurking in the stacks of school and public libraries. Like all of Free Spirit's titles, the book is like a supportive friend: never judgmental, always encouraging. Based on interviews with "straight A" students, this book helps teens understand the differences between goal-directed ambition and out-of-control perfectionism. Filled with solid advice, the book will help perfectionists understand their behavior and become aware of the "mind traps" they fall into, while offering practical strategies. One section discusses why girls are more prone to suffer from perfectionism. **Grades 7—12. PJ**

Reviews: *Booklist* 1/1/1995

---

158   Benson, Peter. ***What Teens Need to Succeed.*** 311 pages.

Free Spirit 1998 Paper 1575420279 $14.95

As the Search Institute message about developmental assets catches on, this prospective how-to book will be remembered as the turning point. Translating research findings into life-improvement suggestions, this might be one of the most important books for any library collection. **Grades 6–12. PJ <LOST>**

Reviews: *SLJ* 4/1/1999, *VOYA* 8/1/1999

---

158   Carlson, Richard. ***Don't Sweat the Small Stuff for Teens: Simple Ways to Keep Your Cool in Stressful Times.*** 242 pages.

Hyperion 2002 Paper 0786887656 $9.95
Hyperion 2000 Paper 0786885971 $11.95

Carlson, a motivational speaker and author of a best selling *Don't Sweat the Small Stuff* series for adults, turns his attention to teens, and he gets theirs. Methods to cope with the daily stresses of teen life played out against the backdrop of schools, family rooms, and fast food restaurants are described. In simple, straightforward language, Dr. Carlson addresses common teen concerns with chapters such as "Make Peace with Your Mistakes," "Be Okay with Your Bad Hair Day," "Turn Down the Drama Meter," and "Notice Your Parents Doing Things Right." **Grades 6–12. PJ**

Reviews: *Booklist* 12/1/2000

---

158   Covey, Sean. ***The 7 Habits of Highly Effective Teens.*** 268 pages.

Simon & Schuster 1998 Paper 0671582755 $12.00

Covey's father's seven-habit shtick made him rich, and now his son keeps the family business cooking with a success guide for teens. Patterned after his father's book and with a similar crisp writing style, Covey provides a step-by-step guide to help teens improve self-image, build friendships, resist peer pressure, achieve their goals, get along with their parents, and make good decisions. The text is augmented with quotes, real-life teen stories, and a few cartoons. **Grades 7–12. PJ**

---

158   Frill, John C. ***The 7 Best Things (Smart) Teens Do.*** 284 pages.

Health Communications 2000 Paper 155874777X $12.95

Written by a husband and wife therapist team, this advice volume contains stories, examples, and strategies meant to provide teens with the tools to thrive in their lives. While the book focuses on teens' assets, attention is paid to at-risk behavior, such as eating disorders and drug abuse, and how to avoid them. **Grades 6–12. PJ**

Reviews: *SLJ* 12/1/2000

---

158 Graham, Stedman. ***Teens Can Make It Happen: Nine Steps to Success.*** 250 pages.

Simon & Schuster 2000 Paper 0684870827 $14.00

Another successful motivational writer turns his sights toward the teen market, offering young people the tools they need to succeed. The message isn't new, but Graham's high-energy prose and his own hard work story make this volume stand out. **Grades 7—12. PJ**

---

158 Hipp, Earl. ***Fighting Invisible Tigers.*** 153 pages.

Free Spirit 1995 Paper 0915793806 $12.95

This enjoyable, easy read offers proven, practical advice to adolescents interested in acquiring stress- and life-management skills. The section "Self-Care for Tiger Bites" offers immediate first aid for those times when fast relief is needed to relieve high levels of stress. **Grades 6—12. PJ**

---

158 Mayall, Beth. ***Get over It!: How to Survive Breakups, Back-Stabbing Friends and Bad Haircuts.*** 119 pages.

Scholastic 2000 Paper 0439114659 $4.99

From *Teen* magazine comes a sassy guide for girls on getting through life's pitfalls. The core advice for almost any situation is the same: stay calm, gather information, express yourself, and then make a decision you can live with, even if it means some short term pain. The book tries to gives teens that one thing that most of them lack: perspective—demonstrating that regardless of the situation, there is always a way to cope and to carry on with life. Often very funny, including some fantasy revenge pranks and teen true confession tales, mostly the book helps teens help themselves survive painful situations, thereby preventing them from taking more drastic measures. **Grades 7—12. PJ**

---

158 McGraw, Jay. ***Life Strategies for Teens.*** 236 pages.

Fireside 2000 Paper 074321546X $14.00

An interesting new subgenre: the teen version of an adult best seller. Jay McGraw, son of best-selling author Dr. Phil McGraw, uses the same themes and gimmicks found in his father's *Life Strategies* to help teens succeed in life. The book is organized around "ten life laws." Each law is explained and expanded, with the central message being that teens should take control of their lives by making good decisions. McGraw encourages teens to overcome obstacles, set goals, and then lay out time-lines and strategies for meeting those goals, all the while pumping up readers in a writing style that one reviewer compared to "the enthusiastic pounding zeal of an aerobics instructor." **Grades 7—10. PJ**

158 Packer, Alex J. **_Highs! Over 150 Ways to Feel Really, Really Good...Without Alcohol or Other Drugs._** 264 pages.

Free Spirit 2000 Paper 1575420740 $15.95

Another great Free Spirit book loaded with positive advice for teens communicated in a friendly, nonpreachy, sometimes funny manner. Packer's offers alternatives to substances for teens, but in doing so, is really helping teens build assets. By increasing their self-esteem, by becoming involved in the community, and in so many other ways, teens can develop the skills they need to resist drugs and alcohol abuse. **Grades 8—12. PJ**

Reviews: _Booklist_ 11/1/2000, _SLJ_ 9/1/2000, _VOYA_ 10/1/2000

158 Shaw, Tucker. **_Who Do You Think You Are?: 12 Methods for Analyzing the True You._** 159 pages.

Puffin 2001 Paper 014131091X $6.99

Self-help books are abundant, as are books on junk science, but this offering from Alloy mixes both strands to come up with a unique volume. While there are certainly longer books on topics such as horoscopes and numerology, the presentation here is lively. In addition to the text, there are quizzes, charts, diagrams, and illustrations to help teen readers understand and make use of the various methods of self-discovery discussed. **Grades 7—12. PJ**

158 Shriver, Maria. **_Ten Things I Wish I'd Known—Before I Went Out into the Real World._** 125 pages.

Warner 2000 Trade 0446526126 $19.95

Although this book's origin is a college commencement speech, older teens will find much here of interest. Shriver illuminates her 10 life lessons with stories, examples, and her own personal experiences, writing, "It is within you to carve out your own future, create your own destiny. I wrote this book so that you might be spared. Not from having to learn the lessons I had to learn. No one can spare you that, because learning is experiential, and you have to do it yourself. As a wise person once told me: If I could spare you the pain you're experiencing, I wouldn't—because I wouldn't want to deprive you of the strength and wisdom you'll gain from having gone through it and come out the other side." **Grades 10—12. PJ**

158 Williams, Terrie. **_Stay Strong: Simple Life Lessons._** 218 pages.

Scholastic 2002 Paper 0439129729 $4.99
Scholastic 2001 Trade 0439129710 $15.95

From its "hip" cover to the introduction by TV pitch-woman-cum-rapper Queen

Latifah, Williams takes a truly fresh approach to the teen advice book. Williams, a successful female African American businesswoman, uses quotes from rappers and other successful African Americans, as well as examples from her own life, to inspire and encourage teens. **Grades 7–12. PJ**

Reviews: *Booklist* 5/15/2001, *SLJ* 6/1/2001, *VOYA* 6/1/2001

---

158 Youngs, Bettie B. ***Taste Berries for Teens: Inspirational Short Stories and Encouragement on Life, Love, Friendship and Tough Issues.*** 344 pages.

Health Communications 1999 Paper 1558746692 $12.95

While this is a *Chicken Soup* knock-off, Dr. Youngs has plenty of experience writing self-help manuals for teenagers as well as speaking/consulting on teen mental health issues. In this volume, Dr. Youngs teams with her daughter to collect writings of teens and then provide commentary on topics such as self-worth, friendship, love and relationships, parents, coping with stress, and decision making. **Grades 6–12. PJ**

---

191 Pirsig, Robert M. ***Zen and the Art of Motorcycle Maintenance.*** 438 pages.

HarperPerennial 2000 Paper 0060958324 $13.00
HarperCollins 1974 Trade 0688002307 $26.00

Declined by 95 publishers before being signed in 1974, *Zen and the Art of Motorcycle Maintenance* has become something of a must-have on the off roads of the literary landscape. Exploring the question of how to reconcile the supremacy of modern technology with the necessity of philosophical and artistic pursuits, Phaedrus (Pirsig) sets off with his son on a cross-country motorcycle trip. During their odyssey, we learn a great deal about keeping a motorcycle in repair, but the lessons are really metaphors for the art of Zen, the becoming one with whatever task presents itself. Offbeat and original, the book works on many levels. **Grades 10–12. PT**

---

248 Dobson, James. ***Life on the Edge.*** 291 pages.

Word 2000 Trade 0849909279 $19.99

Dobson, the leader of the organization Focus on the Family, presents his views on decision making for young people. Issues such as education, relationships, and career choices are discussed, all in the context of leading a healthy Christian life. **Grades 10–12. PJ**

Reviews: *Booklist* 3/15/1995

---

291 Ford, Michael Thomas. ***Paths of Faith: Conversations about Religion and Spirituality.*** 259 pages.

Simon & Schuster 2000 Trade 0689822634 $17.00

Teens are not just searching for their place in the world; many are also wondering about their place in the universe. In this volume, various religious thinkers recall their teens years and the discovery or strengthening of their spiritual side. A dozen different faiths are represented, including Wicca. In addition to the interviews, there are short essays to set up the piece followed by a resource list for teens wanting more information. **Grades 7–12. PJ**

> Reviews: *Booklist* 10/1/2000, *SLJ* 1/1/2001

291 Wilkinson, Philip. ***The Illustrated Dictionary of Mythology.*** 128 pages.

> Dorling Kindersley 1998 Trade 078943413X $24.95

Another fabulous DK offering about a topic that to many teens is their starting off point for reading fantasy. With information about gods and myths from all over the world set side-by-side with colorful DK-quality illustrations, this is a browsing title with reference and readers' advisory value. **Grades 6–12. PJ**

294 Ikeda, Daisaku. ***The Way of Youth: Buddhist Common Sense for Handling Life's Questions.*** 189 pages.

> Middleway 2000 Paper 0967469708 $14.95

A different kind of self-help book for teens based upon Buddhist principles. Using the student/teacher or question/answer style, Ikeda provides teens with the Buddhist perspective on handling most of the issues in their lives. Ikeda is the president of the Soka Gakkai International Buddhist renewal movement and has received the United Nations Peace Award. **Grades 6–12. PJ**

> Reviews: *Booklist* 12/1/2000

297 Wormser, Richard. ***American Islam.*** 130 pages.

> Walker 2002 Paper 0802776280 $8.95

Recently republished in the wake of 9–11, Wormser's book provides a broad overview of the history of Islam and then focuses on the challenges facing Muslims growing up in the United States. **Grades 6–9. PJ**

301 Agee, James. ***Let Us Now Praise Famous Men.*** 471 pages.

> Houghton Mifflin 1989 Paper 0395488974 $16.95
> Marine 2001 Paper 0618127496 $17.00
> Houghton Mifflin 2000 Trade 0395957710 $30.00

What started as a magazine assignment turned into one of the great works of nonfiction as James Agee and Walker Evans set out on assignment to explore the daily lives of sharecroppers in the South. Using text and photo, they captured tenor, texture, and daily harshness of the times. It was recognized by the New York Public Library as one of the most influential books of the 20th century. **Grades 10—12. PJ**

---

301 Allison, Anthony. ***Hear These Voices.*** 16 pages.

Candlewick 2001 Paper 0763613959 $4.99
Dutton 1999 Trade 0525453539 $22.99

The big buzz around young adult fiction in the late 1990s was how it present-ed a bleak view of teenagers. So-called "reality" fiction, it was argued, didn't really reflect the daily life of teenagers. Those critics need to read the stories here about the grimness of the lives of many teenagers. Allison just clicked his camera and turned on his tape recorder, asking questions and recording the answers about the lives of 15 at-risk youths from all over the world. Youths who have been sold into prostitution at age 10, youths whose only homes have been the streets, youths who have been gang-raped, youths who have never known a night without violence in their native lands, and youths who have grown up in circumstances in which it seems not even hope could sur-vive. But it does, as along the way each of these young people has found an adult or an organization of adults who have helped to pull them from the abyss of their existence. As Allison clearly demonstrates by recording the graphic language and gritty lives of these teens, young people should always have hope in a better tomorrow. **Grades 9—12. PJ**

---

305 Alicea, Gil. ***The Air Down Here: True Tales from a South Bronx Boyhood.*** 134 pages.

Chronicle 1995 Trade 0811810488 $14.95

What if S. E. Hinton grew up in the Bronx rather than Tulsa? The result might have looked something like this collection of autobiographical essays by Gil Alicea, penned when he was only 16 years old. The hundred-plus essays are almost prose poems in which Alicea examines his life growing up in the South Bronx. And while the urban landscape of countless TV shows chock-full of sirens and street gangs is the center of many of Gil's sketches, matters closer to home and heart are also explored, with humor often the rhetorical weapon of choice. The essays are about identity as Gil tries to establish his voice and his life as a young Puerto Rican-American in the face of over-hyped stereotypes about city teens. While his words paint the picture vividly, the book is also illustrated with Gil's own black-and-white photos. **Grades 7—10. PJ <LOST>**

Reviews: *SLJ* 3/1/1996, *Booklist* 10/15/95

---

305 Bass. Ellen. ***Free Your Mind.*** 417 pages.

HarperCollins 1996 Trade 0060951044 $15.95

Free Your Mind is a guide for gay, lesbian, and bisexual youth—and their families, teachers, counselors, and friends. The book speaks to the basic aspects of the lives of gay, lesbian, and bisexual youth: self-discovery; friends and lovers; family; school; spirituality; community. Bass mixes practical advice from professionals with voices of gay youth to discuss issues such as coming out, making healthy choices, connecting with other gay youth, and presenting info for adults who want to make the world safer for lesbian, gay, and bisexual youth. **Grades 8–12. PJ**

Reviews: *Booklist* 6/1/1996

305 Brumberg, Joan Jacobs. ***The Body Project: An Intimate History of American Girls.*** 267 pages.

Vintage 1998 Paper 0679735291 $13.00

The author was described by *Entertainment Weekly* as "an academic Judy Blume," and that is not far off. Body image is a major concern for teen girls (not to mention teen and preteen fiction) and Brumberg simply asks, and answers, the question of how that came to be. Using diaries, photos, letters, and other archival material, Brumberg explores girls' attitudes about the size, shape, and workings of their bodies throughout history. **Grades 7–12. PJ**

Reviews: *SLJ* 4/1/1998, *VOYA* 8/1/1998

305 Carroll, Rebecca. ***Sugar in the Raw: Voices of Young Black Girls in America.*** 144 pages.

Crown 1997 Paper 0517884976 $14.00

One of the many books to be built on the foundation provided by *Reviving Ophelia*, this collection of interviews with young, black women aged 11–18 is indeed raw, but also filled with energy, enlightenment, and hope. Carroll talked to 15 young, black women looking for the truth of their lives. They talk about the good, the bad, and the ugly in their lives, but the focus is always on keeping hope alive. **Grades 7–12. PJ <LOST>**

305 Daldry, Jeremy. ***The Teenage Guy's Survival Guide.*** 136 pages.

Little, Brown 1999 Paper 0316178241 $8.95

In this British import, Daldry takes on the usual growing-up questions, but in a flip, often sarcastic, and more than often humorous style. Brutally honest in tone and language, helped along by cartoon illustrations, the whole package is a 90s alterna-tive, edgy version of the old staple *Boys and Sex*. **Grades 7–12. PJ**

Reviews: *Booklist* 5/15/1999, *SLJ* 7/1/1999, *VOYA* 10/1/1999

305 Ford, Michael Thomas. ***OutSpoken: Role Models from the Lesbian and Gay Community.*** 240 pages.

Morrow/Avon 1998 Trade 0688148964 $16.00

Ford interviewed 11 members of the GBLT community. While there are some celebrities here (a cartoonist, a sitcom actor, and a boxer), there are also "normal" people living life out of the closet. Ford asks his subjects about their experiences coming out, their involvement in GLBT issues, and their words of wisdom and inspiration. **Grades 7—12. PJ**

Reviews: *Booklist* 5/1/1998, *SLJ* 6/1/1998

---

305 Gaskins, Pearl Fuyo. ***What Are You?: Voices of Mixed-Race Young People.*** 273 pages.

Henry Holt 1999 Trade 0805059687 $18.95

Gaskin spoke with young people around the country who are of mixed race. For the most part, she gets out of the way and allows her interview subjects, ranging from age 14 to age 26, to tell their own stories. In addition to the oral accounts, there are also poems and essays, as well as Gaskins' occasional commentary. Gaskins, herself a person of mixed-race, brings in the voices of social scientists and psychology to add context, but the colorful words of the young people tell stories as diverse as they themselves are. **Grades 7—12. PJ**

Reviews: *Booklist* 5/15/1999, *SLJ* 7/1/1999

---

305 Gray, Heather. ***Real Girl/Real World.*** 221 pages.

Seal 1998 Paper 1580050050 $14.95

A self-help guide for older teenage girls written from a feminist perspective. The catalog of subjects is similar to other self-help books, but the focus is not only on helping young women build self-esteem but also on placing some topics into a larger social context. While there is old-fashioned advice and how-to information, the bulk of the book records teen voices. The teens quoted offer their own perspectives, sometimes not always the "popular" views. **Grades 8—12. PJ**

Reviews: *Booklist* 10/1/1998, *SLJ* 3/1/1999, *VOYA* 2/1/1999

---

305 Locker, Sari. ***Sari Says: The Real Dirt on Everything from Sex to School.*** 326 pages.

HarperCollins 2001 Paper 0064473066 $11.95

Banned in Iowa (as of this writing), this is indeed the dirt and the real deal. Locker is the *Teen People* online advice columnist and she's got plenty to say, always with a frank, yet friendly, tone. Locker doesn't talk down to her readers, instead she is honest in answering questions. And that's what got the book banned, as some sections of the book were deemed "too sexually explicit." Sex is not the only topic here: Locker is the oracle for all things adolescent, including old saws like friends and cliques, and the stuff of 21st-century teen life like piercing, tattooing, and interracial dating. **Grades 6–12 (mature). PJ**

Reviews: *SLJ* 2/1/2002, *VOYA* 4/1/2002

---

305 Mastoon, Adam. *The Shared Heart.* 87 pages.

HarperTempest 2001 Paper 006447304X $6.95

A collection of portraits and profiles. Photographer Mastoon captures the images of 39 GLBT teens and lays those photos next to short essays in which the subjects write frankly about their sexuality. While readers learn about each person, together the picture and words capture the essence of what it means to be a gay teen; thus, this is as inspirational as it is informative. Emily Saliers of the folk duo the Indigo Girls is blurbed on the jacket saying, "This book will save lives." **Grades 9–12. PJ**

Reviews: *Booklist* 11/15/1997, *SLJ* 2/1/1998

---

305 McCune, Bunny. *Girls to Women; Women to Girls.* 212 pages.

Celestial Arts 1998 Paper 0890878811 $14.95

A collection of short essays, letters, stories, and poems from girls and women around the globe. The format may differ, but the subject remains the same: facing the pressure of growing up female. One teen reviewer on Amazon noted, "I found it very inspirational and encouraging.... it's a book that grows with you. I VERY strongly recommend this book." **Grades 9–12. PJ**

Reviews: *SLJ* 4/1/1999

---

305 Morgenstern, Mindy. *Real Rules for Girls.* 111 pages.

Girl Press 2000 Paper 0965975452 $14.95
Pocket 2002 Paper 0743457250 $15.00

Produced by Girl Press, this is a sassy guidance-laden volume loaded with quips and quotes to help young women understand how to interact with the world around them. The usual suspects of sex and drugs appear, as do parents, pals, and partners. What separates this title from the pack is the smart and occasional smart-ass tone as well as hip retro photos. It is as much about attitude as advice. **Grades 8–12. PJ**

Reviews: *Booklist* 3/15/2000, *SLJ* 3/1/2000, *VOYA* 4/1/2000

---

305 Packer, Alex J. *Bringing Up Parents.* 264 pages.

Free Spirit 1993 Paper 0915793482 $14.95

While most library shelves are loaded with books on parenting teenagers, this is one of the few aimed entirely at the teen side of that relationship. While most teen self-help books touch on improving relationships at home, Packer gives it his full attention in this friendly, funny tome. While certainly not for every teen, this advice book is packed with suggestions and ideas to lessen the seemingly necessary turmoil at home. *Parent's Choice* magazine noted, "This book should be on everyone's required reading list." **Grades 8–12. PJ**

Reviews: *Booklist* 5/1/1993

---

305 Paul, Anthea. *Girlosophy.* 319 pages.

Paul 2001 Paper 1865084328 $16.95

It looks like an over-sized fashion catalog, but it is packed with information to help young women develop their personalities, not their accessories. As the title suggests, the book presents a new way of thinking, with a "new age" bent. There is lots of talk about re-centering and karma, but whatever the means, the ends are to provide young women with the tools to improve their health, expand their intellectual boundaries, and achieve emotional balance. Sequels on the way. **Grades 10–12. PJ**

Reviews: *SLJ* 11/1/2000, *VOYA* 6/1/2002

---

305 Potash, Marlin S. *Am I Weird or Is This Normal?: Advice and Info to Get Teens in the Know.* 271 pages.

Simon & Schuster 2001 Paper 0743210875 $13.00

One of Amazon.com's Best of 2001, this is a different kind of teen advice book, one focusing mostly on girl issues. Teen self-help tomes fill the void left in so many households where parents and children don't talk about important issues and share vital information. In the Potash household, that conversation served as the inspiration for this book co-written by a mother and daughter team. Honest, straight forward, and always positive, the family Potash strives to help girls help themselves by answering common questions, dispensing the occasional nugget of advice, and always stressing issues like self-esteem and self-respect. The usual suspects of sex, puberty, and friendships are covered, always with an eye back to the title and the larger question of what does normal mean? **Grades 8–12. PJ**

Reviews: *Booklist* 8/1/2001

---

305 Rosenberg, Ellen. *Growing Up Feeling Good: The Life Handbook for Kids,* 4th Edition. 544 pages.

Viking 1989 Paper 0140342648 $11.99
Lima Bean 2002 Paper 0971134901 $18.00
Beaufort 1987 Trade 0825304210 $9.95

Oversized and overstuffed with important information for young teens about the changes in their lives and now in its 4th edition, this book guides young people on a wide range of issues, such as friendship, popularity, peer pressure, sex, family issues, and getting along at school. Regardless of the "problem," the answer is based on young people's making healthy choices from solid information and self-confidence. **Grades 6–9. PJ**

305 Scholinski, Daphne. ***The Last Time I Wore a Dress.*** 211 pages.

> Berkley 1998 Paper 1573226963 $13.00
> Putnam 1997 Trade 1573220779 $23.95

A memoir that really sounds too unbelievable to be true. Daphne Scholinski came from a dysfunctional home. Her mother left to pursue her education leaving Daphne and her sister with their abusive father. Like many teens, Daphne started acting out. One of her more defiant acts was to refuse to act at all like a girl. Instead she assumed the persona of a total tomboy. But this rebelliousness was reacted to sharply: she was locked away for three years in a mental hospital, her condition classified as gender identity disorder. In addition to the usual round of therapy, groups, and medications, Scholinski was "force fed" femininity, from wearing make-up to learning how to walk "like a girl." **Grades 7–12 (mature). PJ**

> Reviews: *Booklist* 10/15/1997

305 Sonnie, Amy. ***Revolutionary Voices: A Multicultural Queer Anthology.*** 259 pages.

> Alyson 2000 Paper 1555835589 $11.95

Another book that gives voice to youth to share their experiences, both good and bad. Sadly, in this volume, many of the stories are filled with fear, loneliness, confusion, self-hatred, and outright despair. If these were really voices, many were screaming while others were too choked with tears to speak. Yet even within the most chilling experiences, the very act of sharing the hurt brings hope and support. Unlike most anthologies, this is not merely a collection of prose and poetry, although those are ample; the volume also contains artwork, letters, diaries, monologues, and short plays. With teens from all over the country from so many different backgrounds having their say, this collection really does help give voice to GLBT youth proclaiming pride, even through the memories of pain. **Grades 9–12. PJ**

> Reviews: *Booklist* 12/1/2000, *SLJ* 2/1/2001

305 Weston, Carol. ***Girltalk,*** 3rd Edition. 352 pages.

> HarperCollins 1997 Paper 0060928506 $14.00

Now in its third edition, this "bible" of information for girls 11 through 18 was blurbed by the editor of *YM* magazine as "a must for every young woman's library." **Grades 6–9. PJ**

306 Mannarino, Melanie. ***The Boyfriend Clinic: The Final Word on Flirting, Dating, Guys and Love (Seventeen).*** 120 pages.

HarperCollins 2000 Paper 0064472353 $6.95

Seventeen knows boyfriends. It knows the "right" answers to big questions posed on the lips of its readers: How do I get a boyfriend? Is he the right guy for me? How do I get him to notice me? Should I make the first move? How can I say no without hurting his feelings? How do I know it's really love? Is it okay if I don't want a boyfriend right now? A breezy guide through navigating the dating maze based on the magazine content and teens' question-filled letters. **Grades 7–12. PJ**

Reviews: *Booklist* 3/15/2001

323 Archer, Jules. ***They Had a Dream: The Civil Rights Struggle from Frederick Douglass to Marcus Garvey to Martin Luther King and Malcolm X.*** 258 pages.

Puffin 1996 Paper 0140349545 $6.99

Using these four major figures as his starting point, Archer tells the story of the civil rights movement from the fight for freedom from slavery, to the post-Civil War era, to the civil rights struggle of the 1950s and 1960s. The book concludes with a chapter titled "The Black Struggle Today and Tomorrow," written soon after the Rodney King riots in 1992. More than biography, the tenor of the times is reflected so readers understand the context from which each of these leaders emerged and how their lives changed the landscape of civil rights and American life. **Grades 6–9. PJ**

Reviews: *Booklist* 1/1/1995, *SLJ* 1/1/1995

323 Beals, Melba Pattillo. ***Warriors Don't Cry: A Searing Memoir of the Battle to Integrate Little Rock's Central High.*** 312 pages.

Archway 2000 Paper 0671899007 $5.99
Washington Square 1995 Trade 0671866397 $14.00

In 1957, at the same time the Russians were sending Sputnik into orbit, kicking off the space age, the Civil War was still being fought in Arkansas. It was three years after the famous *Brown v. Board of Education* ruling calling for the end of segregated schools, but a black child had yet to set foot in a Little Rock school. Beals was one of the first of the group who finally made it, accompanied by soldiers from the 101st Airborne. Based on her diary, Beals retells her story about those historic events in an uplifting narrative that brings those events back into focus. **Grades 6–9. PJ**

Reviews: *SLJ* 3/1/1995, *VOYA* 8/1/1995

323 Griffin, John Howard. **Black Like Me.** 192 pages.

Signet 1962 Paper 0451192036 $6.99

As of 1996, this memoir has enjoyed its 35th edition and has well earned its place as an American classic. In 1959, during the peak of racial conflict in the United States, John Howard Griffin took a sojourn through the Deep South disguised as a black man. With his chemically darkened skin, Griffin discovered the truth about segregation in all its stark ugliness. Viewed as a half-human by whites, he encountered ignorance, stupidity, and cruelty, all sparked by his color. He also experienced painful exchanges with a few white southerners who offered him apologies and shame for what "their people" did to him. No history book has ever sustained the suspense, the tension, and the clear banality of evil that is racism the way Griffin's has. The laws may have changed, but *Black Like Me* has lost none of its power or its horror. **Grades 8–12. PT**

---

323 Hamilton, Virginia. **Many Thousand Gone: African Americans from Slavery to Freedom.** 151 pages.

Alfred A. Knopf 1993 Library 0394928733 $18.99
Alfred A. Knopf 1995 Paper 0679879366 $12.95

The focus is more on slavery than on freedom as Hamilton pulls from personal narratives of slaves from the beginning of the slave trade in the United States through the Civil War. The horror of slave life is clearly represented: being bought and sold, families torn apart, and always violence. Coupled with illustrations from Leo and Diane Dillon, Hamilton's text is ultimately not one of defeat or despair, but of courage, faith, and, finally, freedom. **Grades 6–9. PJ**

Reviews: *Booklist* 12/1/1992, *SLJ* 5/1/1993

---

323 King, Coretta Scott. **The Words of Martin Luther King, Jr.** 112 pages.

Newmarket 1991 Paper 093785879X $10.00
Newmarket 1984 Trade 0937858285 $15.95
Newmarket 2001 Paper 1557044503 $6.95

A selected collection of Dr. King's most important texts, such as the "Letter from Birmingham Jail"; the "I Have a Dream" speech; and his Nobel Prize acceptance speech. While reading the speeches is no match for hearing King's rousing voice on tape or watching him on video, these are essential readings for teens interested in history, civil rights, and social justice. **Grades 6–12. PJ**

---

323 Levine, Ellen. **Freedom's Children: Young Civil Rights Activists Tell Their Own Stories.** 167 pages.

Puffin 2000 Paper 0698118707 $6.99

While most of the images of the civil rights movement are of leaders like Dr. King or of marchers joined hand-in-hand, this volume shows the young people who were at the forefront of this political crusade. In this inspiring collection of true stories, 30 African Americans who were children or teenagers in the 1950s and 1960s talk about what it was like for them to fight segregation in the South—to sit in an all-white restaurant and demand to be served, to refuse to give up a seat at the front of the bus, to be among the first to integrate the public schools, and to face violence, arrest, and even death for the cause of freedom. A *School Library Journal* Best Book of the Year and *Booklist* Editors' Choice, this is a great example of "teen voices" telling their own stories: empowering stuff. **Grades 6–9. PJ**

323 McCall, Nathan. ***Makes Me Want to Holler: A Young Black Man in America.*** 416 pages.

Vintage 1995 Paper ISBN: 0679740708 $14.00

Using his own experiences as a backdrop, McCall examines racism in the United States. While McCall was able to make it out of his poor, working class, primarily black neighborhood to achieve success as a reporter for the *Washington Post*, it was not without first spending time in prison for armed robbery. He knows that others have been unable to make the same journey out, blocked by political, social, and cultural walls, as well as succumbing to temptations for short-term success. While the book is inspirational, it is primarily about McCall's anger at the racism that still plagues America. **Grades 9–12. PJ**

323 Meltzer, Milton. ***There Comes a Time: The Struggle for Civil Rights.*** 193 pages.

Random House 2000 Library 0375904077 $18.99
Random House 2002 Paper 0375804145 $8.99
Random House 2000 Trade 0375804072 $16.95

Meltzer's book starts with a scene of four young black men refusing to give up their seats at a lunch counter in the South during the 1960s. That incident, and thousands like it, are the small acts of resistance that mark the civil rights movement in Meltzer's narrative. While he covers the roots of the movement, it is the events of the 1960s that form the bulk of the book. The book ends, perhaps metaphorically, soon after the assassination of Dr. King. Though somewhat lacking in photographs, especially given the stock available, Meltzer manages to put readers in the shoes of those sitting in the back of the bus and the actions it took to stop that insanity. **Grades 6–9. PJ**

Reviews: *Booklist* 2/1/2001, *SLJ* 1/1/2001

323 Parks, Rosa. ***Rosa Parks: My Story.*** 192 pages.

Puffin 1999 Paper 0141301201 $5.99
Dial 1992 Trade 0803706731 $17.99

If there is one moment that epitomizes the civil rights movement, it is the day in Alabama when Rosa Parks said "no" to moving to the back of the bus. Almost every book about the movement features this scene prominently. Parks tells her version of that event. In addition, Parks talks about her role in the civil rights movement after helping launch the bus boycott and, thus, the career of Martin Luther King. Like her act on the bus, her book is straightforward and courageous. **Grades 6–9. PJ**

Reviews: *Booklist* 12/15/1991, *SLJ* 2/1/1992

323 Williams, Juan. ***Eyes on the Prize: America's Civil Rights Years 1954–1965.*** 300 pages.

Viking 1987 Paper 0140096531 $15.95

This companion to the highly acclaimed PBS television series is loaded with photos and quotations from those who participated in the major events of the civil rights movement. Williams, a respected journalist, provides a smooth narrative of the flow of events from *Brown v. Board of Education* through the march on Selma. **Grades 7–12. PJ**

324 Boyers, Sara Jane. ***Teen Power Politics.*** 120 pages.

Twenty-First Century 2000 Library 0761313079 $24.90
Millbrook 2000 Paper 0761313915 $9.95

While the audience might be small, this book packs a big message about how teens can get involved in making a difference in their communities. Filled with first-person accounts of teen activism and some history, Boyers mixes in political cartoons as well as a catchy, almost zine, feel to get her message across. **Grades 6–12. PJ**

Reviews: *Booklist* 11/15/2000, *SLJ* 1/1/2001

325 Bode, Janet. ***The Colors of Freedom: Immigrant Stories.*** 141 pages.

Franklin Watts 1999 Library 0531115305 $24.00
Franklin Watts 2000 Paper 0531159612 $9.95

Bode went through over 1,000 student writings and interviews to create this volume of teen stories. These teens have left their homes in the Caribbean, the Middle East, Africa, and Asia to come to the United States. In their stories, Bode relates the terrible circumstances many left behind, as well as the numerous barriers they face—and often overcome—in their new homeland. **Grades 7–12. PJ**

Reviews: *Booklist* 1/1/2000, *SLJ* 3/1/2000, *VOYA* 8/1/2000

325 Budhos, Marina. ***Remix: Conversations with Immigrant Teenagers.*** 325 pages.

Henry Holt 1999 Trade 0805051139 $16.95

In 14 interviews with new Americans from Latin America, Asia, Europe, Africa, and the Caribbean, Budhos records and retells stories about facing huge obstacles to growing up. But unlike many other authors of the "teens tell their own story" genre, Budhos becomes part of the story herself when she meets a young woman with whom she develops a special kinship. **Grades 9–12. PJ**

Reviews: *Booklist* 9/15/1999, *SLJ* 11/1/1999, *VOYA* 12/1/1999

---

326 McKissack, Patricia C. **Rebels Against Slavery.** 181 pages.

Scholastic 1998 Paper 0590457365 $4.50
Scholastic 1999 Paper 0590662597 $5.99
Scholastic 1996 Trade 0590457357 $14.95

While perhaps Abraham Lincoln is credited with "freeing the slaves," what the McKissacks make clear is that many slaves, like Gabriel Prosser and Nat Turner, were taking matters into their own hands. While documenting the assistance of whites and Native Americans, the spotlight is on the black slaves who not only fought for their own freedom by escaping, but planned and executed schemes whereby other slaves fought their way out of chains. There are photographs of many of the principals of these revolutionary heroes. This is as much a collective biography about courage as it is history. A Coretta Scott King Honor Book and a Best Books for Young Adults selection. **Grades 6–9. PJ <YALSA>**

Reviews: *Booklist* 2/15/1996, *SLJ* 3/1/1996

---

327 Melton H. Keith. **The Ultimate Spy Book.** 176 pages.

Dorling Kindersley 1996 Trade 0789404435 $29.95

In this heavily illustrated DK volume, Melton peeks into the world of espionage, finding it full of amazing gadgets and secret agents. Melton's main task is to separate spy fact from pop culture, James Bond-like fiction. While one part of the book is history, tracing the history of spies, the focus is more on the daggers than the cloak. Melton has amassed a dazzling collection of spy devices, from listening devices to assassination devices. **Grades 6–12. PJ**

Reviews: *Booklist* 8/1/1997, *SLJ* 7/1/1996, *VOYA* 10/1/1996

---

331 Bartoletti, Susan Campbell. **Growing Up in Coal Country.** 127 pages.

Houghton Mifflin 1996 Trade 0395778476 $17.00

An award-winning photo essay about the young boys who worked in the coal mines before the child labor laws. Bartoletti weaves into the text personal details, quotes from those who survived, and family stories to present a true "snapshot" social history of life growing up, and dying early, in coal country. **Grades 9–12. PJ**

Reviews: *Booklist* 12/1/1996, *SLJ* 2/1/1997

---

331 Freedman, Russell. ***Kids at Work: Lewis Hine and the Crusade against Child Labor.*** 104 pages.

Clarion 1998 Paper 0395797268 $9.95
Clarion 1998 Trade 0395587034 $20.00

Freedman is to youth biography what Ken Burns is to documentaries: he chooses interesting subjects and photographs to tell America's story. While this is in part a biography of Lewis Hine, one of the leaders in creating child labor laws, the real subject is the social and political history of early 20th-century America. The photos of children working in mines, factories, and other unsafe conditions are in some ways more shocking today than when Hine took them in his work as an activist in the 1920s. **Grades 6–12. PJ**

Reviews: *Booklist* 1/1/1995, *SLJ* 1/1/1995

331 U.S. Department of Labor (Editor). ***Occupational Outlook Handbook.***

Rosen 2000 Paper 0823925447 $16.95
NTC 2000 Trade 0658002260 $22.95

It seems like a report book and it is not very exciting, but as young adults ask themselves questions about what they want to do with their lives, this chestnut provides roadmaps and reality checks. **Grades 6–12. PJ**

338 Schlosser, Eric. ***Fast Food Nation: The Dark Side of the All-American Meal.*** 356 pages.

Houghton Mifflin 2001 Trade 0395977894 $25.00
HarperPerennial 2002 Paper 0060938455 $13.95

This anti-McDonalds tome will find an audience among certain groups of teenagers. While there is certainly some of *The Jungle*-like description of the meat-packing industry, Schlosser is looking deeper. He looks at the entire chain of food, from farm to market to counter. He exposes some of the fast food chain's ugly secrets. But for all the food, the real concern is people. From the migrant workers who pick the food to those risking their lives in meat-packing plants, to the overworked, overstressed, underpaid, and more than occasionally harassed cadre of teenage workers who fuel a fast food economy. **Grades 10–12. PJ**

Reviews: *Booklist* 1/1/2001

345 Kuklin, Susan. ***Trial: The Inside Story.*** 160 pages.

Henry Holt 2000 Trade 0805064575 $17.95

A look inside the workings of the criminal justice system told through a case study. *School Library Journal* noted that the book was like an episode of television's *Law & Order*, documenting first the crime, then the police investigation, followed by the trial. Like that show, however, the narrative takes several twists and turns, and read-ers are not always sure actually what or how to believe. The text is augmented with stark black-and-white photos of judges and lawyers, as well as the evidence. The appendix includes a simple chronology of the case, notes, and a necessary glossary, although legal terms are defined throughout the book in sidebars. **Grades 7–12. PJ**

Reviews: *Booklist* 12/15/2000, *SLJ* 1/1/2001, *VOYA* 2/1/2001

346 Jacobs, Thomas. ***Teens on Trial.*** 197 pages.

Free Spirit 2000 Paper 1575420813 $14.95

"History is not made by great men" is the underlying theme in this collection about court cases involving ordinary young people. In each case, such as the famous *Tinker v. Des Moines* case from the 1960s, young people had the courage not only to stand up, but to fight for their rights. The cases discussed are all of concern to teens: dress codes, locker searches, school prayer, sexual harassment, birth control, free speech, drug testing, and even the death penalty. The book begins with basic information on the legal system, which is then followed by a thematic arrangement of famous cases. The facts are presented as they would be in court, and then followed with a series of questions asking the reader to think about the issues involved. **Grades 7–12. PJ**

Reviews: *Booklist* 1/1/2001, *SLJ* 1/1/2001

346 Jacobs, Thomas. ***What Are My Rights?*** 199 pages.

Free Spirit 1997 Paper 1575420287 $14.95

Using a simple question-and-answer format, Jacobs answers the title question for young people. The legal jargon and case citing is kept to a minimum as Jacobs explores almost one hundred questions related to the rights of young people. All aspects of teen life as related to the law are examined, such as legal rights at schools, at home, on the job, and within the legal system. **Grades 7–12. PJ**

Reviews: *Booklist* 4/1/1998, *SLJ* 4/1/1998, *VOYA* 6/1/1998

362 Bolnick, Tina S. ***Living at the Edge of the World: A Teenager's Survival in the Tunnels of Grand Central Station.*** 283 pages.

St. Martin 2000 Trade 0312200471 $24.95
Griffin 2001 Paper 0312284071 $14.95

Go Ask Alice in the world of crack. April befriends Tina, and soon both are living among the homeless, mentally ill, and drugged-out in the tunnels of Grand Central Station. She describes quite graphically her spiral into addiction, the horror of every-day life (including a rape scene), and her attempt to rebuild her life. **Grades 10–12 (mature). PJ**

Reviews: *Booklist* 9/1/2000

362 Burch, Jennings. **They Cage the Animals at Night.** 293 pages.

Signet 1985 Paper 0451159411 $5.99

Before *A Child Called It*, there was this story of a young boy abandoned by his mother and put into the social service system, which isn't a safety net; it is a series of beatings and betrayals. One teen reader on Amazon wrote about the effect of the book: "I just cannot believe a little innocent eight-year-old boy was so mistreated!! Poor Jennings was abused so much it isn't even funny!! I've read this book about a thousand times and broke out in sobs when I read that part about Jennings' friend dying!! OMG!! People, the ending is so wonderful!! I think Jennings Michael's eleventh year was his best!! If you are someone who cares deeply about child care, this book is a must-read!!" **Grades 10—12. PJ**

362 Dominick, Andie. **Needles: A Memoir of Growing Up with Diabetes.** 220 pages.

Simon & Schuster 1998 Trade 0684842327 $22.00.

In this painful, and sometimes graphic, memoir, Dominick recalls the dramatic influence diabetes had on her life. She at first follows the path of her sister, almost rebelling against the disease. But when her sister dies young, Dominick begins to rethink her own behavior and relationship with her body. **Grades 9—12. PJ**

Reviews: *Booklist* 9/1/1998, *SLJ* 5/1/1999, *VOYA* 2/1/2000

362 Hayden, Torey L. **Ghost Girl.** 307 pages.

Avon 1992 Paper 038071681X $5.99

The victim of unspeakable ritual abuse, Jadie chooses to remain mute, walking bent over "to keep her insides from falling out." No one, however, seems to find such behavior amiss until Torey Hayden, Jadie's special education teacher, takes an interest in the odd little girl. *Ghost Girl* is a harrowing story, both for Jadie and for Hayden, who risks a great deal in pursuing the truth about the destruction of an eight-year-old's body and soul. Part of the horror arises from the citizens of the town, who are all too willing to look the other way rather than face the outrages Jadie suffered. Not recommended for those disturbed by revelations of graphic sexual abuse. **Grades 9—12 (mature). PT**

362 Hayden, Torey. **Murphy's Boy.** 315 pages.

Avon 1990 Paper 0380652277 $6.50

In the same vein as *Ghost Girl*, this time Hayden rescues Kevin, a traumatized mute; again, the pathos and suspense create a tension that carries the reader through to the end. **Grades 10—12. PT**

362 Hayden, Torey L. **One Child.** 221 pages.

Avon Paper 0380542625 $5.99

Hayden takes on Sheila, an autistic child with a genius IQ. Abandoned by her mother and abused by her alcoholic father, Sheila is considered a hopeless case; mere serendipity drops her into Hayden's classroom rather than being warehoused in a hospital. Hayden's gifts as a writer stand her in good stead here, particularly in a case that does not resolve itself in a happy ending. **Grades 9—12. PT**

362 Hayden, Torey L. **Tiger's Child.** 254 pages.

Avon 1996 Paper 0380725444 $6.50
Macmillan 1995 Trade 0025491504 $21.00

The sequel to *One Child*, *The Tiger's Child* rediscovers Sheila in her early teens. Torey Hayden locates her after years of trying, and the reunion is not an easy one. Thought-provoking and sad, the account of an abused child growing into a confused young adult is a testament both to Hayden's determination never to give up, and to the grievous reality that sometimes in human salvage it may be too late. **Grades 10—12. PT**

362 Kaysen, Susanna. **Girl, Interrupted.** 168 pages.

Vintage 1994 Paper 0679746048 $12.00

Diagnosed with borderline personality disorder, Susanna Kaysen was committed to McLean Hospital in Massachusetts for two years. This short collection of memoir-essays is remarkable in its ability to render the "cuckoo's nest" atmosphere of the place with clarity, empathy, and brutal honesty. She spares neither herself nor the other girls incarcerated with her, and every observation she makes is fascinating. Most 18—year-old girls will find some way to identify with Susanna and her fellow "inmates," because while reality was too much for her, it can often be too much for anyone at that age. The book transcends interest of age or gender, however, with involving passages describing the complex machinations of brain chemistry and the all-too-easy wrong paths it can accidentally take. For the reader who must have a linear narrative, this book might be too much of a challenge, but for those who can take on the ride with the mentally peripatetic writer, the story is its own reward. **Grades 10—12 (mature). PT**

362 Keller, Helen. **The Story of My Life.** 382 pages.

Doubleday 1991 Paper 0553213873 $4.99

Blind and deaf from the age of 19 months, Helen Keller led a life that is the stuff of legend. Coming from an early childhood during which she was little more civilized than an animal, Keller went on to graduate from Radcliffe College in 1904; she wrote this remarkable autobiography as a student there. The public is largely aware of what

Helen Keller called the "most important day I remember in all my life," when Anne Sullivan arrived at the Keller household to bring Keller into the light of language. That event has been well-documented on both stage and screen in *The Miracle Worker*. However, readers of her own story may be surprised to discover her list of lifelong achievements, including the fact that she learned to read and write several languages, was a suffragist, pacifist, and even earned an FBI file through her advocacy of socialism. Spanning the years from the 19th to the 20th centuries; places from Tuscumbia, Alabama, to the lecterns of the world; from an absolute inability to communicate to one of the most powerful voices of our time, Helen Keller's life, in her direct, powerful, incisive prose, is simply a joy for the widest reading audience. **Grades 7–12. PT**

---

362 Kozol, Jonathan. ***Rachel and Her Children.*** 244 pages.

Fawcett 1989 Paper 0449903397 $12.95

Taking a heart-rending look at the heartlessness of a system that allows thousands of innocent children to exist as homeless in this country, *Rachel and Her Children* relies on interviews with the homeless themselves, and the anecdotal narrative serves Kozol's purpose well: the subsisting poor are people just like us, and we should know who they are. **Grades 10–12. PT**

---

362 Levy, Barrie. ***In Love and in Danger: A Teen's Guide to Breaking Free of Abusive Relationships.*** 107 pages.

Seal 1998 Paper 1580050026 $10.95

Opening with three personal narratives of young women in violent dating relationships, this self-help book provides young women with the tools they need to escape such situations. The themes within those three stories about obsession, negative self-image, and gender differences are explored in later chapters. There are profiles of dating abusers, as well as discussion about why dating turns violent. With the author estimating that one out of three high school and college-age youth are victims of dating violence, a volume such as this is essential for every library. **Grades 9–12. PJ**

---

362 Mather, Cynthia. ***How Long Does It Hurt?: A Guide to Recovering from Incest and Sexual Abuse for Teenagers, Their Friends, and Their Families.*** 265 pages.

Chelsea House 1994 Trade 1555426743 $15.00

While many self-help books provide tools for teens to avoid troubled times, this handbook guides young people, in particular women, through the process of healing. The book walks readers step-by-step through the healing process, but also answer questions about the legal, emotional, and social issues they might be facing. It is the type of book that may never circulate and never be asked for, but it is essential as it contains necessary information for young people who often do not know where to turn when faced with sexual abuse. **Grades 7–12. PJ**

Reviews: *Booklist* 8/1/1997

---

362 Pelzer, Dave J. ***A Child Called It.*** 184 pages.

Health Communications 1995 Paper 1558743669 $9.95

This excruciatingly honest portrayal of child abuse from a survivor will hold teens from the very first page. Some of Pelzer's tale sounds almost too horrific to believe, but his voice is so clear throughout that little doubt is raised about the veracity of his tale. Enduring everything from starvation to humiliation to physical punishment, Pelzer's temerity and courage will win over many a reader's heart, especially since it is clear that his experiences have helped to shape him into a compassionate, not bitter, person. They say truth is stranger than fiction. In this case, it may not be stranger, but it is certainly a compelling story that continues in *The Lost Boy* and *A Man Named Dave*. **Grades 9–12. SLB**

Reviews: *SLJ* 12/1/1995

---

362 Stavsky, Lois. ***The Place I Call Home: Voices and Faces of Homeless Teens.*** 172 pages.

Shapolsky 1990 Library 0944007821 $14.95

A book about a social issue that is still as relevant today as the day it was published. In 30 short narratives, the lives of teens who are living, or have lived, on the street are explored. The teens talk about the factors that led them to their circumstances and the various steps many have taken to return to the mainstream. Many fled homes filled with abuse or social situations where they would never be accepted, as is the case in many of the gay youth interviewed. While few of these stories have happy endings, they serve as both a window into a world that many teens need to see and certainly as cautionary tales to help teens make different choices. **Grades 6–12. PJ**

---

363 Piven, Joshua. ***The Worst Case Scenario Survival Handbook.*** 176 pages.

Chronicle 1999 Paper 0811825558 $14.95.

While perhaps not as humorous post–9/11, this volume provides expert advice on how to survive almost any sort of calamity. The gimmick lies in that few people will ever need to learn how to get their heads out from between the jaws of an alligator or how to escape from a swarm of killer bees. Most of these improbable circum-stances are illustrated with drawings that seem smirking in their simplicity. In some ways, this almost resembles a *National Lampoon* version of the *Boy Scout Handbook*, even if the authors primarily play it straight. **Grades 10–12. PJ**

Reviews: *Booklist* 3/15/2001

---

364 Beavan, Colin. *Fingerprints: The Origins of Crime Detection and the Murder Case That Launched Forensic Science.* 232 pages.

Hyperion 2002 Paper 0786885289 $14.95

While DNA evidence is state-of-the-art practice at the end of the 20th century, just one hundred years ago the same debates raged about fingerprints. In a book that reads more like a novel than the study of science, Beaven revisits a brutal murder in 1905 that was solved when Scotland Yard adopted the science of fingerprinting. This is the dramatic human story of how technology found its way into the criminal justice system and of a difficult murder case worthy of *Law and Order.* **Grades 10–12. PJ**

364 Bing, Leon. *Do or Die.* 315 pages.

HarperPerennial 1992 Paper 0060922915 $13.00

Do or Die is an insider account of teenage gangs from a journalist allowed inside this closed and dangerous world. This teenage wasteland is one, according to the blurb, "where teenagers have scrapbooks filled with funeral invitations; where teenage gangsters are kidnapped, tortured, and held for six-figure ransoms; where kids hum the latest movie's theme music while killing people. It's a world of sherms, bangers, ballers, and mummyheads; a world where the strongest feelings of family come from other gang members; a world where the most potent feelings of self-worth come from murder." **Grades 10–12. PJ**

364 Bode, Janet. *Voices of Rape.* 160 pages.

Franklin Watts 1998 Library 0531115186 $22.00
Franklin Watts 1999 Paper 0531159329 $9.95

Personal accounts by victims, offenders, doctors, social workers, and members of the legal system put a face on the crime of rape. Bode looks at date rape, incest, stranger rape, and even rapes against males. **Grades 9–12. PJ**

Reviews: *Booklist* 11/1/1998, *SLJ* 5/1/1999, *VOYA* 8/1/1999

364 Bugliosi, Vincent. *Helter Skelter: The True Story of the Manson Murders.* 528 pages.

W. W. Norton 2001 Paper 0393322238 $13.95

This account by the prosecutor in the notorious California murder case, in which a group of fanatical followers of Charles Manson bloodily dispatched actress Sharon Tate and heiress Abigail Folger, among others, is not completely objective, nor should it be. We can follow the trial as it unfolds, and for young adult readers perhaps unfamiliar with the 1969 slaughter, it reads almost like fiction. This is one case in which truth is certainly stranger than fiction. **Grades 10–12 (mature). PT**

364 Capote, Truman. **In Cold Blood.** 343 pages.

> Random House 2002 Trade 0375507906 $22.00
> Random House 1994 Paper 0679745580 $13.00

This classic in the true crime genre still gets under the skin of readers for a good reason: Capote gets readers into the skin of Dick and Perry. **Grades 10—12. PJ**

---

364 Duncan, Lois. **Who Killed My Daughter?** 265 pages.

> Dell 1994 Paper 0440213428 $7.50

An unexplained murder with a possible psychic connection sounds like the plot of a teen thriller, but it is the real-life story of YA author Lois Duncan. When her own daughter is murdered and the police seem unable to make a case, Duncan goes out on her own with the help of private investigators and psychics to answer the title question. **Grades 8—12. PJ**

---

364 Hinojosa, Maria. **Crews: Gang Members Talk to Maria Hinojosa.** 120 pages.

> Harcourt 1994 Paper 0152002839 $11.00

Why would a young person risk death and injury to join a gang? That question and others about gang life are answered as Hinojosa records her interviews with teens who have dropped into new families. In their own words, these Latino gang members talk about the life they left behind, often families filled with drugs, alcoholism, drug addiction, physical and sexual abuse, and utter hopelessness. Hinojosa, a reporter for National Public Radio, gets the young people to open up about their daily lives, and even reflect upon their pasts and gaze into their uncertain futures. **Grades 6—12. PJ**

> Reviews: *Booklist* 3/15/1995

---

364 Owen, David. **Hidden Evidence: Forty True Crimes and How Forensic Science Helped Solve Them.** 240 pages.

> Firefly 2000 Paper 1552094839 $24.95
> Firefly 2000 Trade 1552094928 $35.00

Owen uses 40 famous crimes to explore the ins and outs of forensic science, complete with gruesome crime scene photos. In each case, scientific procedures were instrumental in discovering the truth. Starting in the late 1700s with a case involving Paul Revere through "prime time" crimes at the end of the 20th century, Owen lays out the history and how-to of forensics, examining a wide range of techniques, such as fingerprinting, autopsies, handwriting analysis, ballistics, hair sampling, blood typing, DNA testing, and toxicology. The book isn't about headlines, but about the painstaking lab work used to catch killers. **Grades 7—12. PJ**

> Reviews: *Booklist* 3/15/2001, *VOYA* 2/1/2001

---

364 Rodriguez, Luis J. ***Always Running: La Vida Loca: Gang Days in L.A.*** 260 pages.

Touchstone 1994 Paper 0671882317 $13.00
Curbstone 1993 Trade 1880684063 $19.95

Before the Ricky Martin song, there was this powerful personal narrative about "the crazy life" of an East L.A. gang member. Like many gang autobios, the book overflows with violence. But as Rodriguez shows, the violence is not only against other gang members and the police, but also self-inflicted. Gang life is not glamorized, but presented as a path of despair and destruction. Rodriguez recorded his experiences as a cautionary tale for young people to learn that behind the aura of gangster life is a reality of heartbreak. **Grades 9–12. PJ**

364 Shakur, Sanyika. ***Monster: The Autobiography of an L.A. Gang Member.*** 383 pages.

Grove 1993 Trade 0871135353 $22.00
Penguin 1994 Paper 0140232257 $13.95

Sanyika Shakur tells his tale of being a leading gangster in L.A. to his time behind bars. This is not preachy, but simply told directly. It moves quickly for reluctant readers, but by the powerful voice of the narrator holds the interest of all. **Grades 8–12 (mature). JW**

365 Gaines, Patrice. ***Laughing in the Dark: From Colored Girl to Woman of Color—A Journey from Prison to Power.*** 295 pages.

Crown 1994 Trade 0517594757 $24.00

An inspirational story of a woman who made a series of dangerous choices under difficult circumstances, but still managed to come out on the other side. Gaines's life was a catalog of social problems: racism, absent fathers, drug use, STD, sexual abuse, physical abuse, and finally a trip to prison. That is all here, but it is the after picture that matters, showing that Sisyphus does get the rock over the hill. **Grades 7–12. PJ**

Reviews: *Booklist* 10/1/1994, *SLJ* 3/1/1995, *VOYA* 1/1/1995

365 Gantos, Jack. ***Hole in My Life.*** 199 pages.

Farrar Straus Giroux 2002 Trade 0374399883 $16.00

While there are several memoirs by writers for young people in which they revisit their childhood, often with bittersweet memories of the faded photo, for Gantos, his late teen years can be found in a mug shot. Desperate for money and with no prospects for any real future, Gantos got involved, unsuccessfully, in trafficking drugs. Rather than a big payoff, he ended up in a medium security prison. While this is in some ways a prison memoir, as Gantos recounts life in the stir, it is just as much about his coming of age as a writer. **Grades 7–12. PJ**

Reviews: *Booklist* 4/1/2002, *SLJ* 5/1/2002, *VOYA* 6/1/2002

---

365 Williams, Stanley. ***Life in Prison.*** 80 pages.

Seastar 2001 Paper 1587170949 $4.95
Seastar 2001 Trade 1587170930 $14.95
Morrow 1998 Library 0688155898 $15.00

The cofounder of the notorious Crips gang tells his story about life on death row in San Quentin State Prison in California. Using "scared straight" tactics, Williams vividly describes life in prison in this hard-hitting cautionary tale first published by Morrow Junior Books. Williams was nominated for the 2001 Nobel Peace Prize for this book and his other activities to discourage young people from following in his path. **Grades 6–12. PJ**

Reviews: *SLJ* 9/1/1998, *VOYA* 4/1/1999

---

370 Llewellyn, Grace. ***Real Lives: Eleven Teenagers Who Don't Go to School.*** 318 pages.

Lowry House 1993 Paper 0962959138 $17.00

A nice companion to her *Teenager Liberation Handbook* (see below), this is a collection of personal essays by 11 teens who eschewed formal schooling. The teens tell not just WHAT they did on a typical "nonschool day" but look into the philosophical basis for unschooling. **Grades 9–12. PJ**

---

370 Llewellyn, Grace. ***The Teenage Liberation Handbook: How to Quit School and Get a Real Life and Education.*** 401 pages.

Lowry House 1991 Paper 0962959103 $14.95
Element 1997 Paper 1862041040 $9.95

A radical book that preaches a simple message to teens: school is a waste of time. Llewellyn isn't advocating home schooling, although she has no problem with that choice since it frees teens from the bonds of their school/prison, but instead advocates unschooling. Llewellyn urges teens to educate themselves: drop out and tune in to libraries, books, and the Internet. She then provides teens with resources to develop their own curriculum in all subject areas. Spicing up this menu of self-motivated learning are quotes about freedom from some of history's great thinkers, as well as continued attacks against institutional schooling. A manifesto that many would find more "dangerous" than any Internet porn. It empowers teens not just to think outside the box, but to live there as well. **Grades 9–12. PJ**

Reviews: *Booklist* 10/15/1991

371   Corwin, Miles. ***And Still We Rise: The Trials and Triumphs of Twelve Gifted Inner-City Students.*** 418 pages.

Harper 2001 Paper 0380798298 $14.00
Morrow/Avon 2000 Trade 0380976501 $25.00

Corwin, a *Los Angeles Times* reporter, spent the 1996–1997 school year with a group of honors students in a South Central L.A. high school. The story of those students, all of them growing up in a life full of poverty and rich in obstacles to success, is not so much about issues, but about inspiration. **Grades 9–12. PJ**

Reviews: *Booklist* 5/15/2000

---

371   Greene, Rebecca. ***The Teenagers' Guide to School Outside the Box.*** 261 pages.

Free Spirit 2000 Paper 1575420872 $15.95

More and more schools are engaging students in community services, distance education, and other alternatives to classroom learning. In another informative book from Free Spirit, teen readers discover all the different ways they can learn, such as volunteering, internships, summer programs, exchange programs, apprenticeships, and the like. Each chapter opens with a series of questions, throughout the text are FYI sidebars providing short factual information, and chapters conclude with sources for more information. **Grades 8–12. PJ**

Reviews: *Booklist* 2/15/2001, *SLJ* 3/1/2001

---

371   Lieberman, Susan Abel. ***The Real High School Handbook: How to Survive, Thrive and Prepare for What's Next.*** 230 pages.

Houghton Mifflin 1997 Paper 0395797608 $9.95

A guidebook to help teens do well during their high school years. Comprehensive, covering just about every aspect of high school life, from teachers to clubs to cliques and everything in between, Lieberman provides teens not so much with advice as with perspective on all of these issues. **Grades 9–12. PJ**

Reviews: *Booklist* 10/15/1997

---

371   McElroy, James T. ***We've Got Spirit: The Life and Times of America's Greatest Cheerleading Team.*** 336 pages.

Berkley 2000 Paper 0425173569 $12.95
Simon & Schuster 1999 Trade 0684849674 $22.00

An excellent entry into the canon of sports literature, even if cheerleading is rarely viewed as such. McElroy, a journalist, follows the cheerleading squad at Greenup County High in rural Kentucky as it prepares for a national championship competition. Other than the activity itself, this book is similar to most others on amateur sports: introducing the team, getting to know each person, and following them as they follow their dreams of glory. But as always, there is more than just the story of one team: McElroy looks at larger themes in American life, like community and teamwork, while exploring issues like sexism. **Grades 7—10. PJ**

373 Carter-Scott, Cherie. *If High School Is a Game, Here's How to Break the Rules: A Cutting Edge Guide to Becoming Yourself.* 163 pages.

Delacorte 2001 Trade 038532796X $12.95

Inside the colorful, oversize format rest the 10 rules of making it through high school. The book uses dialogue, stories, and quotes from teens to talk about the big issues. **Grades 9—12. PJ**

Reviews: *Booklist* 2/15/2001, *SLJ* 3/1/2001, *VOYA* 6/1/2001

391 Miller, Jean-Chris. *The Body Art Book; A Complete Guide to Tattoos, Piercings, and Other Body Modifications.* 192 pages.

Berkley 1997 Paper 042515985X $14.00

Not much more to say other than to report the reaction of one teen reader on Amazon: "This is the best book to get if you are planning on getting tattoos and/or piercing. . . . It has everything you needed to know about what to expect when getting a tattoo or piercing. Also, it talked about symbolism, history, and even the aftercare of tattoos and piercings. . . . I highly recommend this book." **Grades 8—12. PJ**

393 Colman, Penny. *Corpses, Coffins and Crypts.* 212 pages.

Henry Holt 1997 Trade 0805050663 $18.95

Death, they say, is a fact of life, and Colman seeks out all the facts about how death has been treated across countries, cultures, and centuries. The book features photos, illustrations, quotes, and even gravestone carvings. **Grades 6—10. PJ**

Reviews: *Booklist* 11/1/1997, *SLJ* 12/1/1997

395 King, Elizabeth. *Quinceanera: Celebrating Fifteen.* 40 pages.

Dutton 1998 Trade 0525456384 $16.99

A photo essay about two Latino teenage girls celebrating their coming-of-age ceremony. The quinceanera is where the community welcomes its newest adult member with a church service, a feast, and dancing. The tradition, which has its roots in Aztec and Mexican custom, is popular in the United States. **Grades 6—10. PJ**

Reviews: *Booklist* 8/1/1998, *SLJ* 12/1/1998, *VOYA* 2/1/1999

395 Packer, Alex J. ***How Rude: The Teenagers' Guide.*** 465 pages.

Free Spirit 1997 Paper 1575420244 $19.95.

Flip and funny, Packer provides teens with basic etiquette info in an entertaining fashion. Packed with examples of what not to do, the book strives to help teens avoid humiliation as well as how to get along better with peers and adults. **Grades 8—12. PJ <LOST>**

Reviews: *Booklist* 2/1/1998, *SLJ* 2/1/1998, *VOYA* 6/1/1998

398 Cohen, Daniel. ***Real Vampires.*** 114 pages.

Apple 1996 Paper 0590645420 $3.50

Cohen is a master of the reluctant reader book: take a high interest subject, dramatize it, and tell the tale in short punchy sentences. Here, Cohen looks at the supposed real-life inspirations for vampire myths from all over the globe. **Grades 6—8. PJ**

419 Costello, Elaine. ***The Signing: How to Speak with Your Hands.*** 262 pages.

Bantam 1995 Paper 0553375393 $18.95

This revised and expanded edition of the widely used, helpfully illustrated, comprehensive guide to sign language includes easy-to-follow instructions, new signs, information on new technology and education, and more. **Grades 6—12. PJ**

419 Riekehof, Lottie L. ***The Joy of Signing.*** 352 pages.

Gospel Publications 1987 0882435205 $21.99

In this standard work on sign language for the deaf, over 1,500 signs have been clearly illustrated and are grouped by chapter into their natural categories. Line drawings and step-by-step descriptions of hand positions aid rapid learning. **Grades 6—12. PJ**

500 ***DK Nature Encyclopedia.*** 612 pages.

Dorling Kindersley 2001 Trade 0789454793 $49.95

DK does nature in this encyclopedia that is anything but boring and staid. Colorful illustrations abound, and the text describes the rich diversity of life on Earth. Magnificently illustrated, and featuring dramatic time-lapse photographs, this compelling guide gives a fascinating insight into how living things evolve, feed, reproduce, and defend themselves. Explores each major plant and animal group, including plants, birds, and mammals, oh my. **Grades 6—12. PJ**

510 Flannery, Sarah. ***In Code.*** 341 pages.

Workman 2001 Trade 0761123849 $24.99

Sarah Flannery was declared a genius at age 16 when she won a Young Scientist of the Year contest for her creation of a data encryption system faster than any other. The book is not only about the contest and her celebrity, but even more about her process and sense of purpose. While there are some math-heavy chapters, what matters most is Flannery's discovering, thanks to her father, of her own special gifts and her "beautiful mind." **Grades 10–12. PJ**

---

510 Miller, Robert. ***Robert Miller's Algebra for the Clueless.*** 176 pages.

McGraw Hill 1998 Paper 0070434255 $10.95

While the focus here is not on curriculum material, this still demands inclusion. Reading Miller is like working with a funny and empathic tutor: his goal isn't only to educate and improve skills, but also to eliminate anxiety, which is often one of the largest objectives. He breaks down the learning process in an easy, nontechnical way to bridge the gulf between the student, the textbook, and the teacher. It is loaded with easy-to-understand methods as well as full explanations of basic principles. Along the way are lots of short tips, tricks, and tools to help teens not only gather valuable information, but also alleviate scholastic stress. **Grades 7–12. PJ**

---

530 Gott, Richard J. ***Time Travel In Einstein's Universe.*** 291 pages.

Houghton Mifflin 2001 Paper 0395955637 $25.00

Time travel is a huge theme in science fiction literature, but is it just fiction? Gott, a professor of astrophysics at Princeton, seeks to answer that question. For H. G. Wells, time travel was speculation; for Gott, it is pure science. After looking at Wells, plus the vision of others from the creative arts, Gott looks at the various laws of physics, examining how they explain or empower time travel. **Grades 10–12. PJ**

Reviews: *Booklist* 5/1/2001

---

551 Newson, Lesley. ***Devastation! The World's Worst Natural Disasters.*** 160 pages.

Dorling Kindersley 1988 Trade 0789435187: $24.95

A fascinating, heavily illustrated volume about nature's wrath. The scope is broad with the usual suspects like floods and hurricanes, as well as disease, drought, plagues, and famines. While the book also covers destruction to humans throughout history, the most striking parts of the book are more current disasters, thanks to outstanding photographs that demonstrate the devastation that occurs when nature runs amok. **Grades 6–9. PJ**

---

568 Haines, Tim. ***Walking with Dinosaurs.*** 288 pages.

Dorling Kindersley 2000 Trade 0789451875 $25.00

While the fascination with dinosaurs is a little kid thing, for some teens the fascination, no doubt fueled by the *Jurassic Park* movie juggernaut, is still there. While loaded with hundreds of computer-generated illustrations, the storytelling is the hook here. Based on the Discovery Channel television show, the book mirrors a good television documentary by allowing the readers to imagine they are in the time and place of the story. **Grades 6—12. PJ**

Reviews: *Booklist* 3/15/2000

577 Matthews, Anne. ***Wild Nights: Nature Returns to the City.*** 207 pages.

North Point 2002 Paper 0865476411 $13.00
Farrar Straus Giroux 2001 Trade 0865475601 $22.00

Perhaps one fascination that young teens have with animals is that for those that live in cities or suburbs, animals are a mystery. Naturalist Matthews, however, shows in this entertaining and enlightening book that critters are everywhere, but mostly they only come out at night. Bats, coyotes, turtles, and various birds make an appearance in this book as Matthews views New York City as one big zoo, and she is the tour guide to this unique ecosystem. But the book is not just about wild animals, but also about the people she meets who study, feed, and protect the beasts within the city, and about the larger issues of how humanity interacts with and encroaches on nature. **Grades 10—12. PJ**

Reviews: *Booklist* 4/1/2001

590 Croke, Vicki. ***Animal ER.*** 194 pages.

Plume 2000 Paper 0452281016 $12.00

Emergency Vet on the Animal Planet cable network is the stuff that teens were made for: animals, drama, loss, love, and miracles. This book is a behind-the-scenes look at an emergency vet at the Foster Hospital for Small Animals at the Tufts University School of Veterinary Medicine. Croke, a *Boston Globe* reporter, observed operations and interviewed vets as they handled tough cases, from a water dragon with a ruptured ulcer to a dog "de-skinned" in an auto accident. Riveting and informative. **Grades 10—12. PJ**

591 Masson, J. Moussaieff. ***When Elephants Weep.*** 291 pages.

Del Rey 1996 Paper 0385314280 $14.95
Delacorte 1995 Trade 0385314256 $23.95

Prince asked what happens when doves cry, but do they? In this accessible, high information book, a psychoanalyst and zoologist team up to capture the emotional lives of animals. They look at the research and report back on the feelings found in mammals that seem quite human. The informative tone of the piece gives way to a final chapter in which the authors call for more humane treatment of animals, in particular that they no longer be used for testing, clothing, or food. **Grades 10–12. PJ**

Reviews: *Booklist* 5/15/1995; *Booklist* 8/1/1997, *SLJ* 4/1/1996

---

596 Conniff, Richard. ***Every Creeping Thing.*** 256 pages.

Henry Holt 1998 Trade 0805056971 $25.00

This could have been subtitled: all things ugly and gross. For every pleasant fawn, there is a nasty creature lurking about, as Conniff demonstrates in this natural science collection. The behaviors of bats, sloths, grizzlies, weasels, sharks, porcupines, snapping turtles, and other animals that are rarely described with the word "cuddly" are discussed in an engaging style. **Grades 10–12. PJ**

---

600 Macaulay, David. ***The New Way Things Work.*** 400 pages.

Houghton Mifflin 1998 Trade 0395938473 $35.00

Is this a book for children, for adults, or for teens? The answer is all of the above. Macaulay was doing DK style before it existed: telling a great nonfiction story, informing readers, but letting pictures carry the load. In this updated volume, the award-winning author keeps what works, including the mysterious woolly mammoth, walking readers through the ins and outs of technological achievement, but adds a whole lot of new gadgets, primarily in a section called "Digital Domain." For any teen who has ever asked how something works, here is the way. **Grades 6–12. PJ**

Reviews: *Booklist* 12/1/1998, *SLJ* 12/1/1998, *VOYA* 6/1/1999

---

609 James, Peter. ***Ancient Inventions.*** 672 pages.

Ballantine 1995 Paper 0345401026 $20.00
Ballantine 1994 Trade 0345364767 $29.95

Ancient Inventions reveals such facts as medieval Baghdad had an efficient postal service, there were early apartment condos in the American Southwest, that contraceptives were used by the ancient Egyptians, and even that the use of plastic dates as far back as first-century India. A tribute to problem solving through the ages loaded with facts, illustrations, and one surprise after another. **Grades 7–12. PJ**

Reviews: *Booklist* 10/15/1994

---

612 Basso, Michael. ***The Underground Guide to Teenage Sexuality: An Essential Handbook for Today's Teens and Parents.*** 256 pages.

Fairview Press 1997 Paper 1577490347 $14.95

This breakthrough book on teens and sex opened the doors for a new frankness found in later titles. Addressing the book to both teens and adults, Basso uses the book as a means of communication about a subject where there is lots of talk, but little chance of clear, concise, and considerate information to emerge. **Grades 7—12. PJ <LOST>**

Reviews: *SLJ* 8/1/1997

612   Bell, Ruth. ***Changing Bodies, Changing Lives: A Book for Teens on Sex and Relationships.*** 411 pages.

Random House 1998 Paper 081292990X $24.00

One of the most important young adult nonfiction books ever published. A recent updating keeps the information, especially about STDs, current, but the core stuff remains the same: the relationship between physical changes and social changes in the lives of teenagers. Filled with illustrations and cartoons, loaded with examples and quotes from teenagers, and written in a friendly, yet obviously authoritative voice, this belongs in every library that serves teenagers. Although not done in a Q & A format, the book does answer the questions that teens have about their newfound sexuality. **Grades 7—12. PJ**

Reviews: *Booklist* 11/1/1998

612   Drill, Esther. ***Deal with It! A Whole New Approach to Your Body, Brain, and Life As a Gurl.*** 309 pages.

Pocket 1999 Paper 0671041576 $16.95

A teen sex guide with attitude. The authors, who also created the gURL.com Web site, provide a frank, funny, and hip approach to issues related to a young woman's changing body and changing life. In addition to the voices of the authors, comments, advice, and questions from the Web site are reprinted in this volume. Smart layout, lots of illustrations, and great graphics make this a winner. **Grades 7—12. PJ**

Reviews: *Booklist* 10/1/1999

612   Gurian, Michael. ***From Boys to Men: All about Adolescence and You.*** 86 pages.

Price Stern Sloan 1999 Paper 0843174838 $4.99
Price Stern Sloan 1999 Trade 0843174749 $13.89

The author of several books about boys for adults, Gurian provides boys with answers to their most common questions in this heavily illustrated volume. In a conversational style, Gurian deals with issues like sex, dating, and physical develop-ment in a nonthreatening manner. **Grades 6—10. PJ**

Reviews: *SLJ* 7/1/1999

612   Jukes, Mavis. ***It's a Girl Thing. 135 pages.***

Alfred A. Knopf 1996 Paper 0679873929 $12.00

Alfred A. Knopf 1997 Paper 0679887717 $5.99

Using her own experiences growing up as a jumping-off point, Jukes approaches teen girl issues with both honesty and humor. Written more like an article in *Seventeen* than a textbook, Jukes shares information with girls about all the important changes taking place in their bodies and lives as they enter their teen years. The *New York Times Book Review* noted that Jukes "delivers the facts but never talks down, preaches or uses scare tactics." **Grades 6–9. PJ**

Reviews: *SLJ* 6/1/1996

---

612   Jukes, Mavis. ***The Guy Book: An Owner's Manual.*** 152 pages.

Knopf 2002 Library 067990283 $18.99
Knopf 2002 Paper 0679890289 $12.95

While the information presented here can be found in almost any teen sex guide, the selling point here is the format. The format apes that of a car-repair manual, while the illustrations are campy—straight out of a J. Edgar Hoover-approved 1950s hygiene film. The style is as lively as the format as Jukes talks to boys about many topics, but mainly about sex. Sexual health, hygiene, relationships, and identity are all discussed, but the focus is on the chapter "Under the Hood," discussing physical changes. **Grades 6–9. PJ**

Reviews: *Booklist* 1/1/2002, *SLJ* 3/1/2002, *VOYA* 6/1/2002

---

612   Masoff, Joy. ***Oh Yuck! The Encyclopedia of Everything Nasty.*** 212 pages.

Workman 2000 Paper 0761107711 $14.95

We pick, we pee, we poo; that sums up this source for info on all that is scatological and stomach turning. Complete with a cover of a young man with a finger up his nose comes this encyclopedia of grossness, neatly arranged in alphabetical order and wonderfully illustrated with cartoons and photos. It's all good: acne, eye gunk, farts, snot, and, of course, vomit. But people don't have a corner on putridness as the animal kingdom ranks and reeks with maggots, slugs, and rats getting their due. **Grades 6–9. PJ**

Reviews: *SLJ* 5/1/2001

---

612   ***No Apologies: The Truth about Life, Love and Sex.*** 231 pages.

Tyndale 1999 Paper 1561796549 $5.99

This book comes from the conservative Christian group Focus on the Family, producers of *Brio* magazine, and presents abstinence as the only true safe sex. Loaded with accounts of teens who took another path, the book is a cautionary tome of consequences. **Grades 9–12. PJ**

---

612 Pogany, Susan Browning. ***Sex Smart: 501 Reasons to Hold Off on Sex.*** 213 pages.

Fairview 1998 Paper 1577490436 $14.95

Almost the antithesis to the Ponton book (below), this book recommends that teens do not act upon sexual impulses. Using the normal Q & A format, Pogany provides information through the lens of abstinence about a variety of sexual behavior issues. In addition to the content inside, the outside boasts a recommendation from Dr. Laura Schlessinger. Much like Packer's *High*, this self-help book provides teens with alternatives to behaviors that can often have negative consequences. **Grades 7–12. PJ**

Reviews: *VOYA* 4/1/1999

612 Ponton, Lynn E. ***The Sex Lives of Teenagers.*** 2,856 pages.

Plume 2001 Paper 0452282608 $13.00
Dutton 2000 Trade 052594561X $24.95

Although this is primarily aimed at parents of teenagers, there is certainly lots of interesting information here for teens. The book is a series of case studies of various teenagers and their sexual selves. The case studies feature both boys and girls struggling with their changing bodies. In this volume, readers meet teen mothers, a teen boy addicted to porn, victims of sexual assaults, and HIV-infected teens. While those are certainly extreme examples, Ponton points out that all teens have sex lives of some sorts: some act upon their sexual drives, others do not. Some do act responsibly, while others show less restraint; still others have sex forced upon them by adults. **Grades 10–12 (mature). PJ**

612 Shaw, Tucker. ***This Book Is About Sex.*** 167 pages.

Alloy 2000 Paper 0141310197 $5.99

The authors are the sex columnists for the teen Web portal alloy.com. Here they answer, with the male and female perspective side by side, some of the questions that teens ask most frequently about sex. Topics such as STDs, pregnancy, contraception, and sexual identity are all addressed in this volume. There is also a great deal about decision making mixed in with the illustrations and examples, as well as the results of lots of polls for alloy.com about sex, and some quotes from teenagers. **Grades 7–12 (mature). PJ**

Reviews: *Booklist* 2/1/2001

612 Solin, Sabrina. ***The Seventeen Guide to Sex and Your Body.*** 130 pages.

Aladdin 1996 Paper 0689807953 $8.99

Seventeen is a brand name that younger teen girls trust. The book is based on the author's long-running "Sex and Body" column from the magazine. Solin uses the familiar question-and-answer format to provide young women with the information they need to make decisions about their bodies. In addition to providing hard data, written in the typical conversational *Seventeen* style, sidebars called "Do Not Believe" knock down popular myths. The first part of the book focuses mostly on physical changes within girls, although there is a short chapter on male puberty. The second part concerns the opportunities and options that begin to emerge because of those changes. The usual suspects of STD, HIV, pregnancy, contraception, and sexual orientation are covered, as well as resisting sexual pressure, eating disorders, and the influences of drugs and alcohol. **Grades 7–12. PJ**

Reviews: *Booklist* 10/1/1996, *SLJ* 11/1/1996, *VOYA* 6/1/1997

---

613   Cooke, Kaz. ***Real Gorgeous.*** 257 pages.

W. W. Norton 1995 Trade 0393313557 $13.00

A book not about make-up, but instead a manifesto against the fashion, diet, and beauty machines. Cooke makes her points about self-acceptance, empowerment, and self-confidence with wit and style, helped out by cartoons, jokes, and quotes. **Grades 8–12. PJ**

---

613   ***"Go Ask Alice" Book of Answers: A Guide to Good Physical, Sexual and Emotional Health.*** 345 pages.

Owl 1998 Paper 0805055703 $15.95

Failed television talk show host and all-around morality mahatma Dr. Laura led a campaign against the American Library Association for its decision to include the "Go Ask Alice" Web site on Teen Hoopla. That should be recommendation enough for this important book, which answers questions such as: "Is it normal to have sex without experiencing an orgasm?" or "Does smoking pot have long-term consequences?" The "Go Ask Alice" Web site receives over half a million hits a week. **Grades 9–12. PJ**

Reviews: *Booklist* 9/15/1998

---

613   Krizmanic, Judy. ***The Teen's Guide to Going Vegetarian.*** 218 pages.

Penguin Putnam 1994 Paper 0140365893 $10.99
Penguin Putnam 1994 Trade 0670851140 $14.99

A how-to book to help teens lean away from eating meat. The book first lays out the arguments for becoming a vegetarian and describes the different types of diets. The key to the book, however, is the advice it provides teens in managing such a change in their lives, from explaining it to parents to socializing with friends. One teen Amazon reviewer noted the title was "a great resource for any teenager considering vegetarianism." **Grades 6–12. PJ**

Reviews: *Booklist* 2/1/1995, *SLJ* 2/1/1995, *Booklist* 10/1/1994

---

613   Luby, Thia. ***Yoga for Teens.*** 105 pages.

Clear Light 1999 Trade 157416032 $14.95

An instruction book aimed at getting teens started in yoga. The design is simple: positions are illustrated by a photograph of the animal, insect, or object for which it is named. On the facing page, teens demonstrate the posture, which is described in detail in the accompanying text. **Grades 6–12. PJ**

Reviews: *SLJ* 5/1/2000

---

613   Madaras, Lynda. ***What's Happening to My Body Book for Boys.*** 3rd edition. 288 pages.

Newmarket Press 2000 Paper 1557044430 $12.95

The definitive guide on the subject. While lacking the humor in word or text that some other books on puberty exhibit, Madaras counters with a straightforward style that carefully answers the questions boys are posing about their changing bodies. The latest edition is the most practical yet, written in part in response to the thousands of letters received by the author through the years. Mixing in personal experience and anecdotes along the way and augmenting the text with illustrations contribute to a powerful and informative resource. **Grades 6–9. PJ**

---

613   Madaras, Lynda. ***What's Happening to My Body Book for Girls.*** 3rd Edition. 304 pages.

Newmarket Press 2000 Paper 1557044449 $12.95

See the above: same quality, same style, different plumbing. **Grades 6–9. PJ**

---

613   Normandi, Carol Emery. ***Over It: A Teen's Guide to Getting beyond Obsession with Food and Weight.*** 224 pages.

New World 2001 Paper 1577311485 $13.95

The authors examine the factors leading to eating disorders, as well as looking at the cultural, emotional, and physical reasons girls obsess about weight and eating. They go on to offer girls a map and a method for finding a realistic and livable balance. Stories and quotations from girls who have struggled with eating disorders give the book immediacy, and exercises and writing suggestions steer girls toward a healthy self-image and wholesome eating patterns. **Grades 6–12. PJ**

---

614   Giblin, James Cross. ***When Plague Strikes.*** 212 pages.

HarperTrophy 1997 Paper 0064461955 $7.95

Throughout history, epidemics have killed thousands. But even more than ending individual lives, these diseases have dramatically affected all aspects of human life. Giblin is looking at the ripple effects of lethal outbreak on politics, economics, religion, and social structure. Reactions to these plagues have been amazingly similar: mass fear, followed by finger pointing, followed by medical breakthroughs. A multiple-award winner. **Grades 6–12. PJ**

Reviews: *Booklist* 10/15/1995, *Booklist* 8/1/1997, *SLJ* 10/1/1995

---

614 Preston, Richard. ***The Hot Zone.*** 300 pages.

Knopf 1995 Paper 0385479565 $7.99
Knopf 1999 Paper 0385495226 $14.00

Richard Preston has been compared to Stephen King (*The Stand*), and the compliment is all the more impressive because *The Hot Zone* is NON-fiction. An account of the Ebola-virus outbreak in a Washington, D.C., laboratory, the story traces the virus' journey from Africa to the nation's capital in descriptions as chilling and gory as anything King, Koontz, and Freddy could invent together. The most frightening aspect of this exposé is that it is, all of it, true. Not recommended for younger or squeamish readers, it is nonetheless an invaluable revelation of how close we can come to committing accidental bioterrorism on ourselves. **Grades 10–12. PT**

---

616 Cobain, Bev. ***When Nothing Matters Anymore.*** 165 pages.

Free Spirit, 1998 Paper 1575420368 $13.95

From an Amazon teen reviewer: "If you are a depressed teen like I am, I recommend this book for you. It has a lot of survival tips, stories from teens who suffer and have suffered from depression like me and you. Reasons why we become depressed. . . . This book is a survival guide indeed. It helps you understand your depression and it lets you know that you're not the only one suffering from this illness. And there is help out there so if you're a depressed teen please buy this book. It's worth the money and it will start you on the path to a better life." **Grades 8–12. PJ**

Reviews: *SLJ* 3/1/1999, *VOYA* 2/1/199

---

616 Corrigan, Eireann. ***You Remind Me of You.*** 13 pages.

Push 2002 Paper 0439297710 $6.99

A real-life horror show about a young woman's graphic description, in prose and poetry, of her eating disorder. *Wasted* meets *Girl, Interrupted.* **Grades 8–12 (mature). PJ**

Reviews: *SLJ* 8/1/2002

---

616 Gottlieb, Lori. ***Stick Figure.*** 222 pages.

Berkley 2001 Paper 0425178900 $12.00
Simon & Schuster 2000 Trade 0684863588 $22.00

Like many teen girls, Lori Gottlieb became obsessed with recording her thoughts in a journal. There, she could escape her parents and all the noise that surrounded her life growing up in Beverly Hills in the 1970s. Her fixation with self and self-image reaches an apex when she sets a goal to be "the thinnest eleven-year-old on the entire planet." Gottlieb used those journals to create this memoir of her eating disorder, which almost left her for dead. **Grades 9—12 (mature). PJ**

---

616   Grealy, Lucy. ***Autobiography of a Face.*** 223 pages.

HarperCollins 1995 Paper 006097673X $13.00

A hard-hitting personal narrative about a teenager whose face is disfigured by cancer. Grealy's heroic struggle for dignity is a modern retelling of the Elephant Man. Hitting upon all the themes of adolescence, the messages about beauty, acceptance, and loneliness will move almost any young adult reader and has become a "cult" teen favorite. **Grades 10—12. PJ <LOST>**

---

616   Gunther, John. ***Death Be Not Proud.*** 161 pages.

HarperCollins 1998 Paper 0060929898 $11.95

Journalist John Gunther had his greatest literary success with this memoir, recounting the tragic illness and death of his 17—year-old son, Johnny, from brain cancer in 1947. While the medical details are inevitably dated, Gunther's musings on his son's courage and his own pain do seem to defy the test of time. **Grades 10—12. PT**

---

616   Hornbacher, Marya. ***Wasted: A Memoir of Anorexia and Bulimia.*** 298 pages.

HarperCollins 1999 Paper 0060930934 $13.00
HarperCollins 1998 Trade 0553525182 $23.00

An unflinching look at anorexia and bulimia, a near-fatal combination for Marya Hornbacher, *Wasted* pulls no punches, asks for no pity, and offers no excuses. Just the kind of book that's most effective in recounting what has become a sort of plague for young American women: the eating disorder. At 23, Hornbacher recalls that she went on her first diet at age 4, and is mistaken for 36 by a bartender asked to guess her age. Perceiving her short, athletic body to be completely undesirable, Hornbacher came harrowingly close to killing herself through self-starvation, becoming so thin she developed lanugo, a fine hair covering the entire body to keep it from freezing to death. She also spent some time in a psychiatric hospital. A searing condemnation of cultural lessons in beauty. Hornbacher was convinced if she became thin enough she would be transformed into a five-foot, ten-inch blonde. *Wasted* is exceptional reading for anyone interested in what is becoming more and more a fatal disorder. **Grades 10—12 (mature). PT <LOST>**

---

616   Irwin, Cait. ***Conquering the Beast Within: How I Fought Depression and Won . . . And How You Can, Too.*** 105 pages.

Times 1999 Paper 0812932471 $14.00

While almost every teenager experiences times of sadness, some, like Irwin, suffer from full-fledged, crippling depression. In this book, which is part memoir and part self-help guide, Irwin recounts her own story. Institutionalized for clinical depression as early as age 14, Irwin struggled to regain herself through therapy and medication. Inspirational, informational, but also instructive for teens similarly afflicted. **Grades 7–12. PJ**

Reviews: *Booklist* 3/15/2001, *SLJ* 2/1/2000, *VOYA* 2/1/2000

---

616 Nelson, Richard. ***The Power to Prevent Suicide: A Guide for Teens Helping Teens.*** 126 pages.

Free Spirit 1994 Paper 0915793709 $12.95

An informative book to provide teens with the tools they need to understand and assist depressed friends. This isn't about suicide per se, although the book looks at many of the issues. Instead, the purpose is to help teens understand the perspective of a suicidal friend and how they can help that friend to realize that "everybody hurts" and that suicide is never the answer. **Grades 8–12. PJ**

Reviews: *Booklist* 8/1/1994, *VOYA* 12/1/1994

---

616 Schiller, Lori. ***The Quiet Room: A Journey out of the Torment of Madness.*** 270 pages.

Warner 1994 Trade 0446517771 $22.95
Warner 1996 Paper 0446671339 $13.95

The disease of schizophrenia is the subject of this memoir. Schiller describes her decay of her sanity and how she recovered. She doesn't rely on just her own voice to tell the story, but instead friends, family, and mental health professionals also supply their viewpoint on Schiller's transformation. *Publishers Weekly* wrote that *The Quiet Room* is a "stunning story of courage, persistence, and hope." **Grades 10–12. PJ**

---

618 Englander, Annrenee. ***Dear Diary, I'm Pregnant: Teenagers Talk about Their Pregnancy.*** 160 pages.

Annick 1997 Paper 1550374400 $9.95

Ten teenage girls tell their stories, all cautionary tales in one way or another. While each of the girls chose different routes, some having the child, others choosing abortion or adoption, their stories have much in common. In these essays, the girls talk about the choices they made and how these choices have affected their lives. The book ends with a chapter called "You Are Pregnant—Now What?" which provides pregnant teens with important information and resources. **Grades 6–12. PJ**

Reviews: *Booklist* 2/1/1998, *VOYA* 12/1/1997

---

623 Macaulay, David. ***Castle.*** 74 pages.

Houghton Mifflin 1982 Paper 0395329205 $8.95
Houghton Mifflin 1977 Trade 0395257840 $18.00

Of all Macaulay's various books, perhaps this one will resonate most with teens, even if (or because) it did win a Caldecott Honor Citation. Using the "you are there" premise, Macaulay whisks readers back to 13th-century England where a fictional lord is charged by the king with constructing a castle. So how would he undertake such a project? That's the book as Macaulay documents in splendid illustration the various tasks and parts of the castle. Although the focus is on architecture, there is also plenty of social history to be had, with glimpses of the stuff of everyday life as well as the weapons of war. **Grades 6—12. PJ**

629 Ballantine, Richard. ***The Ultimate Bicycle Book.*** 192 pages.

Dorling Kindersley 1998 Paper 0789422522 $13.95

Another lavishly illustrated DK tome concerning many a young teen's main transportation mode. Lots of photos and specs on all types of bikes, as well as info on bicycle maintenance, cycling accessories, training, sport cycling, and more. **Grades 6—9. PJ**

629 Willson, Quentin. ***Classic American Cars.*** 192 pages.

Dorling Kindersley 1997 Trade 078942083X $29.95

Loaded with over 650 full-color photos featuring cars from 1945–1975, the book explores 60 classic cars from U.S. auto companies. **Grades 9—12. PJ**

Reviews: *Booklist* 12/1/1997, *SLJ* 7/1/1998

629 Willson, Quentin. ***The Ultimate Classic Car Book.*** 224 pages.

Dorling Kindersley 1995 Trade 0789401592 $29.95

Featuring cars from all over the world, not just the U.S., this volume is more of the same. **Grades 9—12. PJ**

Reviews: *Booklist* 1/1/1996, *SLJ* 6/1/1996

629 Wilson, Hugo. ***Ultimate Harley Davidson.*** 192 pages.

Dorling Kindersley 2000 Trade 0789451654 $24.95

Hog heaven as Wilson profiles the big bikes from America's most famous motorcycle maker. In addition to hundreds of photos, the text provides an authoritative history of the Harley-Davidson company; interviews with veteran Harley-Davidson employees; a guide to the people, places, and phrases of the Harley world; and a dictionary of "Harleyspeak." **Grades 9—12. PJ**

629 Wilson, Hugo. *The Ultimate Motorcycle Book.* 192 pages.

> Dorling Kindersley 1993 Trade 1564583031 $29.95

A no-brainer in terms of popularity, but the quality of these DK books is amazingly high as DK consistently delivers packages that create a positive reading experience, even if that reading experience consists of flipping pages, looking at pictures, and reading short paragraphs. **Grades 9–12. PJ**

---

629 Wolfe, Tom. *The Right Stuff.* 436 pages.

> Doubleday 2001 Paper 0553381350 $14.95
> Bantam 1988 Paper 0553275569 $7.99

Tom Wolfe's dazzling tome about NASA, the astronauts, and their precursors in daredevil Air Force test pilots has lost none of its appeal over the years. From Chuck Yeager to John Glenn, the whole crew is subjected to Wolfe's particularly irreverent brand of history, and the book's pacing is as swift as any action novel. A great read for high school or older. **Grades 10–12. PT**

---

635 Midkiff, Mary D. *She Flies Without Wings: How Horses Touch a Woman's Soul.* 274 pages.

> Delta 2002 Paper 0385335008 $13.95
> Delacorte 2001 Trade 0385334990 $23.95

What is it about girls and horses? That's the question that author and longtime equestrian Midkiff explores in a book that is as much about spirituality as it is animal husbandry. While using plenty of examples from myth, history, literature, and popular culture, Midkiff also pulls from her autobiography, examining the special kinship between females and equines. Like boys and baseball, there is something magical and magnificent about the connection between girls and horses. With horse stories, the stuff of much juvenile fiction, and the preponderance of horses in fantasy literature, there is a ready-made audience for this work of natural history, psychology, and philosophical musings. **Grades 10–12. PT**

> Reviews: *Booklist* 3/15/2001

---

641 Krizmanic, Judy. *Teen's Vegetarian Cookbook.* 186 pages.

> Puffin 1999 Paper 0140385061 $9.99
> Viking 1999 Trade 0670874264 $16.99

Like any cookbook, this one is loaded with recipes, but the focus here is on nutrition. Since teen bodies are still developing, the nutritional aspects of vegetarian cookery are paramount. A related issue is the hectic lifestyle of teens, which requires recipes that are easy and quick to prepare and those, mostly involving melted cheese as the main ingredient, are included as well. **Grades 7–12. PJ**

> Reviews: *Booklist* 6/1/1999, *SLJ* 6/1/1999, *VOYA* 10/1/1999

646 Alloy staff. ***Do It Yourself Beauty.*** 131 pages.

Penguin Putnam Books 2000 Trade 0141309180 $5.99

According to one teen Amazon reviewer: "You have to get this book." The title doesn't mean that teens can just do their own make-up or hair, but rather that they can create their own beauty tools. **Grades 7–12. PJ**

Review: *SLJ* 12/1/2000

646 Banks, Tyra. ***Tyra's Beauty Inside and Out.*** 202 pages.

HarperCollins 1998 Paper 0060952105 $16.95

The supermodel provides lots of fashion tips and offers advice for young women on other issues in their lives as well, such as drugs and relationships. Banks confesses to suffering from a poor self-image as a teen and hopes her book will allow teens to feel better about themselves, in part by looking better and making wiser decisions. **Grades 7–12. PJ**

Reviews: *SLJ* 8/1/1998, *VOYA* 10/1/1998

646 Brown, Bobbi. ***Bobbi Brown Teenage Beauty.*** 200 pages.

Cliff Street 2001 Paper 0060957247 $18.00
Cliff Street 2000 Trade 006019636X $25.00

Bobbi Brown is the beauty editor of NBC's *Today Show*, doling out make-up tips. In this volume, there is still that kind of information, but Brown is just as concerned with what is going on inside teenage girls, in particular as it relates to self-image and self-confidence. **Grades 7–12. PJ**

Reviews: *Booklist* 3/15/2001, *SLJ* 12/1/2000

649 Zakarin, Debra. ***The Ultimate Babysitter's Handbook.*** 50 pages.

Penguin Putnam 1997 Paper 0843179368 $4.99

A valuable and readable reference for the beginning babysitter with answers to all the questions teens might have about their small business enterprise. Loaded with lots of lists and coupled with illustrations, this slim volume belongs in every babysitter's book bag. **Grades 6–9. PJ**

Reviews: *Booklist* 9/15/1997, *SLJ* 12/1/1997

652 Singh, Simon. ***The Code Book.*** 263 pages.

Vintage Anchor 2000 Paper 0385495323 $14.00
Doubleday 1999 Trade 0385495315 $24.95
Delacorte 2002 Trade 0385729138 $16.95

A fascinating look at the science of cryptography. This is a youth version of Singh's *The Code Book* and has fewer pages and less technical jargon. What remains is the history of how, from the time of Caesar to the time of Bill Gates, people have used codes to keep information secret. With lots of focus on code technology born out of wars, Singh's look at secret language should appeal to curious older teens. **Grades 7—12. PJ**

Reviews: *Booklist* 1/1/2002, *SLJ* 5/1/2002, *VOYA* 8/1/2002

659 Rubinstein, Donna. ***Modeling Life: The One (and Only) Book That Gives You the Inside Story of What the Business Is Like and How You Can Make It.*** 314 pages.

Putnam 1998 Paper 0399524096 $14.00

As the model editor of *Seventeen* magazine, Ms. Rubinstein has launched dozens of careers, such as Niki Taylor, Tyra Banks, Kate Moss, Cameron Diaz, and Liv Tyler. *Modeling Life* shows young hopefuls a model's day-to-day routine, the ups and downs of her career, and how she maintains a balanced life in an ever-changing industry. **Grades 8—12. PJ**

700 Aronson, Marc. ***Art Attack: A Short Cultural History of the Avant-Garde.*** 192 pages.

Clarion 1998. Trade 0395797292 $20.00

YA literature commentator, editor, and publisher Aronson presents teens with a tour of artistic experimentation. Although these movements begin in Paris in the 1830s, the avant-garde is a 20th-century product. Major names, trends, and works are noted; each chapter begins with recommended listening and viewing. By art, Aronson isn't confining himself to what hangs on the walls of museums, but addresses all forms of artistic expression: music, dance, literature, etc. Illustrations abound, as do intellectual connections, as Aronson wants readers to see between the culture shocks. **Grades 6—12. PJ**

Reviews: *Booklist* 7/1/1998, *SLJ* 7/1/1998

704 Bruce-Mitford, Miranda. ***Illustrated Book of Signs and Symbols.*** 128 pages.

Dorling Kindersley 1996 Trade 0614204070 $24.95

DK's bible for the teen looking for body art design. An illustrated guide to more than 2,000 signs and symbols covers the arts, religions, and folklore of cultures across the world. **Grades 7—12. PJ**

720 Glancey, Jonathan. ***The Story of Architecture.*** 240 pages.

Dorling Kindersley 2000 Trade 0789459655 $29.95

The DK style applied to 5,000 years of architecture. From caves to churches to sky-scrapers, it is all here with hundreds of colorful illustrations. **Grades 10–12. PJ**

---

722   Ash, Russell. ***Great Wonders of the World.*** 64 pages.

Dorling Kindersley 2000 Trade 0789465051 $19.95

Another DK winner with lavish illustrations supporting sparse text that tells the stories of the wonders of the ancient world, such as the Great Pyramid at Giza and the Hanging Gardens of Babylon. Packed with facts, colorful illustrations, cross sec-tions, maps, city plans, and even timelines, this is a great browsing book for teens. **Grades 6–12. PJ**

Reviews: *SLJ* 9/1/2000

---

745   Harris, David. ***The Art of Calligraphy.*** 128 pages.

Dorling Kindersley 1995 Trade 1564588491 $24.95

A great DK guide introducing teens to hand lettering. After a short history lesson, the bulk of the book is step-by-step instruction on how to do calligraphy, from choosing the right paper to how to hold the pen. All the major Latin-based scripts are included with hundreds of examples in this lushly illustrated volume. **Grades 7–12. PJ**

Reviews: *Booklist* 8/1/1997, *SLJ* 9/1/1995, *VOYA* 2/1/1996

---

780   Nuzum, Eric D. ***Parental Advisory: Music Censorship.*** 349 pages.

HarperPerennial 2001 Paper 0688167721 $15.00

Since Elvis started shaking his hips, music aimed at the teen audience has been the target of censorship. Like battles over books and video games, the question is always the same: should teens be able to read and listen based on their own wants and needs, or should government be allowed to draw that line? With music, because of its profound influence in the lives of young people, that battle is even fiercer. Looking at a wide variety of cases since the 1950s, Nuzman examines how music censorship has crossed sexual, class, and ethnic lines. In particular, Nuzman sees music suppression as a form of racism, and his censorship chronology in the appendix certainly provides ample ammunition for that viewpoint. The text is aug-mented with lots of photos, including the standard issue shot of smiling white church folks standing around a bonfire burning the latest offering that has chal-lenged the orthodoxy. **Grades 10–12. PJ**

Reviews: *Booklist* 4/15/2001, *SLJ* 9/1/2001, *VOYA* 10/1/2001

---

780   *Vibe* Magazine. ***Hip Hop Divas.*** 211 pages.

Three Rivers 2001 Paper 0609808362 $17.95

While rap music often gets criticized for its blatant sexism, the genre has produced a tremendous amount of female talent. Those artists, such as TLC and Lauryn Hill, are featured in this oversize book celebrating women in hip-hop. The volume is loaded with photos and sidebar lists to complement the biographical essays. **Grades 10–12. PJ**

Reviews: *Booklist* 10/15/2001

---

781   Cool J, L. L. ***I Make My Own Rules.*** 214 pages.

St. Martin 1997 Trade 0312171102 $22.95
St. Martin 1998 Paper 0312967861 $5.99

An interesting combination of autobiography and advice from one of the early hip-hop crossover artists. While Cool's cool is not as high as it once was in the music world, he's still around and his clothes are still everywhere. *Rap Pages* magazine wrote that the book was "a charismatic page-turner . . . entertaining and enlightening." **Grades 7–12. PJ**

Reviews: *VOYA* 6/1/1998

---

781   Dyson, Michael. ***Holler If You Hear Me.*** 292 pages.

Basic Books 2001 Trade 046501755X $24.00

Like Jim Morrison and James Dean, Tupac Shakur remains a cultural icon years after his death at a young age. Not merely writing a biography, Dyson is looking for the "meaning" of Tupac and his almost sacred place among hip-hop-listening youth. While a little dense for some readers, the subject alone makes it an essential purchase. **Grades 10–12 (mature). PJ**

Reviews: *Booklist* 8/1/2001, *VOYA* 4/1/2002

---

781   Hopkins, Jerry. ***No One Here Gets Out Alive.*** 387 pages.

Warner 1995 Paper 0446602280 $7.99

Like Kurt Cobain and Tupac Shakur, Morrison remains an icon and idol for many teens long after his death. Morrison, the son of a military man, grew up rebellious, wore his hair long when it was a political statement, and became not just another rock and roll star, but the "lizard king." Morrison WAS sex, drugs, and rock 'n roll personified. Hopkins talked to everyone who knew Morrison to get the real story, which ends with his predictable death at a young age. **Grades 10–12 (mature). PJ**

---

781   Klosterman, Chuck. ***Fargo Rock City.*** 283 pages.

Pocket 2002 Paper 0743406567 $14.00
Scribner 2001 Trade 0743202279 $23.00

Although set in the 1980s, the theme of the power of music in the lives of teenagers is always contemporary. Part autobiography and part sociology, the book is about "how my life was saved by rock and roll." Growing up, Klosterman isn't one of the cool kids; he's just another grind. Then music, in particular the outlandish sounds of mid–80s heavy metal, takes over his life. It is a coming-of-age story with a three-chord soundtrack cranked up to ten as Klosterman views his life through the lens of metal. **Grades 10–12 (mature). PJ**

781   McIver, Denise L. **Droppin' Science: Straight-Up Talk from Hip Hop's Greatest Voices.** 144 pages.

Random House 2002 Paper 0609807293 $10.95

A book for quotes from the masters of rhymes, lifted from songs and interviews, as well as created just for this volume. The book contains lessons and lyrics from all rap genres, and the themes of hip-hop emerge strongly as some of its best performers boast, curse, and verse about urban landscapes. More than anything, this is an advice book as rappers speak to their audience directly about lessons they've learned, many of them the hard way. **Grades 9–12. PJ**

781   *Rolling Stone* Magazine. **Cobain.** 200 pages.

Little, Brown 1994 Paper 0316880159 $16.95

While Cobain's life was short, his influence upon rock music was large and the shadow cast by his suicide even larger. Dubbed the voice of his generation, Cobain, like Tupac Shakur, died at the height of his fame and talent. Interviews, photos, and essays highlight this volume, which attempts to capture the man and his music, but even more so, documents why his suicide affected so many young people so deeply. **Grades 8–12. PJ**

781   *Vibe* Magazine. **Tupac Shakur.** 159 pages.

Crown 1998 Paper 0609802178 $17.00

In life he was an idol; in death he has become an icon whose words and life still inspire. Similar to the *Rolling Stone* book about Cobain, this is a collection of new and old pieces from the pages of *Vibe*, along with lots and lots and lots of photos. The book also generously quotes from Tupac's gritty rhymes. Essential. **Grades 9–12. PJ**

781   *Vibe* Magazine. **The Vibe History of Hip Hop.** 414 pages.

Three Rivers 1999 Paper 0609805037 $27.50

Similar to *Rolling Stone*'s rock histories, this is the real deal with over 400 pages tracing the history of hip-hop. Like *Vibe* magazine itself, this volume uses plenty of photos and song samples rather than just relying on narrative. The essays here range from basic profiles of major artists to those that dig deeper into the meanings of not only the songs, but also all of hip-hop culture. **Grades 8–12. PJ**

Reviews: *SLJ* 7/1/2000

787　Chapman, Richard. *Guitar.* 240 pages.

Dorling Kindersley 2000 Trade 0789459639 $24.95

With a foreword by Eric "Clapton is God" himself, this oversized heavily illustrated tome looks at the heart of every rock and roll band and tells the story of 300 guitar players for every style of music. **Grades 10–12. PJ**

791　Hamilton, Jake. *Special Effects in Film and Television.* 64 pages.

Dorling Kindersley 1998 Trade 078942813X $17.95

An oversized book jammed with color photos describing special effects and illustrating each effect from a famous movie or television show, such as *The Mask* and *Jurassic Park.* Another DK hit. **Grades 6–10. PJ <TEN>**

Reviews: *Booklist* 8/1/1998, *SLJ* 6/1/1998, *VOYA* 10/1/1998

791　MTV Network. *MTV Uncensored.* 274 pages.

Pocket 2001 Trade 0743426827 $40.00

A heavily illustrated volume, dubbed the network's "gift" to its fans, covers all the scandalous moments in MTV's history. Lots and lots of photos highlight this collection of televised accidents and incidents, although they are sadly sans captions, but then MTV has always focused on vivid images over big vocabulary. **Grades 9–12. PJ**

791　Reeves-Stevens, Judith. *The Art of Star Trek.* 295 pages.

Pocket 1997 Paper 0671017764 $25.00
Pocket 1995 Trade 0671898043 $50.00

A gallery of Star Trek artwork, as well as a tribute to the many artists, designers, and technicians whose diverse talents and imagination created the distinctive look of the Star Trek universe. Every incarnation of Star Trek is explored: the original series, *The Animated Series, Star Trek: The Next Generation, Star Trek: Deep Space Nine,* and *Star Trek: Voyager,* and the films—with the complete behind-the-scenes story of Star Trek's design history. With hundreds of full-color illustrations and photographs, many from private collections, readers can linger on Star Trek's rich visual legacy and trace the evolution of, and images from, their initial conceptions to their final form on television and film screens. **Grades 10–12. PJ**

Reviews: *Booklist* 8/1/1997

796 Armstrong, Lance. ***It's Not about the Bike.*** 275 pages.

> Berkley 2001 Paper 0425179613 $13.00
> Putnam 2000 Trade 0399146113 $24.95

Armstrong is a world-class cyclist and winner of the famed Tour de France whose career was interrupted by cancer. This is a classic cancer survivor story, but just as important is the start of the book, where Armstrong talks about his teen years. Those chapters about his struggle to succeed and to find something that mattered in his life are as moving as any part of the book. **Grades 10–12. PJ**

> Reviews: *Booklist* 5/15/2000, *SLJ* 1/1/2001

796 Barnidge, Tom. ***Best Shots: The Greatest NFL Photography of the Century.*** 160 pages.

> Dorling Kindersley 2001 Paper 0789480751 $19.95
> Dorling Kindersley 1999 Trade 0789446391 $30.00

The rise of professional football goes hand-in-hand with the rise of sports television. Television captured the intensity of football, yet some of the most famous images from the game come from the pages of *Sports Illustrated*. Here, the history of the NFL, and its greatest players and coaches, is told through classic photos. **Grades 7–12. PJ**

796 Bermudez, Ben. ***Go Skate: The Monge's Guide to Skateboarding.*** 200 pages.

> 17th Street Press 2001 Paper 1931497427 $19.95

Skaters can be found near libraries: normally on the front steps performing moves such as ollas, half cabs, or pop shuvits. *Go Skate* is a book for those kids, loaded with tricks and tools, as well as safety tips. With full-color photos on every page and step-by-step instructions for every move, this is the skater's bible. **Grades 9–12. PJ**

796 Brooke, Michael. ***The Concrete Wave: The History of Skateboarding.*** 200 pages.

> Warwick 1999 Paper 1894020545 $19.95

The first book by a major trade publisher about skateboarding, the book features hundreds of photos of skaters and interviews with famous skaters. Definitive and essential. **Grades 7–12. PJ**

796 Brooke, Michael. ***Skate Legends (aka Sk8 Legends).*** 210 pages.

> Olmstead 2001 Paper 1587540150 $19.95

Loaded with color photos, *Skate Legends* provides brief, breezy profiles of 140 skaters, including the top dog, Tony Hawk. **Grades 7–12. PJ**

> Reviews: *SLJ* 5/1/2002

---

796   Colton Larry. ***Counting Coup: A True Story of Basketball and Honor on the Little Big Horn.*** 420 pages.

> Warner 2001 Paper 0446677558 $14.95
> Warner 2000 Trade 0446526835 $24.95

The author spent 15 months observing the Hardin High School girls' basketball team in Crow, Montana. The team is a mix of white girls and Crow Indians. One player stands out—a 17-year-old talented Native American who is good enough to star in college basketball, but whose off-court, small-town rural life (absentee father, alcoholic mother, abusive boyfriend, lots of peer pressure, sexism, and racism) threatens her goals. **Grades 10–12. PJ**

> Reviews: *Booklist* 8/1/2000, *VOYA* 8/1/2001

---

796   Foley, Mick. ***Have a Nice Day: Tale of Blood and Sweat Socks.*** 508 pages.

> Morrow 2000 Paper 0061031011 $7.99

When released, the author was a regular on hit television programs produced by the World Wrestling Federation. While that fame certainly helped to turn the book into a huge bestseller, the story has a timeless quality. Foley was a teenage outsider whose goal, which he rarely shared with anyone, was to become a professional wrestler. The best parts of the book describe the sacrifices he undertook to reach that dream. Foley tells great stories, has a unique sense of humor, and, despite being smacked in the head a few hundred times with steel chairs, has a remarkable memory for detail. **Grades 10–12 (mature). PJ**

---

796   Gottesman, Jane. ***Game Face: What Does a Female Athlete Look Like?*** 223 pages.

> Random House 2001 Trade 0375506020 $35.00

In almost 200 photos, Gottesman answers the title question. While there are pictures of famous female athletes, the book also contains "everyday" girls and women engaged in sports, from basketball to skateboarding. The subjects range from young to old and come from countries other than the United States. The caption of each photo provides the basic information, while there are also quotes and personal narratives scattered throughout the book. When Title IX was passed in 1972, only 1 out of 27 school-age girls played sports, but by the end of the 1990s that number was 1 in 3. The book was published simultaneously with the Smithsonian Institution and was endorsed by both the

Girl Scouts of America and the YMCA. **Grades 10–12. PJ**

Reviews: *SLJ* 10/1/2001

796   Hawk, Tony. ***Hawk: Occupation Skateboarder.*** 289 pages.

Regan 2001 Paper 0060958316 $15.00
Regan 2000 Trade 0060198605 $23.00

Hawk was to skateboarding in the 1990s what Hulk Hogan was to pro-wrestling in the 1980s: the first big breakthrough, crossover celebrity. Within the world of skating, Hawk is/was a legend for many things, but mostly for completing a successful move (the 900) that no one thought possible. In his own story, Hawk tells about growing up on skates. He talks about his setbacks, such as injuries, but focuses on how he developed his unique style. It is also a "behind-the-scenes" look at the skating world, showing the ways in which skaters are used and abused. Finally, Hawk veers from his own course to spin the story of skateboarding and skate legends who came before him. **Grades 7–12. PJ**

Reviews: *Booklist* 3/15/2001

796   Jackson, Phil. ***Sacred Hoops.*** 206 pages.

Hyperion 1996 Paper 078688200X $14.00
Simon & Schuster 2001 0743504003 $18.00

Few coaches in the history of professional sports have won more championships than Phil Jackson, coach of the Chicago Bulls and L.A. Lakers basketball teams. While many pro coaches adopt the famed Lombardi "winning is the only thing" credo, Jackson operates from a different set of values. Probably the only world champion coach to spend his summers coaching basketball on Indian reservations, Jackson is not just about achieving victories, but also enlightenment. Jackson tells stories about his famous players from the Bulls, but as a self-professed Zen Christian, the book is really about principles: teamwork, humility, and positive thinking. **Grades 10–12. PJ**

796   Krakauer, Jon. ***Into Thin Air.*** 293 pages.

Random House 1997 Trade 0679457526 $24.95
Vintage Anchor 1999 Paper 0385494785 $13.00
Doubleday 1998 Paper 0385492081 $7.99

In 1996, Krakauer was commissioned by *Outside* Magazine to do a piece on the commercialization of Everest. Rather than a chronicle about corporate greed, Krakauer ended up with a story of survival. As he tells the tale of the journey up the mountain, Krakauer examines the physical changes occurring in the body, as well as the wealth of life and death decisions faced on a daily basis. Coming closer to the peak, Krakauer is asking the most basic of questions about why man climbs a mountain, learning that "because it's there" is not only a simplification, but perhaps a falsehood. While the book is about scaling a peak, in many ways what Krakauer learns about himself and others applies to the whole range of extreme sports and those who live for the thrill. **Grades 10–12. PJ**

Reviews: *Booklist* 4/1/1997, *SLJ* 11/1/199

---

796 McFarlene, Stewart. ***The Complete Book of T'ai Chi.*** 128 pages.

Dorling Kindersley 1999 Paper 0789442590 $13.95
Dorling Kindersley 1997 Trade 0789414767 $22.95

While perhaps not complete, this is a good basic introduction to the strange-looking, yet oddly effective, Asian exercise ritual that on occasion resembles a martial arts workout. The guts of the book is a detailed, heavily illustrated section, as only DK can do, on the basic movements. With the lure of the East still calling many teens and the stress of everyday shouting at them, this book might be the answer for high school students. **Grades 9–12. PJ**

Reviews: *SLJ* 1/1/1998

---

796 Menzer, Joe. ***The Wildest Ride.*** 331 pages.

Touchstone 2002 Paper 0743226259 $14.00
Simon & Schuster 2001 Trade 0743205073 $24.00

Menzer chronicles NASCAR's evolution from the pastime of moonshine runners to a billion-dollar industry with huge television contracts and bigger corporate sponsors. While he tells the story of the industry, the book excels when Menzer profiles the superstar drivers who have dominated the sport, like Junior Johnson, Richard Petty, Cale Yarborough, and the Allison family. The life and death of Dale Earnhardt, who was the "face" of NASCAR, dominates the end of the book. While it is not reluctant-reader material, the narrative is filled with hot action scenes featuring bigger-than-life personalities. **Grades 10–12. PJ**

---

796 Myers, Walter Dean. ***The Greatest: Muhammad Ali.*** 172 pages.

Scholastic 2001 Paper 0590543431 $4.99
Scholastic 2000 Trade 0590543423 $16.95

As much a tribute as a biography, this is a portrayal of the life of the bigger-than-life Ali. The book kicks off with Ali, at that time Cassius Clay, capturing the World Heavyweight Boxing title (for the first time) in 1964. Myers then revisits the details of Ali's life: growing up in segregated Louisville, his amateur career, and his gold medal victory in the 1960 Olympics. But while Myers gets all the details and big events there, he is also looking at the controversies in which Ali seems to find himself planted right in the center. There is still lots of punch-for-punch coverage of the big fights, and much more focus on the heights that Ali reached as the most famous athlete in the world than on his decline. Plenty of photos add depth to the story of "the greatest." **Grades 6–9. PJ**

Reviews: *Booklist* 1/1/2001, *SLJ* 1/1/2001

---

796   Paulsen, Gary. ***Guts: The True Stories behind Hatchet and the Brian Books.*** 148 pages.

Bantam Doubleday Dell 2001 Trade 0385326505 $16.95
Random House 2002 Paper 0440407125 $5.50

Paulsen relates the fact behind the fiction in the tales of Brian and his hatchet. The research for those books was the most elemental kind: Paulsen's own life as an outdoorsman, a dog musher, and an ambulance driver. Paulsen lays out a section from one of the novels, and then tells readers about his own experiences, as well as other information. For example, he describes how he made his own bows and arrows and takes readers on his first hunting trips, showing the wonder and solace of nature. Like the Brian books, there is plenty of gross-out, including a chapter titled "Eating Eyeballs and Guts or Starving: The Fine Art of Wilderness Nutrition." **Grades 6–9. PJ**

---

796   Paulsen, Gary. ***Woodsong.*** 132 pages.

Aladdin 2002 Paper 0689852509 $5.99
Macmillan 1990 Trade 0027702219 $17.00

An autobiographical account of Paulsen's life in Minnesota and Alaska as he prepares his sled dogs and himself to race the grueling Iditarod. While there is plenty of the man-versus-nature conflict that Paulsen readers expect, it is the relationship with the dogs that drives the book. In one of the early scenes, Paulsen writes with great compassion about the courage of one of his older dogs, and throughout about the connection between man and his four-legged friend. **Grades 7–12. PJ <YALSA>**

Reviews: *SLJ* 10/1/1990

---

796   Pfetzer, Mark. ***Within Reach: My Everest Story.*** 224 pages.

Puffin 1999 Paper 0141304979 $6.99

Pfetzer became instantly famous when he scaled Mt. Everest at age 16, the youngest person ever to make the trek successfully. Told in journal format, this is the story of that harrowing experience. Although there's little true suspense since readers know he survives, Pfetzer adds plenty of heart-stopping scenes that make extreme sports seem like child's play. **Grades 7–12. PJ**

Reviews: *Booklist* 11/15/1998, *SLJ* 11/1/1998, *VOYA* 2/1/1999

796 Ryan, Joan. ***Little Girls in Pretty Boxes: The Making and Breaking of Elite Gymnasts and Figure Skaters.*** 268 pages.

Warner 2000 Paper 0446676829 $13.95

An exposé of the physical sacrifices made by young women in order to achieve success in sports. Inspired in part by the story of one Olympic hopeful who starved herself to less than 70 pounds at the time of her death, Ryan digs deeply into the dark side behind the shining faces of figure skating and gymnasts. Filled with case studies as well as a hard look at the medical evidence, Ryan's book uncovers a scandal where young women, in pursuit of a gold medal and glory, push themselves physically and suffer under the abuse of coaches and parents. **Grades 10–12. PJ**

---

803 Barlowe, Wayne Douglas. ***Barlowe's Guide to Extraterrestrials.*** 120 pages.

Workman 1987 Paper 0894803247 $13.95

A re-released classic guide to extraterrestrials with full-color illustrations of 50 alien denizens from popular science fiction literature. Barlowe imagines monsters, aliens, and hybrid humans from across the field, using over 150 full-color paintings showing each character in full figure but also highlighting distinctive characteristics in detail. **Grades 6–12. PJ**

Reviews: *Booklist* 1/1/1995, *VOYA* 1/1/1995

---

803 Barlowe, Wayne Douglas. ***Barlowe's Guide to Fantasy.*** 120 pages.

HarperCollins 1996 Paper 0061008176 $19.95

Same idea as *Barlowe's Guide to Extraterrestrials*, different genre, just as essential. **Grades 6–12. PJ**

Reviews: *Booklist* 1/1/1995, *VOYA* 10/1/1997

---

803 Pringle, David (Editor). ***The Ultimate Encyclopedia of Fantasy.*** 256 pages.

Overlook Press 1999 Trade 0879519371 $29.95

This bountifully illustrated volume features an introduction by Terry Prachett and entries on most well-known fantasy authors, movies, and television shows. There are sections on fantasy subgenres, famous characters, and well-known "worlds," like Narnia, Discworld, and Earthsea. While ultimate, it is not totally comprehensive and is, of course, dated. Regardless, there is enough good stuff here about topics of interest to teen readers that it is well worth owning in any collection. **Grades 6–12. PJ**

---

808 Bell, Janet Cheatham (Editor). ***Stretch Your Wings: Famous Black Quotations For Teens.*** 150 pages.

Little, Brown 1999 Paper 0316038253 $8.95

A wonderful source for inspiration featuring great names from African American history. Writers, rappers, athletes, political leaders, and others are captured with their advice, wisdom, and some humor in this Bartlett's for young people of color. **Grades 7—12. PJ**

> Reviews: *SLJ* 12/1/1999, *VOYA* 2/1/2000

808 Duffy, Carol Ann (Editor). ***I Wouldn't Thank You for a Valentine: Poems for Young Feminists.*** 104 pages.

> Henry Holt 1997 Paper 0805055452 $6.95

A collection of almost 100 poems, including authors Maya Angelou, Alice Walker, and Nikki Giovanni. While subject matter varies, most center on the theme of the different roles women assume: friend, mother, daughter, etc. **Grades 7—12. PJ**

> Reviews: *Booklist* 1/1/1995, *SLJ* 1/1/1995, *VOYA* 1/1/1995

808 Duffy, Carol Ann (Editor). ***Stopping for Death: Poems of Death and Loss.*** 134 pages.

> Henry Holt 1996 Library 0805047174 $14.95.

Teens. Poetry. Death. Do the math. Over 80 poems from many authors spanning many centuries. **Grades 7—12. PJ**

> Reviews: *Booklist* 8/1/1996, *SLJ* 8/1/1996, *VOYA* 10/1/1996

808 Okutoro, Lydia Omolola (Editor). ***Quiet Storm: Voices of Young Black Poets.*** 128 pages.

> Hyperion 1999 Library 0786824034 $17.49
> Hyperion 1999 Trade 0786804610 $16.99
> Hyperion 2002 Paper 0786813202 $4.99

Black, however, doesn't mean exclusively African American; this book features young people of color from England, Canada, the West Indies, and several African countries. That said, the works of Angelou, Hughes, and other African American poets introduce each chapter, and there are biographical sketches to close out the book. **Grades 9—12. PJ**

> Reviews: *VOYA* 12/1/1999, *SLJ* 7/1/1999, *Booklist* 6/15/1999

808 Vecchione, Patrice (Editor). ***Truth and Lies.*** 142 pages.

> Henry Holt 2000 Trade 0805064796 $17.00

Vecchione gathers poems from across time and geography to tackle the issue of truth. The poems are book-ended with a preface by Vecchione explaining the premise and then a short biographical sketch of each of the poets. These anthology collections provide teens with an opportunity to explore the works of many writers, and to explore the many sides to one question. **Grades 7–12. PJ**

Reviews: *Booklist* 12/15/2000, *SLJ* 2/1/2001, *VOYA* 2/1/2001

---

810 Bolden, Tonya (Editor). ***33 Things Every Girl Should Know: Stories, Songs, Poems and Smart Talk by 33 Extraordinary Women.*** 159 pages.

Crown 1998 Paper 0517709368 $13.00

Thirty-three extraordinary women offer stories, songs, poems, and smart talk in this collection that will give every adolescent girl reason to feel hopeful about making the transition from girlhood to womanhood. **Grades 6–9. PJ**

Reviews: *Booklist* 5/15/1998, *SLJ* 5/1/1998

---

810 Estepa, Andrea (Editor). ***Starting with I: Personal Essays by Teenagers.*** 199 pages.

Persia 1997 Paper 089255228X $13.95

These 35 essays written by teenagers were first published by *New York Connections*, a magazine of teen writing. The essays here are about big issues (death, love) and little ones (getting a haircut), but all carry the authentic voice of teenagers using writing as a way of knowing. **Grades 7–12. PJ**

Reviews: *Booklist* 9/15/1997, *SLJ* 10/1/1997, *VOYA* 10/1/1997

---

810 Franco, Betsy (Editor). ***Things I Have to Tell You: Poems and Writing by Teenage Girls.*** 63 pages.

Candlewick 2001 Paper 0763610356 $8.99
Candlewick 2001 Trade 0763609056 $15.99

A book of raw images; some in the black-and-white photos, most in the unpro-fessional but wildly passionate writings of 30 teen girls. The usual subject suspects are here: dating, drugs, body image, family, love, etc. But these poems are about voice, about young women finding their own truth through words. **Grades 7–12. PJ**

Reviews: *Booklist* 3/15/2001, *SLJ* 5/1/2001, *VOYA* 10/1/2001

---

810 Franco, Betsy (Editor). ***You Hear Me? Poems and Writing by Teenage Boys.*** 107 pages.

Candlewick 2000 Trade 0763611581 $14.99

A collection of writing, mostly poems, by boys working out their lives—and their fears, hurts, frustrations, and hopes—on paper for all to see. **Grades 7–12. PJ**

Reviews: *Booklist* 10/1/2000, *SLJ* 10/1/2000, *VOYA* 12/1/2000

810   Heron, Ann (Editor). ***Two Teenagers in Twenty: Writings by Gay and Lesbian Youth.*** 186 pages.

Alyson 1995 Paper 1555832822 $12.95

Although the book contains some materials previously published in the break-through *One Teenager in Ten* (1983), there are plenty of new voices here as well as the specter of AIDS, which was still lurking in the shadows in the early 1980s. The book is a collection of first-person narratives of teens talking about growing up gay in America. All of the passages deal in some part with coming out, but even more on what is going on inside of each person who grapples with what it means to be gay and a member of a minority. **Grades 9 –12. PJ**

810   Jacob, Iris (Editor). ***My Sisters' Voices.*** 246 pages.

Henry Holt 2002 Trade 080506821X $13.00

My Sisters' Voices is a passionate and poignant collection of writings by teenage girls of African American, Hispanic, Asian American, Native American, and bi-racial backgrounds. Jacobs solicited contributions from teen girls across the country to "speak out" about the issues in their lives. These poems and essays are the authentic voices from young women coming of age, many of them struggling with social issues such as poverty, racism, sexism, and identity. But for all the big issues that surround them, the young women write just as openly and honestly about their daily lives: school, family, work, and relationships. **Grades 7–12. PJ**

Reviews: *Booklist* 3/1/2002

810   Macy, Sue (Editor). ***Girls Got Game: Sports Stories.*** 152 pages.

Henry Holt 2001 Trade 0805065687 $16.95

Edited by women's sports historian Sue Macy, this collection of prose and poetry is about the love affair between females and sports. Noted YA authors Virginia Euwer Wolff and Jacqueline Woodson, along with 11 others, craft words to capture the female athlete in action. While the "big ones" are here, more interesting are the stories on the fringe sports, like synchronized swimming, tetherball, horseback riding, and stickball. The book ends not only with short biographical notes, but with a short summary of each author's own athletic achievements. **Grades 6–9. PJ**

Reviews: *Booklist* 6/1/2001, *SLJ* 7/1/2001, *VOYA* 8/1/2001

810   Meyer, Stephanie H. (Editor). ***Teen Ink: Our Voices, Our Visions.*** 361 pages.

Health Communications 2000 Paper 1558748164 $12.95

Written entirely by teens, *Teen Ink* uniquely captures the essence of adolescence in this collection of prose and poetry. Pieces for this book were chosen from more than 300,000 submissions to *Teen Ink* magazine. In addition, more than 3,800 students helped evaluate the final selections for the book. The book focuses on teen issues such as friends, family, fitting in, romance, heroes, and the lack of those things in teen lives. This isn't great art; it is honest self-expression and its value is to validate and inspire other teens. In these words and images, young people will find mirrors for their own lives, worries, and wishes. According to the editors, this book "represents some of the best stories, poems, essays and artwork we've published over the last decade." As of this writing, there have been three sequels. **Grades 7—12. PJ**

Reviews: *SLJ* 2/1/2001

---

810   Nam, Vickie (Editor). **YELL-Oh Girls.** 297 pages.

Quill 2001 Paper 0060959444 $13.00

Asian-American young women speak out in this anthology of stories, essays, letters, and poetry about what it is like growing up in two cultures. There are over 80 entries, few over four pages long. The contributors are primarily high school and college students from all the United States and Canada. The arrangement is thematic and each ends with a short essay by an established Asian-American writer reflecting on her teen years. Like most anthologies featuring "amateur" writing, the sentiment and intensity of emotion often outweigh the skill. But the theme here is the classic one: what does it feel like to be an outsider? The young women writing here reflect upon their unique isolation: feeling unaccepted by mainstream America, yet also feeling the pull, often by parents, to retain elements of their ethnic heritage. Trying to walk this line and live this contradiction provides the fuel for these writings. **Grades 10—12. PJ**

Reviews: *Booklist* 7/1/2001, *SLJ* 10/1/2001, *VOYA* 2/1/2002

---

810   Nikkah, John (Editor). **Our Boys Speak: Adolescent Boys Write about Their Inner Lives.** 220 pages.

St. Martin 2000 Paper 0312262809 $12.95

First Ophelia spoke, now young men get their turn in this collection of essays, diary fragments, short stories, and poems penned by teenage boys. The book is divided into thematic chapters, unified by authentic voices writing about learning hard lessons as well as about typical "guy stuff." Nikkah introduces each of the chapters, then lets the boys fill the pages, staking out what boys think, feel, and care about as they turn from boys to men. **Grades 7—10. PJ**

Reviews: *Booklist* 7/1/2000, *SLJ* 2/1/2001

---

810   Stevens, Ilan (Editor). **Wachale: Poetry and Prose about Growing Up Latino.** 146 pages.

Cricket 2001 Trade 0812647505 $16.95

Wachale is Spanish for "watch out," which is an apt descriptor for this collection of prose and poetry from Latino writers. The range is vast, with writers not only from Mexico and Latin America, but also from Cuba and the Dominican Republic. The poetry is presented in both English and Spanish, while the prose is primarily in English, although sprinkled with many Spanish phases. In addition to essays and folktales, many of the prose pieces are personal narratives about the Latino coming-of-age experience. Each work kicks off with a short bio sketch of the author. **Grades 6—8. PJ**

---

810   Woodson, Jacqueline (Editor). ***Way Out of No Way: Writings About Growing Up Black in America.*** 172 pages.

Edge 1996 Trade 0805045708 $15.95

Woodson has collected coming-of-age stories, poems, and parts of novels from the foremost black writers, from James Baldwin to Toni Morrison, in this thin volume from Holt's Edge series. **Grades 7—12. PJ**

---

811   Adoff, Arnold (Editor). ***I Am the Darker Brother: An Anthology of Modern Poems by African Americans.*** 208 pages.

Aladdin 1997 Paper 0689808690 $4.99
Simon & Schuster 1997 Trade 0689812418 $17.00

A young adult poetry classic first published in 1968 that collects the best poems by African American authors. A new edition adds 21 additional poets, 10 of them women. The poems are arranged by themes, following introductions by critic Rudine Sims Bishop and poet Nikki Giovanni. In addition to the poems themselves, there are brief biographies of each of the poets, including Maya Angelou and United States poet laureate Rita Dove. Hazel Rochman of *Booklist* called it an "essential purchase." **Grades 6—9. PJ**

Reviews: *Booklist* 2/15/1997, *SLJ* 5/1/1997, *VOYA* 06/01/1997

---

811   Adoff, Arnold. ***Slow Dance Heartbreak Blues.*** 80 pages.

HarperCollins 1995 Trade 0688105696 $15.95

Poems are matched with photo collages in a collection of coming-of-age poems. The collages and Adoff's use of language give the book an urban tone as many of the poems focus on teens growing up under the dark clouds of street life. **Grades 6—9. PJ**

Reviews: *Booklist* 12/1/95, *VOYA* 6/1/1996

---

811   Angelou, Maya. ***The Complete Collected Poems of Maya Angelou.*** 273 pages.

Random House 1994 Trade 067942895X $24.00

Angelou is a remarkably gifted modern poet and her collection shows it. Highly accessible and enduring, these poems are a wonderful way to introduce the poetry-traumatized to the "real thing," and they are strong enough to engage those comfortable with poetics and their challenges. **Grades 10—12. PT**

---

811   Anglesey, Zoe (Editor). ***Listen Up! Spoken Word Poetry.*** 197 pages.

One World 1999 Paper 0345428978 $14.50

Another poetry slam by-product featuring a collection of poems by young people that probably sound better than they read, especially if heard in a dimly lit room with lots of coffee flowing. **Grades 10—12. PJ**

Reviews: *Booklist* 3/15/1999

---

811   Carlson, Lori M. (Editor). ***Cool Salsa: Bilingual Poems on Growing Up Latino in the United States.*** 123 pages.

Fawcett, 1995 Paper 044970436X $5.50
Edge 1994 Trade 0805031359 $16.95

Thirty-six poets are featured in this collection, which captures the rhythm and textures of the Latino teen experience. The poems, many first written in English and then translated into Spanish, are organized by themes, such as school, parties, and food. Dealing with joy and sorrow, good times and bad, this collection is a must for any library collection serving Latino teens (in other words, just about every collection). **Grades 7—12. PJ**

Reviews: *Booklist* 11/1/1994, *SLJ* 8/1/1994

---

811   cummings, e. e. ***100 Selected Poems.*** 212 pages.

Grove 1959 Paper 0802130720 $11.00

With his constant creed of experimentation mixed with his ability to use simple images to capture complex emotions, cummings is read in school, but will also be read for pleasure and inspiration by young budding poets. **Grades 10—12. PJ**

---

811   Fletcher, Ralph. ***Buried Alive: The Elements of Love.*** 46 pages.

Atheneum 1996 Trade 0689805934 $14.00

A short, but intensely entertaining, collection of free-verse poems about teen romances, crushes, and heartbreaks told from a variety of teen viewpoints. **Grades 6—12. PJ**

Reviews: *Booklist* 5/1/1996, *SLJ* 5/1/1996, *VOYA* 10/1/1996

---

811   Fletcher, Ralph. ***I Am Wings: Poems About Love.*** 48 pages.

Bradbury 1994 Trade 0027353958 $14.00

Booklist noted this slender volume of poems was "more dramatic monologue than poetry." The book is divided into two sections: falling in love and falling out of love. In a sense, the poems create a short narrative about one teenage boy's emotional experience, rendered with simple language and recognizable images. **Grades 6–12. PJ**

Reviews: *Booklist* 3/15/1994, *SLJ* 6/1/1994

---

811   Giovanni, Nikki. ***Ego-Tripping and Other Poems for Young People.*** 52 pages.

Lawrence Hill 1993 Paper 1556521898 $10.95

One of the all-time classics of teen poetry has recently been re-released and expanded with 10 new poems. The style remains the same: Giovanni's empowering words, which are filled with celebration without minimizing hard times, talk about growing up African American. **Grades 6–9. PJ**

---

811   Giovanni, Nikki. ***Love Poems.*** 96 pages.

Morrow 1997 Trade 061420397X $12.00

The love between mother and daughter, the lasting passion between man and woman, and the wonderful froth of romance all find their way into Nikki Giovanni's sparkling verse; layers of meaning and wit make up this cake of a collection suitable for a wide range of readers. The joy of rereading contradicts the adage that you can't eat your cake and have it, too! **Grades 10–12. PT**

---

811   Giovanni, Nikki. ***The Selected Poems of Nikki Giovanni.*** 292 pages.

Morrow 1996 Trade 0688140475 $22.00

It has been said that Giovanni is a poet for those who don't care for poetry; certainly the selections in this collection are both inviting and accessible to the reader who has little experience with the challenges of reading verse. An artist, a woman, an African American, a political figure, a daughter, a lover, Nikki Giovanni explores the complexities of her many selves in poetry that is at once compelling and singular. **Grades 10–12. PT**

---

811   Glenn, Mel (Editor). ***Class Dismissed: High School Poems.*** 96 pages.

Houghton Mifflin 1991 Library 0899190758 $13.95

Teens who think they hate poetry will find a surprise here—poems about teens to whom they can relate and poems that will make them understand other teens a little better. Teens who enjoy poetry will likewise find these poems accessible and interesting portraits. Speaking of portraits, the photographs that accompany the poems are superb, balancing and supporting them. The teen angst, joys, and challenges that live in these poems can be appreciated by teens today as much as they were 20 years ago. **Grades 8–12. DT**

---

811   Glenn, Mel. **Split Image.** 159 pages.

HarperTempest 2002 Paper 0060004819 $6.95
HarperCollins 2000 Trade 0688162495 $15.95

Glenn captures the duality in the lives of many teenagers. During the day Laura Li
is a parent's picture of perfection: obedient, kind, and a good student. By night,
Laura hits the clubs trying to dance free of the weight of being good all the time.
Told in poems by a wide section of voices from Laura's who each have their own
images of Laura, Glenn trims off another slice of high school essence. **Grades
9—12. PJ**

Reviews: *Booklist* 4/1/2000, *SLJ* 6/1/2000, *VOYA* 10/1/2000

811   Glenn, Mel. **Who Killed Mr. Chippendale: A Mystery in Poems.** 100
       pages.

Puffin 1999 Paper 0140385134 $5.99
Lodestar 1996 Trade 0525675302 $14.99

A popular high school teacher is shot dead and everyone around him has an idea of
"whodunit." In a series of connected free-verse poems, students and teachers each
have their say. While the BIG mystery is exposed, just as important are the small
ones revealed by the teen voices. The popular teacher, it turns out, was not the only
one with secrets in the school. **Grades 7—12. PJ**

Reviews: *Booklist* 6/1/1996, *SLJ* 7/1/1996

811   Gordon, Ruth (Editor). **Pierced by a Ray of Sun.** 105 pages.

HarperCollins 1995 Library 0060236140 $15.89
HarperCollins 1995 Trade 0060236132 $15.95

Feelings of loneliness, isolation, and alienation are a part of almost every teen's coming-of-age experience. Gordon collects a wide range of poems and poets addressing
these emotions. **Grades 6—12. PJ**

Reviews: *Booklist* 5/1/1995, *Booklist* 8/1/1997, *SLJ* 6/1/1995

811   Greenberg, Jan (Editor). **Heart to Heart: New Poems Inspired by
       Twentieth-Century American Art.** 80 pages.

Harry N. Abrams 2001 Trade 0810943867 $19.95

Award-winning YA novelist Greenberg created this unique collection of poems laid
next to the artworks that inspired them. The poems are as varied as the poets, with a
wide range of styles and forms represented. The artwork, all reproduced in large,
full-color spreads, is not simply paintings, but prints, sculpture, and even photo-

graphs. Poets include Jane Yolen, Nancy Willard, X. J. Kennedy, Naomi Shihab Nye, and Angela Johnson. **Grades 6—9. PJ <PRINTZ>**

> Reviews: *Booklist* 3/15/2001, *SLJ* 4/1/2001, *VOYA* 8/1/2001

---

811   Herrera, Juan Felipe. ***Laughing Out Loud, I Fly.*** unpaged.

> HarperCollins 1998 Trade 0060276045 $15.95

A collection of poems in English and Spanish are set against images from Mexican folk art. Winner of the 2000 Pura Belpré Award. **Grades 6—12. PJ**

> Reviews: *SLJ* 5/1/1998, *VOYA* 6/1/1999

---

811   Janeczko, Paul B. ***How to Write Poetry.*** 117 pages.

> Scholastic 2001 Paper 0590100785 $6.95
> Scholastic 1999 Trade 0590100777 $12.95

The award-winning poet shares with teens everything he knows about writing poetry. The book is smartly organized into five chapters: "Getting Ready," "Starting to Write," "Writing Poems That Rhyme," "Writing Free Verse Poems," and "When Your Poem Is Finished." In each chapter, Janeczko provides instruction, inspiration, and plenty of examples. The examples are sometimes from his own work, sometimes from that of other poets, and, on occasion, from teen poets. There are plenty of writing exercises and other poem starters, as well as instructions on poetry pitfalls to avoid. **Grades 6—9. PJ**

---

811   Janeczko, Paul B. (Editor). ***Place My Words Are Looking For.*** 150 pages.

> Macmillan 1990 Trade 0027476715 $17.00

An anthology, not just of poems, but also about poetry. The works of over 40 poets representing a wide range of styles are presented. But the real hook is the story behind the poem as each poet talks about his or her art. **Grades 6—9. PJ <YALSA>**

---

811   Johnson, Dave (Editor). ***Movin': Teen Poets Take Voice.*** 52 pages.

> Orchard 2000 Trade 053130258X $15.95
> Orchard 2000 Paper 0531071715 $6.95

Poets House and the New York Public Library sponsored a series of teen poetry workshops in branch libraries. At these workshops, teens not only read and listened to poetry, but also had a chance to create some of their own. The best of those poems are reprinted here, augmented by drawings from award-winning picture-book illustrator Chris Raschka. **Grades 7—12. PJ**

> Reviews: *Booklist* 3/15/2000, *SLJ* 5/1/2000, *VOYA* 6/1/2000

---

811   Kaufman, Alan (Editor). **The Outlaw Bible of American Poetry.** 685 pages.

Thunder's Mouth 1999 Paper 1560252278 $24.95

Before there were Def poetry slams, there were the beat poets smashing through convention with raw verse and rhyme. The singer-songwriters followed the beats in the
rock generation, most notably Bob Dylan. This volume collects the best of these fringe
poets who, Kaufman writes, "don't get taught in American poetry 101." The canvas is
broader still as stand-up comics like Lenny Bruce and Richard Pryor are featured, as are
activists like Che Guevara as well as performance artists. The book isn't a collection of
poems in any traditional sense, but rather words wrapped in an attitude of rebellion
and edgy expression, staking out new territory. Slammers, ranters, punks, and rappers
will find inspiration within the many pages. In addition to the words themselves, there
is information about the writers, interviews, news clippings, and photographs, including photographs of clubs and cafes. **Grades 10—12 (mature). PJ**

811   Kherdian, David (Editor). **Beat Voices.** 212 pages.

Henry Holt 1995 Trade 0805033157 $14.95

"I saw the best minds of my generation" begins Allan Ginsberg's *Howl,* the poem that
kicks off this collection celebrating the beat generation of the 1950s. As the book
begins with the definitive poem of the beat movement, it ends with a long excerpt
from the prose apex: Kerouac's is-it-fact-or-is-it-fiction opus, *On the Road.* In between
these bookends are the voices of others who heard the rallying cry of the beats and set
out to revolutionize writing. The beats were outsiders using words as their weapons
of rebellion, setting the stage for the experimentation of the 1960s. In addition to the
works, there are biographical sketches for each writer, many who failed to live long or
successful lives after breaking through as part of the beat scene. Just as pop music was
forming into rock and roll, the beats were taking the language and action of the
streets, in particular drug use, and putting it on the page. **Grades 8—12. PJ**

Reviews: *Booklist* 5/15/1995, *SLJ* 11/1/1995, *VOYA* 10/1/1995

811   Kilcher, Jewel. **Night Without Armor.** 138 pages.

HarperCollins 1999 Paper 0061073628 $11.00
HarperCollins 1998 Trade 0060191988 $18.00

Although she's a musician with a couple of huge-selling albums to her name, Jewel
Kilcher fancies herself a poet. In this collection of 80+ free-verse poems, Kilcher
tackles a wide variety of topics and textures. Growing up on a small farm in Alaska,
Kilcher's very much in tune with environment, and many of the poems reflect upon
the natural world. Yet, as the title suggests, like so many young poets, it is the world
of the self that most concerns her in these poems that tingle on the raw nerve of
honest self-expression. **Grades 8—12. PJ**

811   Myers, Walter Dean. **Harlem.** unpaged.

Scholastic 1997 Trade 0590543407 $16.95

Myers writes the text in the form of poetry while his son provides the art in the media of collage in this living tribute to Harlem. Yet, both rise above the limits of those words: the text isn't as much poetry as it is a song, which makes sense as music coming from the streets and songwriters of Harlem drives the work. The collages are also more than that; they are meant not to illustrate, but illuminate and inspire. **Grades 8—12. PJ**

Reviews: *Booklist* 2/15/1997, *SLJ* 2/1/1997

811   Nye, Naomi Shihab (Editor). **What Have You Lost?** 205 pages.

HarperTempest 2001 Paper 0380733072 $9.95
Greenwillow 1999 Trade 0688161847 $18.95

An intriguing title question, for loss is certainly one of the most common emotions felt by young people as they come of age. Loss of innocence, loss of loved ones, and sometimes even a loss of perspective: all of those and more are covered by this collection of over 140 poets. While there are some "names" here, many of the poets are being published for the first time. The book is illustrated with black-and-white photos of teens. While they don't comment directly upon individual poems, collectively the photos demonstrate the strength in the faces of these young people, as well as a reminder that loss isn't like a photograph: loss is not simply black-and-white, but rather an experience with many colors and textures. **Grades 6—12. PJ**

Reviews: *Booklist* 4/1/1999, *SLJ* 4/1/1999, *VOYA* 10/1/1999

811   Plath, Sylvia. **Collected Poems.** 351 pages.

HarperCollins 1992 Paper 0060909005 $17.50

It seems sometimes as if the Sylvia Plath mystique is about to overload her reputation as poet, and that is a shame. So gifted was Plath that her work is still required reading for many graduate students of literature, and this collection bears out that longevity. Among her nearly perfect poems are "Lady Lazarus," "Ariel," "Daddy," "Snakecharmer," and "Kindness." These, however, are a mere handful of the dozens of works here (all post—1956), all so crystalline that reading them is like beholding pieces of fabulously cut glass. Plath was a very serious linguistic artist, and often her meanings require study, thought, and debate. The high school junior who adores *The Bell Jar* would have to be a very advanced scholar indeed to parse out many of these poems. Recommended for the sophisticated reader and any who love the complexities of poetry at its most challenging and brilliant. **Grades 9—12. PT**

Reviews: *Booklist* 1/1/1995, *Booklist* 8/1/1997

811   Rosenberg, Liz (Editor). ***The Invisible Ladder: An Anthology of Contemporary Poems.*** 210 pages.

Henry Holt 1996 Trade 0805038361 $18.95

The poems selected by Rosenberg were not written for young people. Instead they demonstrate that "adult" poets can speak to the emotional experience of teens. The book is arranged alphabetically by author and features 38 poems and poets. In addition to the poems themselves, there are photos of each poet both as an adult and as a young person, as well as a short narrative about the poem or writing process. **Grades 7—12. PJ**

Reviews: *Booklist* 9/15/1996, *SLJ* 2/1/1997, *VOYA* 2/1/1997

---

811   Shakur, Tupac. ***The Rose That Grew from Concrete.*** 149 pages.

Simon & Schuster 2000 Trade 0671028448 $20.00

Tupac's poetry is as essential to a collection serving teens as *The Outsiders* or *Holes*. What matters here is not the poetry itself, but rather the effect these words and images have, on young men in particular. Tupac's message is about rising above circumstances and being true to oneself. **Grades 7—12. PJ**

Reviews: *Booklist* 3/15/2001, *SLJ* 7/1/2000, *VOYA* 10/1/2000

---

811   Soto, Gary. ***Neighborhood Odes.*** 68 pages.

Harcourt 1992 Trade 0152568794 $15.95

A small collection of verse for younger teens focusing on growing up Latino. **Grades 6—9. PJ**

Reviews: *Booklist* 6/15/1992, *SLJ* 5/1/1992

---

811   Von Ziegesar, Cecily. ***Slam.*** 157 pages.

Penguin Putnam 2000 Trade 0141309199 $5.99

Featuring an intro by musician/poet/angst teen-icon Tori Amos, this is a wide collection of verse, from Shakespeare to the Beastie Boys. Dubbed by one Amazon teen reviewer as "the best teen poetry book out there!" **Grades 7—12. PJ**

---

811   Watson, Esther Pearl (Editor). ***The Pain Tree: And Other Teenage Angst-Ridden Poetry.*** 62 pages.

Houghton Mifflin 2000 Paper 0618047581 $6.95
Houghton Mifflin 2000 Trade 0618015582 $16.00

Despite the tongue-in-cheek title, this is a slender volume of poems written by and for teens. The editors used Web sites, teen Web portals, and even teen magazines to find submissions, augmenting them with excellent illustrations. **Grades 7—12. PJ**

Reviews: *Booklist* 3/15/2001, *SLJ* 9/1/2000, *VOYA* 6/1/2000

---

812   Miller, Arthur. ***Death of a Salesman.*** 139 pages.

Penguin 1998 Paper 0141180978 $10.00

"Attention must be paid," cries Willy Loman's wife, considering the plight of her husband, the traveling salesman whose life is unraveling faster than he can pull it together, and in her words lie the crux of the play. Low man, indeed, Willy has built his career on hard work and illusion, with the first surrendering to the destruction of the second. Willy's relationships with his two sons, his boss, his wife, and even himself come under scrutiny during the course of three acts, and all are found pathetically wanting. Arthur Miller wrote this play as a "tragedy of the common man," formulating the theory that Greek tragedy, in which the heroes were usually gods or kings, no longer had reflective bearing on modern society. Like its classical counterparts, however, the play ends with Willy's death, not by the forces of fate or gods, but by his own hand in his shabby basement, a symbol for the depths to which the so-called common man can, unawares, fall. Generally on the main course menu for students of American literature, Miller's most famous work is simply a necessity for any collection. **Grades 6—12. PT**

---

812   Zindel, Paul. ***The Effect of Gamma Rays on Man in the Moon Marigolds.*** 128 pages.

Bantam 1970 Paper 0553280287 $5.99

This Pulitzer Prize-winning play centers on the fractured family life of an eccentric woman and her two teenage daughters. Biting dialogue and poetic monologues make this of interest to both young actors and avid readers. **Grades 7—12. PJ**

---

813   Singer, Marilyn (Editor). ***Stay True: Short Stories for Strong Girls.*** 204 pages.

Apple 1999 Paper 0590360337 $4.99

As a nice companion to all the various collections of writings by teen girls comes this anthology of short stories about the adolescent female experience. Although there are only a few well-known names here (Norma Fox Mazer, M. E. Kerr, and Rita Williams Garcia), the themes within these stories should be quite recognizable to young adult readers. Most of the stories are about teen girls developing a strong sense of self, often in the face of negativity from their families, friends, and peers. **Grades 6—9. PJ**

Reviews: *Booklist* 4/1/1998, *SLJ* 5/1/1998

---

813   Carlson, Lori M. (Editor). ***American Eyes: New Asian-American Short Stories for Young Adults.*** 144 pages.

Fawcett 1996 Paper 0449704483 $5.50

A collection of short stories by 10 young Asian-American writers about bridging the gap between childhood and adulthood, as well as between two cultures—one that lives for the moment, the other that respects the past. A starred review in *School Library Journal* noted that the book "crackles and burns, warms and illuminates." **Grades 7–12. PJ**

Reviews: *Booklist 3/15/1998*

---

816   Canfield, Jack (Editor). ***Chicken Soup for the Teenage Soul: Letters.*** 325 pages.

Health Communications 2001 Paper 1558748040 $12.95
Health Communications 2001 Trade 1558748059 $24.00

A collection of letters written by teenagers in response to the best-seller, *Chicken Soup for the Soul.* The letters are by broad themes, such as "overcoming obstacles" and "helping others." The editors often tack notes onto the end of the letters referring teens to sources of information or additional resources. The book concludes with brief biographical sketches of both the letter writers and the editors**. Grades 6–12. PJ**

Reviews: *SLJ 7/1/2001*

---

817   Northcutt, Wendy. ***Darwin Awards: Evolution In Action.*** 327 pages.

Dutton 2000 Trade 0525945725 $17.95
Plume 2002 Paper 0452283442 $10.00

A book that seems to answer the age-old question: "Just how stupid can a person be?" The book is loaded with short, funny anecdotes and news reports of humans at their absolute dumbest, such as looking to see if a gas tank is full and deciding to use a match for illumination. Funny, and kind of scary. **Grades 10–12. PJ**

---

817   Onion Staff. ***Our Dumb Century: The Onion Presents 100 Years of Headlines from America's Finest News Source.*** 164 pages.

Three Rivers Press 1999 Paper 06098084618 $16.00

What happens when the funniest humor site on the Web goes into print? Simply, the funniest history lesson imaginable, with mock headlines and stories covering the big events of the 20th century. Funny, and in very bad taste, such as a caption of FDR asking, "Why does our joyless President never dance?" The bad taste is matched only by the four-letter words and preoccupation with sex jokes. This is not PG–13 material; it also might be the funniest work available for high school students who get it. **Grades 10–12 (mature). PJ**

817 Stewart, Jon. ***Naked Pictures of Famous People.*** 163 pages.

HarperCollins 1999 Paper 0688171621 $14.00

Stewart is the host of Comedy Central's *Daily Show*, quite possibly the funniest half-hour on television. But unlike most comedians, Stewart didn't just fill a book with jokes or greatest hits from his acts, instead he created a collection of fantastically funny comic essays. All of these are high on the bad-taste meter, such as his mock Larry King interview with Hitler or a fake exchange of letters between Princess Di and Mother Teresa. Smart comedy for sophisticated teens who take pride in getting the references. **Grades 10–12 (mature). PJ**

818 Canfield, Jack (Editor). ***Chicken Soup for the Teenage Soul I.*** 354 pages.

Health Communications 1997 Paper 1558744630 $12.95
Health Communications 2001 Trade 1558744681 $24.00

Stories, poems, sketches, and short essays written (and edited by) teenagers designed to show the writers and the readers that they are not alone. The essential experience of adolescence, in all of its "angsty" glory, is the central theme of these writings dealing with topics such as betrayal, friendship, first love, lost love, and finding a place in the world. As of this writing, there are two sequels: *Chicken Soup for the Teenage Soul II* and *Chicken Soup for the Teenage Soul III.* **Grades 6–12. PJ**

Reviews: *SLJ* 10/1/1997

818 Poe, Edgar Allan. ***The Raven and Other Poems and Tales.*** 256 pages.

Bulfinch Press 2001 Trade 0821227726 $16.95

American inventor of the detective story, perfector of the horror tale, and creator of some of the most popular poetry in American letters, Edgar Allan Poe's work still retains its popular appeal over 150 years after original publication. His work remains required reading in schools, appears at Halloween readings, has been made into dozens of films (most notably Roger Corman's, all of which take gigantic liberties with Poe's texts), has inspired paintings and tribute stories, and is among the most recognizable and constant allusions on the literary scene. This collection of 16 poems and tales is illustrated with appropriately creepy renderings by Daniel Alan Green that bring an added depth. While the poetry works easily for most reading levels, the horror stories are laden with 19th-century vernacular and the long, baroque sentences Poe was most fond of, and are not readily accessible to many of the under-high-school-aged. **Grades 6–12. PT**

823 Fonstad, Karen Wynn. ***Atlas of Middle Earth.*** 219 pages.

Houghton Mifflin 1992 Paper 0395535166 $19.95
Mariner 2001 Paper 0618126996 $24.00

With *The Hobbit* always listed as one of teens' favorite books, this book is a must for every collection. Not just some cheap tie-in to go along with the movie, this is a serious, yet entertaining, work that brings Middle Earth if not to life, then at least to scale. The author used not only Tolkien's texts but also drafts, edited sections, and other data to create a colorful series of maps. Like any good historical atlas, in addition to the general maps there are also documents for specific battles, specific locations, and thematic representations. **Grades 8–12. PJ**

---

823 Hoff, Benjamin. ***The Tao of Pooh.*** 158 pages.

> Puffin 2001 Paper 0140067477 $11.95
> Dutton 1982 Trade 0525244581 $19.95

Children love Winnie-the-Pooh, while many college students explore Eastern religion: the two are combined in this popular volume. One of the world's great Taoist masters isn't Chinese, or a venerable philosopher; he is Milne's effortlessly calm, still, reflective bear, Winnie-the-Pooh. While Eeyore frets and Piglet hesitates and Rabbit calculates and Owl pontificates, Pooh just is. **Grades 10–12. PJ**

---

823 Kronzek, Allan. ***The Sorcerer's Companion: A Guide to the Magical World of Harry Potter.*** 286 pages.

> Broadway Books 2001 Paper 0767908473 $15.00

One of the keys to the success of the Harry Potter books was author J. K. Rowling's ability to strike a chord with readers. In this volume, the authors find the notes within those chords. The 84 entries are arranged in alphabetical order, most essays running between two and four pages. The "stuff" of the Potter books—owls, amulets, wizards, magic, love potions, and spells—are all explained. Fans of the Rowling books will learn here how she drew deeply on English literature, legend, folklore, and folk medicine, as well as ancient history, to create Harry Potter's magical world. **Grades 6–12. PJ**

> Reviews: *SLJ* 12/1/2001, *VOYA* 2/1/2002

---

827 Lewis, C. S. ***The Screwtape Letters.*** 128 pages.

> HarperSanFrancisco 2001 Paper 0060652934 $10.00
> HarperSanFrancisco 2001 Trade 0060652896 $19.95

C. S. Lewis, philosopher, theologian, creator of famous children's literature, had his greatest adult success with *The Screwtape Letters*, and rightly so. Echoing Mark Twain's *Letters from the Earth*, Lewis' premise explores what might happen if Satan got a yen to correspond with his nephew "Wormwood" to advise him on the best methods for perverting human love. There's a certain glee in Screwtape's intellectualizing, reminiscent of Lord Chesterfield's letters to his son on how to conduct oneself as a successful gentleman ("Never apologize, never explain"); that's part of the fun of what is essentially a philosophical treatise on How to Beat the Devil at His Own Game (If You Read between His Lines). Be aware: this is NOT for children, either in

subject or execution. It is, however, Lewis' best in a long line of brilliant works.
Grades 10–12. PT

---

860 Nye, Naomi Shihab (Editor). ***The Tree Is Older Than You Are: A Bilingual Gathering of Poems and Stories from Mexico with Paintings by Mexican Artists.*** 111 pages.

Aladdin 1998 Paper 0689820879 $13.00
Simon & Schuster 1995 Trade 0689802978 $19.95

This gathering of poems and stories, told in both the original Spanish and translated into English, transcends borders as it invites readers into a shared world of ideas, visions, and dreams. Sixty-four great Mexican writers and painters are collected here.
Grades 6–9. PJ

Reviews: *Booklist* 9/15/1995, *SLJ* 10/1/1995

---

892 Gibran, Kahlil. ***The Prophet.*** 96 pages.

Walker 1986 Paper 0802725325 $7.95
Random House 1973 Trade 0394404289 $15.00

For the last 80 years, Gibran's poetics have stirred readers to comfort and contemplation. *The Prophet* muses on marriage, love, work, moderation, pleasure, friendship: in short, all the aspects of life that make it worth living. Despite sneering from distant corners of the intelligentsia, *The Prophet* continues to evoke, inspire, and bring its readers to peace. The young reader can discover the prophet's words; the older reader may revisit them with the advantages of experienced life. **Grades 10–12. PT**

---

910 Callahan, Steven. ***Adrift.*** 234 pages.

Ballantine 1987 Paper 0345410157 $12.95

An amazing true story of survival. Steven Callahan set sail in his small sailboat from the Canary Islands, bound for the Caribbean. Six days out the sloop sank, and Callahan found himself adrift in the Atlantic in a five-and-a-half-foot inflatable raft with only three pounds of food and eight pints of water. He would drift for 76 days over 1,800 miles of ocean before he reached land and rescue. **Grades 9–12. PJ**

Reviews: *Booklist* 1/1/1995, *SLJ* 1/1/1995

---

910 Junger, Sebastian. ***The Perfect Storm.*** 226 pages.

HarperCollins 1998 Paper 006101351X $6.99
HarperCollins 1999 Paper 0060977477 $14.00
Random House 2000 Trade 037541651X $22.95

"This man wrote; he put down on a scrap of paper the last moments of twenty men in this world. Then he corked the bottle and threw it overboard." So Sebastian Junger introduces us to the men of the *Andrea Gail* (a name that turned out to be unfortunate, indeed), a ship lost to the "perfect storm," which blew into Nova Scotia and the northeastern part of the United States in October 1991. The crew of six was lost in the Atlantic, and Junger manages to weave the threads of their stories into the fabric of the freak storm's birth, growth, and ultimately fatal power. Working from survivors' accounts, published material, media reviews, and his own and other eyewitnesses' testimony, he builds the story to its inexorably tragic end, giving the reader a good deal of fishing and maritime information along the way. Perhaps the book is not the best choice for those trying to conquer aquaphobia, but for everyone else, it is a splendid mix of history and historical imagination. **Grades 10—12. PT**

Reviews: *SLJ* 11/1/1997

---

910 Read, Piers Paul. ***Alive.*** 352 pages.

Avon 1992 Paper 038000321X $7.99

Novelist Piers Paul Read turns his hand to nonfiction with *Alive*, and his hand is deft, indeed. What begins as a rugby team's trip to a tournament turns into a modern day Donner party after their plane crashes off the radar in the Andes. Of 32 survivors, only 16 made it out alive. While it is an account of the extremes a human being will endure to survive, it is also a story of love, courage, loyalty, and sacrifice. Some of the boys, knowing death is fast approaching, beg the stronger ones to make use of their bodies when they've gone, becoming symbols for the triumph of the human spirit. Such a history would suffer from garishness in lesser hands, but Read handles the sensitive material superbly, and the narrative unfolds with the suspense of a novel. Certainly very accessible prose, but some younger readers might not be ready for the subject matter. **Grades 7—12. PJ**

---

917 Krakauer, Jon. ***Into the Wild.*** 207 pages.

Doubleday 1997 Paper 0385486804 $12.95
Random House 1996 0679450254 $18.00

Krakauer's nonjudgmental adventure tale of a young man from a wealthy family who gives away his possessions, walks into the Alaska wilderness, and dies. The book isn't afraid to leave questions unanswered and allows Chris McCandless' desire to move away from society an opportunity to speak for itself. **Grades 10—12. JW**

Reviews: *Booklist* 12/1/1995

---

919 Armstrong, Jennifer. ***Shipwreck at the Bottom of the World.*** 134 pages.

Crown 1999 Trade 0517800136 $18.00
Crown 1999 Library 0517800144 $19.99

Crown 1900 Paper 0375810498 $11.95

The story of the Shackelton shipwreck was hidden from history for some time until the past few years, when it became a cottage industry. This heavily illustrated volume is aimed at young readers, but it is still rich in detail. The gripping tale of a group of men who are stranded without hope, yet still fight on. **Grades 6—9. PJ**

Reviews: *Booklist* 12/1/1998, *SLJ* 4/1/1999

920 Hansen, Joyce (Editor). ***Women of Hope: African Americans Who Made a Difference.*** 31 pages.

Scholastic 1998 Cloth 0590939734 $16.95

Twelve famous African American women, such as writer Alice Walker and activist Fannie Lou Hamer, are featured in this slender volume. The text is secondary to a splendid series of black-and-white photos that show the strength in the faces and bodies of African Americans who made a difference, primarily by showing valor in the face of tribulation. **Grades 6—9. PJ**

921. Angelou, Maya. ***I Know Why the Caged Bird Sings.*** 281 pages.

Bantam 1983 Paper 0553279378 $5.99
Random House 1970 Trade 0394429869 $20.00

Angelou's masterpiece. A series of memories of her childhood and youth, some of which is fairly ugly, the book is accessible to all readers and paints a raw picture of racism, sexism, and sexual abuse without being graphic, didactic, or crude. **Grades 10—12. PT <YALSA>**

921 Brooks, Polly. ***Beyond the Myth.*** 176 pages.

Houghton Mifflin 1999 Paper 0395981387 $8.95

Focusing on one year of Joan of Arc's life to tell the story, Brooks also provides readers with a glimpse into the political and social climate of 15th-century France. Brooks shows how a spirited young woman became a patron saint and a symbol to women across the years. **Grades 6—9. PJ <YALSA>**

921 Brown, Claude. ***Manchild in the Promised Land.*** 415 pages.

Simon & Schuster 1999 Paper 0684864185 $13.00

A tale of the streets that reads like fiction, but seems more like an autobiography. Published in the 1960s, it was a landmark book looking at the underclass in Harlem through the story of one young man who made it through to the other side, but not before experiencing a life of crime, violence, and poverty. **Grades 10—12. PJ**

921   Carroll, Jim. **Basketball Diaries.** 212 pages.

Penguin 1995 Paper 0140249990 $13.00

A controversial choice for any collection, especially in light of the movie version
starring Leonardo DiCaprio, which features a fantasy sequence of a trench-coat-
wearing teen using bullets to gain revenge on those who have tormented him.
Carroll is a cutting-edge New York poet, songwriter, heroin addict, street hustler, and
pal to the Rolling Stones. This book purports to be his actual diaries from his teen
years, when he was growing up in the 1960s on the "mean streets" of New York. The
language is as raw as the emotional expression that one might expect from an angry,
confused young man. **Grades 8—12 (mature). PJ**

921   Conway, Jill. **The Road from Coorain.** 238 pages.

Vintage 1990 Paper 0679724362 $12.00

This is a remarkable journey that reads like fiction, and all the more memorable because it
is autobiography. From the grasslands of Australia, where Jill Kerr Conway grew up on an
isolated sheep ranch, to Northampton, Massachusetts, the book chronicles her rise from
backwoods nobody to first woman president of Smith College. Rich in detail, and smooth
in prose, Conway's memories are a delight, and an especially good recommendation for the
reader ready to venture into contemporary biography, not to mention a flat contradiction
to those naysayers who insist that the American Dream is dead. **Grades 10—12. PT**

921   Dahl, Roald. **Boy: Tales of Childhood.** 160 pages.

Penguin 1984 Paper 0140089179 $9.95
Farrar Straus Giroux 1984 Trade 0374373744 $17.00

A good argument could be made that all of Dahl's books might be considered part of
a core collection for young adults. His humor, irreverence, and storytelling skills
make his works a favorite to folks of all ages, but this autobiographical volume will
suffice since it provides the real life inspiration for his best-known works. However,
his boyhood was not all fun and games as caning was the rule of the day in British
schools for rule-breakers like Dahl. **Grades 7—12. PJ**

921   Donofrio, Beverly. **Riding in Cars with Boys: Confessions of a Bad Girl
Who Makes Good.** 204 pages.

Penguin 2001 Paper 0140296298 $13.00
Penguin 1992 Paper 0140156291 $13.00.

With a catchy subtitle and a semi-successful movie behind it, this is a memoir of
Donofrio's wild times during the 1960s. A rebellious teen whose father is a police
officer is a recipe for risky behavior, which Donofrio engages in eagerly. Pregnant by
her senior year in high school and soon to get heavily into drugs, she's a "bad girl"

cliché. That is part of the story; the other is how she turned her life around, primarily through the power of reading. An entertaining, inspiring read that bears occasional resemblance to the Drew Barrymore film. **Grades 10—12 (mature). PJ**

921   Freedman, Russell. ***Eleanor Roosevelt: A Life of Discovery.*** 198 pages.

Clarion 1997 Paper 0395845203 $10.95
Clarion 1993 Trade 0899198627 $17.95

Freedman plus photo-essay equals lots of awards, such as Best Book for Young Adults, Notable Books, *Booklist* Editors' Choice, Golden Kite Award, *Boston Globe/Horn Book Award, Bulletin of the Center for Children's Books* Blue Ribbon Winner, *Horn Book* Fanfare Selection, Newbery Honor Book, *Publishers Weekly* Best Books of the Year, and *School Library Journal* Best Books of the Year. **Grades 6—12. PJ <YALSA>**

921   Freedman, Russell. ***Franklin Delano Roosevelt.*** 150 pages.

Clarion 1992 Paper 0395629780 $8.95
Houghton Mifflin 1990 Trade 089919379X $18.00

Another photo essay by Freedman, which won just about every award and honor for which it was eligible. The stories of Roosevelt's personal struggles are juxtaposed with the troubles faced by the nation he led from 1933 to 1945. **Grades 6—12. PJ**

Reviews: *SLJ* 12/1/1990

921   Freedman, Russell. ***Lincoln: A Photobiography.*** 200 pages.

Houghton Mifflin 1987 Paper 0395518482 $7.95
Houghton Mifflin 1987 Trade 0899193803 $18.00

A description of the boyhood, marriage, and young professional life of Abraham Lincoln, using photos and selections from Lincoln's own writings. In addition to winning the Newbery Award, this title was also named *Booklist* Editors' Choice, ALA Best Book for Young Adults, ALA Notable Book, *Horn Book* Fanfare Selection, *Publishers Weekly* Best Books of the Year, and *School Library Journal* Best Books of the Year. **Grades 6—10. PJ <YALSA>**

921   Hansberry, Lorraine. ***To Be Young, Gifted, and Black.*** 266 pages.

Vintage 1995 Paper 0679764151 $12.00

Liberally sprinkled with half-century-old African American slang, this autobiography of the author of the play *A Raisin in the Sun* may prove challenging for less sophisticated readers. That said, the late Hansberry's book is valuable not only for the information it imparts, but for the pleasure of reading about the world, difficult as it might be, through her eyes. **Grades 10—12. PT**

921 Haskins, James. ***The Life and Death of Martin Luther King, Jr.*** 150 pages.

Morrow 1992 Paper 0688116906 $6.95

Haskins is the author of more than a hundred books, with many of them aimed at teaching African American history to young people. In this short but powerful work, Haskins examines the impact of Dr. King, as well as the circumstances of his death and the highpoints of his life. **Grades 6—9. PJ**

921 Marrin, Albert. ***Commander in Chief: Abraham Lincoln.*** 246 pages.

Dutton 1997 Trade 0525458220 $25.00

Marrin, like his doppelgänger Russell Freedman, is to youth biography and history what Ken Burns is to documentary filmmaking. He relies very heavily on primary source material to shape the image of his subject: The details make the man. At the same time, like Burns and Freedman, Marrin looks at the big picture and places his subjects within the context of the times, focusing always on how that person changed those times. Using an engaging style that brings in texture but doesn't get buried in it, Marrin gives readers a portrait of Lincoln, the imperfect person facing incredible pressures and making the best decisions possible, while keeping them grounded in his basic beliefs about humanity and the role of government. **Grades 7—12. PJ <TEN>**

Reviews: *Booklist* 12/15/1997, *SLJ* 2/1/1998

921 McCourt, Frank. ***Angela's Ashes.*** 364 pages.

Simon & Schuster 1996 Trade 0684874350 $25.00

Son of a drunken, wastrel father and a despairing, poverty-stricken mother, Frank McCourt grew up in the slums of Limerick, Ireland, in the kind of environment that would have done the urchins of Charles Dickens proud. His brothers and sisters died regularly from disease and starvation, and his mother, the anchor of the family, battled depression resulting from an almost inhuman struggle to keep her children alive. A memoir that reads with the fluidity of a novel, McCourt's autobiography is sometimes difficult to take in its endless catalog of deprivation, but it is also consistently fascinating. **Grades 10—12 (mature). PT**

Reviews: *Booklist* 8/1/1996, *Booklist* 8/1/1997, *SLJ* 6/1/1997

921 Mowat, Farley. ***Woman in the Mists: The Story of Dian Fossey and the Mountain Gorillas of Africa.*** 380 pages.

Warner 1998 Paper 0446387207 $10.95

Mowat uses letters, journal entries, and other documents to provide readers with insight into the real Dian Fossey. This moving portrait of one of the best known scientists served as the basis for a successful motion picture. **Grades 8—12. PJ**

921 Myers, Walter Dean. ***Bad Boy.*** 214 pages.

> HarperCollins 2001 Library 0060295244 $15.89
> HarperTempest 2002 Paper 0064472884 $6.95
> HarperCollins 2001 Trade 0060295236 $15.95

Perhaps one of the reasons that Myers has been so successful as a young adult novel-ist is that his teen years were in many ways the stuff of teen literature. He struggled with identity, in particular what it meant to be black. He asked questions about his place in the world and what effect the events of the world (WWII) had on his life. He was an outsider, although not an outcast, who was looking for that one thing he could do well: which was writing. Rich in detail about Harlem in the 1940s, this is an entertaining, informational, but mostly inspirational volume for young men of color. **Grades 7—10. PJ**

> Reviews: *Booklist* 5/1/2001, *SLJ* 5/1/2001, *VOYA* 6/1/2001

921 Myers, Walter Dean. ***Malcolm X: By Any Means Necessary.*** 210 pages.

> Scholastic 1994 Paper 0590481096 $4.50

Myers employs his skills as a storyteller to sketch the life of the civil rights leader Malcolm X. Myers follows the life of Malcolm Little from petty criminal to one of the most influential figures of the 1960s. Black-and-white photos accompany the easy-to-read text. **Grades 6—9. PJ**

> Reviews: *Booklist* 8/1/1997

921 Salzman, Mark. ***Lost in Place.*** 273 pages.

> Random House 1995 Paper 0679767789 $13.00

A memoir of growing up in suburban America in the 1970s that touches on many timeless themes. Salzman's place in the world is perfectly normal: nice suburban home, professional parents, and standard-issue brothers and sisters. So Salzman's fas-cination with all things from the East, such as Kung Fu and Zen Buddhism, make him stand apart from the crowd. Like any YA novel about an outsider, *Lost in Place* has Salzman both delighting in iconoclasm but also longing for acceptance. **Grades 10—12. PJ**

> Reviews: *Booklist* 9/1/1995, *SLJ* 12/1/1995

921 Scott, Darrel. ***Journal of Rachel Scott: A Journey of Faith at Columbine High.*** 149 pages.

> Nelson 2001 Trade 0849975948 $9.99

The title is slightly misleading: these are not Rachel's true journals; instead they have been pasted together by her mother from Rachel's diary and other writings, as well as her drawing. The book ends with her entry for 20 April 1999, the day of her death during the shooting at Columbine High School. Following that entry is a short essay by Rachel's mother about her own journey to forgiveness and acceptance. The writing is nothing special, but Rachel's story is an important one. Readers are also encouraged throughout to reflect upon their own feelings and faith. **Grades 6–9. PJ**

Reviews: *SLJ* 8/1/2001

---

921 Vizzini, Ned. ***Teen Angst? Naaah—a Quasi-Autobiography*** 221 pages.

Free Spirit 2000 Paper 1575420848 $12.95
Laurel-Leaf 2002 Paper 044023767X $5.50

Unlike many personal narratives about teen years, Vizzini doesn't have far to look back, having published this when he was barely 20 years old. The book is a series of essays, some of which have been previously published, about teen life in these United States. There are pieces on parents, peers, pushing through school, smoking dope, playing Nintendo, and the rest of the adolescent experience. What Vizzini lacks in insight, he makes up for in wit, as many of the pieces, most accompanied with annotations in the margin, are LOL funny. **Grades 8–12. PJ**

Reviews: *Booklist* 10/15/2000, *SLJ* 11/1/2000

---

921 Wright, Richard. ***Black Boy.*** 501 pages.

HarperCollins 1998 Paper 0060929782 $13.00

One of the most influential voices in Black American literature, Richard Wright published this autobiography in 1945, but critical acclaim first arrived some 20 years later. Initially thought to be an attack on the White South, *Black Boy* pulls no punches and asks for no pity as it describes a childhood unknown to most middle-class Americans. Reared in the Jim Crow South in Mississippi and Tennessee, Wright recalls growing up poor, black, and despised. From such beginnings grew a writer whose understanding of what it is to be a 20th-century American is so penetrating that race is only one factor in his complex life journey. **Grades 10–12. PT**

---

921 X, Malcolm. ***The Autobiography of Malcolm X.*** 500 pages.

Ballantine 1992 Trade 0345379756 $25.00
Ballantine 1989 Paper 0345350685 $7.99
Ballantine 1992 Paper 0345376714 $15.00

Based upon his interviews by Alex Haley, this is the story of Malcolm X's traumatic childhood, which was plagued by racism; his years as a drug dealer and pimp; his conversion to the Nation of Islam while in prison; his subsequent years of militant activism; and the turn late in his life to more orthodox Islam. *Time* magazine recently named this book One of the Top Ten Works of Nonfiction for this century.

Essential for any library serving older teenagers who want to understand the Black Muslim movement and its charismatic leader, and who will also find inspiration in Malcolm X's spiritual renewal. **Grades 10—12. PJ**

---

940 Bachrach, Susan D. ***Tell Them We Remember.*** 109 pages.

> Little, Brown 1994 Paper 0316074845 $14.95
> Little, Brown 1994 Trade 0316692646 $21.95

Anne Frank was not the only one: this is the story of the other children murdered during the Holocaust. The volume was produced in association with the U.S. Holocaust Memorial Museum, using their vast archives of photos and documents. It features short selections, covering all aspects of the Holocaust. Photos supplement the text, although in many ways the photos are more powerful than any words. There are sidebar stories that focus on individual children. An excellent one-volume introduction to the Holocaust. **Grades 6—9. PJ**

> Reviews: *Booklist* 1/1/1995, *SLJ* 1/1/1995, *VOYA* 1/1/1995

---

940 Bitton-Jackson, Livia. ***I Have Lived a Thousand Years: Growing Up in the Holocaust.*** 224 pages.

> Aladdin 1999 Paper 0689823959 $4.99
> Simon & Schuster 1997 Trade 0689810229 $17.00

A Holocaust memoir describing the life of a 13-year-old Jewish girl during the Nazi invasion of Hungary in 1944. There are scenes of death camps, torture, forced labor, and mass graves. But, like many Holocaust memories, it is a story of hope, survival, and the power of love. **Grades 6—9. PJ**

> Reviews: *Booklist* 3/15/1997, *SLJ* 5/1/1997

---

940 Boas, Jacob. ***We Are Witnesses: Five Diaries of Teenagers Who Died in the Holocaust.*** 196 pages.

> Scholastic 1996 Paper 059084475X $4.50
> Henry Holt 1995 Trade 0805037020 $17.95

First-person accounts, including a selection from Anne Frank, of teens' coming of age in a land of genocide. **Grades 7—12. PJ <YALSA>**

> Reviews: *Booklist* 5/1/1995, *SLJ* 7/1/1995

---

940 Frank, Anne. ***The Diary of a Young Girl.*** 308 pages.

> Bantam 1993 Paper 0553296981 $4.99
> Doubleday 1995 Trade 0385473788 $26.00

Anne Frank's account of her short girlhood before entering hiding and her three years in an attic evading the Nazis has never waned in its power and pathos. Compelling to all readers from age 10 onward, the story is a simple and beautifully written account of one of the darkest periods in human history filtered through the eyes of a 13–year-old girl struggling with all the normal uncertainties of growing up, albeit in the most frightening of circumstances. For any reader, the *Diary* is fascinating and readily accessible, and always repays multiple readings. The newest edition includes passages originally omitted by Otto Frank, Anne's father, and gives insight into the complexities of the Franks' marriage and Anne's own approaching womanhood—a womanhood, sadly, she never lived to experience. **Grades 6–12. PT**

Reviews: *Booklist* 1/1/1995, *Booklist* 8/1/1997

---

940 Gies, Frances. ***The Knight in History.*** 255 pages.

Harper & Row 1987 Paper 0060914130 $14.00

Chivalry is alive and well in many of the fantasy novels that teens devour regardless of page counts. This book provides them with some truth behind the myth of the age of knights. Gies has written extensively on the Middle Ages, and this volume seems to draw together all the best information about the life and times of members of the chain mail brigades. **Grades 10–12. PJ**

Reviews: *Booklist* 8/1/1997

---

940 Gies, Miep. ***Anne Frank Remembered.*** 252 pages.

Simon & Schuster 1988 Paper 0671662341 $14.00

The Diary of a Young Girl is one of the most famous autobiographies, so it is not strange that those who sheltered Anne Frank and her family would come forward to tell her story from their point of view. Gies talks about her own experience in detail, while adding new light to the well-known portrait of a young girl growing up in the Holocaust. **Grades 6–9. PJ**

---

940 Gut Opdyke, Irene. ***In My Hands: Memories of a Holocaust Rescuer.*** 276 pages.

Knopf 1999 Library 0679991816 $19.99
Knopf 2001 Paper 0385720327 $12.00
Knopf 1999 Trade 0679891811 $18.00

Irene Gut's story is that of another type of Holocaust survivor: a story about those Gentiles who dared to help Jews escape and fight back. In the fall of 1939, the Nazis march into Poland, and Irene's days of training to be a nurse end quickly. She is forced into the service of the German army, working as a waitress in an officers' club. She uses that position to steal food and supplies for the Jews in the ghetto as well as to gather information for the Russians. She also smuggled Jews out of the work camps, ultimately hiding a dozen people in the home of a Nazi major, whose mistress she has become to aid those in hiding. *SLJ* noted, "No matter how many Holocaust stories one has read, this one is a must, for its impact is so powerful." **Grades 6—9. PJ**

Reviews: *Booklist* 6/1/1999, *SLJ* 6/1/1999

---

940 Houston, Jeanne Wakatsuki. ***Farewell to Manzanar.*** 177 pages.

Bantam 1983 Paper 0553272586 $5.99
Houghton Mifflin 2002 Trade 0618216200 $15.00

Jeanne Wakatsuki was seven years old in 1942 when her family was uprooted from their home and sent to live at Manzanar internment camp—with 10,000 other Japanese Americans. This is her story of what she and her family did in order to survive the ordeal. Yet, for every distraction that she could create to take her mind off her plight, she never could forget that she was a native-born American citizen who had been imprisoned without a trial and whose only crime was the color of her skin.
Grades 6—9. PJ

Reviews: *Booklist* 1/1/1995

---

940 Lobel, Anita. ***No Pretty Pictures: A Child of War.*** 193 pages.

Avon Camelot 2000 Paper 0380732858 $5.95
Greenwillow 1998 Trade 0688159354 $15.95

Lobel is known as a creator of children's picture books and for her pretty pictures, but her life as a child was anything but pretty. Between the ages of 5 and 10, Lobel's life was in constant danger, first moving and hiding from the Nazis, then finally being captured and sent to a concentration camp. Having survived, Lobel waited for years to tell her story, then did so, not as an adult looking back, but from the perspective of a child taking in the horror all around her. As if this were not horrible enough, she also was charged with caring for a younger brother's survival. A remarkable story of a childhood lost. **Grades 6—9. PJ <TEN>**

Reviews: *Booklist* 8/1/1998, *SLJ* 9/1/1998

---

940 Meltzer, Milton. ***Never to Forget: The Jews of T.*** 217 pages.

HarperCollins 1991 Paper 0064461181 $7.95

Meltzer is one of the great nonfiction writers for youth, primarily because he never writes about subjects; he writes about people. He takes big events and issues apart, always looking at the human element. He's not a reporter; he's not objective. There are no "two sides" to his books: there is good and there is evil; there is right and wrong. Meltzer relies heavily on first-person accounts, letting the victims tell the tale, allowing the staggering stats and numbing film clips to be replaced by tales of human suffering and superhuman courage. One of the best easy-to-read histories of the Holocaust, the book received numerous awards upon and after its publication, including Notable Children's Books, *School Library Journal* Best Book, *New York Times* Outstanding Children's Books, and the Sidney Taylor Book Award from the Association of Jewish Libraries. **Grades 6 —9. PJ**

---

940 Meltzer, Milton. ***Rescue: The Story of How Gentiles Saved Jews in the Holocaust.*** 258 pages.

HarperCollins 1991 Paper 0064461173 $7.95

A companion to *Never to Forget*, this was published around the time that the film *Schindler's List* was released. Meltzer tells the stories of the other Oscar Schindlers who risked their own lives and livelihoods to save Jews from the death camps. The stories read like small adventure tales with ordinary people taking extraordinary efforts to save even one life. Another heavily awarded book, *Rescue's* awards include Notable Children's Books, *School Library Journal* Best Books, and a Best Books Selection. **Grades 6—9. PJ**

---

940 Nelson, Peter. ***Left for Dead: The USS Indianapolis and a Young Man's Search for Justice.*** 201 pages.

Random House 2002 Library 0385900333 $17.99
Random House 2002 Trade 0385729596 $15.95

Sharks, government intrigue, war, survival, guts, and glory . . . plus a young teen trying to rewrite history. All in a nonfiction book that many of the boys will find to be a must-read. **Grades 6—9. MA**

Reviews: *Booklist* 4/1/2002, *VOYA* 8/1/2002

---

940 Rochman, Hazel (Editor). ***Bearing Witness: Stories of the Holocaust.*** 135 pages.

Orchard 1995 Trade 053109488X $15.95
Orchard 1995 Library 0531087883 $16.99

The title is misleading; this impressive collection contains much more than stories. There are personal narratives and interviews, as well as other genres, such as a film script and a comic strip. The comic strip is from *Maus* creator Art Spiegelman who, like the other authors, tells his family's tale of courage. The editor shows in this eclectic selection that regardless of how the tale is told, the Holocaust must be remembered, retold, and re-experienced. **Grades 7—12. PJ**

Reviews: *Booklist* 6/1/1995, *SLJ* 9/1/1995

---

950 Higa, Tomiko. ***The Girl with the White Flag.*** 127 pages.

Kondansha 1995 Paper 4770019467 $9.95

The author recounts how she was separated at age seven from her family on the

Okinawa battlefields during World War II, searched for her lost sisters for seven weeks, and eventually found the strength to survive on her own. **Grades 7–12. PJ**

951 Jiang, Aut Li. ***Red Scarf Girl.*** 285 pages.

> HarperTrophy 1998 Paper 0064462080 $6.99
> HarperCollins 1997 Trade 0060275855 $16.95

The winds of political upheaval often inspire great literature, and *Red Scarf Girl* is no exception. The year Ji-li turned 12, her whole world changed. An excellent academic and a student leader, Ji-li seemed to have had it all. But that was the year of China's Cultural Revolution, which led to a dramatic shift in status. Young people like Ji-li, who were on the top of the social order, sank to the bottom. Under an endless assault of propaganda from the government and hazing from the community, Ji-li's family lived every day in fear of arrest, assault, or even worse. When her father is finally arrested, Ji-li is forced to choose between her family and her future. **Grades 6–12. PJ**

> Reviews: *Booklist* 10/1/1997, *SLJ* 12/1/1997

951 Mah, Adeline Yen. ***Chinese Cinderella: True Story of an Unwanted Daughter.*** 205 pages.

> Bantam Doubleday Dell 2001 Paper 0440228654 $5.99
> Bantam 1999 Trade 0385327072 $16.95

Adeline Yen Mah's cruel stepmother dominated her childhood. While not a fairy tale, this personal narrative is packed with scary images of a powerless young woman yearning to escape to a better life. The answer is not Prince Charming, but education. In particular, it is through reading that Yen Mah first escapes her harsh daily life, but then discovers the power of literature in her life. Teens who feel like outcasts in their own families will find inspiration in this story. **Grades 7–12. PJ**

> Reviews: *Booklist* 10/1/1999, *SLJ* 10/1/1999

959 Denenberg, Barry. ***Voices from Vietnam.*** 251 pages.

> Scholastic 1997 Paper 0590435302 $4.99.

An oral history tracing the U.S. involvement in Vietnam, beginning in late 1940 and going through the last helicopter to leave the roof of the embassy in 1975. The narrative is told using letters and personal accounts of soldiers, military and political leaders, diplomats, intelligence officers, medical personnel, Vietnamese citizens, journalists, and members of the antiwar movement. **Grades 6–10. PJ**

> Reviews: *Booklist* 2/15/1995, *SLJ* 3/1/1995

959   Kovic, Ron. ***Born on the Fourth of July.*** 208 pages.

Simon & Schuster 1996 Paper 067173914X $6.99

Ron Kovic's transformation from regular guy to Vietnam vet is a harrowing story, and he writes it without euphemism or flinching. Source for the film starring Tom Cruise, Kovic's account of war and "recovery" is a good choice for students of history or anyone wanting an unvarnished view of the United States' involvement in the Vietnam "conflict." **Grades 10—12. PT**

---

959   Ung, Loung. ***First They Killed My Father.*** 240 pages.

HarperPerennial 2001 Paper 0060931388 $13.00
HarperCollins 2000 Trade 0060193328 $23.00

Written in the present tense, the book actually looks back at the years from 1975 to 1979 in Cambodia under the nightmare regime of Pol Pot. The brutality seems unending—beatings, starvation, attempted rape, mental cruelty—and yet the narrator (a young girl) never stops fighting for escape and survival. Sad and courageous, her life and the lives of her young siblings provide quite a powerful example of how war can so deeply affect children—especially a war in which they are trained to be an integral part of the armed forces. **Grades 10—12. PJ**

Reviews: *Booklist* 12/15/1999, *SLJ* 7/1/2000

---

959   Wallace, Terry. ***Bloods.*** 311 pages.

Ballantine 1985 Paper 0345311973 $6.99

Award-winning oral history of the experience of African American soldiers in Vietnam. Stark in language and loaded with gripping stories, this is an excellent nonfiction companion to *Fallen Angels* by Walter Dean Myers. **Grades 10—12 (mature). PJ**

---

973   Bolden, Tonya. ***33 Things Every Girl Should Know About Women's History: From Suffragettes to Skirt Lengths to the ERA.*** 240 pages.

Crown 2002 Library 0375911227 $18.99
Crown 2002 Paper 0375811222 $12.95

This slim volume uses photo essays, poems, drama, and letters to walk through women's history. Organized chronologically, the book begins with Abigail Adams's 1776 letter to her husband, but the book is not just a gathering of archives. Reading more like a long magazine article and loaded with illustrations, this is an empowering, engaging, inspiring, and informative look at the role women have played in shaping American history. **Grades 6—9. PJ**

Reviews: *Booklist* 3/1/2002, *SLJ* 4/1/200

---

973 Davis, Kenneth C. ***Don't Know Much About History: Everything You Need to Know about American History but Never Learned.*** 462 pages.

Avon 1991 Paper 0380712520 $14.00.

Using a question-and-answer format, Davis offers a radically different history education than that found in most high schools. Beginning with Columbus's voyage and continuing up until the Clinton years, Davis sets up myths and then shatters them. **Grades 8–12. PJ**

973 Loewen, James W. ***Lies My Teacher Told Me.*** 372 pages.

Touchstone 1996 Paper 0684818868 $15.00
New Press 1994 Trade 156584100X $24.95

Unlike some other works of this nature, which are more for infotainment, Loewen's work has a serious social and political purpose. It is not merely a matter of textbooks getting facts wrong, but rather the near total avoidance of race, gender, and class that Loewen wishes to expose. His vehicle is to take ten common topics in history texts, from the landing of the Pilgrims to the war in Vietnam, and illustrate time and time again how 12 standard issue history textbooks got it wrong. **Grades 9–12. PJ**

973 McPherson, James M. ***Battle Cry of Freedom.*** 904 pages.

Ballantine 1989 Paper 0345359429 $18.00
Oxford 1988 Trade 0195038630 $45.00

A Pulitzer Prize-winning history of the Civil War that brings to life the major players as well as the grunt soldiers. Proclaimed as an instant classic upon its release, this is the best one-volume work on the war and its background. **Grades 10–12. PJ**

Reviews: *Booklist* 1/1/1995, *Booklist* 8/1/1997

973 Wolfe, Tom. ***The Electric Kool-Aid Acid Test.*** 433 pages.

Doubleday 1999 Paper 0553380648 $14.95
Bantam 1883 Paper 0553264915 $7.50

If Jack Kerouac had lived a generation later, he might have written this psychedelic version of *On the Road.* Tom Wolfe joined Ken Kesey and his Merry Pranksters as they crossed country in a Day-Glo-painted VW bus, dropping acid and stirring up revolution. Fortunately for the reader, Wolfe declined all offers of LSD, so his account of this outrageous road trip is as reliable as Wolfe is going to get. Considered one of the inimitable chronicles of the 60s, this Acid Test is for everyone who remembers being there, those who were there but forgot, and those who only wished they'd been born in time to join in "tootling the multitudes." **Grades 10–12. PT**

973 Zinn, Howard. ***A People's History of the United States.*** 702 pages.

HarperPerennial 2001 Paper 0060937319 $18.00
HarperCollins 1999 Trade 0060194480 $35.00

Zinn, a historian and social activist, presents a different view of history—one focus-ing not on the accomplishments of "dead rich white guys," but one that includes the stories of blacks, women, war protesters, labor activists, and other groups whose voices are left unheard in most standard textbooks. **Grades 10–12. PJ**

974 Murphy, Jim. ***Blizzard: The Storm That Changed America.*** 136 pages.

Scholastic 2000 Trade 0590673092 $18.95

Murphy uses big events to look at historical changes. Just as the great fire in Chicago altered the history of the city, so did the great snowstorm of 1888 in New York City change the destiny and design of the Big Apple. The photographs, maps, and illustra-tions drive the point home about the powerful intensity of the storm that killed almost 800 people. The gimmick here is Murphy tells about the storm from many viewpoints, each "person" based on personal accounts from survivors as well as newspaper accounts. **Grades 6–9. PJ**

Reviews: *Booklist* 2/15/2001, *SLJ* 12/1/2000

975 Murphy, Jim. ***The Great Fire.*** 144 pages.

Scholastic 1995 Trade 0590472674 $18.95

Like Russell Freedman and Albert Marrin, Jim Murphy is working in the documen-tary-book format. Like a filmmaker, he makes history come alive in oversized volumes built on archival records, personal accounts, and a generous use of photographs, maps, and illustrations. While the center of the book is the Chicago Fire itself, Murphy looks at the context, complications, and the consequences of the event.
Grades 6–9. PJ

Reviews: *Booklist* 6/1/1995, *SLJ* 7/1/1995

978 Savage, Candace. ***Cowgirls.*** 134 pages.

Ten Speed 1996 Paper 0898158303 $25.95

A wonderful mix of photos and words tells the history of cowgirls. Savage amasses photos, illustrations, personal histories, letters, and lots of quotations to let young readers learn about these talented performers and young women in the West.
Grades 10–12. PJ

Reviews: *Booklist* 9/1/1996

CHAPTER 2

FICTION

Abelove, Joan. ***Saying It Out Loud.*** 136 pages.

> Dorling Kindersley 1999 Trade 0789426099 $15.95
> Puffin 2001 Paper 0141312270 $5.99

A tearjerker that transforms itself into literature about a teenage girl coping with her mother's illness. Mindy is a typical 16-year-old claiming her independence from her mother and feeling nothing but scorn for her detached father. She is thrust back into the family unit when her mother discovers she has a brain tumor. Told in a series of journal entries, the book chronicles Mindy's mother's slow and painful death, which is parallel to Mindy's coming of age. More complex than a Lurlene McDaniel offering, the issue is not death, but the grief, fear, and utter terror of loneliness that Mindy faces. **Grades 6—9. PJ**

> Reviews: *Booklist 9/1/1999, SLJ 9/1/1999*

Achebe, Chinua. ***Things Fall Apart.*** 215 pages.

> Anchor 1996 Paper 0385474547 $9.95
> Simon & Schuster 1989 Paper 067168762X $4.50
> Alfred A. Knopf 1992 Trade 0679417141 $14.50

Teen readers will have a positive reading experience with this novel concerning the theme of courage under the blood red skies of violence. The novel chronicles the life of Okonkwo, the leader of an Igbo (Ibo) community, from his banishment for accidentally killing a clansman through his seven years of exile to his return. While there are larger themes, such as the effects of colonialism in Africa, the real story is about living life as an outcast: a very powerful chord among teens of any color. **Grades 9—12. PJ**

> Reviews: *Booklist 8/1/1997*

Adams, Douglas. ***The Hitchhiker's Guide to the Galaxy.*** 215 pages.

> Pocket 1982 Paper 0671664964 $4.50.
> Ballantine 1997 Paper 0345418913 $12.95

Ballantine 1995 Paper 0345391802 $7.50

The classic, funny SF book features Arthur Dent, the nebbishy Everyman, caught up by intergalactic hitchhikers when Earth is wiped out to make way for an interstellar equivalent of a freeway exchange. As the weirdness escalates, the British humor gets both drier and wonkier. This is for fans of the *Red Dwarf* BBC series and *Monty Python and the Holy Grail.* The increasingly ill-named Hitchhiker's Trilogy is continued in *The Restaurant at the End of the Universe, Life, the Universe and Everything,* and *So Long, and Thanks for All the Fish.* **Grades: 7–12. KE <YALSA>**

Reviews: *Booklist* 1/1/1995, *VOYA* 1/1/1995.

Adams, Richard. **Watership Down.** 429 pages.

HarperPerennial 2001 Paper 0060935456 $13.00
Avon 1976 Paper 0380002930 $7.99

If rabbits, real rabbits, had a culture, religion, and mythology, this is what it would look like. With the depth and detail of background characteristic of J. R. R. Tolkien, the world of rabbits is richly imagined. When their habitat is threatened by destruction, a small band break away from their home warrens on a quest to find a safe place of their own. War, sex, romance, and danger drive the story forward, and the depth of characterization gives it heart. Fans of *Mrs. Frisby and the Rats of NIMH* or the mythopoeic Firebringer, as well as readers of "quest" fantasy, will find this deeply satisfying. **Grades: 7–12. KE <YALSA>**

Reviews: *Booklist* 1/1/1995

Alexander, Lloyd. **The Iron Ring.** 283 pages.

Puffin 2000 Paper 0141311959 $2.99
Puffin 1999 Paper 0141303484 $4.99
Dutton 1997 Trade 0525455973 $16.99

A young hero comes of age in an unusual fantasy setting: medieval India. After losing a rash bet to a mysterious late-night visitor, the young king Tamar's finger is marked by an iron ring: the symbol that his kingdom, possessions, and even his life are forfeit. Honor demands that he undertake a perilous journey to deliver the prize to the kingdom of the victor. Along the way, the reader enjoys discovering medieval Indian society, while our hero discovers true love, loyalty, and a sense of responsibility and duty to his people. A satisfying read for Alexander's many fans and for those who enjoy fantasy adventure. **Grades: 6–9. KE**

Reviews: *SLJ* 5/1/1997

Alexander, Lloyd. **Westmark.** 144 pages.

Firebird 2002 Paper 0141310685 $5.99

Book one of the Westmark Trilogy. In the imaginary, but utterly realistic, late-Renaissance kingdom of Westmark, Theo, a young printer's apprentice, runs afoul of the law, and his life and livelihood are destroyed. Suddenly the world he thought he understood is turned on its head, and he perceives the injustices and corruption that rot his government and his society. As he falls in with quirky and shady characters—Count Las Bombas, the charlatan; Musket, the dwarf; and Mickle, the street-wise urchin—he lurches from danger to danger. Theo's adventures continue in *The Beggar Queen*, in which Mickle comes into her own, and *Kestrel*, in which the revolution takes a surprising turn. As in all of Alexander's stories, coming of age, love, and loyalty are strong themes. Although his fantasy fans may be disappointed by the lack of magic, young teen readers of historical adventure will happily follow Theo's exploits. **Grades: 6—9. KE**

Almond, David. ***Heaven Eyes.*** 233 pages.

> Laurel-Leaf 2002 Paper 0440229103 $5.50
> Delacorte 2001 Trade 0385327706 $15.95

A surrealistic tale of four children who escape on a makeshift raft from a riverside English orphanage only to run aground onto a dark alternate reality called Black Middens. There they meet "Heaven Eyes," a ghostly child with webbed fingers, and her frightening, inarticulate "Grampa," and their plans for escape and freedom are subsumed in their murky and freakish new life. As with all of Almond's books, reality and magic, terror and light are fused to create an eerie mood. The complex relationship among the children drives the story forward, and the resolution, one of hope and redemption, make this a satisfying read. **Grades: 6—9. KE**

> Reviews: *Booklist* 1/1/2001, *SLJ* 3/1/2001

Almond, David. ***Kit's Wilderness.*** 240 pages.

> Bantam Doubleday Dell 2000 Trade 0385326653 $15.95
> Bantam Doubleday Dell 2001 Paper 0440416051 $4.99

An evocative sense of place—an English coal-mining village—and the theme that past and present are connected by our art and the stories that we tell, are the great strengths of this book. When 13-year-old Christopher Watson (Kit) moves to live with his grandfather, an old miner, he becomes involved in a creepy game of "Death" played out near the monument of an 1821 mining disaster. The edge between the living and the dead, past and present, blurs eerily in both Kit's mind and the reader's. Though the plot tends to meander, a hopeful ending makes *Kit's Wilderness* another compelling book of magical realism. **Grades 6—9. KE <PRINTZ>**

> Reviews: *Booklist* 1/1/ 2000, *SLJ* 3/1/ 2000, *VOYA* 4/1/2000

Almond, David. ***Skellig.*** 182 pages.

> Yearling 2000 Paper 0440416027 $4.99

Laurel-Leaf 2001 Paper 0440229081 $4.99
Delacorte 1999 Trade 038532653X $16.95

Preteen Michael's life is in chaos: his family has moved and his baby sister is in hospital and probably dying. Behind the house, however, he finds a dilapidated barn and a mysterious, and probably inhuman, creature, and across the way he finds a strange girl—and a potential friend. In sorting out his sorrow and the strangeness that enters his life, Michael finds meaning and friendship. The reader will turn the pages hoping to understand the Skellig's secrets and to find out whether Michael's sister will survive. Almond has created poetic magical realism for young teens. **Grades: 6—9. KE**

Reviews: *Booklist* 2/1/1999, *SLJ* 2/1/1999

Anaya, Rudolfo. ***Bless Me, Ultima.*** 262 pages.

Warner 1994 Paper 0446600253 $6.99
Warner 1999 Paper 0446675369 $12.95

Although this is an often-assigned classic, many teens will enjoy this novel, which touches the hot spots of adolescence. The book chronicles the coming of age of a Chicano boy in New Mexico in the 1940s. With themes related to social justice, morality, identity, and acceptance, this thin volume stands the test of time and transcends cultures. **Grades: 8—12. PJ**

Anderson, Laurie Halse. ***Fever 1793.*** 251 pages.

Aladdin 2002 Paper 0689848919 $5.99
Simon & Schuster 2000 Trade 0689838581 $16.00

Anderson tells the story of the yellow fever epidemic in Philadelphia near the end of the 18th century, which killed off one-tenth of the city's population, as well as the story of a young girl's coming of age. The central character is 16-year-old Mattie Cook, whose mother and grandfather run a pre-Starbucks coffee house popular with the locals. While the plague rages, business drops off and the body count begins to mount (including those close to Mattie), and those who can afford to flee head for higher ground. The disease hits closer to home when Mattie's mother is inflicted, causing Mattie and the rest of her family to leave the city. The book is rich in historical details: there is even a "bring out your dead" scene, and corpses begin to pile up near the docks. Each chapter begins with an actual diary entry taken from the later 1700s and the book concludes with notes about the research. **Grades: 6—9. PJ**

Reviews: *Booklist* 10/1/2000, *SLJ* 8/1/2000

Anderson, Laurie Halse. ***Speak.*** 197 pages.

Farrar, Straus & Giroux 1999 Trade 0374371520 $16.00
Penguin Putnam 2001 Paper 014131088X $7.99

The great irony of the book is that the voice of the narrator Melinda is so strong in the telling of her story, even though it is a story of how she rarely speaks. Due to an incident which remains unnamed throughout most of the book, Melinda is treated like an outcast at her school, a social leper, and a poster child for peer rejection. She is slowly slipping out of life, cutting class, avoiding school, and growing mute. At home, the situation is no better; she communicates with her parents through notes on the fridge. While the outside world doesn't hear Melinda's voice, readers do as her interior monologue shows a young woman limping each day through her pain, using humor and sarcasm as her crutches. When the book's secret is revealed, so is Melinda's voice, and she confronts the school's poster boy for perfection about his not-so-perfect past. **Grades 8–12. PJ <PRINTZ>**

Reviews: *Booklist* 9/15/99, *SLJ* 1999, *VOYA* 12/1/99

Andrews, V. C. ***Flowers in the Attic.*** 412 pages.

Pocket 1995 Paper 0671729411 $7.99

No critical barbs can derail the franchise that refused to let the author's death stand in the way of selling books. This is the book that started it all, although later came prequels and sequels and spin-offs too numerous to mention, but all in need of owning. An old-time gothic that works for teens because it hits upon the key issues of adolescent angst, speaks to teens' worst nightmares, and puts teen characters at risk again and again and again. **Grades 10–12. PJ**

Anthony, Piers. ***On a Pale Horse.*** 325 pages.

Ballantine 1989 Paper 0345338588 $6.99

Book one of the *Incarnations of Immortality* series begins when a young suicide, Zane, shoots Death rather than die. Unfortunately, he still loses his life, as he is forced to become the new avatar of Death, ending the lives of others. Zane quickly discovers that other Avatars exist, including Satan, whom Zane must thwart if he is to save the life of the woman he loves. The first book, original, clever, and quickly told, neatly sets up and answers, "What if an ordinary man became Death itself?" Teens of all ages are likely to be intrigued by the premise and more than satisfied by the fast-paced story and world of immortals. The other titles in the series, *And Eternity* (God), *Bearing an Hourglass* (time), *With a Tangled Skein* (fate), *Wielding a Red Sword* (war), *Being a Green Mother* (nature), and *For Love of Evil* (Satan) are likely to be in demand. They are uneven in quality and the premise becomes unwieldy before its conclusion. **Grades: 6–12. KE**

Anthony, Piers. ***A Spell for Chameleon.*** 344 pages.

Ballantine 1987 Paper 0345347536 $6.99

Bink is an ordinary young man in a land where everyone has magic—or else! If he doesn't find some magic soon, he'll be exiled and lose the lady he imagines he adores. His quest takes him across the now familiar and very popular landscape of Xanth, where he comes of age and discovers true love. Younger teens adore Piers Anthony's deft mix of puns, tongue-in-cheek pokes at fantasy conventions, and sword-and-sorcery action adventure. While the first four novels (*A Spell for Chameleon, The Source of Magic, Castle Roogna,* and *Centaur Aisle*), should be read in order as a connected series, subsequent books are increasingly stand-alone titles. **Grades: 6—12. KE**

Anthony, Piers. ***Split Infinity.*** 350 pages.

Ballantine 1987 Paper 0345354915 $6.99

Book one of the original *Apprentice Adept* series features an exotic science fictional confection: The decadent planet Proton, so rich in energy resources, and so perfect that noncitizens are willing to sign on as naked serfs, and the annual games, or "Tourney," to win the one coveted citizenship are extensive, inventive, and attended galaxywide by sports fans. When Stiles, a talented young serf and games master, is nearly murdered, he escapes into Phaze, a parallel world run entirely by magic, only to discover that his alternate self in this world has already been murdered. He must win the Tourney on Photon and solve the murder on Phaze if he is to save himself and the two worlds he loves. The world-building is inventive, the adventure fast-paced, the characters appealing, and both older and younger teens should be quickly hooked. Stiles' story is continued in *Blue Adept* and *Juxtaposition.* Later titles (*Out of Phaze, Robot Adept, Unicorn Point,* and *Phaze Doubt)* use the setting and many of the characters, but do not continue this story. They're unexceptional, but Anthony fans and fans of the original series will probably want them. **Grades 10—12. KE**

Asimov, Isaac. ***I, Robot.*** 272 pages.

Bantam Books 1991 Paper 0553294385 $7.50

This classic science fiction book is a series of connected short stories introducing the cool logic and cruel technological fate of the three laws of robotics, which don't quite compute. Asimov's prose might be a bit much for reluctant readers, but the story is strong enough to engage those wanting or needing challenges. **Grades 8—12. PT**

Atkins, Catherine. ***When Jeff Comes Home.*** 231 pages.

Puffin 2001 Paper 0698119150 $6.99
Putnam 1999 Trade 0399233660 $17.99

A novel with the spark, and occasional sordidness, of a true crime tale. A stranger abducts Jeff at knifepoint. For over two years, Jeff travels with "Ray" and suffers sexual abuse. He is finally returned to his family, but the events of his past haunt him on a daily basis, especially since his abductor is still lurking in the background. Jeff didn't come of age naturally; instead the events of his life thrust him dramatically and tragically into a world of paranoia, anger, and hatred, much of it self-directed. **Grades: 10–12. PJ**

Reviews: *Booklist* 10/15/1999, *SLJ* 2/1/2000, *VOYA* 12/1/1999

Atwater-Rhodes, Amelia. ***Demon in My View.*** 192 pages

Bantam Doubleday Dell 2000 Trade 038532720X $9.95
Bantam Doubleday Dell 2001 Paper 0440228840 $4.99

Jessica Allodola is a high school senior who pens vampire tales under a pseudonym but manages to remain invisible at her high school. Jessica thinks she might have found new friends, only to discover that one of them is a vampire. From merely writing about vampires to actually knowing one, Jessica learns they are anything but fictional as she fights for her soul in a rip-roaring teen angst-with-a-side-of-fangs fest. **Grades 7–10. PJ**

Reviews: *SLJ* 5/1/2000

Atwater-Rhodes, Amelia. ***In the Forests of the Night.*** 160 pages.

Bantam Doubleday Dell 1999 0385326742 $8.95
Bantam Doubleday Dell 2000 0440228166 $4.99

It is 1684 in Concord, Massachusetts. Rachel is 17 years old, but becomes immortal when she is bitten by a vampire and turned into one of the undead. The story cuts to 300 years after the event, to Riska (the vampire's new name), who spends her nights hunting the streets of New York City. The plot moves back and forth across time and kicks in when another vampire enters the picture, seeking to harm Riska. Good stuff, but of most interest is simply that the author wrote this when she was 13. **Grades 7–10. PJ**

Reviews: *Booklist* 6/15/1999, *SLJ* 7/1/1999, *VOYA* 8/1/1999

Atwater-Rhodes, Amelia. ***Shattered Mirror.*** 227 pages.

Delacorte 2001 Trade 0385327935 $9.95

Watch out Buffy, here comes Sarah: she's not just a vampire hunter—she's also a teen witch. But unlike Buffy, who has a posse in tow, Sarah keeps to herself. The plot kicks in when Christopher arrives at her school. He is a vampire trying to pass as a normal high school student who wants to know Sarah better. Drawn to him despite her better judgment, Sarah's forced to admit that there's room for gray in her otherwise black-and-white world of good versus evil—until she meets Nikolas, Christopher's twin and one of the most hunted vampires in history. That's when the fun really begins. **Grades: 7—10. PJ**

Reviews: *Booklist* 9/1/2001, *SLJ* 9/1/2001, *VOYA* 12/1/2001

Atwood, Margaret. ***The Handmaid's Tale.*** 311 pages.

Doubleday 1998 Paper 038549081X $12.95

Margaret Atwood is probably one of the most important writers of our time, and this is the book that made such adulation clear. A novelist who began as a poet, in this book Atwood clearly shows the power of her language: spare, clear, and emotionally jolting. Accessible to all readers, although only the more sophisticated are likely to enjoy the full sting of the satire. **Grades: 9—12. PT <YALSA>**

Reviews: *Booklist* 8/1/1997, *VOYA* 1/1/1995

Austen, Jane. ***Pride and Prejudice.*** 269 pages.

HarperPerennial 1999 Paper 0060933259 $20.00
Modern Library 2000 Paper 0679783261 $7.95
Signet Classic 1996 Paper 0451525884 $4.95

One of the great novels of the early 19th century (set in the late 18th), this is not a book for reluctant readers. The prose is thick, sentences long, references unfamiliar (it helps to know what a barouche is), and the love story of Lizzy and Darcy is as far from graphic as you're ever going to get. That said, for those ready to handle it, P&P is a must-read. For those not yet ready, *Sense and Sensibility* is a great choice, telling basically the same story in a simpler construction and fewer subplots. **Grades 7—12. PT**

Avi. ***The Blue Heron.*** 192 pages.

Simon & Schuster 1992 Library 0027077519 $17.00
Morrow/Avon 1993 Paper 0380720434 $4.50

Against the backdrop of a shimmering summer at the lake, Avi explores the family dynamics in a story centered on 12-year-old Maggie. Her relationship with her father is in crisis, but unlike most young adult novels, *Blue Heron* portrays a crisis stemming from the changing behavior of the adult character. Maggie tries to reach out to her father, but fails. She finds solace in watching a blue heron on the lake and in developing new friendships with former enemies, including a neighborhood bully. **Grades 6—8. PJ <YALSA>**

Reviews: *SLJ* 4/1/1992

Avi. ***The Man Who Was Poe.*** 200 pages.

Avon Flare 1991 Paper 0380711923 $5.99
Camelot 1997 Paper 0380730227 $5.95

Avi intersects his fictional storyline with the real biography of Edgar Allan Poe. In this tale, Poe meets a forlorn man named Edmund who, like so many Poe characters, has a life shrouded in mystery. Edmund has a missing twin sister, and Poe becomes involved in unraveling the mystery of her disappearance, all the while using Edmund to pursue his own agenda. Part mystery, part historical fiction, and all together suspenseful. **Grades: 7–12. PJ**

Reviews: *Booklist* 4/15/1995

Avi. *Nothing but the Truth.*

Avon Flare 1995 Paper 038071907X $5.99
Orchard 1991 Trade 0531059596 $16.95

A breakthrough book for Avi, who is experimenting with ways to tell a story by creating a novel in documents: memos, letters, news reports, and so forth. The premise is simple: ninth-grader Philip, an all-around good kid, gets in trouble for disobeying the rule about standing in respectful, silent attention during the daily playing of the national anthem. Soon everyone, from the school board to the national media, becomes involved, and the reader must determine the truth from a variety of vantage points. **Grades: 6–12. PJ <YALSA>**

Reviews: *Booklist* 9/15/1991, *SLJ* 9/1/1991

Avi. *True Confessions of Charlotte Doyle.* 212 pages.

Avon Flare 1995 Paper 0380714752 $5.99
Avon Camelot 1997 Paper 0380728850 $5.99
Orchard 1990 Trade 053105893X $18.95

In an old-fashioned story of the sea set in 1832, 13-year-old Charlotte Doyle finds herself the only passenger aboard a sailing ship bound from England to Rhode Island. Bad turns to worse when the crew launches a mutiny against the ship's evil captain. A Newbery Honor Book. **Grades: 6–9. PJ**

Reviews: *Booklist* 1/1/1995, *SLJ* 9/1/1997

Avi. *What Do Fish Have to Do with Anything? And Other Stories.* 155 pages.

Candlewick 1997 Paper 0763604127 $6.99
Candlewick 1997 Trade 0763603295 $16.99

A collection of stories slicing through the life of younger teens. In these readable and memorable stories, each of the protagonists must face something he or she fears, from something as banal as a teacher to a troubling phone call that comes every day at the same time. **Grades 6–9. PJ <TEN>**

Reviews: *Booklist* 11/15/1997, *SLJ* 12/1/1997

Avi. ***Wolf Rider: A Tale of Terror.*** 202 pages.

> Aladdin 1993 Paper 0020415133 $4.99
> Atheneum 2000 Trade 0689841590 $17.00

Andy picks up the phone only to hear a voice say, "I just killed someone." That hook alone (which would be used over and over and over again in numerous thrillers) kicks the story off with a bang and the suspense rarely lets up. **Grades: 6–12. PJ**

> Reviews: *Booklist* 1/1/1995, *SLJ* 1/1/1995, *VOYA* 1/1/1995

Baldwin, James. ***If Beale Street Could Talk.*** 197 pages.

> Delta 2000 Paper 0385334591 $11.95
> Dell 1974 Paper 0440340608 $6.99

Baldwin's most accessible book for teens, the tale of Tish and her incarcerated boyfriend Fonny's doomed love has Romeo and Juliet qualities. As always, Baldwin uses fiction to tell readers hard facts about the treatment of blacks in America and, in this case, how they are treated in the criminal justice system. **Grades: 10–12. PJ**

Banks, Russell. ***Rule of the Bone.*** 400 pages.

> HarperTrade 1996 Paper 0060927240 $13.00

For the mature teen reader seeking challenge after *Maniac Magee*. Chappie is a punked-out teen living with his mother and abusive stepfather in an upstate New York trailer park. During this time, he slips into drugs and petty crime, eventually landing on the street. He assumes the identity of "Bone" and begins a journey of self-discovery, along the way meeting people as beat-up and been-down as he. Yet, Bone struggles on, eventually landing in Jamaica in search of his real father. A big book written for adults with huge appeal to teen readers looking for a story that makes the adolescent search for identity into an epic. **Grades 10–12 (mature). PJ**

> Reviews: *SLJ* 4/1/1995

Barker, Clive. ***Thief of Always.*** 225 pages.

> HarperTrophy 2002 Paper 0064409945 $5.95
> HarperCollins 1997 Paper 006105769X $4.50

Barker is a Renaissance man; he pens best-selling horror novels, writes and directs blockbuster films (*Hellraiser* series), and has great influence on other writers, in particular graphic novelists. This novel, aimed at young readers, uses a classic set-up: a bored boy accidentally finds a door that allows him to travel to another reality. But because it is Barker, the trip is a dark ride into horror, magic, and mystery. **Grades: 6–9. PJ**

Bauer, Cat. ***Harley Like a Person.*** 248 pages.

> Winslow 2000 Paper 189081749X $6.95
> Winslow 2000 Trade 1890817481 $16.95

Like many teens, 14-year-old Harley feels out of place. But in her case, those feelings of isolation are intense, and she is convinced that she, with her artistic leanings, could not be the child of her alcoholic, abusive father and her enabling, romance-novel-reading mother. The search for identity, which is found in most YA novels, becomes a real life mystery as Harley tracks down clues to find her real father. **Grades: 7–12. PJ**

> Reviews: *Booklist* 6/1/2000, *SLJ* 5/1/2000, *VOYA* 10/1/2000

Bauer, Joan. ***Hope Was Here.*** 192 pages.

> Penguin Putnam 2002 Paper 0698119517 $5.99
> Penguin Putnam 2000 Trade 0399231420 $16.99

Bauer scored a Newbery Honor for this book about a funny, tender, and tough 14-year-old named Hope. Abandoned by her mother at age two, Hope has been under the care of her Aunt Addie, who makes a fine mother and an even better cook. When they relocate from the noise of New York City to the quiet of a small Wisconsin town, things really heat up. With her usual wit, Bauer serves up a coming-of-age story with a side order of romance—and even a slice of political intrigue. **Grades 7–12. PJ**

> Reviews: *Booklist* 10/15/2000, *SLJ* 11/1/2000, *VOYA* 2/1/2001

Bauer, Joan. ***Rules of the Road.*** 201 pages.

> Puffin 2000 Paper 0698118286 $5.99
> Putnam 1998 Trade 039923140 $16.99

Jenna loves her job at Gladstone's Shoe Store and loves having her driver's license. When she is asked to chauffeur the owner of the shoe store chain on a trip from Illinois to Texas, Jenna jumps at the chance. Bauer's humor and humanity shine through as Jenna journeys not only down the road but forward into her confident, competent self. **Grades: 7–12. PJ <YALSA>**

> Reviews: *Booklist* 2/1/1998, *SLJ* 3/1/1998

Bauer, Joan. ***Squashed.*** 194 pages.

> Puffin 2000 Paper 0698119177 $5.99
> Putnam 2001 Trade 039923750X $16.99

Ellie wants two things: her body to get smaller and her prize pumpkin to get bigger so she can win the county fair first prize. In her first novel, Joan Bauer introduces her trademark spunky lead heroine who's got wit and knows how to use it. Adding in thieves who want to steal her prize pumpkin and a cute new boy at school who threatens to steal Ellie's heart, Bauer creates a humor-filled coming-of-age story.

Squashed won the Delacorte Press Prize for an Outstanding First Young Adult Novel and launched a stellar career. **Grades: 7—12. PJ**

Bauer, Marion Dane (Editor). ***Am I Blue.*** 273 pages.

HarperTrophy 1995 Paper 0064405877 $6.99

This is a collection of 16 short stories by writers such as Francesca Lia Block, Nancy Garden, M. E. Kerr, Lois Lowry, William Sleator, Jacqueline Woodson, and Jane Yolen around the theme of growing up gay or lesbian or having gay or lesbian parents or friends. **Grades: 7—12. PJ**

Reviews: *Booklist* 3/15/1998, *Booklist* 8/1/1997

Beatty, Paul. ***The White Boy Shuffle.*** 225 pages.

Picador 2001 Paper 031228019X $13.00

Beatty, a hip-hop poet, tells the story of two very different L.A. neighborhoods. The main character, Gunnar, spends his teen years in black-Latino-Asian West Los Angeles, even though he was reared like the Fresh Prince of Bel Air. There's no sitcom smugness here: Gunnar gains fame and starts calling for the mass suicide of the black race. Beatty spears everything, but mostly political correctness, and spares no one his comic lash, including Martin Luther King, Jr., Kirkus called it "a wildly inventive debut that veers between spirited brilliance and Def Comedy Jam vulgarity." **Grades 10—12 (mature). PJ**

Bennett, Cherie. ***Life in the Fat Lane.*** 272 pages.

Bantam Doubleday Dell 1999 Paper 0440220297 $4.99

Lara is living the dream life: pretty, great boyfriend, lots of friends, queen of the prom, and a healthy, if sometimes inflated, self-image. But all that is challenged when Lara starts inexplicably gaining weight because of a rare metabolic disorder. While that is a soap opera hook, the real story here is how Lara feels about herself and how everyone around her treats her now that she is living life in the fat lane. **Grades 6—9. PJ**

Reviews: *Booklist* 1/1/1998, *SLJ* 3/1/ 1998

Bennett, Cherie. ***Searching for David's Heart.*** 176 pages.

Scholastic 1988 Paper 0590306731 $4.50

Bennett presses all the right buttons. At a party, Darcy gets into a disagreement with her older brother David. She takes off running and he chases her, gets hit by a car, and dies. But wait, he's an organ donor. Obsessed with her role in David's death, Darcy enlists her best friend to set out on a cross-country journey to meet the person who received David's heart. **Grades 6—9. PJ**

Bennett, James. ***Blue Star Rapture.*** 134 pages.

> Aladdin Paperbacks 2001 Paper 0689841507 $4.99
> Simon & Schuster 1998 Cloth 0689815808 $16.00

An interesting boy-meets-girl story with lots of twists. TJ is a star basketball player and, with his friend Tyron, who has a learning disability, is attending a summer basketball camp to hone his skills. TJ is Tyron's protector. Sneaking out of camp one night, TJ encounters LuAnn, a pregnant young woman from the Christian camp nearby. This meeting of opposites drives the story onward while forcing TJ to look inward at some of his own choices. **Grades 8—10. PJ**

> Reviews: *Booklist* 9/1/1988, *SLJ* 6/1/1988, *VOYA* 12/1/1998

Bennett, James. ***Squared Circle.*** 247 pages.

> Scholastic 2002 Paper 0590486721 $4.99

Sonny is an all-American high school basketball player. Everything has always come easy for him on the court, but, now in college, he is struggling with his grades and with social acceptance. His troubles increase when an NCAA investigation into player recruiting is launched and his attempts to join a fraternity find him the victim of a vicious, and graphically described, hazing incident. Bennett's good at the sport scenes and even better at showing Sonny's struggles. **Grades: 9—12. PJ**

Berry, James. ***Ajeemah and His Son.*** 83 pages.

> HarperTrophy 1994 Paper 0064405230 $4.99

In 1807, at the height of the slave trade, Ajeemah and his son, Atu, are snatched by slave traders from their home in Africa. They are taken to Jamaica and sold to neighboring plantations, never to see one another again. One of the most critically acclaimed YA books of the early 1990s, it captured honors such as Notable Children's Book; YALSA's Best Books; *Booklist*'s Books for Youth, Editor's Choices; and a Coretta Scott King Honor citation. **Grades: 6—9. PJ**

> Reviews: *Booklist* 8/1/1997, *SLJ* 1/1/1995

Berry, Liz. ***China Garden.*** 285 pages.

> Avon Tempest 1999 Paper 0380732289 $6.95

Set in the Brontë-esque Ravensmore estate, teenage Clare gets wrapped up in mystery and intrigue. There are mysterious strangers on motorcycles, psychic visions, a trip to Stonehenge, and, of course, a deep, dark secret in this classic gothic with a coming-of-age story, romance, and some new age magic. **Grades: 6—9. PJ**

> Reviews: *Booklist* 3/15/1996, *SLJ* 5/1/1996

Blatty, William Peter. **_The Exorcist._** 340 pages.

HarperCollins Paper 0061007226 $5.99

This is one of those miraculous books that manages to be accessible to all readers without oversimplifying its prose. There's a lot going on here that was not in the film, so that might be a selling point to those convinced of the "saw the movie, don't need to read the book" platitude. NOT a good read for the faint of heart, even so many years after its publication. **Grades 10–12 (mature). PT**

Bloch, Robert. **_Psycho._** 212 pages.

St. Martin 1989 Paper 0812519329 $4.95

One of the masters of the horror genre in the 50s, Bloch wrote many episodes of _The Twilight Zone_, and his stories reflect the message that things that go bump in the night are searching for those who deserve them. The novel manages to be even more terrifying than the Hitchcock film, no easy task. While the book is old, the themes are not, and the notion of the serial killer lurking in the shadows continues to resonate. **Grades 10–12 (mature). PT**

Block, Francesca Lia. **_Dangerous Angels._** 478 pages.

HarperCollins 1998 Paper 0064406970 $12.00

Love as a dangerous angel is the central theme of all of Block's books, in particular the Weetzie Bat saga. Those five slim novels (_Weetzie Bat, Witch Baby, Cherokee Bat and the Goat Guys, Missing Angel Juan,_ and _Baby Be-Bop_) are collected here in one volume. Set against the backdrop of the almost magical Los Angeles skyline, Block weaves her story of an extended "family" of teens—some gay, some straight, all ungodly unique—who are searching for real life in a fairy tale surrounding. It is all told in prose that sounds like poetry, filled with popular culture images and hipster slang. **Grades: 9–12. PJ**

Block, Francesca Lia. **_Echo._** 215 pages.

HarperCollins 2001 Library 0060281286 $14.89
HarperCollins 2002 Paper 0064407446 $6.99
HarperCollins 2001 Trade 0060281278 $14.95

This is about a girl growing up in Los Angeles. Ultimately it is about love and angels—I cried "yes!" with catharsis at the end—but it is also about vampires, suicide attempts, and despair, and about feeling completely unloved by parents and peers. For readers who like something a little "edgy." **Grades: 9–12. (Annotation by Hope Baugh)**

Reviews: _Booklist_ 8/1/2001, _SLJ_ 8/1/2001, _VOYA_ 10/1/2001

Block, Francesca Lia. ***Girl Goddess #9.*** 192 pages.

> HarperCollins 1988 Paper 006447187X $4.95
> HarperCollins 1996 Trade 0060272112 $14.95

A collection of nine short stories built around the theme that "in every girl is a goddess." The stories are arranged chronologically, beginning with one about a toddler and ending with a young woman entering college. L.A. is the central setting for all the stories except the quasi-novella "Dragons in Manhattan." Block's interest is exploring what love, and sometimes sex, means in the life of young women, as well as the power of friendship and family. None of these young women have it easy; stories contain scenes of suicides, interracial relationships, and even sex changes, but like the characters in the Weetzie Bat books, all these young women live happily. Two of the stories, "Blue" and "Winnie and Cubby," have been previously published in YA anthologies. **Grades 9—12. PJ**

Block, Francesca Lia. ***The Hanged Man.*** 137 pages.

> HarperCollins 1994 Library 0060245379 $15.89
> HarperTrophy 1999 Paper 0064408329 $8.99

Despite the usual beauty of Block's words and images, this is an ugly book about sexual abuse and incest. Laurel is haunted by dark thoughts of her father, who perpetuated the abuse, and of her mother, who accepted it. Casual sex, group sex, anorexia, abortion, suicide, and heroin-use shape and scar Laurel's life. This is not the feel-good book of the season or your father's young adult novel. While this is a thin book, it is weighty in subject matter, artful writing, and mature themes. **Grades: 10—12 (mature). PJ**

> Reviews: *Booklist* 9/15/1994, *SLJ* 9/1/1994, *VOYA* 1/1/1995

Block, Francesca Lia. ***Rose and the Beast: Fairy Tales.*** 229 pages.

> HarperCollins 2000 Library 0060281308 $14.89
> HarperTrophy 2001 Paper 0064407454 $6.95
> HarperCollins 2000 Trade 0060281294 $14.95

It was inevitable that Block, who uses fairy tales as her foundation, would want to put her spin on some old favorites. In this collection of stories, Block takes Snow White, Thumbelina, Cinderella, Rose Red and Rose White, and other characters away from Disneyland, setting them under other parts of the shining, bright southern California sky. In these versions, Sleeping Beauty pricks her arm with a heroin needle, Prince Charming is a middle-aged man turned on by a comatose Snow White, while the Snow Queen is a sex goddess. The stories are from childhood, but the concerns are those of teens: identity, independence, and acceptance. **Grades: 9—12 (mature). PJ**

> Reviews: *Booklist* 8/1/2000, *SLJ* 9/1/2000, *VOYA* 2/1/2001

Block, Francesca Lia. ***Violet and Claire.*** 176 pages.

> HarperCollins 1999 Trade 0060277491 $14.95
> HarperCollins 2000 Paper 0064472531 $6.95

What happens when opposites attract? Violet is Goth from head to toe and obsessed with putting her dark vision under the bright lights of a movie set. Claire is the waif, the shy young poet, who actually dresses herself in wings. Their friendship, born from pain, much of it self-inflicted, is the real star of the show. **Grades 9—12. PJ**

> Reviews: *Booklist* 9/1/1999, *SLJ* 9/1/1999

Block, Francesca Lia. ***Weetzie Bat.*** 88 pages.

> HarperTrophy 1989 Paper 0064408183 $7.95

See annotation for *Dangerous Angels.* This is a stand-alone copy of the one that started it all and is well worth having in any collection trying to serve the hip and well-read teen. **Grades: 9—12. PJ <MOCK> <YALSA>**

> Reviews: *Booklist* 1/1/1995, *Booklist* 8/1/1997, *VOYA* 1/1/1995

Bloor, Edward. ***Tangerine.*** 294 pages.

> Scholastic 2001 Paper 0439286034 $4.99
> Harcourt 1997 Trade 015201246X $17.00

A mysterious eye injury in early childhood has left seventh-grader Paul Fisher legally blind and unlikely to follow in the footsteps of his football-star older brother. When his family moves to Tangerine, Florida, a bizarre series of natural disasters and a shift to a tough urban middle school allow Paul to shine on the soccer field and see the truth about his community and his family's secrets. The tight third-person viewpoint keeps the reader focused on Paul's adventures, while the suspense of this young teen's growing realization of "what really happened," the unusual setting, and the sports action keep the pages turning. **Grades: 7—12. KE <MOCK> <YALSA>**

> Reviews: *Booklist* 5/1/1997, *SLJ* 4/1/1997

Blume, Judy. ***Forever.*** 212 pages.

> Pocket Books 1989 Paper 0671695304 $6.99
> Simon & Schuster 1982 Library 0027110303 $16.00

Controversy follows Judy Blume like a hungry mongrel. Too bad, because this very accessible book is an accurate picture of teenage love and betrayal. No matter what the pseudo-righteous say, Blume understands YA readers, and particularly girls. This subject matter is what they are interested in and will read, however reluctantly they open the pages of any other books. **Grades 8—12 (mature). PT**

Blume, Judy. *Tiger Eyes.* 206 pages.

> Dell 1982 Paper 0440984696 $4.99
> Simon & Schuster 1982 Trade 002711080 $16.00

After 15-year-old Davey's father is killed in a hold-up, Davey escapes by visiting family in New Mexico. In her new home, she contains to mine her emotional self as she falls in love for the first time. Blume's only pure YA novel is almost perfect. **Grades: 6–9. PJ**

Borland, Hal. *When the Legends Die.* 216 pages.

> Bantam 1984 Paper 0553257382 $5.99

Yet another assigned book that teen readers also find on their own and with good reason. A young Native American's family is killed, forcing him to live independently, but also without identity, as he rejects both the white race and his own heritage. **Grades 7–12. PJ**

Boylan, James. *Getting In.* 342 pages.

> Warner 1998 Paper 0446674176 $14.00

Three adults and four high school seniors head off for a tour of Ivy League schools. From that simple premise comes a funny novel about families, friends, fears, and finalizing college plans. The ensemble teen cast of Juddy (surfer dude), Polo (yuppie), Dylan (sensitive and shy), and Allison (sensitive and not shy) gives it teen movie feel, and that's not a bad thing. **Grades: 10–12. PJ**

> Reviews: *Booklist* 8/1/1998

Bradbury, Ray. *Fahrenheit 451.* 192 pages.

> Del Rey 1991 Paper 0345342968 $6.99
> Simon & Schuster 1993 Trade 067187036X $22.00

Long a staple of English Department curricula, this is a very compelling story of censorship gone mad, and the prose offers both accessibility and challenge. Horror story, political satire, and meditation on the irreplaceable value of books in a free society, this one counts as a must-read. **Grades: 8–12. PT**

Bradley, Marion Zimmer. *The Mists of Avalon.* 876 pages.

> Ballantine 2000 Trade 0345441184 $30.00
> Ballantine Paper 0345350499 $16.95

A groundbreaking, feminist, neo-pagan retelling of the Arthurian romance from the viewpoint of the women of Camelot, *The Mists of Avalon* easily crosses the boundary of genre fantasy into literary or even historical fiction. Morgaine (Morgan Le

Fay) and Gwenhwyfar (Guinevere) battle for the love of princes, control of the king-dom, and the coming rise of Christianity over aboriginal paganism. This is sure to be popular with many older teen girls and some young men looking for another take on a famous legend. The adventures continue in several sequels: *The Forest House, Lady of Avalon,* and *Priestess of Avalon.* In this interesting derailing of the usual perspec-tive, Camelot is undermined as much by the conflict between the new Christianity and the old goddesses as anything. *Mists* is a staple in the Arthurian legends and sophisticated story-telling, but far less challenging than *Morte d'Artur* or *The Once and Future King.* A good beginning for readers without previous knowledge of the myths, and an excellent supplement to those with more extensive backgrounds in the subject. **Grades 10–12. KE/PT**

Brashares, Ann. ***The Sisterhood of the Traveling Pants.*** 304 pages.

Bantam Doubleday Dell 2001 Trade 0385729332 $14.95
Random House 2003 Paper 0385730586 $8.95

Four teenage girls who are best friends spend a summer apart, connected by the magic of the "traveling pants," which they mail to one another to take turns wearing during all the trials and joys that they each experience. This book is funny, creative, and has great characters. Teens will find a reflection of themselves, or at least other teens they know, in this sometimes passionate, sometimes sad, always compelling, and unique story. **Grades 6–9. (Annotation by Diane Tuccillo)**

Reviews: *SLJ* 8/1/2001, *Booklist* 8/1/2001, *VOYA* 10/1/2001

Bridgers, Sue Ellen. ***Home Before Dark.*** 212 pages.

Replica 1998 0735100535 $29.95

Life on the road is all that Stella has really known in her first 14 years of life as she travels with her parents from town to town in their old station wagon. When her father finally decides to settle, Stella's dream of home is realized, but sometimes dreams coming true isn't always an easy thing. This novel was named the *New York Times* Outstanding Book of the Year. **Grades: 6–9. PJ <HIPPLE>**

Brin, David. ***Postman.*** 294 pages.

Bantam 1990 Paper 0553278746 $6.99

An epic post-apocalyptic science fiction classic about Gordon Krantz, who is looking for hope and heroes, with his nation in ruins. He finds it in himself when he takes on the role of connecting scattered survivors as the first step to a restored United States. **Grades 10–12. PJ**

Reviews: *Booklist* 1/1/1995, *VOYA* 1/1/1995

Brontë, Charlotte. ***Jane Eyre.*** 312 pages.

> Bantam 1983 Paper 0553211404 $4.95
> Modern Library 2000 Paper 0679783326 $7.95
> Signet 1997 Paper 0451526554 $4.95
> Penguin 1996 Paper 0140434003 $7.95

While this novel is a part of the "core of the core" collection, caution is a byword here. This is NOT appropriate reading for young adults lacking extensive experience in challenging fiction. Heavily decorative, the style is laden with many of the conceits common to the 19th century, not the least of which are the many passages written in French. For those ready for Charlotte Brontë's most celebrated book, however, here is reading joy meant to be experienced repeatedly. **Grades: 7–12. PT**

Brontë, Emily. ***Wuthering Heights.*** 320 pages.

> Puffin 1995 Paper 0140366946 $4.99
> St. Martin's 1992 Paper 0312035470 $12.10
> Modern Library 1994 Trade 067960135X $17.95

Arguably the greatest novel of the 19th century, Emily Brontë's masterpiece is no piece of cake. Despite what many film versions would have you believe, there is a great deal more to the story than the mythic love affair between Heathcliff and Cathy. Unfolding from the memories of seven different people (one character told another who told another who told another and so on and so on), the plot is highly complicated, reveals itself non-chronologically, and turns on obscure and complex English inheritance laws. Inexperienced readers simply will not be afforded the almost infinite rewards of mastering *Wuthering Heights*, while those who can take it on may count it as one of the richest reading adventures of their lives. **Grades: 8–12. PT**

Brooks, Bruce. ***Midnight Hour Encores.*** 192 pages.

> HarperTrophy 1988 Paper 0064470210 $5.95

As she drives with her father across the country in search of the mother who abandoned her, a 16-year-old musician discovers what it takes to be independent while truly learning to love. Sibilance is a complex character whose story touches many teens. **Grades: 7–12. PJ**

Brooks, Bruce. ***Moves Make the Man.*** 280 pages.

> HarperCollins 1984 Library 0060206985 $15.89
> HarperTrophy 1996 Paper 0064405648 $5.95
> HarperTrophy 1995 Paper 0064470229 $5.99

Brooks' debut novel still amazes with the richness of the storytelling; the strength of the main characters, Jerome and Bix; the witty dialogue; the taut sports scenes; and the themes of friendship and racial injustice. **Grades: 7–12. PJ <HIPPLE><MOCK> <YALSA>**

Brooks, Terry. *Magic Kingdom for Sale—Sold!* 324 pages.

> Ballantine 1998 Paper 0345317580 $6.99

Brooks brings his talent for writing exciting fantasy adventure to an amusing world all his own: The Magic Kingdom of Landover. When Ben Holiday, discouraged by the death of his young wife, answers the bizarre "want ad" in his big city newspaper, he finds himself the unlikely knight-in-shining-armor and owner of a magical kingdom in a fantasy world parallel to our own. The kingdom is on the brink of ruin, and Ben must fight an evil demon lord to save his new possessions and the people (and creatures) there for whom he is the last hope. The underdog makes good, a hopeless man finds a purpose in life, and an action-packed fantasy adventure ensues, making this a popular choice for most teens, young or old. Series titles include *The Black Unicorn, Wizard at Large, The Tangle Box,* and *Witches' Brew.* **Grades 7–12. KE <YALSA>**

Brooks, Terry. *Sword of Shannara.* 726 pages.

> Ballantine 1986 Paper 0345336860 $9.95
> Del Rey 1995 Paper 0345314255 $7.99
> Ballantine 1996 Paper 0345909577 $6.99

What many enjoy about Tolkien—the sense of history, the careful language, and the epic character—many others would just as soon avoid. They want the grand plot, elves and dwarves, and huge battles and giant quests. Brooks more than delivers with every title in the Shannara series. From the first series (*The Sword of Shannara, The Elfstones of Shannara,* and *The Wishsong of Shannara*), which are Tolkien redux down to nearly every plot element and character, through subsequent adventures (*The Heritage of Shannara* series, the prequel, and *The Voyage of the Jerle Shannara* series) Brooks expands the fantasy world he borrowed and makes it his own. With every one of the titles, readers enjoy the epic adventures of wizards, rings, elves, and magic. Popular with nearly every teen who likes Big Thick Fantasy books, but often not with serious Tolkien fans. **Grades: 7–12. KE**

Bujold, Lois McMaster. *Curse of Chalion.* 442 pages.

> Eos 2001 Trade 0380979012 $25.00

Cazaril, a crippled warrior and galley slave, is assisted by an old friend into a court position as tutor to the royal heir. This is no sinecure; Cazaril is immersed in court intrigue, the passions of willful and dangerous teenage royals, murderous magic, and an ancient curse. How to save the kingdom, unite the young lovers, and survive to, perhaps, find a love of his own, drive many a fantasy adventure novel, though few are as well constructed and well told as this one. The sense of place, an alternate medieval

Spain, is solid; religion, utterly consonant with the medieval worldview, takes a modern twist with a five-part godhead. Teen fans of Big Fat Fantasy Quests will take to Cazaril's adventures, while mature readers who enjoy thoughtful alternate realities, such as *The Mists of Avalon*, should not pass this by. **Grades: 10–12. KE**

Reviews: *Booklist* 5/1/2001, *SLJ* 10/1/2001, *VOYA* 12/1/2001

Bujold, Lois McMaster. ***The Warrior's Apprentice.*** 311 pages.

Baen 2002 Paper 067172066x $6.99
Nesfa 2002 Trade 1886778272 $25.00

Eighteen-year-old Miles Vorkosigan, a severely physically handicapped young nobleman on a militaristic planet where "mutants" have routinely been killed at birth, may have just failed his physical entrance exams to the Empire's military academy. However, nothing will stop him from an extraordinary military career. With the assistance of his bodyguard, Bothari; his best friend, Elena; and a lot of fast-talking and clever maneuvering, Miles shanghais a small mercenary fleet and jumpstarts his career as "Admiral Naismith"—only to discover that making his dream real costs more than he can bear to pay. The Vorkosigan or Nexus series by Bujold is unusual in that each title can stand alone, but the whole is still greater than the sum of its parts. Miles' parents' stories are told in the prequels, *Shards of Honor* and *Barrayar*, the latter with excellent thematic riffs on love and motherhood in wartime. His own adventures continue in *The Vor Game, Cetaganda, Borders of Infinity, Brothers in Arms, Mirror Dance, Memory, Komarr, A Civil Campaign*, and *Diplomatic Immunity*. Older fans of military science fiction, *Ender's Game*, or any underdog-makes-good coming-of-age adventure fiction will appreciate Miles' saga. **Grades: 10–12. KE**

Bunting, Eve. ***Jumping the Nail.*** 148 pages.

Harcourt 1993 Paper 0152413588 $6.00

One of the better books for adults about teens is called *The Romance Is Risk*; this slender novel explores the same territory, examining risk-taking teens succumbing to the power of peer pressure. The story concerns a group of just-graduated high school seniors facing tough choices about their future and their relationships. The Nail is a cliff that some leap from to prove themselves, but the metaphor for how teens can lose perspective is as robust as the narrative drive on this overlooked novel. **Grades: 9–12. PJ**

Bunting, Eve. ***Someone Is Hiding on Alcatraz Island.*** 144 pages.

Berkley 1986 Paper 0425102947 $4.99

A nail-biter about a teenager on the run from a gang of toughs. Danny makes the mistake of choosing Alcatraz Island as his hiding place, setting up an adventure story that doesn't linger on details and keeps the action moving. **Grades 7–10. PJ**

Bunting, Eve. ***Sudden Silence.*** 107 pages.

Fawcett 1992 Paper 0449703622 $6.99

Bunting does her usual bang-up job of showing "good kids" who get into bad trouble. Teenager Jesse is obsessed with finding the hit-and-run driver who killed his brother. He enlists the help of his dead brother's girlfriend, Chloe, but that only creates more emotions that Jesse isn't sure how to handle. Simple, direct, and captivating. **Grades: 6—9. PJ**

Burgess, Anthony. ***A Clockwork Orange.*** 192 pages.

W. W. Norton 1996 Paper 0393312836 $13.00

If there were ad posters for this novel, they might shout "Learn a New Language! Read *A Clockwork Orange!*" Famous for uncompromising violence, a hideous process of "redemption," and a perverse protagonist eliciting sympathy and horror simultaneously, the book presents one central difficulty. The characters speak in a London slang invented by Burgess so complicated that many editions feature a glossary. Be certain that yours does. Without it, the book can be impenetrable for many readers. Teens, especially males, respond enthusiastically, and Burgess' masterwork is a must-read, not only for literary education, but for the social implications of the culture in which we live. Brilliant, stunning, and the most vicious of satires. **Grades: 10—12 (mature). PT**

Burgess, Melvin. ***Lady: My Life As a Bitch.*** 256 pages.

Henry Holt 2002 Trade 0805071482 $16.95

Transformational literature has huge YA appeal. The idea of slipping out of human skin and turning into another form works in both high art and popular pulp, not to mention the central theme of Animorphs, which many 21st-century teens cut their teeth on. Take that idea and mix it with gritty realism and you have *Lady*, a book about a risk-taking, self-absorbed teen girl who gets turned into a dog by an alcoholic bum with magical powers. This book comes complete with its own tag line: "If you gotta be a dog, be a bitch." *SLJ* noted that "this seductive volume is as raw and ravenous as its subject." **Grades 9—12 (mature). PJ**

Reviews: *SLJ* 7/1/2002, *VOYA* 8/ 1/2002

Burgess, Melvin. ***Smack.*** 250 pages.

Avon 1999 Paper 0380732238 $6.99
Henry Holt 1998 Trade 080505801X $16.95

The *VOYA* review has the best description of this tale of a teen heroin addict: "It not only has sex and drugs and rock 'n roll, but it has elements far more rare. It does exactly what teenagers want a book to do. It tells the truth. It doesn't preach. It makes you think . . . As addictive as the drug it profiles. You will not be able to put it down." **Grades 9–12 (mature). PJ**

Reviews: *Booklist* 4/15/1998, *SLJ* 5/1/1998

Butler, Octavia E. ***Parable of the Sower.*** 299 pages.

Warner 1995 Paper 0446601977 $5.99
Warner 2000 Paper 0446675504 $13.95

Butler, Octavia E. ***Parable of the Talents.*** 305 pages.

Seven Stories Press 1998 Trade 1888363819 $24.95
Warner 2000 Paper 0446675784 $13.95

From global warming to the collapse of the U.S. government through worldwide economic disaster, Octavia Butler has created dystopia on a grand scale, then grounded it and given it a human face: 18-year-old Lauren Olamina. Told in diary form, Lauren's journey begins in *Parable of the Sower*, when her fragile, walled Southern California community is destroyed. The post-holocaust survival story is given depth by Lauren's struggle to accept her own nature: a hyperempathy syndrome that forces her to share others' conscious pains and pleasures, and her own growing religious sensibilities and search for the nature of God. Both the quality of Butler's writing and Lauren's distinctive voice make this a compelling read for mature teens, and it should appeal to both hard science fiction readers and those who enjoy feminist literary fiction. Lauren's journey continues in *Parable of the Talents* as she shapes her new religion, creates a godhead, and determines the ultimate future of humanity in the face of new crises. **Grades: 10–12. KE**

Reviews: *Booklist* 1/1/1995 (*Parable of the Sower*)
Reviews: *Booklist* 11/1/1998, *VOYA* 12/1/1999 (*Parable of the Talents*)

Butler, Octavia. ***Wild Seed.*** 306 pages.

Warner 2001 Paper 0446676977 $13.95
Warner 1980 Paper 0446606723 $6.50

Doru is a shape-changer, taking the bodies of ordinary men as he wills, even farming humanity to create better forms for his use. Anyanwu is a "wild seed," unpredictable, uncontrollable, and beyond Doru's power. When the lives of these two powerful beings intersect, their relationship allows Butler to explore the conflict between male and female on a grand scale. Beautiful writing and distinctive voices for her characters are Butler's strengths, while the bizarre scenarios will hook any mature teen who enjoys speculative fiction. The universe of cloned humanity and strange evolution is continued in her novels *Mind of My Mind, Patternmaster, Clay's Ark,* and *Survivor.* **Grades: 10–12. KE**

Cabot, Meg. ***The Princess Diaries.*** 224 pages.

> HarperCollins 2001 Paper 0380814021 $5.99
> HarperCollins 2000 Trade 0060292105 $15.89

A fairy tale in the form of a young adult novel. Mia is a typical teenager, lacking self-esteem and obsessively recording every detail of her life in her diary. Her life changes one fine day when her jet-setting father tells her she is to become princess of the principality of Genovia (located closer in spirit to Monaco than Fredonia). Her grandmother becomes her tutor in all things royal with comically disastrous results. Throw in a romance, Mia's honest and hilarious voice, and no wonder this was a huge hit on the page and screen. **Grades 6–10. PJ**

> Reviews: *Booklist* 10/15/2000, *SLJ* 10/1/2000, *VOYA* 4/1/2001

Cabot, Meg. ***Princess in the Spotlight (Princess Diaries II).*** 274 pages.

> HarperCollins 2001 Library 0060294663 $15.89
> HarperCollins 2001 Trade 0060294655 $15.95
> HarperCollins 2002 Paper 0064472795 $5.99

The book's tag line announces the theme: "No one ever said being a princess was easy." A lot happens to Mia in just 13 days, including an interview that calls for spin control, a secret admirer who won't call for a date, and a grandmother who continues to call her on the carpet for not acting royal enough. Mia is still sassy, smart, and still searching in this entertaining sequel. **Grades 7–10. PJ**

> Reviews: *Booklist* 10/1/2000, *SLJ* 11/1/2000, *VOYA* 10/1/2001

Cabot, Meg. ***Princess in Love (Princess Diaries III).*** 240 pages.

> HarperCollins 2003 Paper 0064472809 $6.99
> HarperCollins 2002 Library 0060294671 $15.99
> HarperCollins 2002 Trade 006029468X $15.89

In the third installment, Mia still bristles under her grandmother's overbearing ways, still worries about love (she has a boyfriend but he may not be right for her), and like any teenager, princess or not, she still has school worries. **Grades 7–10. PJ**

> Reviews: *Booklist* 7/1/2002, *VOYA* 6/1/2002

Cadnum, Michael. ***Edge.*** 142 pages.

> Penguin Putnam 1999 Paper 0140387145 $5.99

Zachary is adrift in the world. He has cut himself off from most of his past, dropped out of high school, broken up with his girlfriend, lost touch with his best friend, and seems content in his discontent. Then a random act of violence enters his life—his father is shot during a carjacking—and his life begins to spin out of control. When it appears that the person arrested for shooting and paralyzing his father will go free because of a lack of evidence, Zachary becomes obsessed with seeking vengeance. Retrieving a gun he acquired years ago, Zachary is determined to see that justice is done. The tension builds as readers watch the gun introduced in Chapter One, knowing that it will reappear, and then wonder, when it does reappear, how Zachary will handle the choice between right and righteous revenge. **Grades 8–10. PJ**

Reviews: *Booklist* 6/15/1997, *SLJ* 7/1/1997

Cadnum, Michael. ***In a Dark Wood.**** 246 pages.

Orchard 1998 Library 0531330710 $18.99
Orchard 1998 Trade 0531300714 $17.95
Puffin 1999 Paper 0141306386 $5.99

Cadnum normally pens teen novels, horror fiction, and poetry. He has an ear for language, an eye for graphic detail, and a bias toward characters under layers of stress and clouds of violence. It is that formula dropped into Sherwood Forest that creates *In a Dark Wood*. Cadnum's young adult novels are hard edged and suspenseful; the "battle" between the sheriff (who tells the story) and Robin Hood is no less so. One sequel as of this writing. **Grades: 7–12. PJ**

Reviews: *Booklist* 3/1/1998, *SLJ* 4/1/1998, *VOYA* 8/1/1998

Cadnum, Michael. ***Redhanded.**** 176 pages.

Penguin Putnam 2000 Trade 0670887757 $15.99

Like most Cadnum young male protagonists, Steve is disconnected from his world, especially from his parents. He escapes to a local gym, where he learns how to box and how to cheat. His best friend, Raymond, wants to cheat death and engages Steve and another friend in a series of hazards, done for no other reason than the thrill of almost being caught. *Redhanded* explores ground similar to that examined in the out-of-print and near-perfect *Breaking the Fall*, about risks and relationships. **Grades 7–10. PJ**

Reviews: *Booklist* 10/1/2000, *SLJ* 11/1/2000

Camus, Albert. ***The Stranger.**** 184 pages.

Random House 1989 Paper 0679720200 $9.95
Random House 1988 Trade 0394533054 $25.00

Certainly a classic, *The Stranger* is not for everyone. Originally published in French, the novel comes with two stumbling blocks for less sophisticated readers. It reads less well in translation, and it personifies the existential movement. Long a staple of advanced English and French classes, this is an excellent choice for readers interested in existential satire. Otherwise, despite its status as "easy" reading and the fact that it is a "thin one," it is probably not recommended for reluctant readers. **Grades 10—12 (mature). PT**

Canty, Kevin. ***Into the Great Wide Open.*** 244 pages.

> Vintage Anchor 1997 Paper 0679776524 $13.00

The scene is the sprawl of suburbia, a teenage wasteland. Kenny's family hasn't fallen apart, it has self-destructed. His mother is in an institution, his brother in exile, and his father is all about abuse and alcohol. He thinks he's the only one with such problems until he meets a girl (Junie) spit out of the same suburban hell, and they try to heal each other. **Grades 10—12 (mature). PJ**

Card, Orson Scott. ***Enchantment.*** 390 pages.

> Del Rey 2000 Paper 0345416880 $6.99
> Ballantine 1999 Trade 0345416872 $25.00

A young Ukrainian-American graduate student, Ivan Smetski, finds himself transported to ninth-century Russia to live out the role of the prince in the Russian version of "Sleeping Beauty." Part fantastic historical fiction, part fairy tale adventure, Ivan's romance with his beauty takes them back and forth in time as they thwart the creepiest of evil witches: Baba Yaga. Card's sweet and satisfying romance has enough action to please most fantasy adventure fans, and young women ready to graduate from *Ella Enchanted* or McKinley's *Beauty* will adore this one. **Grades: 7—12. KE**

> Reviews: *Booklist* 3/1/1999, *SLJ* 12/1/1999, *VOYA* 10/1/1999

Card, Orson Scott. ***Ender's Game.*** 226 pages.

> TOR 1992 Paper 0312853238 $13.95
> TOR 1994 Paper 0812550706 $6.99
> TOR 1991 Trade 0312932081 $24.95

This book is the perfect blend of high concept and adventure. It is especially intriguing because the main character begins the book at age 6 and at the end is only age 12, yet acts and thinks far beyond his years. Higher-level readers will enjoy the political intrigue raised by Ender's older siblings, while all will enjoy the clearly blocked action in the battle room. This book is especially good for hooking the elusive "teen boy reader," and has as a bonus being the first in a series. This is one that I can't keep on the shelves at my library—probably because I'm always handing it out. **Grades: 6—12. (Annotation by Spring Lea Boehler)**

Card, Orson Scott. ***Ender's Shadow.*** 379 pages.

> TOR 2000 Paper 0812575717 $7.99
> TOR 1999 Trade 031286860X $24.95

Those who loved *Ender's Game* will welcome the retelling of the events of that book from the viewpoint of his young teammate, Bean. From the ugly streets of Amsterdam, this ruthless, and borderline psychopathic child joins Ender in Battle School and in the fight to destroy the alien Buggers. Bean's tormented childhood, his fragmented attempt to connect on an emotional level with his teammates, and his efforts to shed what he considers (rightly) to be a monstrous nature lend a human depth to a story of war and political conflict. Bean's story and those of Ender's child teammates continue in *The Shadow of the Hegemon* and *Shadow Puppets*, in which Bean and Peter Wiggins, Ender's brother, struggle for control of post-war Earth. Card's winning combination of bright, alienated children facing war and political intrigue with courage, loyalty, and love will draw teen fans of all ages. **Grades: 6—12. KE**

Reviews: *Booklist* 7/1/1999

Card, Orson Scott. **Homebody.** 291 pages.

HarperCollins 2000 Paper 0061093998 $6.99
HarperCollins 1998 Trade 0060176555 $24.00

Don Lark, a man who lost his entire family in a car crash, finds a purpose in life by buying and restoring junked house for others to enjoy. His latest project, the Bellamy mansion in North Carolina, involves not just fixing up an old building, but the lives of those associated with its old tragedies, including those no longer among the living. Of course Don faces danger, disaster, and finds true love, but the journey keeps the reader turning the pages. Teens who like their ghost stories without horror and their suspense mixed with sweet romance will enjoy Card's contemporary ghost story. **Grades: 7—12. KE**

Reviews: *SLJ* 8/1/1998, *VOYA* 8/1/1998

Card, Orson Scott. **Lost Boys.** 544 pages.

Morrow/Avon 1993 Paper 0061091316 $6.99

While Card received no credit, it is obvious that the hit movie *The Sixth Sense* owes a debt to this story about a family living in a small North Carolina community whose son is "slipping away" from them and merging himself into a video game. At the same time, young boys are disappearing. *Lost Boys* has an ending as moving as any Card has ever written. Overlooked, given Card's massive output. **Grades 9—12. PJ**

Card Orson Scott. **Seventh Son.** 241 pages.

TOR 1988 Paper 0812533054 $6.99
TOR 1987 Trade 0312930194 $17.95

In an alternate United States, where work-a-day folk magic is part of ordinary life, and history took a few different turns, a young boy, Alvin Maker, is the seventh son of a seventh son. From his birth throughout his childhood, adolescence, and manhood, evil powers have recognized his ability to change the course of the world for the better and have tried to kill him. Alvin must master his powers, survive the threats against him, and stay true to his better nature. The series is an extended coming-of-age novel in an intriguing America that might have been. Other books in the series are *Red Prophet, Prentice Alvin, Alvin Journeyman,* and *Heartfire.* **Grades: 7—12. KE**

Card, Orson Scott. ***Speaker for the Dead.*** 415 pages.

> TOR 1992 Paper 0312853254 $13.95
> TOR 1986 Trade 0312937385 $24.95
> TOR 1991 Paper 0812550757 $7.99

The tormented child-soldier of *Ender's Game* is now a 30-ish wanderer still deeply troubled by his unwitting alien mass destruction during the war. When Ender Wiggin's travels take him to the Portuguese-colony planet Lusitanian, he has a chance at absolution with a second, seemingly deadly alien race: the pequeninos. The well-developed characters and their culture ground the exotic setting, while the emotional and social conflicts among the colonists and the horrific alien dangers drive the plot. Younger fans of Ender Wiggin will find *Speaker for the Dead* an intellectual stretch, while mature teens will appreciate the compassion and insight Card brings to the conflict between the demands of survival and human decency. **Grades: 7—12. KE <YALSA>**

Cart, Michael (Editor). ***Love and Sex: Ten Stories of Truth.*** 225 pages.

> Simon & Schuster 2001 Trade 0689832036 $18.00

Award-winning authors such as Joan Bauer, Emma Donoghue, Angela Johnson, Chris Lynch, Garth Nix, Sonya Sones, and Shelley Stoehr examine the real deal of teen relationships. The teens here are gay and straight, active and abstinent, horny and horrified, yet all are searching for answers even if sometimes they are not sure or are too shy to even ask the question. **Grades 7—12. PJ**

> Reviews: *SLJ* 6/1/2001, *VOYA* 6/1/2001

Cart, Michael. ***My Father's Scar.*** 192 pages.

> St. Martin's Press 1998 Paper 031218137X $11.95

Marketed to both teen and adult audiences, the first novel by *Booklist's* Michael Cart was a crossover success. College freshman Andy Logan looks back on his life, which has not been without considerable pain. Growing up gay in a straight world and alienated from his alcoholic father and distant mother, Andy comes of age alone and in the closet. **Grades 10—12 (mature). PJ**

Cart, Michael (Editor). ***Tomorrowland: Ten Stories About the Future.*** 198 pages.

Scholastic 2000 Paper 0590376799 $4.99
Scholastic 1999 Trade 0590376780 $15.95

An interesting mix of writers, from the wacky shenanigans of Jon Scieszka to the twisted vision of Rodman Philbrick to the compassion of Lois Lowry, creates this collection of teens across time and space. But like *Star Wars* and *Star Trek*, the beeping sounds and bright lights in science fiction can't hide the essence of these stories: love, hate, and an unbending faith in humanity. **Grades: 6–12. PJ**

Reviews: *SLJ* 9/1/1999, *VOYA* 12/1/1999

Carter, Alden. ***Between a Rock and a Hard Place.*** 224 pages.

Scholastic 1999 Paper 0590374869 $4.99

Mark and his cousin Randy are less than thrilled about their extended family's wilderness adventure: a 10–day canoe trip through the Minnesota lake country. When the two boys get cut off first from the others, and then from their supplies, they learn to rely on each other and their wits to survive. *Hatchet* times two. **Grades 7–10. PJ**

Reviews: *Booklist* 1/1/1996, *SLJ* 12/1/1995, *VOYA* 4/1/1996

Chbosky, Stephen. ***Perks of Being a Wallflower.*** 256 pages.

Pocket Books 1999 Trade 0671027344 $12.00

This is the best of the best. You want angst? You want great characters and a protagonist who, while damaged somehow, manages to pin down the subtlest emotions and ironies of life? Read *Perks* and "feel infinite." **Grades 9–12. (Annotation by David Lane)**

Reviews: *Booklist* 2/15/1999, *SLJ* 6/1/1999, *VOYA* 12/1/1999

Childress, Alice. ***A Hero Ain't Nothin' but a Sandwich.*** 126 pages.

Puffin 2000 Paper 0698118545 $5.99
Putnam 1989 Trade 0698202783 $15.95

A young adult classic originally published in 1973 tells the story of Bennie, a 13-year-old heroin addict. While the short annotation makes it seems like a mid–70s problem novel of the week, it is much more. Childress cares about charters, community, and courage, not just a problem in need of a quick fix. **Grades: 7–12. PJ <YALSA>**

Childress, Alice. ***Rainbow Jordan.*** 146 pages.

Avon Flare 1982. Paper 0380589745 $4.99

Rainbow is 14 years old and caught up in the system of child services. She's getting ready to head to another foster home, wondering all the while where her heart really belongs and when she will be tough enough to have a home of her own. **Grades: 6—12. PJ**

Christie, Agatha. ***And Then There Were None.*** 218 pages.

St. Martin 2001 Paper 0312979479 $5.99

Christie is like your favorite cafeteria—lots of variety, but you know exactly what you're getting. A group of the "veddy British" gather together, there's a murder, one of them did it (but who?), and one of Christie's legendary sleuths (Miss Marple, Inspector Poirot), spends the remainder of the novel unmasking the culprit. Christie is a master, and has remained so for over half a century. As much novel of manners as mystery, any one of her books is a good choice for the reader moving beyond the simpler versions of the whodunit and ready for more sophistication in character, plot, and prose. **Grades: 8—12. PT**

Cisneros, Sandra. ***The House on Mango Street.*** 134 pages.

Vintage 1991 Paper 0679734775 $9.95
Random 1994 Trade 067943335X $24.00

Cisneros, a writer from San Antonio, Texas, captures the Hispanic experience beautifully (the episode about the Anglo Barbie dolls is especially choice), and does so in prose that is easily digested. An excellent recommendation for young adult readers, particularly those who may feel outside the mainstream of a culturally white society. **Grades 6—12. PT**

Clements, Andrew. ***Things Not Seen.*** 251 pages.

Philomel 2002 Trade 0399236260 $15.99

One fine morning Bobby awoke, looked in the mirror, and noticed he wasn't there. He has always felt invisible, locked out of the popular cliques at school and dateless, so he shouldn't be surprised when it really happens. Told in first person, Bobby's transformation is complicated by a car accident involving his parents, which leaves him alone in the world, with no body, not even his own, near. **Grades 6—9. PJ**

Reviews: *Booklist* 4/15/2002, *SLJ* 3/1/2002, *VOYA* 2/1/2002

Cofer, Judith Ortiz. ***An Island Like You: Stories of the Barrio.*** 176 pages.

Peter Smith 1998 Trade 0844669679 $20.25
Penguin Putnam 996 Paper 014038068X $5.99

A collection of stories captures the lives of different teenagers growing up in a Puerto Rican neighborhood in New Jersey. In addition to the challenges facing all teens, the Latino youth in these stories feel the push and pull of trying to thread the needle of bi-lingual culture. **Grades 7–10. PJ**

Reviews: *Booklist* 11/15/1997

Cole, Brock. ***The Facts Speak for Themselves.*** 184 pages.

Puffin 2000 Paper 0141306963 $5.99
Front Street 1997 Trade 1886910146 $16.95

The cutting edge of edgy books. Linda is old beyond her years, only 13 but already experienced in acting as caregiver to her brother after her father dies and her mother reacts to his death by living life with wild abandon. Linda's entanglement with an older man ends with the man's murder. What matters here isn't the plot, but the tone and texture. The story spills out of Linda, void of emotion as she merely recites the facts of her life, when a social worker seeks the truth behind the murder. She is dispassionate about the dysfunction that swallows her, and that distance is disturbing. **Grades 9–12 (mature). PJ**

Reviews: *Booklist* 10/1/1997, *SLJ* 10/1/1997

Cole, Brock. ***The Goats.*** 184 pages.

Starburst 1990 Paper 0374425752 $5.95

Two social misfits are marooned on an island overnight without their clothes—a traditional summer camp prank. Although the plot sounds like a cross between *Hatchet* and the teen flick *The Blue Lagoon*, the two characters (simply called boy and girl) may begin the story as victims, but end anything but. It was both a BBYA and a Quick Picks choice. **Grades: 6–9. PJ <HIPPLE><MOCK>**

Colfer, Eoin. ***Artemis Fowl.*** 277 pages.

Hyperion 2002 Paper 0786817070 $6.99
Miramax 2001 Trade 0786808012 $16.95

Marketed as a Harry Potter clone, *Fowl* is less about high fantasy and more about he-man fights. Artemis Fowl is a boy-genius and the last in line of a legendary Irish crime family. With a trusty but wisecracking sidekick and more gadgets than the latest James Bond opus, Fowl cooks up a plan to regain his family's gold and glory. This has blockbuster movie tie-in written all over it. The first in a series. **Grades: 6–12. PJ**

Reviews: *Booklist* 4/15/2001, *SLJ* 5/1/2001, *VOYA* 8/1/2001

Coman, Carolyn. ***Many Stones.*** 159 pages.

Puffin 2002 Paper 0142301485 $5.99
Front Street 2000 Trade 1886910553 $15.95

The title refers to the heavy weights on the life of 16-year-old Berry, who lives with her mother in the D.C. suburbs. She is estranged from her father, yet she agrees to accompany him on a long and painful journey. They are going to South Africa for a memorial service for Berry's older sister, who was murdered while working as a school volunteer in Capetown. Just as the country of South Africa is attempting to heal the division after years of struggle, Berry and her father try to reconcile as well. **Grades: 6—9. PJ <PRINTZ>**

Reviews: *Booklist* 11/1/2000, *SLJ* 11/1/2000

Coman, Carolyn. ***What Jamie Saw.*** 126 pages.

Puffin 1997 Paper 0140383352 $5.99
Front Street 1995 Trade 1886910022 $13.95

This is an excellent example of the problems with defining young adult literature. On the face of it, a book narrated by a nine-year-old is a book for children, not teens. But with its powerful first image of a baby being hurled against the wall, this searing look at domestic violence is obviously not kid stuff. The protagonist, Jamie, and her mother escape the destroyer of their lives, but the pain lingers as they try to repair what has been broken. A teacher plays the role of supportive adult in this moving book about a child hurled into a harsh adult experience. **Grades: 6—9. PJ**

Reviews: *Booklist* 12/15/1995, *SLJ* 12/1/1995

Conford, Ellen. ***Crush.*** 138 pages.

HarperCollins 1998 Trade 0060254149 $15.95

Conford explores the comedic possibilities of high school dating rituals in this series of stories. The stories all center on the "big" event: a Valentine's Day dance. For some, having a date is a lock, while for others it is a matter of luck. Either way, wacky complications ensue. **Grades: 6—9. PJ**

Reviews: *Booklist* 1/1/1998

Conrad, Pam. ***Prairie Songs.*** 167 pages.

HarperCollins 1987 Library 006021337X $15.89
HarperTrophy 1987 Paper 0064402061 $5.99

Louise lives with her family in the vast prairie of Nebraska. Her life is simple and beautiful, just like the poetry she writes. Beauty enters her life in a different way when a doctor and his wife, Emmeline, move nearby. While for Louise life on the prairie is a dream, for Emmeline it soon becomes a nightmare. The *Bulletin for the Center for Children's Books* called this a "touching and effective story, with strong characterization and a spare, dramatic style." **Grades: 6—12. PJ**

Cook, Karin. **What Girls Learn.** 304 pages.

> Vintage 1998 Paper 0679769447 $13.00

This tale of two sisters coping with their mother's cancer is for Lurlene McDaniel fans wanting to branch into adult fiction. Tilden is 12 and the good daughter; Liz is a year younger but a whole lot wilder. They fight, bicker, and bond, but their relationship changes first with a sudden move from Atlanta to Long Island and then with the news that their mother has breast cancer. Cook captures the hope and heartache of teen girls confronting and coping with crisis in this moving first novel. **Grades: 9–12. PJ**

> Reviews: *Booklist* 2/15/1997, *SLJ* 7/1/1997, *VOYA* 8/1/1998

Cooney, Caroline B. **Both Sides of Time.** 210 pages.

> Delacorte 1995 Trade 0385729480 $15.95
> Delacorte 1997 Paper 0440219329 $4.99

Annie graduates from high school, but there is little joy in her life. She longs for a different life, one filled with the stuff of the romance novels she devours. While visiting an old mansion, a freak storm occurs that magically hurls Annie back 100 years; there she meets the man of her dreams only to learn that in the realization of dreams begins responsibilities. Followed by *Out of Time* and *Prisoner of Time*. **Grades: 6–9. PJ**

> Reviews: *Booklist* 8/1/1997

Cooney, Caroline B. **Burning Up.** 232 pages.

> Delacorte 1999 Trade 0385323182 $15.95
> Laurel-Leaf 2001 Paper 0440226872 $5.50

Cooney normally keeps it light, but here she uses a mystery tale to tackle the issue of racism head on. Fifteen-year-old Macey decides to research the burning of a barn and death of a black school teacher in her hometown for a school project, but no one wants to talk about it. When arson strikes a black church, Macey is convinced there is a connection between the two events and that someone close to her might be involved. Great suspense; good substance. **Grades: 6–9. PJ**

> Reviews: *Booklist* 12/1/1998, *SLJ* 2/1/1999, *VOYA* 2/1/1999

Cooney, Caroline B. **Driver's Ed.** 184 pages.

> Delacorte 1994 Trade 0385320876 $16.95
> Laurel-Leaf 1996 Paper 0440219817 $5.50

The very definition of a page-turner. From a great title to a dynamic cover, Cooney writes up a storm in a wonderful book that will appeal to the most reluctant reader because of the plot, but can be enjoyed by avid readers because of the themes and characters. Remy and Morgan meet in a driver's ed class and begin a light-hearted romance. One night they take a stop sign from an intersection. They see it only as a joke, but the result is a tragic accident that leaves a young mother dead. How they deal with their guilt and its effects upon their feelings for each other makes for a poignant story of two teens suddenly faced with the consequences of their actions. **Grades: 7—12. PJ**

Reviews: *Booklist* 6/1/1994, *SLJ* 8/1/1994, *VOYA* 1/1/1995

Cooney, Caroline B. ***The Face on the Milk Carton.*** 184 pages.

Laurel-Leaf 1994 Paper 0440220653 $5.99
Bantam 1996 Trade 038532328X $15.95

One day at school, Janie looks down at her milk carton. Looking back at her is the face of a young child, kidnapped over a decade ago and still missing. Janie realizes that day that she is the face on the milk carton. Romance, mystery, and action drive the plot, while bigger issues of identity and family hover in the background for teens wanting to dig deeper. Followed by two less than successful, yet still necessary, sequels: *Whatever Happened to Janie* and *Voice on the Radio.* **Grades: 6—9. PJ**

Cooney, Caroline B. ***Flight 116 Is Down.*** 201 pages.

Scholastic 1993 Paper 0590444794 $4.99.

Heidi lives a rich and sheltered life. She's never wanted for anything, expect to prove herself. Her chance comes when a 747 crashes into the woods behind her house. The story is told in "real time," which adds even more intense heat to an already flaming plot. A novel about how people react when faced with immediate and unexpected crisis sadly strikes an even more powerful chord post 9—11. **Grades: 6—9. PJ <YALSA>**

Cooney, Caroline B. ***Hush Little Baby.*** 258 pages.

Scholastic 1999 Paper 0590819747 $4.99

What a hook! Kit's life revolves around her friends, her clothes, her younger sister, and her unrequited love for Rowen. One day, her stepmother hands her a package, then drives away forever. The package turns out to be a baby, and it turns Kit's dull life into a high-octane adventure. **Grades 6—9. PJ**

Cormier, Robert. ***After the First Death.*** 233 pages.

Dell 1991 Paper 0440208351 $5.50

As a teen, I read this book and hurled it against the wall when I got to its uncompromising finish. This story of a terrorist takeover of a bus of school children is as immediate as the headlines. **Grades: 6—12. (Annotation by Angela Benedetti) <MOCK><YALSA>**

Cormier, Robert. ***Beyond the Chocolate War.*** 278 pages.

Dell 1986. Paper 04409058X $5.50

The sequel continues to look at the sordid and twisted happening at Trinity High begun in *The Chocolate War*. This novel focuses on evil Archie and his right-hand man, Obie, as they dish out punishments at the year's end. But perhaps the last course for Archie will be his just desserts. The final scene, featuring a homemade guillotine, was considered over the top when it was published; in the age of Columbine, it somehow seems a more disturbing image. **Grades: 6—12. PJ**

Cormier, Robert. ***The Bumblebee Flies Anyway.*** 241 pages.

Dell 1991 Paper 044090871X $4.99

As in *I Am the Cheese*, a young man is trapped, this time in a mental institution. Something is going on behind the scenes, but he can't quite figure it out. His life is in danger; he's a human guinea pig, but he's not so sure he wants to go along with the plan. Another Cormier creation disturbs the universe, which always bites back. **Grades: 6—12. PJ**

Cormier, Robert. ***The Chocolate War.*** 253 pages.

Dell 1991 Paper 0440944597 $5.50

Cormier grips his readers with the opening line: "They murdered him," and never lets go in this tale which, as he says, shows us clearly that "Evil will triumph—if allowed to do so." A classic. **Grades: 6—12. (Annotation by Dr. Lois Stover) <HIPPLE> <YALSA>**

Cormier, Robert. ***Fade.*** 310 pages.

Dell 1991 Paper 0440210917 $5.50

A science fiction premise about Paul, a young man who has the power to disappear, is also a riveting account of a young man's coming of age. This ability to disappear allows Paul to observe others. He is like an omniscient narrator; he sees all, but no one sees him. What he sees is not always pretty, such as random acts of violence. His thoughts are not always pure; he is a teen boy after all. But as in all Cormier books, the main character doesn't really pull the strings together until the end, thus producing an explosive climax. **Grades: 8—12 (mature). PJ <HIPPLE><YALSA>**

Cormier, Robert. ***I Am the Cheese.*** 233 pages.

Dell 1991 Paper 0440940605 $5.50

Cormier pushes readers in this novel-in-fragments about 14-year-old Adam Farmer's attempt to solve the mystery of his own life. Told in a series of tape transcripts,

Adam is discovering who he is and who he isn't. It is Kafka for teens as Adam answers the questions of government agents holding him captive. Chilling is too lame a word to describe the finale. **Grades: 6–12. PJ <YALSA>**

Cormier, Robert. ***In the Middle of the Night.*** 182 pages.

Laurel-Leaf 1997 Paper 0440226864 $5.50

A book about guilt that has a thriller premise (don't answer the phone) yet digs deep as it examines the ideas of justice, revenge, and forgiveness. Eight years before Denny was born, his father was involved in a tragic accident that killed 22 children. Now Denny is 16, and all he wants is to be like other kids his age, but he isn't allowed to answer the telephone, and his family is constantly moving from town to town—all because people can't forget what happened long ago. When Denny defies his parents one afternoon and answers the telephone, he finds himself drawn into a plot for revenge that may prove deadly. While not thematically as robust as other Cormier works, it is one of his most readable narratives. **Grades: 7–12. PJ**

Reviews: *Booklist* 4/1/1995, *SLJ* 5/1/1995

Cormier, Robert. ***The Rag and Bone Shop.*** 128 pages.

Bantam 2001 Library 0385900279 $17.99
Delacorte 2001 Trade 0385729626 $15.95

Did Cormier save the best for his last? His final novel is as disturbing as anything he has ever written, perhaps more so given the constant 2002 newspaper headlines about missing young girls killed by people they know. Twelve-year-old Jason is accused of the brutal murder of a young girl. A special investigator is sent in to learn the truth, or at least to get a confession. The ending is worthy of Hitchcock: a shocking twist of events that horrifies and haunts. A fitting finale to a remarkable career. **Grades: 7–12. PJ**

Reviews: *Booklist* 7/1/2001, *SLJ* 9/1/2001, *VOYA* 10/1/2001

Cormier, Robert. ***Tenderness.*** 240 pages.

Delacorte 1997 Trade 0385322860 $16.95
Laurel-Leaf 1998 Paper 0440220343 $5.50

Another stroll in the dark-park vision of the master of the horror held in the human heart. This is a love story; a Cormier love story. The hero is Eric Poole, recently released from a juvenile correctional facility after serving time for murdering his mother and stepfather. The heroine is Lori, a runaway who has developed a crush on Eric via the media. Twisting the tale tighter is the fact that Eric believes that Lori is a witness to his other murders, which are as yet undiscovered. Add to the mix Eric's uncomfortable fixation with young women who remind him of his mother, adding a theme of incest. Lori may be the victim, but she is no innocent as she trades sexual favors to get what she wants. What both teens claim to want on the surface is tenderness, affection, and human connection, but neither has any experience in these matters. The novel is thought-provoking, shocking, and challenging as Cormier attacks the bottom line of what a young adult novel can or should be about. **Grades: 9–12 (mature). PJ <TEN>**

Reviews: *Booklist* 2/1/1997, *SLJ* 3/1/1997, *VOYA* 4/1/1997

Cormier, Robert. ***We All Fall Down.*** 193 pages.

Bantam 1993 Paper 0440215560 $5.50

Beginning with an incredible first chapter describing an act of vandalism and ending with a violent act and a vow for vengeance, Cormier takes a paperback-thriller setup and creates literature. The story revolves around one of the vandals, one of the victims, and "the avenger." The Cormier slant, of course, is that none of the characters is exactly what he or she seems. **Grades: 8–12. PJ <MOCK>**

Reviews: *Booklist* 11/15/1991, *SLJ* 1/1/1995, *VOYA* 1/1/1995

Crane, Stephen. ***The Red Badge of Courage.*** 208 pages.

Bantam 1986 Paper 0553210114 $3.95
Modern Library 2000 Paper 0679783202 $8.95
Modern Library 1998 Trade 0679602968 $15.95

A basic ingredient in the recipe for a school's English curriculum, Crane's account of a boy's illusions shattering on the battlefields of the Civil War is timeless, classic, and a must-read for everyone. The lesson that must be relearned by every generation, that the bloody badge of courage is a hard and fatal way to grow up, is beautifully recounted and never more timely than now. **Grades 8–12. PT**

Creech, Sharon. ***Chasing Redbird.*** 272 pages.

HarperCollins 1997 Library 006026988X $16.89
HarperCollins 1997 Trade 0060269871 $16.99
HarperTrophy 1998 Paper 0064406962 $5.99

Zinny is the middle daughter in a large farm family. When her beloved aunt suddenly dies, Zinny feels lost and without purpose. Without any help, she takes on a project to clear an overgrown trail near the farm. As she works on the trail, Zinny works out her own life and her place in the world. Yet there is more than a coming-of-age story here as the clear trail leads to an uncovering of family secrets. **Grades: 6–8. PJ**

Reviews: *Booklist* 3/15/1997, *SLJ* 4/1/1997

Creech, Sharon. **Walk Two Moons.** 280 pages.

> HarperCollins 1994 Library 0060233370 $17.89
> HarperCollins 1994 Trade 0060233346 $16.99
> HarperTrophy 1996 Paper 0064405176 $6.50

Thirteen-year-old Sal's mother has disappeared, supposedly to Idaho and supposedly with a promise to return. When she doesn't come back, Sal and her grandparents set off on a car trip from Ohio to bring her home. Along the way, Sal passes time on the journey by telling her grandparents the story of a "friend" named Phoebe whose mother has also disappeared. The novel won the Newbery Medal, with the selection committee noting, "The book is packed with humor and affection and is an odyssey of unexpected twists and surprising conclusions." **Grades 6—8. PJ <HIPPLE>**

> Reviews: *Booklist* 11/15/1994, *SLJ* 10/1/1994

Creech, Sharon. **The Wanderer.** 320 pages.

> HarperCollins 2000 Library 0060277319 $15.89
> HarperCollins 2000 Trade 0060277300 $15.95
> HarperTrophy 2002 Paper 0064410323 $5.99

Thirteen-year-old Sophie boards the *Wanderer*, a sailboat, with her three uncles and her cousins Cody and Brian. The trip from Connecticut to England is told at first through Sophie's journal, but then shifts to Cody's point of view. As the two narrators tell the tale, one of occasional adventure and comedy, readers want to learn the truth about Sophie as Creech again uses a journey to unlock a young person's search for self. **Grades 6—9. PJ**

> Reviews: *Booklist* 4/1/2000, *SLJ* 4/1/2000

Crichton, Michael. **The Andromeda Strain.** 252 pages.

> Ballantine 1992 Paper 0345378482 $7.99
> Random House 1987 Trade 0394415256 $26.95

In the age of anthrax anxiety, this science fiction novel about a group of scientists trying to save the world from itself is still relevant and wonderfully readable. **Grades 10—12. PJ**

Crichton, Michael. **Jurassic Park.** 399 pages.

> Random House 2002 0553755994 $9.99
> Random House 1990 0394588304 $17.00
> Alfred A. Knopf 1990 Trade 0394588169 $27.95

There might have been a movie about a theme park full of dinosaurs that goes horribly wrong. If not, sounds like a good premise for one. **Grades 8—12. PJ**

Crutcher, Chris. ***Athletic Shorts: Six Short Stories.*** 154 pages.

> Dell 1992 Paper 0440213908 $4.99
> Greenwillow 1991 Trade 0688108164 $16.95
> HarperTempest 2002 Paper 0060507837 $6.99

A collection of six short stories, five of them published for the first time. Five stories contain characters from Crutcher's novels; Angus Bethune is a new character and appears in a story that had already been published in a collection of young adult short stories. The plots in each story all lead to a decision by the protagonist. The common theme to the stories, and Crutcher's rich oeuvre, is about a healing vision that empowers kids to do their best in tough situations. **Grades 7—12. PJ <MOCK×YALSA>**

> Reviews: *Booklist* 10/15/1991, *SLJ* 9/1/1991

Crutcher, Chris. ***Chinese Handcuffs.*** 202 pages.

> Dell 1991 Paper 0440208378 $4.99
> Greenwillow 1989 Trade 0688083455 $16.95

High school junior Dillon refuses to participate in any school sports. He believes that too many coaches "have somehow confused athletic commitment with patriotism and human spiritual values, among other things." Dillon instead trains for triathlons because "it's so mental" and "you do it all for yourself." As the story unfolds, Dillon has much pain to deal with in his own life, as well as in that of his new girlfriend, Jennifer. He tries to ease his pain by attempting to understand his brother's decision to kill himself. Dillon becomes deeply involved with Stacy, his brother's girlfriend, and in the life of Jennifer, only to discover that both women are hiding something from him, and from everyone. Along the way, Dillon finds himself in conflict with the principal of his school and members of his brother's old motorcycle gang. But his greatest conflicts are within himself. He was unable to "save" his brother; thus, he sets out to save Jennifer from her stepfather, who is sexually abusing her. Crutcher's most controversial novel is a kitchen sink of suffering, but his healing vision makes it all work. **Grades 7—12. PJ <HIPPLE>**

> Reviews: *SLJ* 4/1/1989

Crutcher, Chris. ***Crazy Horse Electric Game.*** 215 pages.

> Greenwillow 1987 Trade 0688066836 $16.99

Growing up in the shadow of his father, his small town's biggest sports hero, Willie succeeds at his one last chance to become a hero during a championship baseball game. Soon after, however, his dream life is shattered during a water-skiing accident. The head injury affects his coordination, his communication, but mostly his self-esteem. He feels that he has failed his family and runs off one night without telling anyone. He lands on the tough streets of Oakland, where a street gang attacks him. A bus driver, Lacey, rescues him from both the gang and his spinning-out-of-control life by enrolling him in an alternative school called One More Last Chance High School (OMLC). At the school, Willie starts his road to rehabilitation through basketball, Tai Chi, and the support of teachers and other students. He forgives himself, but when he returns home, he learns that the cliché that you can't go home again is born in truth. **Grades 7—12. PJ**

Crutcher, Chris. **Ironman.** 228 pages.

> Laurel-Leaf 1996 Paper 044021971X $4.99
> Greenwillow 1995 Trade 068813503X $16.99

Angry father and stubborn sons is the theme of Crutcher's novel, told in a series of letters from teen jock Beau Brewster to talk-show host Larry King. The letters give Beau a chance to exorcise all his demons, but mostly his rage. An argument with a faculty member lands Beau in anger-management classes. There, Beau learns that others share his problems, and, in some cases, such as Shelly, with whom he falls in love, the problems are even sometimes worse. **Grades 7—12. PJ <HIPPLE> <MOCK> <YALSA>**

> Reviews: *Booklist* 3/1/1995, *SLJ* 3/1/1995

Crutcher, Chris. **Running Loose.** 190 pages.

> Dell 1993 Paper 0440975700 $5.50
> Greenwillow 1983 Trade 068802002X $18.99

Louis Banks has it all: dream car, dream girl, and he is a football star to boot. But when he takes an ethical stand against his coach, his world begins to fall apart, piece by piece. Finally there is nothing left, except whatever Louie can find within himself. **Grades 7—12. PJ <YALSA>**

Crutcher, Chris. **Staying Fat for Sarah Byrnes.** 216 pages.

> Laurel-Leaf 1995 Paper 044021906X $5.50
> Greenwillow 1993 Trade 0688115527 $16.95

School Library Journal called it a "masterpiece," and even that might be falling short. Eric was the fat boy and Sarah was the ugly girl, and they were friends. When Eric takes up swimming, he pulls away from his old friends, including Sarah. Eric attempts to rekindle the friendship after Sarah's suicide attempt, but with limited success. Questions of good and evil, right and wrong, and means and ends clatter about in both the dialogue and action in one of Crutcher's finest works. **Grades 7—12. PJ <HIPPLE><YALSA>**

> Reviews: *Booklist* 3/15/1993, *SLJ* 3/1/1993

Crutcher, Chris. **Stotan.** 183 pages.

> Dell 1988 Paper 0440200806 $4.99
> Greenwillow 1986 Trade 0688057152 $16.95

Walker and three of his swimming buddies see that their coach, Max II Song, has posted a sign looking for volunteers for Stotan Week. The week turns out to be a rigorous experience, both physically and emotionally, for Walker, Nortie, Lion, and Jeff. Each of the young men is battling personal demons and all are combating a group of bully bigots at their school. During a swim meet, the one member who seems to have no problems, Jeff, collapses. He is soon diagnosed with terminal leukemia. The other swimmers stay together and enter the four-man relay event with only three men: their tribute to their fallen friend. A great novel about the power of friendship. **Grades 7–12. PJ**

Reviews: *SLJ* 5/1/1986

Crutcher, Chris. ***Whale Talk.*** 224 pages.

Laurel-Leaf 2002 Paper 0440229383 $5.50
Greenwillow 2001 Trade 0688180191 $15.99
Greenwillow 2001 Library 0060293691 $15.89

Cutter High School is no place for T. J. Jones. He's black, Japanese, and white, and his adoptive dad is an ex-hippie. He sees a therapist, who has helped him deal with his anger. But like Tom Joad, when T. J. senses an injustice resulting from the jock culture running Cutter High, he is there. He assembles a group of high school misfits to form a swim team with the sole purpose of getting one member of the squad, the brain-damaged Chris Coughlin, a varsity letter. Along the way, T. J. encounters bullies, racists, and pain from his own past, all in order to do the right thing. **Grades 7–12. PJ**

Reviews: *Booklist* 4/1/2001, *SLJ* 5/1/2001, *VOYA* 6/1/2001

Curtis, Christopher Paul. ***Bud, Not Buddy.*** 256 pages.

Delacorte Press 1999 Trade 0385323069 $16.95
Random House 2002 Paper 0440413281 $5.99

This Newbery Award winner features a spunky ten-year-old narrator/protagonist. The novel is set in Michigan during the depression, but Curtis mixes plenty of giggles in with issues of growing up black in America. **Grades 6–8. PJ**

Reviews: *Booklist* 9/1/99, *SLJ* 9/1/1999, *VOYA* 2/1/2000

Curtis, Christopher Paul. ***The Watsons Go to Birmingham—1963.*** 210 pages.

Dell 1997 Paper 0440414121 $5.99
Laurel-Leaf 2000 Paper 044022800X $5.99
Delacorte 1995 Trade 0385321759 $16.95

One of the most honored debut novels ever tells the story of the Watson family's trip from their home in Flint, Michigan, to Birmingham, Alabama, right in the eye of the storm of the civil rights movement. Mostly funny and always moving, this is really a children's book, but the appeal to teens cannot be denied. **Grades 6—10. PJ <HIPPLE>**

Reviews: *Booklist* 8/1/1995, *SLJ* 10/1/1995

Cushman, Karen. ***Catherine Called Birdy.*** 169 pages.

HarperTrophy 1995 Paper 0064405842 $6.50
Clarion 1994 Trade 0395681863 $16.00

Told in diary format, Cushman spins the tale of a 14-year-old girl growing up at the end of the 13th century. Although she is the daughter of a knight, her life never seems easy. Each day brings a new set of obstacles for her to overcome, but they make her stronger. Cushman's debut novel was a 1995 Newbery Honor Book as well as a BBYA and Quick Picks selection, ALA Notable Book, *Booklist* Editors' Choice, a *Horn Book* Fanfare Selection, and one of *School Library Journal*'s best books of the year. **Grades 6—9. PJ <MOCK><YALSA>**

Reviews: *Booklist* 4/15/1994, *SLJ* 9/1/1997

Cushman, Karen. ***The Midwife's Apprentice.*** 112 pages.

HarperTrophy 1996 Paper 006440630X $5.99
Clarion 1995 Trade 0395692296 $10.95

One of the most honored young adult books of the past few years tells the story of Alyce, a young woman growing up in medieval England. After failing at her first attempt to make a life for herself, Alyce runs away from her village to "find herself" but finds only hardships along the way. By the time she returns from her exile, she is confident and brave. **Grades 6—9. PJ <YALSA>**

Reviews: *Booklist* 3/15/1995, *SLJ* 5/1/1995

Danziger, Paula. ***Can You Sue Your Parents for Malpractice?*** 152 pages.

Paperstar 1998 Paper 0698116887 $4.99 .

"It's absolutely disgusting being 14. You've got no rights whatsoever. Your parents get to make all the decisions: Who gets the single bedroom. How much allowance is enough. What time you must come in. Who is a proper friend. What your report card is supposed to look like. And what your parents don't tell you to do, the school does." So begins the tale of high school freshman Lauren Allen, who decides to fight for her right to be a teen. **Grades 6—9. PJ**

Davis, Jenny. ***Checking on the Moon.*** 208 pages.

Scholastic 1991 Library 0531085600 $17.99
Scholastic 1991 Trade 053105960X $16.95

With Davis' touching novel *Sex Education* out of print, this novel will have to represent the work of this unprolific, but powerful, writer. Twelve-year-old Cab spends the summer in her mother's hometown of Pittsburgh. But the neighborhood that Cab's mother grew up in, and where Cab will be staying with her grandmother, has changed from a working class community to a near slum filled with vacant stores, homeless people, gangs, poverty, and the threat of violence. After a series of events bring crime closer to home, Cab decides to become involved in the community and work for positive change. **Grades 6—10. PJ**

Davis, Terry. ***If Rock and Roll Were a Machine*** (scheduled to return to print spring 2003)

It would be a motorcycle. Fast, black, and shiny. Bert is searching for a truth just as simple: who he is. He thought he knew, but his fifth-grade teacher took it away. Now, a high school junior, Bert is seeking answers and a little bit of payback. **Grades 9 and up. PJ <MOCK>**

Davis, Terry. ***Vision Quest.*** 312 pages.

Eastern Washington University Press 2002 0910055793 $15.95

John Irving called the story of high school wrestler Lowden Swain "the truest novel about growing up since *The Catcher in the Rye*." This book is better than the movie, better than the hype, and due back in print. Like his friend Chris Crutcher, Davis presents the story of a young man on the brink of manhood who still has a few demons to slay and wrestles not just with his unbeatable foe on the mat, but with his place in the world. **PJ**

De Lint, Charles. ***Trader.*** 325 pages.

TOR 1997 Paper 0812551575 $6.99

A kind and talented maker of guitars wakes up in another, less scrupulous, man's body. The guitar-maker finds out what it is like to be homeless, but also realizes that he has certain strengths that are his no matter what body he is in. Alternate worlds and shamanic journeying merge with contemporary urban life and settings in a rich, believable way. **Grades 10—12. (Annotation by Hope Baugh)**

Dean, Pamela. ***Tam Lin.*** 468 pages.

TOR 1992 Paper 0812544501 $4.99

A fine fairy tale, Dean's novel also works well as a young woman's exploration of her sexuality and the intellectual awakening and camaraderie of college life. Janet Carter's subtle romance with a young man doomed to be the next sacrifice to hell is thoroughly embedded in the liberal college experience. Give *Tam Lin* to any bright teenage girl looking forward to college who enjoys novels with depth, complexity, and strong female heroines. This is also part of Windling's excellent Fairy Tale Series, which reworks old stories for modern readers. **Grades 10–12. KE**

Reviews: *Booklist* 4/15/1991

Deaver, Julie Reece. ***Say Goodnight, Gracie.*** 224 pages.

HarperCollins 1989 Paper 00644700–5 $5.99
HarperCollins 1988 Trade 006021418X $15.00

When a drunken driver kills her best friend, Jimmy, 17-year-old Morgan must learn to cope with his death and face life without him. Expertly written, this book carefully relays the deep affection two people, who are truly best friends, feel for one another. At the same time, it shows the depth and struggle of the grieving process and how even the most difficult experiences can be managed. Teens face all kinds of loss and grief, and many times they don't know how to deal with those things or that others have the same painful feelings. This book will show them how one teen persevered. **Grades 8–10. (Annotation by Diane Tuccillo)**

Reviews: *Booklist* 4/1/1988

Dessen, Sarah. ***Dreamland.*** 250 pages.

Puffin 2002 Paper 0142300675 $5.99
Viking 2000 Trade 0670891223 $15.00

Caitlin has lived in the shadow of her older, almost perfect sister, Cass, all of her life. Desperate for attention and something of her own, Caitlin hooks up with Rogerson, a senior at her high school with a shady past. She is drawn to him and nothing, not even the abuse she suffers at his hands, seems able to pull her away. **Grades 9–12. PJ**

Reviews: *Booklist* 11/1/2000, *SLJ* 9/1/2000

Dessen, Sarah. ***Keeping the Moon.*** 228 pages.

Puffin 2000 Paper 0141310073 $5.99
Viking 1999 Trade 0670885495 $15.00

Colie used to be fat, but even though her body size has changed, her body image is much the same. She gets a chance to start over, spending time with her aunt in a small North Carolina town. She develops a new set of friends, a crush on an artistic young man, and some new insights about her life. **Grades 7–12. PJ <TEN>**

Reviews: *Booklist* 9/1/1999, *SLJ* 9/1/1999, *VOYA* 12/1/1999

Dessen, Sarah. ***Someone Like You.*** 288 pages.

Puffin 2000 Paper 0141302690 $5.99

Viking 1998 Trade 0670877786 $16.99

A tale of teen friendship that survives many rough patches. Halley and Scarlet's junior year is interrupted by Halley's relationship and Scarlet's pregnancy, complicated even more by the death of Scarlet's boyfriend in an accident. Despite the tragic elements, the story, told in Halley's voice, is upbeat, sometime humorous, and always hopeful, showing that true friendship can withstand any storm. **Grades 7—12. PJ**

Reviews: *Booklist* 6/1/1998, *SLJ* 6/1/1998, *VOYA* 8/1/1998

Dessen, Sarah. ***That Summer.*** 208 pages.

Scholastic 1996 Trade 053109538X $16.95
Scholastic 1996 Library 053108888X $17.99
Penguin Putnam 1998 Paper 0140386882 $5.99

Perhaps this could have been called "two summers," as the book ricochets in time between Haven's life at age 15 and back to the summer when she was just 11. She'd rather look back because the present, with her perfect sister's wedding, her father's remarriage, and her abnormal growth spurt, is anything but pleasant. **Grades 6—10. PJ**

Reviews: *Booklist* 10/15/1996, *SLJ* 10/1/1996, *VOYA* 12/1/1996

Deuker, Carl. ***On the Devil's Court.*** 252 pages.

Avon 1991 Paper 0380708795 $5.99

Joe Faust (get it?) is a high school senior who seems to have lost his magic for shooting hoop. The answer to his dreams is a nightmare; he makes a deal with the devil for one star season in exchange for his soul. **Grades 7—12. PJ <YALSA>**

Dick, Philip K. ***Do Androids Dream of Electric Sheep?*** 244 pages.

Ballantine 1996 Paper 0345404475 $13.00

The novel, which served as the basis for *Blade Runner*, is a cult classic. It is set in the year 2021 after a war has killed off most of the population. Those who remain try to repopulate the planet, even if it means creating cyborgs. When good science goes bad, it is up to one man to round up and retire the faux-humans before they take over. **Grades 7—12. PJ**

Dickens, Charles. ***A Christmas Carol.*** Page count varies with edition.

Signet 1997 Paper 0451522834 $3.95
Bantam 1995 Paper 0553212443 $3.95
Modern Library 1995 Trade 0679601791 $14.95

Charles Dickens may be the greatest storyteller of the 19th century, but he is no picnic for less-able readers. While his prose is beautiful, it is also complex, ornate, and heavily reliant on references to the culture of his own time and place. Many younger readers simply cannot penetrate the customs of his country. That said, for those ready to take him on, Dickens is an unforgettable experience. *A Christmas Carol* survives because its story is universal. Scrooge has been reborn in many films, in many personas, but the song remains the same: generosity, kindness, and love give you immortality. The opposite gives you hell in the memories of those remaining after your death. Dickens' saintly children are generally less interesting than his more dimensional adults, but the mix is always a great discovery for the reader yet to encounter them. **Grades 6—12. PT**

Dickens, Charles. ***David Copperfield.*** Page count varies with edition.

> Bantam 1981 Paper 0553211897 $5.99
> Oxford 1999 Trade 0192100432 $18.00

Dickens said himself that Copperfield was the character whose life most resembled his own. From the disaster of debtors' prison, to the realization he must make his own way in life, from Micawber to Aunt Betsy Trotwood, the novel is full of people so real most readers speak of them as if they *were* real. A great read for those ready for a long (and we do mean long) and satisfying immersion into Dickens' fictionalized life and times. **Grades 8—12. PT**

Dickens, Charles. ***Great Expectations.*** Page count varies with edition.

> Viking 1997 Paper 0140864172 $10.95
> HarperPerennial 1999 Paper 0060933232 $22.00
> Signet 1960 Paper 0451526562 $4.95

Great Expectations follows Pip as he emerges into manhood, but the bulk of the story is his youth and the many odd characters crossing his path. This novel is not really the best introduction to Dickens, but for the seasoned reader, it's a fine choice. **Grades 7—12. PT**

Dickens, Charles. ***A Tale of Two Cities.*** Page count varies with edition.

> Random 1990 Paper 0679729658 $10.00
> Modern Library 1996 Trade 0679602089 $18.50

This is probably Dickens' masterpiece. It is at once an emotionally wrenching story of love and sacrifice and a mystery enticing the reader on to the last page. Madame DeFarge and Sydney Carton are the yin and yang of evil and good, and their parallel story lines finally cross in one of the most dramatic scenes in literature. By the time Carton has come to his farewell, "It is a far, far better thing I do," most readers have surrendered to weeping. A must-read for able readers. **Grades 9—12. PT**

Dickinson, Peter. **Eva.** 219 pages.

Dell 1990 Paper 0440207665 $5.50

Fourteen-year-old Eva wakes up in a hospital bed and learns there was only one way to save her life after being in a terrible crash—to transplant her brain into the body of a female chimpanzee! There is only one way to promote this book—to be up front with teens that it sounds like a very weird story, but even so to give it a chance. It really makes teens think! Teens here in Mesa have read and reread this book; they enjoy talking about it (we had our most successful book discussion on it); and many even share it with their parents! Teens have told me the book drives them crazy in its premise and complexity—and they love it! **Grades 6–12. (Annotation by Diane Tuccillo) <YALSA>**

Dickinson, Peter. **The Ropemaker.** 376 pages.

Delacorte 2001 Trade 0385729219 $15.95.

Dickinson presents a classic coming-of-age story nestled inside a fantasy. The book is set in "the Valley," which is protected from the evil Empire by Tilja, an enchanted forest. Over time, the power of the forest begins to fade, forcing a small group, including teenager Tilla, to embark on a journey to find a wizard who can restore the magic of the forest. **Grades 7–12. PJ <PRINTZ>**

Reviews: *Booklist* 10/15/2001, *SLJ* 11/1/2001, *VOYA* 12/1/2001

Doherty, Berlie. **Dear Nobody.** 185 pages.

Beech Tree 1994 Paper 0688127649 $5.95.
Orchard 1992 Trade 0531054616 $16.95.

The winner of the 1992 Carnegie Medal deals with teen pregnancy head-on. Rather than bringing them closer together, Helen and Chris's teenage romance explodes when Helen learns she is pregnant. How each character deals with the forthcoming baby and the pain of loss is explored in prose that *SLJ* called "some of the loveliest, most lyrical to be found in YA fiction." **Grades 7–12. PJ**

Reviews: *Booklist* 10/1/1992, *SLJ* 10/1/1992

Donoghue, Emma. **Kissing the Witch.** 240 pages.

HarperCollins 1997 Trade 0060275758 $15.95.

This collection of 13 revisionist fairy tales focuses on the women in the stories and surprise endings. Many of the stories involve lesbian relationships, including a retelling of Cinderella in which she runs off with her fairy godmother. The reviewer for the *New York Times* noted that even though the book is "ostensibly for children from 12 to 17, a 12-year-old would have to be especially savvy in the ways of relations between the sexes to appreciate what is being reworked here. These fairy tales are for sophisticated readers." **Grades 9–12 (mature). PJ**

> Reviews: *Booklist* 6/1/1997, *VOYA* 8/1/1997

Draper, Sharon M. ***Darkness Before Dawn.*** 256 pages.

> Simon Pulse 2002 Paper 0689851340 $5.99
> Atheneum 2001 Trade 0689830807 $16.95

The third Hazelwood High title focuses on high school senior Keisha, whose senior year is loaded with loss. Her ex-boyfriend has killed himself, while a good friend dies in an auto accident. Attempting to fill those voids, she enters into an unwise relationship with one of the school's coaches. Kind of an urban version of *Hatchet* in which Keisha has numerous obstacles to overcome and few tools for survival. **Grades 7–12. PJ**

> Reviews: *Booklist* 1/1/2001, *SLJ* 2/1/2001

Draper, Sharon M. ***Forged by Fire.*** 156 pages.

> Aladdin 1998 Paper 0689818513 $4.99
> Atheneum 1997 Trade 068980699X $16.00

This is not so much a sequel as a companion to *Tears of the Tiger*. While that book told the story of Andy after the fatal alcohol-fueled auto accident that killed Robert Washington, this book focuses on Gerald, another member of the basketball team in the car that night. Alcohol also fuels problems at home; Gerald's drunken stepfather poses a danger to his half-sister Angel, and it is up to Gerald to protect her from becoming just another victim. **Grades 7–12. PJ**

> Reviews: *Booklist* 2/15/1997, *SLJ* 3/1/1997, *VOYA* 6/1/1997

Draper, Sharon M. ***Romiette and Julio.*** 240 pages.

> Aladdin 2001 Paper 0689842090 $4.99.
> Atheneum 1999 Trade 0689821808 $16.00.

The *West Side Story* version of Shakespeare's play for the AOL generation, including lots (and lots) of chat. The relationship between Julio (Hispanic boy) and Romiette (African-American girl) sets up this modern spin on the age-old tale of forbidden and doomed love. **Grades 7–12. PJ**

> Reviews: *Booklist* 9/15/1999, *SLJ* 9/1/1999, *VOYA* 12/1/1999

Draper, Sharon M. ***Tears of a Tiger.*** 162 pages.

> Aladdin 1996 Paper 0689806981 $4.99
> Atheneum 1994 Trade 0689318782 $16.00.

Like Avi's *Nothing but the Truth*, this story of a high school scandal is told mainly through documents. An auto accident kills an all-star basketball player, but the driver of the car, Andy, survives. Andy soon wishes, however, that he had died because feelings of shame and guilt overwhelm him. **Grades 7—12. PJ <YALSA>**

Reviews: *Booklist* 1/1/1995, *SLJ* 2/1/1995

Duane, Diane. ***So You Want to Be a Wizard.*** 400 pages.

Harcourt Children's Books 2001 Paper 015216250X $6.50

When Nita, a much-bullied teen finds *So You Want to Be a Wizard* in her library's career section, she's eager to defend herself. She soon discovers that she's been granted power, as has a boy, Kit, only to defend others. Teen crises, along with family and relationship troubles, ground Nita and Kit's initiation into magic, while a trip into a deadly machine world to fight the Long Power provides page-turning action. Nita and Kit continue to put their hearts and lives on the line "for Life's sake" in the sequels: *Deep Wizardry, High Wizardry, A Wizard Abroad,* and *The Wizard's Dilemma.* **Grades 6—10. KE**

Reviews: *SLJ* 12/1/1998

Dumas, Alexandre. ***The Count of Monte Cristo.*** Page count varies with edition.

Modern Library 2002 Paper 037576030X $12.95
Bantam 1985 Paper 0553213504 $6.50
Signet Paper 1988 0451521951 $6.95

An annual best-seller since its publication in 1844, *The Count of Monte Cristo* is a sweeping historical romance set in post-Napoleonic France. Falsely accused of treason, Edmund Dantes is imprisoned in Chateau d'If and manages a miraculous escape after 20 years, many spent plotting revenge on those who ruined him. Part history, part love story, part thriller, the *Count* has something for everyone. For the reader unaccustomed to European topical references, this long novel offers a challenge. The story is far more complex and layered than the 2001 movie of the same name. **Grades 8—12. PT**

Dumas, Alexandre. ***The Man in the Iron Mask.*** Page count varies with edition.

Oxford 1998 Paper 0192838423 $13.95
Signet 1992 Paper 0451525647 $6.95

The opening pages of this novel suggest to the reader that Dumas has returned to his theme of the righteous, unjustly imprisoned for the greed and ambition of the evil. However, although *Iron Mask* begins in the Bastille, it is not a companion book to *The Count of Monte Cristo.* Rather, it is the fifth of six volumes detailing the adventures and intrigues of the Three Musketeers. It also has very little to do with any of the movies made of *Iron Mask;* so readers who request it based on cinematic experience should be warned they are asking for much, much more than the film story. For skilled readers, who might enjoy *Mask* more if they follow the tale from its beginning and in order: *The Three Musketeers, Twenty Years After, The Vicomte de Bragelonne,* and *Louise de la Valliere.* The final volume in the series is *Son of Porthos.* Should you purchase all the titles, do so from the same house; different publishers pick up the stories in different places. Unabridged editions run sometimes over a thousand pages. There are good abridged versions, but diehard Dumas fans might take exception to them. Some archaic vocabulary ("girdle" for belt, etc.) and a heavy dose of historic topicality will make Dumas hard going for inexperienced readers, but among those with the skills and a love for Athos, Porthos, Aramis, and D'Artagnan (never static characters), the Musketeer serial evokes fiercely loyal readers. **Grades 8—12. PT**

Dumas, Alexandre. **The Three Musketeers.** Page count varies with edition.

Oxford 1998 Paper 0192835750 $8.95
Bantam Paper 1990 0553213377 $5.95
Modern Library 2000 Trade 0679603328 $24.95

First in the series, this novel introduces us to D'Artagnan, his initiation into the Musketeers, and his growing loyalty to and his friendship with Athos, Porthos, and Aramis. The plot centers on the four intrepid guards' adventures in protecting the queen from the evil and Machiavellian Cardinal Richelieu. Language selection and a background rich in centuries-old French and European political intrigue makes the *Musketeers* a challenge for the reader who requires a less detailed setting and more contemporary vocabulary. **Grades 8—12. PT**

Duncan, Lois. **Daughters of Eve.** 256 pages.

Dell 1990 Paper 0440918642 $4.99

The Stepford wives visit high school as Duncan looks at high school clubs, conformity, and covens. **Grades 6—8. PJ**

Duncan, Lois. **Down a Dark Hall.** 192 pages.

Bantam Doubleday Dell 1990 Paper 0440918057 $4.99

Her books may have come into vogue with the motion picture *I Know What You Did Last Summer,* but this book is perhaps one of her best. Kit is a young girl who is entering a boarding school for the first time, one that is housed in a dark and mysterious mansion. The headmistress puts her ill at ease as does her oppressive bedroom. It isn't long at all before she and the other students are experiencing strange dreams and exhibiting odd behavior. The mystery of what is actually going on at the school will have readers on the edge of their seats and clamoring for more of her books when they are finished. **Grades 6—8. (Annotation by Spring Lee Boehler)**

Duncan, Lois. *I Know What You Did Last Summer.* 199 pages.

> Pocket Books 1997 Paper 0671017225 $4.99

This is the book that became, much to Duncan's chagrin, the foundation for a block-buster movie and a blueprint for the teen thriller trend of the 1990s about a group of friends, an accidental murder, and payback time. **Grades 7–12. PJ**

Duncan, Lois (Editor). *Night Terrors: Stories of Shadow and Substance.* 222 pages.

> Simon & Schuster 1997 Paper 0689807244 $3.99
> Simon & Schuster 1996 Trade 068980346X $16.00

A nice collection of stories about things that go bump in the night by authors such as Joan Lowery Nixon, Richard Peck, Chris Lynch, and Annette Curtis Klause. There are stories about ghosts, deranged killers, and even one on the "Bogey Man."
Grades 6–10. PJ

> Reviews: *Booklist* 5/15/1996, *SLJ* 6/1/1996

Duncan, Lois. *Stranger with My Face.* 250 pages.

> Dell 1990 Paper 0440983568 $4.99

Laurie's life is falling apart. Her friends are making accusations, and she feels anxious all the time, as if she's being watched. Her paranoia turns out to be well founded when paranormal circumstances lead to a pair of Lauries. **Grades 6–8. PJ**

Duncan, Lois. *Summer of Fear.* 217 pages.

> Dell 1977 Paper 044098324X $4.99

From the moment Rachel's cousin Julia arrived that summer, she seemed to seep into Rachel's life like a poison. Everyone else was enchanted by her—including Rachel's boyfriend. Rachel figured out right away that Julia wasn't a good person, but she had no idea that she was pure evil. **Grades 7–12. PJ**

Duncan, Lois. *The Third Eye.* 224 pages.

> Bantam Doubleday Dell 1991 Paper 0440987202 $4.99

When a child goes missing, high school senior Karen is faced with a choice. All she wants to do is fit in, but her psychic powers, including her ability to see the missing child, are bound to set her apart. **Grades 6–8. PJ**

Duncan, Lois (Editor). *Trapped: Cages of Mind and Body.* 240 pages.

> Aladdin 1999 Paper 0689830823 $4.99

Simon & Schuster 1998 Trade 068981335X $16.00

Popular YA authors such as Rob Thomas, Joan Bauer, Walter Dean Myers, and Francesca Lia Block contribute stories around the theme of containment. Most stories are not, as one might expect from a Duncan-edited collection, horror or suspense; rather, a variety of genres are explored, including romance, fantasy, and humor. **Grades 7—12. PJ**

Reviews: *Booklist* 7/1/1998, *SLJ* 6/1/1998, *VOYA* 8/1/1998

Easton, Kelly. ***The Life History of a Star.*** 208 pages.

Simon Pulse 2002 Paper 0689852703 $6.99
McElderry 2001 Trade 068983134X $16.00

A novel in diary form about Kristin Folger's 14th year, when the whole world, and her body, seem at war with her. It is 1973 in California, but nothing is groovy. She hates her body, her school, and her parents; she hates her whole life. Coming of age is hard enough to begin with, but Kristen has to do it in the shadow of a "ghost" (her Vietnam-vet brother) who haunts her thoughts. **Grades 7—12. PJ**

Reviews: *Booklist* 4/15/2001, *SLJ* 7/1/2001

Eddings, David. ***Guardians of the West.*** 454 pages.

Ballantine 1998 Paper 0345352661 $6.99

The Belgaird redux: All the familiar elements are here as Garion and his friends from the first series are reunited to save their kingdom from the Dark Prophecy, which is once again threatening the Prophecy of Light. Fans of the first series will demand this and the other titles in Mallorean series: *King of the Murgos, Demon Lord of Karanda, Sorceress of Darshiva,* and *Seeress of Kell.* **Grades 6—10. KE**

Eddings, David. ***Pawn of Prophecy.*** 262 pages.

Ballantine 1986 Paper 0345335511 $6.99

Garion is a teenage farm boy until his "Aunt Pol" and her disreputable tramp father turn out to be powerful sorcerers, and he is embroiled in an epic quest to save his land from enslavement to a prophesied evil god and its followers. Eddings' adventures have engaging male (and female) heroes, and the nonstop action is leavened by the often-humorous foibles and relationships among them. One of the first (and best) of the "Tolkien-lite" adventure series, Eddings books are a fine transition for middle school students not yet ready for the violence of a Robert Jordan, while older teens who enjoy adventure gaming (like D&D) will find it an enjoyable romp. Other books in the Belgaird saga are *Queen of Sorcery, Magician's Gambit, Castle of Wizardry,* and *Enchanters' End Game.* **Grades 6—10. KE**

Ellison, Ralph. ***Invisible Man.*** 572 pages.

Random 1992 Trade 0394603389 $18.50

Since its publication in 1952, this shattering novel of race in America has become a foundation stone in literature. Remarkably, a first novel by an unknown writer, *Invisible Man* won the National Book Award, was 19th place on Modern Library's list of 100 top English language novels of the 20th century, and has sustained its power as a book capable of changing readers' lives. Ellison's prose is direct, clear, powerful, and beautiful. All levels of readers can find the grief Ellison profoundly recounts in a double tragedy: growing up black in a racist society, and the pitfalls of simply growing up with no guidance or truth as to one's own identity. The final line tells it all: "And it is this which frightens me: Who knows but that, on the lower frequencies, I speak for you?" **Grades 10–12. PT**

Ende, Michael. ***The Neverending Story.*** 448 pages.

Puffin 1997 Paper 0140386335 $7.99
Dutton 1997 Trade 0525457585 $22.99

Targeted for the young adult audience, the tale of Bastian Bux is not a challenge to more advanced teens. Bastian feels compelled to steal a book, whereupon his life and the adventures in the land of Fantastica begin to merge. The twinned stories end with Bastian emerging from his quest stronger and more grown up. **Grades 6–12. PT**

Engdahl, Sylvia Louise. ***Children of the Star.*** 648 pages.

Meisha Merlin 2000 Paper 1892065142 $18.00

Long before there was *The Giver*, Engdahl was writing challenging science fiction about hope in the face of seemingly necessary despair. Noren is a teenage atheist challenging the caste system of the City and determined to oppose their control of the machinery (which the villagers take for divine power) that enables the toxic soil to be farmed and the mutagenic water to be drunk. Utterly committed to the truth and refusing to recant his opinions in the face of torture and death, only a cruel librarian will reveal to the reader that the deception is necessary: the City, Noren's destiny, and his society seemingly doomed to extinction. *Children of the Star* contains the original three books, *This Star Shall Abide, Beyond the Tomorrow Mountains,* and *The Doors of the Universe*. Thoughtful characterization, intelligent philosophy (without preaching or lecturing), and a page-turning mood of desperate action will draw in older readers of intelligent speculative fiction. **Grades 8–12. KE**

Engdahl, Sylvia Louise. ***Enchantress from the Stars.*** 288 pages.

Firebird 2003 Paper 0142500372 $6.99
Walker 2001 Trade 0802787649 $18.95

A long time ago, in a galaxy far, far away, an advanced civilization studies other cultures via the Anthropology Service, a group so dedicated that they will allow themselves to die before tampering with the lives and culture of the "Younglings" on other planets. The broad sweep of the tale is grounded in the perspective of three teenagers: Elana, the inadvertent member of the Anthropology Service team studying Andrecia; Georyn, a local boy from Andrecia's medieval culture, who hopes to save his village from a "dragon"; and XXX, the invader from a nearby planet whose bulldozers and mining equipment seem like magic to Georyn and primitive technology to Elana. The three-way storyline is skillfully handled, the viewpoints making the lesson for understanding and self-sacrifice without ever preaching. An excellent title to give to younger teens or those who "don't like SF"; older readers won't want to miss the sequel, *The Far Side of Evil*, in which XXX goes undercover in a totalitarian society on the brink of nuclear war. **Grades 7–12. KE**

Esquivel, Laura. ***Like Water for Chocolate.*** 245 pages.

> Anchor 1994 Paper 038542017X $11.95
> Doubleday 1992 Trade 0385420161 $23.00

A wonderful introduction to the literary form of magical realism, this first novel from Esquivel unfolds a nearly mythological love story between Tita de la Garza, the youngest of three daughters, and Pedro, who marries Tita's older sister. Family tradition forbids the youngest daughter to marry, and Pedro thinks the only way to be close to Tita is to take the role of her sister's husband. Filled with recipes and home remedies that serve as metaphors for the central story, this novel is a delight for all levels of readers. **Grades 10–12 (mature). PT**

> Reviews: *Booklist* 9/15/1992

Farmer, Nancy. ***The Ear, the Eye and the Arm.*** 311 pages.

> Firebird 2002 Paper 0141311096 $6.99
> Orchard 1994 Trade 0531068293 $18.95

Three mutant detectives in a future Zimbabwe are hired by the local warlord to rescue his children from kidnappers. All is not as it seems, however, and the story shifts from the children's viewpoint to the detectives', revealing, in the process, a fascinating Africa that never was. The action is nearly constant and leavened with slapstick humor. A must for younger fans of science fiction or adventure. The wise librarian will purchase the Firebird Press reprint with the very cool cover rather than the somewhat dweeby-looking original. **Grades 7–12. KE <YALSA>**

> Reviews: *Booklist* 4/1/1994

Farmer, Nancy. ***A Girl Named Disaster.*** 306 pages.

> Puffin 1996 Paper 0140386351 $5.99
> Orchard 1996 Trade 0531095398 $19.95

Orchard 1996 Library 0531088898 $20.99

A coming-of-age and adventure story set in Africa. Nhamo lives with her grand-mother: her mother is dead and her father is away in the mines. She is promised in marriage, but the night before the wedding, at her grandmother's urging, she runs away. Her trip to Zimbabwe to find her father is full of danger, but Nhamo grows in strength along the journey, buoyed by conversations with her dead mother. An interesting glimpse into another culture that resonates with themes any teen can relate to. **Grades 6–9. PJ <YALSA>**

Reviews: *Booklist* 9/1/1996

Fast, Howard. ***April Morning.*** 184 pages.

Bantam 1983 Paper 0553273221 $6.99

Howard Fast transfers the American teenage boy's grappling with war and soldier-ing to Lexington and Concord, as Adam signs on with the Revolutionary Army and reflects on life in the world beyond his farm. Good historical fiction; easily accessi-ble. **Grades 6–12. PT**

Feist, Raymond E. ***Faerie Tale.*** 544 pages.

Bantam 1989 Paper 0553277839 $5.99

Along with Robert Jordan, Feist is an overlord of dark fantasy. While he has numer-ous sagas and series in print, this stand-alone volume, perhaps, is most important to a library collection and seems ripe for "Hollywoodization." The Hastings family is picture perfect, until they move into a new home teeming with fairies and other icons from Irish mythology. These are not quite charming little gnomes; rather they represent to the Hastings family a real threat, as it seems their house is the battle-field for an upcoming war. A horror novel built on a fantasy foundation that is a great read for teens. **Grades 8–12. PJ**

Ferris, Jean. ***Bad.*** 192 pages.

Aerial 2001 Paper 0374404755 $5.95
Farrar Straus Giroux 1998 Trade 0374304793 $17.00

Dallas wants to fit in; that is no crime. But when the fitting in involves an attempted robbery, Dallas is the only one caught, while her new "friends" go free. Her father, hoping to teach her a lesson, refuses to take custody, and Dallas is forced to spend six months in a juvenile detention facility. There she endures the daily grind of life behind bars and the daily testing from the other residents. **Grades 7–12. PJ**

Reviews: *Booklist* 10/1/1998, *SLJ* 12/1/1998

Ferris, Jean. ***Love Among the Walnuts.*** 214 pages.

> Puffin 2001 Paper 0141310995 $5.99
> Harcourt 1998 Trade 0152015906 $16.00

A weird title matches the wacky Rube Goldberg plot about how a young man tries to protect his very rich parents from being murdered by some very evil relatives. And these are the normal characters. A teen reviewer on Amazon wrote: "I couldn't put it down, and finished it in less than a day. I even read it again, which is something I almost never do. The Walnuts helped me to realize what a great life I had, but made it fun to do. *Love among the Walnuts* also makes people believe that money really doesn't make life perfect, and that it can make more problems than happiness."
Grades 6—10. PJ

> Reviews: *SLJ* 8/1/1998, *VOYA* 2/1/1999

Fine, Anne. ***Flour Babies.*** 178 pages.

> Laurel-Leaf 1995 Paper 0440219418 $4.50

Simon Martin and his chums at school are under-whelmed by their assignment: learning about parenting by carrying around and caring for, a bag of flour. But what Simon thinks is going to be an easy task with plenty of comic possibilities has other sides, such as the way the assignment makes him think about his relationship with the father who abandoned him. *Booklist* noted the novel was a "poignant, gloriously funny book with a strong message for readers." **Grades 7—9. PJ**

> Reviews: *Booklist* 4/1/1994

Fitzgerald, F. Scott. ***The Great Gatsby.*** 170 pages.

> Simon & Schuster 1996 Trade 0684830426 $25.00
> Simon & Schuster 1995 Paper 0684801523 $12.00

One of the core of the core, *The Great Gatsby* has, since its publication in 1925, entered into legend among American letters. After falling from favor, along with its author, in the 1940s, the novel returned to print in 1950, averaging sales of 300,000 copies a year, every year. The story of Jay Gatsby, Nick Caraway, Nick's cousin Daisy, and her husband Tom Buchanan is in reality the recounting of the failure of the American Dream. The romance of illusion cannot stand against the brutality of reality, as the characters learn to their sorrow and to ours. Fitzgerald is arguably one of the two or three great American writers of the 20th century, and his work is both complex and accessible to those without complex reading skills. **Grades 9—12. PT**

Flake, Sharon G. ***Money Hungry.*** 127 pages.

> Jump at the Sun 2001 Library 078682476X $16.95
> Jump at the Sun 2001 Trade 078680548X $15.99

Raspberry and her mother have run away from her drug-addicted father only to find themselves with few resources and even homeless for a short time While her mother works two jobs and attends school, Raspberry helps out by earning money any way she can as she adjusts to life in the projects. Although she's only 13, Raspberry is forced to sacrifice her childhood, and even her friends (who all have problems of their own), just to survive. *Booklist* noted the novel's "razor-sharp dialogue and unerring details evoke characters, rooms, and neighborhoods with economy and precision, creating a story that's immediate, vivid, and unsensationalized." **Grades 6—12. PJ**

Reviews: *Booklist* 6/1/2001, *SLJ* 7/1/2001, *VOYA* 2/1/2002

Flake, Sharon G. ***The Skin I'm In.*** 171 pages.

Jump at the Sun 2000 Paper 0786813075 $5.99
Jump at the Sun 1998 Trade 0786804440 $14.95

Thirteen-year-old Maleeka is the victim of black-on-black teasing because of her very dark skin. She's unsure of herself and has no close friends. It is only when a teacher befriends her that Maleeka starts to accept the skin she is in. A small story that speaks volumes about identity and alienation. **Grades 6—10. PJ**

Reviews: *Booklist* 9/1/1998, *SLJ* 11/1/1998

Fleischman, Paul. ***Bull Run.*** 104 pages.

HarperCollins 1993 Library 0060214473 $16.89
HarperTrophy 1995 Paper 0064405885 $4.99

Another literary experiment from the Newbery Award-winning author. Is it a novel? A play? A series of monologues? Whatever the form, the story is that of the first great battle of the Civil War told by voices black and white, male and female, Rebel and Union. A huge hit with book reviewers, who showered it with awards and honors, such as *SLJ* Best Book; *Booklist*'s Books for Youth, Editors' Choices; Scott O'Dell Award for Historical Fiction for Children; and YALSA Best Books. Grades **6—12. PJ <YALSA>**

Reviews: *Booklist* 1/15/1993

Fleischman, Paul. ***Mind's Eye.*** 108 pages.

Bantam Doubleday Dell 2001 Paper 0440229014 $5.50
Henry Holt 1999 Trade 0805063145 $15.95

Written entirely in dialogue, *Mind's Eye* tells how 16-year-old Courtney, who is paralyzed and abandoned in a convalescent home, and her elderly roommate embark on an imaginary journey with a bittersweet, disturbing ending. **Grades 7—12. (Annotation by Jill Patterson)**

Reviews: *Booklist* 9/1/1999, *VOYA* 12/1/1999

Fleischman, Paul. ***Whirligig.*** 133 pages.

> Laurel-Leaf 1999 Paper 0440228352 $4.99
> Henry Holt 1998 Trade 0805055827 $16.95

Sixteen-year-old Brent wants to be popular. When an incident at a party leads to his humiliation, he decides to take his own life by crashing his car. The resulting accident, however, causes the death of another. Seeking to atone for his deed, Brent undertakes, at the request of the mother of the deceased, a cross-country journey to build memorials at the four corners of the U.S. *Whirligig* has been called a groundbreaking work. **Grades 6—9. PJ <YALSA>**

> Reviews: *Booklist* 4/1/1998, *SLJ* 4/1/1998

Flinn, Alex. ***Breathing Underwater.*** 272 pages.

> HarperTempest 2002 Paper 0064472574 $7.99
> HarperCollins 2001 Trade 0060291982 $15.99
> HarperCollins 2001 Library 0060291990 $16.89

Perhaps the clearest demonstration of Flinn's talent here is the way she can so clearly portray abusive behavior from the point of view of the abuser who does not realize that what he is doing is wrong! I felt so sorry for Nick's girlfriend, and so happy that she escaped. And yet, when I read Nick's story, I couldn't help but find sympathy for him as well, despite the fact that his behavior turned my stomach. The clever interlacing of past and present narrative through journal entries was well done and never gave away elements of the story too soon. Flinn's book may have been written as a warning to potential abuse victims or abusers, but it is more than just a poster from an action group. Her characters are real, their foibles are believable, and their stories will have readers hanging on to the very end. **Grades 8—12. (Annotation by Spring Lea Boehler)**

> Reviews: *Booklist* 8/1/2001, *SLJ* 5/1/2001, *VOYA* 6/1/2001

Fox, Paula. ***The Eagle Kite.*** 212 pages.

> Laurel-Leaf 1996 Paper 0440219728 $4.50
> Orchard 1995 Library 0531087425 $16.99

While many of the first "round" of novels for teens about AIDS have gone out of print or not aged well, Fox's book still resonates. Liam's father is dying of AIDS, from a blood transfusion Liam is told. But as his father wastes away, a teenage boy grows into a man and discovers the power of acceptance and love. **Grades 7—12. PJ**

> Reviews: *Booklist* 2/1/1995, *SLJ* 4/1/1995

Frank, E. R. ***America.*** 256 pages.

> Atheneum 2002 Trade 0689847297 $18.00

Frank turns the stuff of urban mythology into flesh, bone, and soul. The book opens with the main character, America, recovering from a suicide attempt. The teen's past, described in graphic detail, includes abandonment, sexual abuse, racism, alcoholism, a crack-addicted birth mother, and even attempted murder. America's present is spent trying to recover by working with a caring therapist. **Grades 9—12 (mature). PJ**

Reviews: *Booklist* 2/15/2002, *SLJ* 3/1/2002

Frank, E. R. *Life Is Funny.* 263 pages.

Puffin 2002 Paper 0142300837 $7.99
DK 2000 Trade 078942634X $19.99

Life may be funny, but it is not always pretty. A series of interconnected stories describe the sometimes harsh daily lives of 11 teens coming of age in Brooklyn. The characters represent all "types," yet they also come alive in their stories, which all read, in some ways, like mini-problem novels. The experiences of these 11 teens include tales of teen pregnancy, dating violence, spousal abuse, drug abuse, racism, and alcoholism. And hope. **Grades 9—12. (mature) PJ**

Reviews: *Booklist* 3/15/2000, *SLJ* 5/1/2000

Furlong, Monica. *Juniper.* 198 pages.

Borzoi 1992 Paper 0679833692 $4.99

Before the word "Wicca" entered the teen lexicon, before Silver Ravenwolf's *Teen Witch* became a young adult collection staple, there was *Juniper.* Monica Furlong's medieval tale about a healer named Euny, who teaches a spoiled palace brat the Craft of the Wise, was among the first and still is the best portrayal of witchcraft in teen fiction. **Grades 6—12. (Annotation by Jennifer Hubert) <LOST>**

Furlong, Monica. *Wise Child.* 240 pages.

Random 1989 Paper 0394825985 $4.99

The central character, the "wise child," is adopted by Juniper (see above) and taught the ways of white, or good, magic. But her birth mother appears and attempts to bring her over to the "dark side." An ALA Notable Children's Book and an IRA/CBC Young Adults' Choice. **Grades 6—12. PJ**

Gaiman, Neil. *American Gods.* 465 pages.

HarperCollins 2002 Paper 0380789035 $7.99
Avon 2001 Trade 0380973650 $26.00

Shadow is fresh out of prison and has recently returned from his wife's funeral. He is then told, by the mysterious stranger known only as Mr. Wednesday, that Shadow's boss is also dead, so why not come to work for Mr. Wednesday? The veil is removed; Mr. Wednesday is really the Norse god, Odin. Shadow's job is to help Odin round up the other "old" gods of Norse mythology in preparation for a battle with the new gods of America: greed, speed, and all things modern. Loaded into this fable are fight scenes and lots of weirdness as Shadow makes his away across these United States with the corpse of his dead wife, which won't stay in the ground, popping in on him. **Grades 10–12. PJ**

Reviews: *VOYA* 2/1/2002

Gaiman, Neil. **Neverwhere.** 337 pages.

Morrow/Avon 1998 Paper 0380789019 $6.99
Morrow/Avon 1997 Trade 0380973634 $24.00

Richard Mayhew turns his successful yuppie life upside down when he rescues what appears to be a teenage girl living on the streets. However, he has been catapulted into London Below, a world of magic and horror, which connects with London Above only, and in part, by London's Underground. Once touched by magic, he finds it increasingly difficult to return to normal life, as job, bank account, and girlfriend appear to evaporate, while strange and sinister powers turn their attention to controlling or destroying him. Originally a BBC series (and cult favorite), the story is extremely cinematic with (for Gaiman) a surprisingly fast-paced plot loaded with cliffhangers. Both fantasy and horror fans will find much to their liking here: The clever and detailed magical world and the skillful handling of suspense, terror, and a mood of relentless doom are made accessible to the reader by the intelligent and likable "Everyman" protagonist. **Grades 10–12. KE**

Reviews: *Booklist* 5/15/97

Gaiman, Neil. **Stardust.** 238 pages.

DC Comics 1999 Paper 156389470X $19.95
HarperCollins 2001 Paper 0060934719 $13.00
Avon 1999 Trade 0380977281 $22.00

Stardust's epic journey in the name of love revolves around the book's main character, Tristan, who actually tries to "catch" a falling star. Set in a land of magical make-believe, Gaiman loads up the stories with the usual suspects of witches, goblins, ogres, and gnomes, as well as enough dark shadow to keep even the Brothers Grimm happy. A rich stew of fantasy classics and fairy tale clichés layered thick, all driven by Gaiman's wit. **Grades 7–12. PJ**

Reviews: *Booklist* 11/1/1998, *SLJ* 2/1/1999, *VOYA* 10/1/1999

Gaines, Ernest J. ***The Autobiography of Miss Jane Pittman.*** 245 pages.

> Bantam 1982 Paper 0553263579 $6.50
> Houghton Mifflin 1998 Trade 0395869935 $16.60

In the 31 years since its publication, *Autobiography*, a novel, has lost none of the power evoked from the remarkable story of Miss Jane Pittman, a child at the close of the Civil War, who endures through the civil rights movement 100 years later. Of enormous scope, filled with a panoply of fascinating characters, this fictionalized history of the United States' most tumultuous years is given sharp resonance through the tape-recorded recollections of an 110-year-old black woman who has literally seen it (just about) all. Gaines' style is deceptively simple, though some dialect ("sable" for "saber") can be challenging for less able readers. **Grades 7–12. PT**

Gallo, Donald R. (Editor). ***No Easy Answers: Short Stories About Teenagers Making Tough Choices.*** 323 pages.

> Laurel-Leaf 1999 Paper 0440413052 $5.50

This anthology features stories about teens put to a test, not in school, but in trying to make the right choices in their lives. The stories are not always about making the choice, but about the consequences of those decisions. There are "big" choices, such as handling an unexpected pregnancy, and smaller ones about working out family dynamics. Gallo has a lineup of YA all-stars penning tales: M. E. Kerr, David Klass, and Virginia Euwer Wolff. Both a BBYA and a Quick Pick selection. **Grades 7–12. PJ**

> Reviews: *Booklist* 11/15/1997, *VOYA* 10/1/1997

Gallo, Donald R. (Editor). ***On the Fringe.*** 221 pages.

> Penguin Putnam 2001 Trade 0803726562 $17.99

The most common theme of all literature for young adults is that of the "outsider." Here, Gallo pulls together some of the finest YA writers to face that theme head-on. There are stories from Joan Bauer, Ron Koertge, Angela Johnson, Graham Salisbury, M. E. Kerr, Will Weaver, and Alden Carter. Writing partly in response to the events at Columbine High School, the authors attempt to understand and illuminate teens who are outside of "normal" high school life. **Grades 7–12. PJ**

Gantos, Jack. ***Desire Lines.*** 138 pages.

> Farrar Straus Giroux 1997 Trade 0374317720 $16.00

An amazingly harsh novel about homophobia. The main character, Walker, seems likable enough, even heroic as he liberates animals from his high school's science lab. But he is also without close friends and enjoys his isolation; he lacks a center. When a fire-and-brimstone preacher comes to town, Walker latches onto him and his message. He then "outs" a lesbian couple, and the wheels of murders are set in motion. **Grades 7—12. PJ**

Reviews: *VOYA* 10/1/199

Gantos, Jack. ***Joey Pigza Swallowed The Key.*** 153 pages.

HarperTrophy 2000 Paper 0064408337 $5.99
Farrar Straus Giroux 1998 Trade 0374336644 $16.00

For all the press about attention deficit disorder in kids, it was never addressed directly until Gantos gave voice to Joey Pigza, the boy who can't sit still. The havoc the disease wreaks in Joey's life, albeit sometimes with more than a little humor, is the centerpiece of the first book in the series. **Grades 6—9. PJ**

Reviews: *Booklist* 12/15/1998, *SLJ* 12/1/1998

Garden, Nancy. ***Annie on My Mind.*** 233 pages.

Aerial 1992 Paper 0374404143 $5.95

This breakthrough lesbian love story is the only book to appear on all four of YALSA's Best of the Best lists. But what do teens think about it? This is from one Amazon review: "The book is AMAZING; it tells how they really feel and I could relate to it. I think most gay, lesbian, or bi-sexual people (teens) can. Even if you're straight I suggest you read this book. Definitely read it if you just want to try and understand." **Grades 7—12. PJ <MOCK><YALSA>**

Garland, Sherry. ***Song of the Buffalo Boy.*** 232 pages.

Harcourt 1994 Paper 0152000984 $6.00
Harcourt 1992 Trade 0152771077 $16.00

Loi is a pariah in her village in Vietnam, the child of a woman from the village and an American solider. For 17 years, she has felt little but scorn from those around her. When she meets Khai (the buffalo boy), she finds love for the first time, but the objections of those around her threaten her happiness. Loi changes from outcast to being in exile when she and her boyfriend flee her village and head to Ho Chi Minh City. **Grades 7—12. PJ**

George, Jean Craighead. ***My Side of the Mountain.*** 177 pages.

Puffin 2001 Paper 0141312424 $5.99
Dutton 1988 Trade 0525463461 $15.99

A Hans Christian Andersen Award Honor book, a Newbery Honor book, and an ALA Notable Book, *My Side of the Mountain* recounts the adventures of young Sam Gribley, who runs away from home and winds up in the Catskill Mountains. With few initial skills in survival, Sam manages to discover the secrets of living off the land and surviving loneliness, fear, and the lure of comforts he left behind in the city. With freedom comes maturation; as Sam realizes his love for adventure he manages to begin the process of becoming a man. His year in the Catskills is reminiscent of Thoreau's sojourn on Walden Pond, but written for younger readers. The story continues in *Julie* and *Julie's Wolf Pack.* **Grades 6—8. PT**

Gibson, William. ***Neuromancer.*** 271 pages.

> Ace 1995 Paper 0441569595 $6.99
> Ace 2000 Paper 0441007465 $13.95
> Ace 1994 Trade 0441000681 $21.95

Winner of the triple crown of science fiction—the Hugo Award, the Philip K. Dick Award, and the Nebula Award—*Neuromancer* invented the fictional universe of cyberspace. "Cyberpunks" cruise Virtual Reality to escape their own bodies, or the "world of meat," and auction their skills to the highest corporate bidders. The information superhighway becomes the new Old West, and our hero, Case, rides it at his peril. A traditional adventure unspooled in most untraditional venues, *Neuromancer* is an important signpost on the road to technological science fiction. **Grades 10—12. PT**

Gilmore, Kate. ***Exchange Student.*** 217 pages.

> Houghton Mifflin 1999 Trade 0395575117 $15.00

What would a foreign exchange student look like in the year 2094? For starters, he would be seven feet tall. Daria's family, who owns a breeding zoo, welcomes a student (Fen) from the planet Chela. He's an alien mood-ring whose skin changes color to match his emotions. Think of *My Favorite Martian* in high school, with a little bit of Star Trekian moralizing about how humans have little respect for their environment. **Grades 6—9. PJ**

> Reviews: *Booklist* 9/15/1999, *SLJ* 10/1/1999

Gilstrap. John. ***Nathan's Run.*** 293 pages.

> Warner Books 1997 Paper 0446604682 $6.99

Although the eponymous Nathan is only 12, this *Fugitive*-type novel is not for young readers. Plenty of violence and gore surround Nathan Bailey, an orphan accused of murdering a police officer. As the subject of a national "boyhunt," Nathan finds an unlikely ally: a national radio talk-show host who gives his story coast-to-coast exposure. The reader holds his breath, along with a nation, following Nathan's strategies to elude capture and prove his innocence while discovering his own strongest weapon: the truth. **Grades 9—12. PT**

> Reviews: *SLJ* 4/1/1997

Goldman, William. ***The Princess Bride/25th Anniversary Edition.*** 399 pages.

> Ballantine 1998 Trade 034543014X $24.95
> Del Rey Paper 0345348036 $6.99

For those whose only experience with this title is the movie, a surprise awaits. Goldman, a successful screenwriter, redirects his gifts for humor, romance and suspense into a charming fable of love and heroics, a fairy tale for grownups. *Newsweek* declared of Goldman's book: "His swashbuckling fable is nutball funny . . . A 'classic' medieval melodrama that sounds like all the Saturday serials you ever saw feverishly reworked by the Marx Brothers." A retooling of S. Morgenstern's *Classic Tale of True Love and High Adventure* (the subtitle), this novel, according to Goldman, is "The Good Parts Version." We would agree. **Grades 9—12. PT**

Goldstein, Lisa. ***Dark Cities Underground.*** 252 pages.

> TOR 2000 Paper 0312868278 $13.95
> TOR 1999 Trade 0312868286 $22.95

Although the mythical stories of Isis, Osirus, and Set form the backbone of *Dark Cities*, it would be an unkindness to reveal this to a teen reader: Goldstein's characters have fallen, puzzle-like, into a magical reality that lies side-by-side with our own and is linked across the world via its subways. As the heroine, a single mother and writer, and the hero, an aging man whose mother stole his childhood to make him the central character of her popular children's fantasy series, try to solve the puzzle, readers are gradually drawn into their fantastical and increasingly creepy world. Older fans of Neil Gaiman and Tim Powers should find this particular fantasy universe very appealing. **Grades 10—12. KE**

> Reviews: *Booklist* 5/15/1999

Grant, Cynthia D. ***Mary Wolf.*** 166 pages.

> Simon & Schuster 1997 Paper 0689812922 $4.50
> Atheneum 1995 Trade 068980007X $16.00

Cynthia Grant gave us a young adult book that wasn't about cliques, peer pressure, or addiction. Instead, she described a teen with a moral core who is forced to play the parent to her own mother and father, who live in complete denial of the desperation of their homeless situation. A well-articulated tribute to the strength and reason of teenagers. **Grades 8—10. (Annotation by Jennifer Hubert) <LOST>**

> Reviews: *Booklist* 10/1/1995, *SLJ* 10/1/1995, *VOYA* 12/1/1995

Grant, Cynthia D. ***White Horse.*** 157 pages.

> Aladdin Paperbacks 2000 Paper 06898326X: $4.99

Not a sequel to *Black Beauty*, but rather a penetrating novel about heroin. The story is told in two voices. The first voice belongs to Raina, a 16-year-old pregnant teenager who is living a *Go-Ask-Alice*-type existence after running away from her abusive home life. The other voice is that of an adult, Margaret Johnson, a teacher at Raina's school, who isn't strung out on drugs, but rather burnt out on teaching and feeling betrayed by the choices she has made in her life. One day Ms. Johnson reads Raina's journal about her journey of pain and faces yet another hard choice. Underrated. **Grades 8–12 (mature). PJ**

Reviews: *Booklist* 10/15/1998, *SLJ* 12/1/1998, *VOYA* 12/1/1998,

Greenberg, Joanne. ***I Never Promised You a Rose Garden.*** 300 pages.

Signet 1964 Paper 0451160312 $6.99
NAL 1977 0451137477 $3.95

Readers as young as 10 have been captivated by this painful novel of descent into and recovery from mental illness. Sixteen-year-old Deborah Blau suffers a long, nightmarish bout of insanity that lands her in a hospital where she witnesses all the ways the mind can betray itself. Adult readers who themselves have battled mental diseases have said this work may be a novel, but it reads like truth; they found both accuracy and hope in its pages. A serious work of fiction that anyone can access. **Grades 6–12. PT**

Greenberg, Joanne. ***In This Sign.*** 275 pages.

Henry Holt 1984 Paper 0805007229 $12.00

Once again, Joanne Greenberg takes a difficult, often misunderstood subject and clarifies it in a dramatic novel. Janice and Abel, both deaf, marry and rear a hearing daughter, who must then live in a world they abhor. The resolution of Janice and Abel's fear and distrust of hearing society through their child is a story for any age and reading ability. **Grades 10–12. PT**

Greene, Bette. ***Summer of My German Soldier.*** 230 pages.

Puffin 1973 Paper 014130636X $6.99
Dial 2003 Trade 0803728697 $16.99

This National Book Award finalist in 1973 concerns 12-year-old Patty Bergen and her coming of age during one summer of World War II. As unlikely as it seems, her small Arkansas town becomes the site of a prison camp for Germans, and she finds that life is more complex than Jews versus Germans or Allies versus Axis. Falling for Anton, a young Nazi escapee, Patty comes to terms with what she is willing to risk, and to lose, for the price of giving her heart. **Grades 6–12. PT**

Griffin, Adele. ***Amandine.*** 220 pages.

Hyperion 2001 Library 0786825308 $16.89
Hyperion 2001 Trade 0786806184 $15.74

Delia is a newcomer to DeWolf High School and is looking to make friends.
Although there is clearly something "off" about Amandine, Delia, partially from her
parents' urging and partially from her own fascination, seeks her friendship. Delia
tells stories, mocks classmates, dresses in costume, draws grotesques figures in her
sketchbook, but mostly is talented in the art of deception. When she decides to end
the friendship, Amandine wants revenge in this twisted tale of high school friendship and betrayal. **Grades 6—12. PJ**

Reviews: *Booklist* 9/15/2001, *SLJ* 11/1/2001, *VOYA* 12/1/2001

Griffin, Adele. ***Other Shepards.*** 218 pages.

Hyperion 1998 Library 0786823704 $15.89
Hyperion 1998 Trade 0786804238 $14.95

Holland and Geneva are the only Shepard children, their three older siblings having
died in a tragic accident before either of them were born. Reminded constantly of
"the other Shepards," the sisters find their world brightened by the arrival of Annie,
a young artist who loves life. By blending family dynamics with a surprising ghost
story, Griffin created a truly unusual coming-of-age narrative. **Grades 6—9.
(Annotation by Jennifer Hubert) <LOST>**

Reviews: *Booklist* 8/1/1998, *SLJ* 9/1/1998, *VOYA* 10/1/1998

Grimes, Nikki. ***Bronx Masquerade.*** 167 pages.

Dial 2002 Trade 0803725698 $16.99

Every Friday in a high school in the Bronx, students in Mr. Ward's English class get
their turn at the microphone. Grimes allows each student to speak in a collection of
poems and poetry forms to create a realistic portrait of teenagers. While the voices
and rhythms are contemporary, the "types" are well worn and so are all the issues.
From jock to beauty queen to doper, these teens use words to work out their lives.
They are not types at all, but young people coming of age in a world that is sometime uncaring, uncompromising, and never uncomplicated. **Grades 7—12. PJ**

Reviews: *Booklist* 2/15/2002, *SLJ* 1/1/2002, *VOYA* 2/1/2002

Guest, Judith. ***Ordinary People.*** 263 pages.

Viking 1982 Paper 0140065172 $11.00

Alternating narratives between Conrad Jarrett and his father, Calvin, *Ordinary People*
is the story of an American family destroyed by extraordinary circumstance. Conrad's

older brother, the golden boy, dies in a freak boating accident, and Con's mother, Beth, seems to blame Conrad. The story commences as Con returns home after a year in a psychiatric hospital for a suicide attempt. How these three ordinary people survive, or not, in a world that has proven itself capricious and deadly is a story of strength, faith, love, ultimate failure, and ultimate success. **Grades 7—12. PT**

Guterson, David. ***Snow Falling on Cedars.*** 345 pages.

> Vintage 1995 Paper 067976402X $14.00
> Harcourt 1994 Trade 0151001006 $21.95

It is a testament to the extent this novel has been celebrated that there are Cliffs Notes™ available, and, for the less able reader, such assistance might be helpful. Set in the 1950s, the novel is ostensibly about a murder trial; however the important action on an island north of Puget Sound has much more to do with fresh memories of World War II and the Japanese internment camps. Winner of the PEN/Faulkner Award, this is a fascinating exploration of racism in a fishing community long settled by Japanese Americans and their Caucasian counterparts. Evocative and descriptive, the book is noted for its lush descriptions. **Grades 10—12 (mature). PT**

> Reviews: *Booklist* 8/1/1994

Guy, Rosa. ***Disappearance.*** 245 pages.

> Dell 1992 Paper 0440920647 $4.99

Imamu is recently transplanted from his broken Harlem home to a Brooklyn brown-stone. After being acquitted of murder, Imamu is taken in by the wealthy Aimsley family, who help him get a new start in life. Then, their youngest daughter disappears. A fine mystery that also tackles issues of race, class, and guilt. **Grades 6—12. PJ <YALSA>**

Guy, Rosa. ***Friends.*** 203 pages.

> Bantam 1996 Paper 0440226678 $5.50

Phyllisia is having a hard time fitting in at her school in Harlem. She has recently moved to New York from Jamaica, and everything about her—her clothes, her accented English—make her an easy target for ridicule. Edith is no stranger to feeling like an outsider, so she befriends Phyllisia. Both girls find that while they have much in common, there are other things in their lives driving them apart. **Grades 6—12. PJ <YALSA>**

Haddix, Margaret Peterson. ***Among the Hidden.*** 153 pages.

> Aladdin 2000 Paper 0689824750 $4.99
> Simon & Schuster 1998 Trade 0689817002 $16.00

In a society sometime in the future, families are limited to two children. Luke is the third child, a shadow child. His entire life has been spent in hiding from the Population Police. Just when it looks as if he will be revealed, he makes a discovery of his own: another shadow child. A suspenseful book that works because it pushes all the right buttons with young teen readers, including the need for sequels: *Among the Impostors* and *Among the Betrayed*. **Grades 6—8. PJ**

Reviews: *SLJ* 9/1/1998, *VOYA* 10/1/1998

Haddix, Margaret Peterson. ***Don't You Dare Read This Mrs. Dunphrey.*** 108 pages.

Aladdin 1997 Paper 0689815433 $4.99
Simon & Schuster 1996 Trade 0689800975 $16.99

When Tish's 10th-grade English teacher, Mrs. Dunphrey, assigns students to keep a journal, Tish is less than thrilled. She is bored at school and preoccupied with daily existence. Her mother is severely depressed and it's up to Tish to take care of her and her younger brother. Bad turns to worse when Tish's abusive father returns home. Desperate for a way to channel her turbulent home life and emotional distress, Tish begins writing in the journal, remembering that she can mark passages that she doesn't want her teacher to read. A BBYA and Quick Picks selection. **Grades 7—10. PJ**

Reviews: *Booklist* 10/15/1996, *SLJ* 10/1/1996, *VOYA* 12/1/1996

Haddix, Margaret Peterson. ***Just Ella.*** 185 pages.

Aladdin 2001 Paper 0689831285 $4.99
Simon & Schuster 1999 Trade 0689821867 $17.00

What if Prince Charming wasn't all that? Haddix picks up the story of Cinderella after happily ever after to create a strong coming-of-age story in which Ella comes to realize that there is more to life than being queen of the ball. Prince Charming turns out to be vapid, boring, and more than a little bit overbearing as he molds Ella into his vision. The dream life for Ella turns out to be quite the nightmare until she meets Jed. He is one of her tutors and the catalyst for her change into a strong young woman. The only problem remaining is that Prince Charming has no intention of breaking the engagement. So once again, Cinderella needs to escape, but this time, she has to be her own "fairy godmother." **Grades 6—10. PJ**

Reviews: *Booklist* 9/1/1999, *SLJ* 9/1/1999, *VOYA* 12/1/1999

Hamilton, Virginia. ***Plain City.*** 194 pages.

Point Signature 1993 Paper 0590473654 $4.99

An intriguing novel about identity starring a young girl with changeable blue-green eyes. Bulaire doesn't fit in anywhere, in part because she doesn't know much about her family history. Her father is dead, or is he? Her journey to find herself, both real and metaphorical, make up the bulk of this thin novel that will force readers to think at the same time they are slack-jawed in support of Bulaire's quest. **Grades 7–12. PJ**

Reviews: *Booklist* 1/1/1995, *SLJ* 1/1/1995

Hamilton, Virginia. ***Sweet Whispers, Brother Rush.*** 215 pages.

HarperTrophy 1983 Paper 0380651939 $5.95
Philomel 1982 Trade 0399208941 $21.99

Hamilton's masterpiece about history that haunts one family, literally. The main character is Tree, a 14-year-old girl without much a childhood. She has given it over to care for her brother, Dab, who is retarded. But when Tree hears whispers in the night, she thinks she has a chance to live a different life, if only for a while. A great combination of mystery, history, and coming of age, this book won a Newbery Honor citation and continues to be a favorite. **Grades 7–12. PJ**

Reviews: *Booklist* 8/1/1997, *Booklist* 2/15/2001

Hamilton, Virginia. ***White Romance.*** 240 pages.

Harcourt Children's Books 1989 Paper 0152958886 $3.95

Swept away by the illusions of romance, Talley Barbour, a black high school student, falls for a devastatingly handsome white classmate. Hamilton's finest pure young adult novel about teen issues. **Grades 8–10. PJ**

Reviews: *Booklist* 10/15/1987, *SLJ* 11/1/1988

Hautman, Pete. ***Mr. Was.*** 216 pages.

Aladdin 1998 Paper 0689819145 $4.99

I give this book to every new teen who asks for a good read. It's a great sci-fi mystery, fast-paced and clever. How'd you like to go back 50 years in time and live your life in order to prevent your mother's murder? **Grades 7–12. (Annotation by David Lane)**

Reviews: *Booklist* 9/15/1996, *VOYA* 12/1/1996

Hautman, Pete. ***Stone Cold.*** 163 pages.

Aladdin 2000 Paper 0689833210 $4.99
Simon & Schuster 1998 Trade 0689817592 $16.00

Denn has always been a bit of a hustler. When his father splits, he starts his own business to help support his mom and pay for college. But when some pals introduce him to playing poker, Denn gets hooked. It is like an addiction: it is something that started as fun, but soon gambling takes over Denn's life. Big stakes replaces nickel and dime games with friends. Along his journey to the big time, Denn meets several

characters who try to steer him clear, but like a junkie needing a fix, Denn is addicted to the game. **Grades 7–12. PJ <LOST>**

Reviews: *Booklist* 9/15/1998, *SLJ* 9/1/1998

Hautzig, Deborah. ***Second Star to the Right.*** 176 pages.

Penguin Putnam 1999 Paper 0141305800 $5.99

Leslie Hiller is a bright, attractive, talented teenager who leads a privileged life in
New York City. She is also a perfectionist. When Leslie starts to diet, she finds herself becoming obsessed, getting thinner and thinner, until she is forced to realize
that her quest for perfection is killing her. The landmark novel about anorexia ner-
vosa now includes an afterword by the author that links the events in the book with
her own experiences. **Grades 7–10. PJ**

Heinlein, Robert A. ***The Moon Is a Harsh Mistress.*** 383 pages.

Ace 1987 Paper 0441536999 $5.50
St. Martin's 1997 Paper 0312863551 $14.95
St. Martin's 1996 Trade 0312861761 $24.95

In 2076, the Lunar colony is kept poor and subservient by the Earth-based corporate
governments, but revolution is brewing. Mannie, a computer technician, is drawn
into the fight almost against his will: It is through his eyes that we come to understand lunar and earth societies and the unfolding war for freedom and to appreciate
its bittersweet conclusion. Heinlein keeps the action going as he speculates about the
nature of machine intelligence emerging from complex systems, alternative marriage
arrangements, and the price of freedom. In what is perhaps his best novel, Heinlein
has neatly balanced politics, a mature sexuality, and an exciting plot to create a very
satisfying read for mature teens and adults. **Grades 10–12. KE**

Heinlein, Robert A. ***Starship Troopers.*** 309 pages.

Ace 1987 Paper 0441783589 $6.99
Amereon 1976 Trade 0848810457 $24.95

After high school graduation, Johnny joins the Government Service to impress a
girl—she's signing on as a pilot. It's only a two-year hitch, and when its over he's
earned voting rights—but boot camp turns out to be more than he bargained for, and
the "short term" may turn out to be for the rest of his life (what there is of it) when
Earth is attacked by aliens. Part survival story, as Johnny endures boot camp and warfare, and part coming-of-age novel, as a boy accepts responsibility for his life and puts
it "between his loved ones and the war's desolation," *Starship Troopers* is also intelligent political speculation on the nature of citizenship. Though younger teens will get
a kick out of the story, it's older teens, who are up to the challenge of Heinlein's ideas,
who will find this provocative book most appealing. **Grades 10–12. KE**

Heinlein, Robert A. ***Stranger in a Strange Land.*** 408 pages.

> Ace 1987 Paper 0441790348 $7.99
> Ace 1991 Paper 0441788386 $16.95

More proof that those seeking the "truth" need only to look toward science fiction. This Hugo winner was a touchstone of the 1960s. Valentine Michael Smith is the only survivor on the first manned mission to Mars. Only a child at the time, he is not cast into darkness, but instead Martians raise him as their own. When he returns to Earth, he has no knowledge of life on the planet. Circumstances conspire, and soon he becomes a new messiah, and you know that's not going to be good for anyone. **Grades 8–12. PJ**

Heller, Joseph. ***Catch-22.*** 415 pages.

> Simon & Schuster 1996 Paper 0684833395 $12.00
> Simon & Schuster 1999 Trade 0684865130 $26.00

They're all here: Yossarian, Snowden, Milo Minderbinder, Major Major, the Chief, Dunbar, and Orr among the collection of loonies in residence in the madhouse of World War II. Stationed in Italy, Yossarian flies bombing missions over Germany and plots ways to escape the war. The only method is to snag a medical diagnosis of insanity, and thus be grounded, but there's a catch. To ask for the "crazy" label in order to be grounded proves you can't be crazy, because only a sane man would want to escape to the safety of grounding; if you were really crazy, you would claim to be sane. Therefore, back in the air you go. Catch-22. As the Catch-22 is circular logic, so is the plot of the book. It goes in circles, pausing only long enough for another character to die, some in grisly fashion, until no one is left but Yossarian. And what happens to him? Readers looking for a chronological plot line and an ending to relieve the endless frustration of military sensibilities should avoid Catch-22. For everyone else, it may be the greatest anti-war satire ever written. **Grades 10–12. PT**

Hemingway, Ernest. ***The Old Man and the Sea.*** 93 pages.

> Scribner 1995 Paper 0684801221 $10.00
> Scribner 1996 Trade 0684830493 $20.00

Ernest Hemingway once observed "No son of a bitch that ever won the Nobel Prize ever wrote anything worth reading afterwards." This sentiment did not prevent him, however, from accepting the Nobel, which he won after the publication of this novella, which went a long way in securing him the prize. Published in 1952, it has remained the quintessential Hemingway for over half a century and is still a staple in the country's English classes. All of Hemingway's classic themes are here: grace under pressure; courage in the face of certain defeat; man pitting himself against his most worthy enemy, nature. Santiago is old and ill, riddled with skin cancer, and scarred from years of hauling heavy fishnets. Though he manages by the end of the book to reel in the giant marlin, the prize for his excruciating battle is a shark-ravaged skeleton, hardly a prize about which to boast. In typical Hemingway fashion, however, the old man has won. Life, like fishing, is less about the catch and more about the fight. **Grades 8—12. PT**

Herbert, Frank. ***Dune.*** 517 pages.

> Bantam 2001 Paper 0553580302 $6.99
> Berkley 1999 Trade 044100590X $24.95

In a far distant future, a single planet, Arrakis, holds the resources that a far-flung empire requires for its survival. So when House Harkonnen is replaced by House Atreides, sabotage and treachery ensue: the Atreides family is murdered, and young Paul Atreides left to die on the violent and deadly desert planet. Taken in by the native Fremen, Paul discovers that he is more than just the heir to an interstellar dukedom, but the end result of a generations-long genetic experiment: He has been bred to become the new messiah. With its baroque plot, intricately realized future civilizations, and mystical subtext, *Dune* is both a thrilling and intense read. Older teens will eagerly demand the sequels, *Dune Messiah, God Emperor of Dune, Heretics of Dune,* and *Chapterhouse Dune*—but only the last title fulfills the promise of the first adventure. Brian Herbert, Frank Herbert's son, and Kevin Anderson, the popular *Star Wars* novelist, have written a series of preludes to *Dune.* These novels, which include *Dune: House Atreides; Dune: House Harkonnen; Dune: House Corrino; Dune: Butlerian Jihad; Dune: The Machine Crusade;* and *Dune: The Battle of Corrin,* will be welcomed by fans, but are not a part of the original story. **Grades 8—12. KE**

Herrera, Juan Felipe. ***Crashboomlove: A Novel in Verse.*** 155 pages.

> University of New Mexico Press 1999 Paper 0826321143 $11.95

César Garcia is 16 years old and looking for answers. His father has deserted his family, and his mother seems more interested in retelling her own past than in dealing with the present or César's future. César just can't seem to fit in anywhere, but every day he is looking for his place. *Booklist* called this novel in verse about the Latino teen experience a "must purchase." **Grades 9—12. PJ**

> Reviews: *Booklist* 2/1/2000, *SLJ* 3/1/2000, *VOYA* 10/1/2000

Hesse, Hermann. ***Siddhartha.*** 153 pages.

> Bantam 1982 Paper 0553208845 $5.99

Rejecting sensuality as comfortless and suffering as useless, Siddhartha searches for enlightenment in this mid-century classic; Hilda Rosner's translation from the German is the standard, though other versions are available. The son of a Brahmin, Siddhartha is born with gifts thought to be inherent to the aristocracy: good looks, intelligence, and personal magnetism. None of these, however, offer him the meaning of life, and he turns away from a privileged life to seek true happiness. Hesse sends his protagonist to cross paths with several people from whom he can learn, Govinda, Samanas, Kamala, and Vasudeva. He learns, but accepts from none of them, including Gotama the Buddha. In the end, he discovers enlightenment with the phrase: "The world, Govinda, is perfect at every moment." Hermann Hesse received the Nobel Prize for Literature in 1946, and his works are considered basic text in the Western canon. *Siddhartha* is an excellent beginning for those philosophically searching. **Grades 9—12. PT**

Hesse, Hermann. ***Steppenwolf.*** 309 pages.

Henry Holt 1990 Paper 0805012478 $13.00

Again, Hesse explores the meaning of life through the soul searching of a single man. The going here is a bit tougher than with *Siddhartha*. The book is of greater length and detail, and may not be the best choice for first-time Hesse readers. However, for devotees, it's a good second course in the philosophical meal. **Grades 9—12. PT**

Hesse, Karen. ***Out of the Dust.*** 227 pages.

Scholastic 2000 Paper 043913112X $3.95
Apple 1999 Paper 0590371258 $4.99
Scholastic 1997 Trade 0590360809 $15.95

Hesse won the 1998 Newbery for this free-verse novel about one girl's hard life during the Great Depression. As if the crippling economy weren't enough, Billie Jo's life is filled with storms. The weather outside creates dust storms, but the real hard weather is in her house. Her father is dying of skin cancer, her mother is killed in a horrific accident, and her dreams of being a pianist are stolen from her in the same accident. Set against the bleak Oklahoma sky during the height of the Dust Bowl, this historical novel tells a story as gritty and gripping as any contemporary, edgy novel. In addition to the Newbery, the book won the Scott O'Dell Award for Historical Fiction. **Grades 6—10. PJ <HIPPLE>**

Reviews: *Booklist* 10/1/1997, *SLJ* 9/1/1997

Hesse, Karen. ***Witness.*** 161 pages.

Scholastic 2001 Trade 0439271991 $16.95

Hesse mixes together a series of seemingly incompatible elements. This is a historical novel written in free verse featuring a murder mystery that is somehow connected to the Ku Klux Klan. Like Paul Fleischmann, Hesse uses multiple narrators (11) to tell the tale about what happens in a small Vermont town in the 1920s as the characters all reveal their views on race. Hesse challenges readers to think not only about social-justice issues, but also about the form of literature itself in this poem as play as novel. **Grades 6—10. PJ**

Reviews: *Booklist* 9/1/2001, *SLJ* 9/1/2001, *VOYA* 10/1/2001

Hesser, Terry Spencer. ***Kissing Doorknobs.*** 149 pages.

>   Laurel-Leaf 1999 Paper 0440413141 $5.50
>   Delacorte 1998 Trade 0385323298 $15.95

This is the best novel I've ever read in terms of the author's ability to make me become the character, to feel all her tensions and to experience, with her, her struggles with obsessive-compulsive disorder. It's well researched, alive with voice, and very realistic in presenting what it's like to live with an intense mental illness. **Grades 6—10. (Annotation by Dr. Lois Stover) <YALSA>**

>   Reviews: *Booklist* 6/1/1998, *SLJ* 6/1/1998, *VOYA* 12/1/1998

Hinton, S. E. ***The Outsiders.*** 188 pages.

>   Puffin 1997 Paper 014038572X $6.99
>   Viking 1967 Trade 0670532576 $16.99

Every year a new generation of readers discovers Ponyboy and becomes engrossed in his story; every year, as I reread it, I find myself in awe yet again of Hinton's knack for telling a story, creating voice, giving me the details of a very different kind of life from what I've experienced. We're all outsiders; Ponyboy speaks to everybody. **Grades 7—10. (Annotation by Dr. Lois Stover) <HIPPLE>**

Hinton, S. E. ***Rumble Fish.*** 132 pages.

>   Dell 1989 Paper 0440975344 $5.99

A quick read from Hinton about the relationship between brothers. Rusty worships his older brother, the Motorcycle Boy, and he wants to be like him: the toughest kid on the block. But a series of incidents occur that make Rusty question not just who he is, but what he wants to be. **Grades 7—10. PJ**

Hinton, S. E. ***Taming the Star Runner.*** 181 pages.

>   Dell 1989 Paper 0440204798 $5.50

Travis seems akin to Tex: his girl and his horse are his main concerns, along with writing. He's also like Rusty from *Rumble Fish* or the greasers in *The Outsiders* with the cool exterior he projects. His mother can't raise him, so she sends him off to an uncle's ranch in the country. There Travis encounters the Star Runner, a horse so wild that no one can seem to tame it. The pairing of the "wild" horse and the "wild" teen is obvious, and effective. Although not as successful or as popular as Hinton's other works, its strong message and authentic voice make it essential for any collection. **Grades 6—10. PJ**

Hinton, S. E. ***Tex.*** 194 pages.

>   Laurel-Leaf 1989 Paper 0440978505 $5.50

The focus is not on a "family" of young men as in previous Hinton novels, but on the changes in the life of Tex, a sensitive young man looking for his place in the world. It is almost a western, as two main thrusts in his life are his horse and his girl, Jamie. Life is not without trouble as his dad has been away for five months, his brother Mason is negative, and Tex is certain that the only way to make anything of himself is to get out of Oklahoma. More a character study than a fully realized novel, this still has high appeal to young teens, especially boys. **Grades 6—10. PJ**

Hinton, S. E. ***That Was Then, This Is Now.*** 159 pages.

> Dell 2001 Paper 0440220122 $5.99

A tale of two best friends, Mark and Bryon, who grow up together, only to grow apart. The two have always been close, but Bryon notes that a rift is developing between them; he also notices that he is changing and maturing, while Mark is not. When Bryon learns of Mark's involvement in selling drugs, he is forced to make a hard decision between right and wrong, between trust and betrayal. **Grades 7—10. PJ**

Hobbs, Will. ***Bearstone.*** 144 pages.

> Morrow/Avon 1991 Paper 0380712490 $4.95
> Atheneum 1989 Trade 0689314965 $17.00

VOYA called this story about a troubled, young Native American boy "a must purchase." Cloyd is only 14 years old, but he seems a lot older. He has grown up mostly alone in a desolate part of Utah, without parents and without going to school. He finally finds a home in the mountain of Colorado, where he lives with an old rancher, but the call of the wild remains strong. When Cloyd discovers an artifact in a burial ground, it puts him on a path toward finding his roots and finding his true self. **Grades 7—10. PJ**

Hobbs, Will. ***Downriver.*** 204 pages.

> Bantam 1992 Paper 0440226732 $5.50

Jessie and six other troubled teens escape their adult leader at the outdoor education program where they have been sent to mend their ways, then steal the leader's river running gear and head down the Colorado through the Grand Canyon. There is a well-balanced cast of rebellious girls and boys, lots of compelling adventure, romances and breakups, good versus evil, a captivating setting, and worthwhile messages without preaching. **Grades 6—12. (Annotation by Diane Tuccillo) <YALSA>**

Hobbs, Will. ***Far North.*** 226 pages.

> Avon Camelot 1997 Paper 0380725363 $5.99
> Morrow 1996 Trade 0688141927 $15.95

It starts with a similar premise to that of *Hatchet*: A plane crashes in a remote northern wilderness. But rather than telling of a sole survivor, this tells the story of Gabe, his buddy Raymond, and the mysterious Johnny Raven, a wise, older Native American man. Raven helps the boys survive the winter and encounters with a collection of wild animals. In addition to the fast-paced action, there are some larger themes working here that make the book work on more than one level. **Grades 6—9. PJ <YALSA>**

Reviews: *Booklist* 7/1/1996, *SLJ* 9/1/1996

Hobbs, Will. ***Maze.*** 198 pages.

Avon Camelot 1999 Paper 038072913X $5.99
Morrow 1998 Trade 0688150926 $15.95

Rick has had a hard life, in and out of foster homes. Trouble comes into his life again when he is sentenced to serve time in a juvenile correctional facility. But there is no peace there either, so he runs again only to find himself lost in a wilderness. He is rescued by a scientist who is working with condors and who enlists Rick's help, but also teaches him how to hang glide. Add in a group of thugs out to do both Rick and the birds harm to create a masterful adventure tale about a boy lost in the "maze" of self-hatred. Rick eventually finds himself by helping others. **Grades 6—9. PJ**

Reviews: *Booklist* 9/1/1998, *SLJ* 10/1/1998, *VOYA* 2/1/1999

Holland, Isabelle. ***The Man Without a Face.*** 159 pages.

HarperTrophy 1987 Paper 0064470288 $4.95

An important book that nobody talks about much anymore, despite a filmed adaptation starring Mel Gibson. Charles is 14 years old and has grown up without a father, or with any strong relationship to any adult. That changes with his involvement with the reclusive Justin McLeod, who becomes his tutor. McLeod, known as the man without a face by the locals, is also a man with secrets. **Grades 7—12. PJ**

Holt, Kimberly Willis. ***When Zachary Beaver Came to Town.*** 227 pages.

Yearling 2001 Paper 0440229049 $5.50
Henry Holt 1999 Trade 0805061169 $16.95

Holt won the National Book Award for youth literature with this character-heavy novel about life in a small Texas town where nothing much ever happens. Toby's life in tiny Antler is pretty boring, although not without problems as his mother bolts to become a country western star while the girl he has a mad crush on could not care less. But Toby's problems seem small—literally and figuratively—when the sideshow comes to town with the world's fattest boy, 600-pound Zachary Beaver, as the star. **Grades 6—9. PJ**

Reviews: *Booklist* 9/15/1999, *SLJ* 11/01/1999

Hoover, H. M. *Another Heaven, Another Earth.* 212 pages.

Starscape 2002 Paper 0812567617 $5.99

There's a dearth of first-rate serious science fiction for children or the middle school crowd, but H. M. Hoover is an exception. Popular in the 1980s, most of her best books are, in 2002, out of print. In this recent reprint, a far-off space colony has achieved a precarious, but satisfying, existence when it is rediscovered, and threatened, by Earth. Told from the viewpoint of Gareth, a colonial teenage girl, and the would-be helpful scientists, the story will resonate with current concerns about first- and third-world societies. The pacing is somewhat slow in places, but the exotic setting and the well-realized character of Gareth should keep younger readers hooked. **Grades 7–12. KE**

Hoover, H. M. *Orvis.* 300 pages.

TOR 2002 Paper 0812557352 $5.99

Two boys in a future environment, where most of Earth is abandoned and humanity lives in orbital habitats or other planets, become involved with a renegade robot, "Orvis." Embedded in the standard chase-and-rescue futuristic adventure is a deft exploration of artificial intelligence, identity, and freedom. This is serious science fiction for the younger teen and a welcome addition to the TOR (the premier SF publisher for adults) "Starscape" line for that audience. **Grades 10–12. KE**

Horowitz, Anthony. *The Devil and His Boy.* 182 pages.

Puffin 2001 Paper 0698119134 $5.99
Philomel 2000 Trade 0399234322 $15.99

Short chapters crammed with action structure this adventure story set in England in 1593. Rescued from a Dickensian existence working in the Pig's Head Inn, young Tom Falconer takes off with a mysterious man promising him a new life. The man is murdered, and Tom's adventures are launched. Eventually he winds up with a group of traveling players whose production, *The Devil and His Boy*, is, unknown to Tom, a ruse to overthrow Queen Elizabeth; of course, he winds up saving her. Parts of the story are based in fact, but there's plenty of swash and buckle to keep things lively. Excellent reading for younger teens wanting a fast, easy read with realistic historical detailing. **Grades 6–9. PT**

Reviews: *Booklist* 1/1/2000, *SLJ* 4/1/2000, *VOYA* 4/1/2000

Howe, James. *Misfits.* 274 pages.

Atheneum 2001 Trade 0689839553 $16.00

On the TV show *The Wonder Years*, Kevin noted that the most important thing in middle school isn't who you are, but whom you sit next to at lunch. As the title suggests, this book examines a group of kids who are at a table all to themselves. Bobby is fat, Joe is gay, Skeezie is just strange, while Addie looks all right. She's a little tall for a girl, but mostly she is mouthy, which gets her exiled to the misfit table. There is plenty of plot here about student council elections, but the red meat is the theme of how kids on the fringe are treated. **Grades 6—9. PJ**

Reviews: *Booklist* 11/15/2001, *SLJ* 11/1/2001, *VOYA* 12/1/2001

Howe, James. ***The Watcher.*** 172 pages.

Aladdin 1999 Paper 0689826621 $8.00
Aladdin 2001 Paper 0689835337 $4.99
Atheneum 1997 Trade 0689801866 $16.00

A novel that seems more likely to come from Chris Crutcher than the author of a story about a ghostly bunny. Although set primarily on a sun-drenched beach, this is a dark novel about three young people drowning in their pain. Evan, the lifeguard, seems to have it all together, but at home things are falling apart. Chris, a younger lifeguard, wants to save lives to make up for the one that was lost: his younger brother's death in an accident years past but haunting him still. And Margaret (aka the Watcher) the young girl who observes Evan and Chris, then imagines them in the rich fantasy life that she clings to in order to escape the horror taking place in her house. As in Crutcher, it is only when the three young people reach out to each other that they can rescue their own lives. **Grades 7—12. PJ**

Reviews: *Booklist* 6/1/1997, *SLJ* 5/1/1997

Hrdlitschka, Shelley. ***Dancing Naked.*** 249 pages.

Orca 2001 Paper 1551432102 $6.95

When Kia becomes pregnant after her first sexual encounter, she plans to have an abortion. At the 11th hour, however, she changes her mind. The book, narrated in e-mails, journal entries, and dialogue, chronicles the baby's development inside her womb, but mostly Kia's transformation. Kia is confused by the various reactions from her friends and family to her situation. *Booklist* noted that the title was "recommended purchase for all libraries serving young adults." **Grades 9—12 (mature). PJ**

Reviews: *VOYA* 4/1/2002

Hugo, Victor. ***The Hunchback of Notre Dame.*** Page count varies with edition.

Laurel-Leaf 1996 Paper 0440226759 $4.50
Puffin 1997 Paper 0140382534 $4.99

More properly titled *Notre-Dame de Paris*, Victor Hugo's masterpiece centers on the deformed bellringer of Notre Dame, Quasimodo; his unrequited love for the beautiful gypsy Esmerelda; and, completing the triangle, the archbishop Claude Frollo, ruined by his lust for the same woman. Hugo, the quintessential Romantic, believed not only that love happened at first sight, but that it happened "in this way and in this way only" (*Les Misérables*). Never has an ideal been so forcefully or colorfully played out than in *The Hunchback*. Against a huge cast of vivid characters, the plot roils and complicates itself, with Esmerelda falling in love with Captain Phoebus, who, appropriate to his name, shines like the sun and burns the innocent gypsy girl. The unabridged edition is necessary to any good collection, but an abridged volume is recommended for readers new to the Hugo experience or for those who might be intimidated by very long books with lots of detours from the main plot line. For unabridged versions, translations by Walter Cobb or by Lee Fahnestock and Norman MacAfee are recommended. **Grades 6—12. PT**

Hugo, Victor. ***Les Misérables.*** Page count varies with edition.

> Signet 1987 Paper 0451525264 $7.95
> Random 1995 Paper 067986668X $3.99
> Modern Library 1992 Trade 0679600124 $22.95

Victor Hugo's masterpiece remains alive and vibrant a century and a half after its initial publication, in part because of its popularity as a stage musical and a Disney movie. Both incarnations, however, hardly do justice to this sprawling novel of love, loss, honor, revenge, damnation, salvation, and social injustice. The story of Jean Valjean, sent to the Bastille for 14 years for stealing a loaf of bread for his starving family, has lost none of its power, and the love story between Cosette, his ward, and Marius remains as fresh as ever. From Fantine to Javert, the obsessed gendarme, the novel is peppered with unforgettable characters and tells a story that could not help but become immortal. This is a giant of a novel, and the Charles Wilbour translation is recommended, particularly for the abridged edition. For the unabridged, Fahnestock and MacAfee have updated the language, but based their translation on Wilbour's excellent earlier work. Perhaps the younger reader is not ready for the scope of *Les Misérables*, but everyone else will indeed find that reading it will "light up the night." **Grades 7—12. PT**

Hurwin, Davida Wills. ***Time for Dancing.*** 257 pages.

> Puffin 1997 Paper 0140386181 $5.99

Best friends' (Juliana and Samantha) lives are shattered when one is stricken with lymphoma. This is a tearjerker that rises above the rest through engaging storytelling, vivid characters, and authentic dialogue. The book, told by the girls in alternating chapters, begins with the future looking bright for both girls in their senior year as they consider their possible futures. The book then traces the effect of Julie's disease, not only on her body but also on the fabric of the friendship. **Grades 7—12. PJ <YALSA>**

> Reviews: *Booklist* 11/1/1995, *Booklist* 8/1/1997, *SLJ* 10/1/1995

Huxley, Aldous. **_Brave New World._** 311 pages.

HarperPerennial 1998 Paper 0060929871 $11.95

In an awfully perfect world, things are perfectly awful. This classic novel of a modern dystopia has been in print for 70 years and shows no signs of fading from the landscape. Indeed, Huxley's warnings of a society controlling its members through drugs, sex, and instant-gratification entertainment may seem more chillingly realistic now than when it was originally conceived. This quintessential satire takes its title from Shakespeare's _The Tempest_ ("O brave new world/That hath such people in it!"), and turns it on its ear. Bernard Marx, (yes, as in THAT Marx), lives amid a society that has achieved the original Marx's ideal, and he despises it. Feel bad? Take soma, the party drug, and go on a mental holiday. Sex (though not portrayed graphically) is free with any partner of your choosing. Babies grow in tubes, and a rigid class structure is preordained. For diversion, attend the "Feelies" (movies with full sensory perception). In other words, welcome to a life where all needs are met, and the only crime is thinking on your own. Bernard's escape to an Indian reservation where the inhabitants actually read books (Shakespeare!) and ponder philosophy is the apex of the novel. While the climax may seem a bit heavy handed, Huxley's take on modern socialism still has bite. Recommended for all reading levels. **Grades 9—12. PT**

Irving, John. **_The World According to Garp._** 437 pages.

Ballantine 1990 Paper 034536676X $7.99
Ballantine 1997 Paper 0345418018 $14.00

A Modern Library edition evinces that _Garp_ is officially a classic, and deservedly so. Akin to Dickens in scope, Irving's masterpiece is a landscape filled with wildly diverse characters: insane feminists with amputated tongues (to sympathize with a famous rape victim), a unicycle-riding bear, lobotomized ball turret gunners, and more. The climactic scene consists of simultaneous events: Garp's wife is busy with an adulterous affair while Garp amuses his beloved sons with a trifle of a car trick that defines everything that follows for the rest of the novel. Irving's substantial writing gift is never more apparent than in this scene, which will leave readers flabbergasted and gasping for breath. Despite the near continuing presence of death, Garp maintains an almost childlike optimism for the world to which he gives his name. Multilayered, the prose is still uncomplicated enough to entice almost any level of reader and should be considered part of the "core of the core" collection. **Grades 10—12 (mature). PT**

Jackson, Shirley. **_We Have Always Lived in the Castle._** 214 pages.

Viking 1984 Paper 0140071075 $10.95

With her celebrated economy of words and deliciously twisted descriptions, Shirley Jackson once again does what she does better than anyone. Long before Stephen King and Dean Koontz, Jackson was creating a universe in which the "normal" functions against the backdrop of a reality that is anything but. The Blackwood family resides near a village in which "the men stayed young and did the gossiping and the women aged with gray evil weariness"; most of the Blackwoods have died mysteriously of poisoning. The novel's appealing narrator, Merricat Blackwood, tells us she likes most things except dogs, noise, and washing herself. When a cousin arrives with plans of his own for the Blackwood fortune and for the family itself, Merricat, as befitting her name, must spring into action. No one else in the writing world has a voice like Shirley Jackson, and this funny, macabre story certainly proves it. **Grades 7–12. PT**

Jacques, Brian. ***Redwall.*** 351 pages.

    Firebird 2002 Paper 0142302376 $7.99
    Philomel 2000 Paper 0399236295 $12.99
    Putnam 1986 Trade 0399214240 $23.99

When the idyllic Abbey of Redwall is under threat from the rat warlord, Cluny the Scourge, the orphaned mouse Matthias is determined to save his home. Finding the lost and legendary sword of Martin the Warrior is his only hope. Each short chapter ends in a cliffhanger, the characters are very appealing, and the animal world of Redwall is lovingly detailed. Sure to please most middle-school students, and many older teens who enjoy fantasy adventure in a faux-medieval setting will be hooked by the series. For a complete listing of titles in the order they ought to be read, visit the official Web site at www.redwall.org/dave/library.html. **Grades 6–8. KE**

Jenkins A. M. ***Breaking Boxes.*** 182 pages.

    Laurel-Leaf 2000 Paper 0440227178 $4.99

What happens when a regular guy of modest means reveals to his privileged best friend that his older brother is gay? Jenkins explores classism, the complications of male adolescent friendship, and the subtlety of homophobia in this thought-provoking first novel. **Grades 9–12. (Annotation by Jennifer Hubert) <LOST>**

    Reviews: *SLJ* 10/1/1997, *VOYA* 12/1/1997

Jenkins A. M. ***Damage.*** 186 pages.

    HarperCollins 2001 Library 0060291001 $15.89
    HarperCollins 2001 Trade 0060290994 $15.95

Austin Reid is the stuff high school dreams are made of: good looking "stud" football star dating the prettiest girl in school and hanging out with great friends. But behind those actions is the turmoil taking place in Austin's mind. Jenkins has Austin refer to himself in the second person, underscoring Austin's detachment from his own life as depression and suicidal thoughts begin to overtake him. As the depression grows, so does Austin's introspection as he searches for answers to rescue himself from the abyss. With an interesting cast of stock secondary characters, including the loyal best friend and the brutal football coach, and an unflinching commitment to the gritty nature of describing teen life, Jenkins creates a memorable novel. **Grades 7—12. PJ**

Reviews: *Booklist* 9/15/2001, *SLJ* 10/1/2001

Johnson, Angela. ***Heaven.*** 138 pages.

Aladdin 2000 Paper 0689822901 $4.99
Simon & Schuster 1998 Trade 0689822294 $16.00

Marley grows up in a small Ohio town called Heaven. To 14-year-old Marley, it is the right name as she feels safe and secure in a caring community, with good friends and loving supportive parents. But soon Marley learns that her "parents" are not really her parents, but instead her aunt and uncle. Once that secret is revealed, Marley comes to realize that almost everyone in her perfect little town has secrets. But the question for Marley is no longer about who she was, but about who she is. Johnson's lyric style meshes perfectly with Marley's confused pursuit of her identity. **Grades 7—10. PJ**

Reviews: *Booklist* 9/15/1998, *SLJ* 10/1/1998

Johnson, Angela. ***Humming Whispers.*** 121 pages.

Orchard 1995 Library 0531087484 $14.99
Orchard 1995 Trade 0531068986 $15.95
Point Signature 1995 Paper 0590674528 $4.99

When Sophy's older sister Nicole turned 14, she began to hear voices. Diagnosed as a schizophrenic, Nicole is on medication (Sophy hopes) and is living a somewhat normal life, but Sophy still worries about her. But mostly, Sophy worries about herself. She is a bright student, a talented dancer, and about to turn 14 herself. She wonders if she, too, will hear the voices and begin to act strangely. Sophy tells the story in almost a stream-of-consciousness narrative, pouring out her fears. **Grades 7—10. PJ**

Reviews: *Booklist* 2/15/1995, *SLJ* 4/1/1995, *VOYA* 6/1/1995

Johnson, Angela. ***Toning the Sweep.*** 103 pages.

Scholastic 1994 Paper 0590481428 $4.99
Orchard 1993 Trade 0531054764 $15.95

Poet-turned-novelist Johnson beautifully renders this Coretta Scott King Award-winner about three generations of one African American family. Emily and her mother gather at her grandmother's house to help her move. Grandma Ola is dying of cancer and wants to spend her remaining days with her family back in Cleveland. During the journey, the three women share their stories of growing up in the United

States. Ola recalls the lynching of her husband, while Emily and her mother share painful experiences from their lives. Yet the journey and sharing of the stories help the women bond, heal, and move forward. **Grades 7–10. PJ**

Reviews: *Booklist* 4/1/1993, *SLJ* 9/1/1998

Jones, Diana Wynne. ***Fire and Hemlock.*** 432 pages.

HarperCollins 2002 Trade 0060298855 $16.95
HarperCollins 2002 Paper 006447352X $6.95

One of the finest retellings of the Tam Lin ballad, it also happens to be an eerie coming-of-age novel for teenage girls, as young Polly's perception of her musician friend, Thomas Lynn, changes from girlhood through puberty. Jones takes a subtle approach to fantasy, as the stories Polly writes about Thomas eerily play out within the framework of growing pains, divorce, and ordinary life. It becomes clear only near the very end that Thomas is scheduled for mortal sacrifice, and Polly must pay with her heart to save him. Readers who enjoy romantic fiction and magical realism will return to reread this challenging book again and again. **Grades 8–12. KE**

Jones, Diana Wynne. ***Hexwood.*** 295 pages.

HarperTrophy 2002 Paper 0064473554 $6.99
Greenwillow 2002 Trade 006029888X $16.99

Jones's most challenging novel weaves Arthurian myth and legendry into the story of a suburban British woodland haunted by something very, very strange. Told from the viewpoint of a teenage girl, the wood, the strange creatures she finds there, a far-off alien power and their unwilling slaves, the story can be pieced together by the reader—but time and causality are flexible, and most of the characters mistaken as to who and what they are. Jones has mastered the deft character sketch, creating sympathetic characters and pathos very quickly. Despite the large cast, readers will move from character to character with increasing anticipation. *Hexwood* offers a very satisfying final resolution, rewards multiple readings, and should prove to be a fine puzzle book for good readers willing to stretch their horizons. **Grades 7–12. KE**

Jones, Diana Wynne. ***Howl's Moving Castle.*** 212 pages.

HarperCollins 2001 Paper 006441034X $6.95
HarperCollins 2001 Trade 0060298812 $16.95

Jones is famous for her inventive spins on old stories and legends, grounding them with realistic heroes and heroines. Here, teenage Sophie, the eldest of three sisters in a fairy tale world, is wryly aware of what her fate holds. So when the evil enchantress curses her with instant old age, she accepts her fate and ends up as housekeeper to the wicked magician Howl in his mobile castle. Of course, the enchantress and the magician are at odds, the castle cursed, and Sophie herself capable of solving the puzzles and winning true (if unexpected) love once she sets her contrary mind to it. Although younger readers may have to struggle a bit to keep up with the plot twists, older readers who liked *Ella Enchanted* will by charmed by the humor, suspense, and entertaining characters. **Grades 7–12 . KE**

Reviews: *SLJ 8/1/96*

Jordan, Robert. ***The Eye of the World.*** 670 pages.

TOR 2000 Paper 081257995X $3.99
TOR 1990 Paper 0812500482 $14.95

Rand is a teenager with friends and a happy future with his family in the isolated countryside. His lot, however, is to be born in "interesting times" and his destiny to become the Christ for his world, and, in the process, be destroyed. In the initial volume, however, his goal, and that of his young friends, is to survive catastrophe—invasion by monsters, war, and famine—and to begin to understand his role. This is the premier Big Quest series, hugely popular with older teens, and surprisingly restrained in its approach to graphic violence and sexuality. Once this is part of your collection, your young patrons will demand the continuing (and still not complete) saga—all 10 volumes! **Grades 10–12. KE**

Jordan, Sherryl. ***The Raging Quiet.*** 266 pages.

Aladdin 2000 Paper 0689828772 $8.00
Simon & Schuster 1999 Trade 0689821409 $17.00

When Marnie, a young serf, marries the younger son of the local lord, her life takes an ugly turn. Immediately uprooted from home and family to a distant seacoast village, she is regarded with suspicion by the hard-hearted local peasantry and nightly raped by her husband. His untimely death and her lonely friendship with the other village outcast, a deaf-mute boy, bring her under suspicion of witchcraft. Readers looking for fantasy adventure will not be nearly as pleased as those who enjoy solid historical fiction. Jordan's anonymous medieval setting is rock solid, and if Marnie is rather exceptional for her time, mature teens will be too caught up in her dramatic story to care. **Grades 7–10. KE**

Reviews: *Booklist 5/1/1999, SLJ 5/1/1999, VOYA 8/1/1999*

Jordan, Sherryl. ***Secret Sacrament.*** 338 pages.

HarperCollins 2001 Library 0060289058 $17.89
HarperCollins 2001 Trade 006028904X $15.95

Gabriel's life as a healer is driven by the rejection of his authoritarian father and the childhood memory of a gang rape and murder he witnessed but did not try to prevent. In Jordan's fantasy setting, the city state of Navora has long dominated the tribal Shinali, but the young protagonist may become the prophesied force for change. The depth of characterization and themes of transcendent love and sacrifice deepen this fantasy adventure, even as political intrigue, demonic magic, and desperate choices keep the reader turning the pages for more. **Grades 7—10. KE**

Reviews: *Booklist* 2/15/2001, *SLJ* 2/1/2001, *VOYA* 6/1/2001

Jordan, Sherryl. **Wolf Woman.** 162 pages.

Houghton Mifflin 1994 Trade 0395709326 $13.95

Raised by wolves, but "rescued" by a prehistoric tribe, 16-year-old Tanith has never quite fit in. Her people hunt and kill the wolves to which she feels akin, yet she is falling in love with a young man from another tribe. When catastrophe strikes, Tanith's place in the tribe is challenged, and she must choose between a young man she loves and the emotional wholeness of a life with the wolves. There's a nice tension between action and angst: This compelling historical fantasy and strong female protagonist should appeal to a wide range of teenage girls. **Grades 6—10. KE**

Reviews: *Booklist* 11/15/1994, *SLJ* 10/1/1994, *VOYA* 1/1/1995

Kafka, Franz. **The Metamorphosis and Other Stories.** 98 pages.

Macmillan 1993 Trade 0684194260 $25.00
Scribner's 2000 Paper 0684800705 $12.00

Known for its famous opening line, "When Gregor Samsa woke up one morning from unsettling dreams, he found himself changed in his bed into a giant cockroach," Kafka's most famous image has much more for the reader than its nightmarish beginning. (Some translations give us "vermin" or "insect." Your choice.) Variously interpreted over the last century as an allegory, either social or religious; a case history of psychoanalysis; or a bad drug trip, *The Metamorphosis* remains a testament to the power of imagination and the reality it can create. Though various translations differ slightly, they all have in common the unadorned prose of the original, all the more shocking in contrast to its subject matter. **Grades 10—12. PT**

Keneally, Thomas. **Schindler's List.** 400 pages.

Simon & Schuster 1993 Paper 0671880314 $14.00
Simon & Schuster 1994 Trade 0671516884 $25.00

Based on the true story of Oskar Schindler, a German industrialist and war profiteer, this novel recounts Schindler's "conversion" from Nazi sympathizer to rescuer of over 1,300 Jews from the gas chambers. The most unlikely of heroes, Schindler used his contacts in the Nazi hierarchy to conscript Jewish workers for his manufacturing plants, thus averting their path to Auschwitz. Winner of both the Booker Prize and the *Los Angeles Times* Award for Fiction, Keneally's prose is so compelling that it is difficult to remember his work is fiction. He captures the dichotomy of Schindler's nature vividly: a man profiting from evil who risked his life to save the "enemies" of his state. Steven Spielberg's film has become part of the American cinematic landscape, and as powerful as it is, it falls far short (perhaps fortunately) in describing the unspeakable horrors of the Cracow ghetto, the camps, and the general disdain for the basic decencies of humanity the Nazis were so easy to claim. For the more sensitive reader, the book may be too challenging in its details, but it is highly recommended for all students of history and fiction. **Grades 10–12. PT**

Kerouac, Jack. *On the Road.* 310 pages.

Penguin USA 1972 Paper 0140042598 $12.95
Viking 1997 Library 0670874787 $24.95
Penguin 1999 Paper 0140283293 $15.00

A barely fictionalized autobiography, *On The Road* is the bible of the Beat Movement and a seminal work of the hipsters who defined it. Like Odysseus before him, Kerouac heeds the siren call of the road and chronicles his adventures in clear, sharp, distinctive prose. Sal Paradise, a WWII veteran in his late 20s (the book was written in the 1940s, but found no publisher until 1957), takes a train out of New York, and by whatever transportation he can manage heads across the country seeking adventure and enlightenment. He gets both, in spades. And as soon as circumstances heat up, like Homer's fabled traveler, Sal lights out for the next location. *On the Road* is both wonderful pleasure reading and a map of the mind for an entire generation. **Grades 10–12 (mature). PT**

Kerr, M. E. *Deliver Us from Evie.* 177 pages.

HarperTrophy 1995 Paper 0064471284 $5.99

Evie is 18 years old. She lives in a small Midwestern town, and she is in love with the daughter of the town's wealthy banker. Told from the point of view of Evie's younger brother, Parr, this was a turning-point novel for Kerr. After years of writing for young adults, this was the first novel in which Kerr dealt with lesbianism head-on. The town is against Evie and her partner, who decide they would rather be together than be accepted by their families. Rich in the details of small town life and richer still in the emotional roller coaster of the narrator, Parr, as he balances his love for his sister with what everyone else thinks, this breakthrough book was named a Best Books and a Quick Picks selection. **Grades 7–12. PJ <HIPPLE>**

Kerr, M. E. *Gentlehands.* 183 pages.

HarperTrophy 1990 Paper 0064470679 $5.95

Buddy is desperately in love with Skye Pennington, who is as rich and sophisticated as her name sounds. He knows he will never be accepted into her world; he is not cut from the same cloth. Buddy finds no support from parents, so he reaches out to his estranged grandfather in a search for approval and advice. Just when it seems that the Romeo and Juliet tale will have a happy ending, Buddy learns that his grandfather is not quite the esteemed man he thought he was; instead Buddy learns that his grandfather is probably a Nazi war criminal. **Grades 7–12. PJ <MOCK>**

Kerr, M. E. **Night Kites.** 216 pages.

Farrar Straus Giroux 1986 Trade 0060232536 $12.95
HarperTrophy 1987 Paper 0064470350 $5.95

Erick has always been on the inside: good grades, good friends, and a good life. That all is shattered when two outsiders break into his world. The first is his best friend's girlfriend, Nicki, a punk rocker wanna-be, with whom Erick falls madly in love. The second is his older brother, Pete, who is dying of AIDS. One of the first AIDS novels, the message from Kerr is about not being afraid to be a "night kite," someone who lives life not grounded by what others think and is willing to take risks. **Grades 8–10. PJ**

Reviews: *SLJ* 5/1/1986

Kesey, Ken. **One Flew over the Cuckoo's Nest.** 311 pages.

Penguin 1995 Paper 0140236015 $15.99
Penguin 1999 Paper 014028334X $15.00
Viking 2002 Trade 0670030589 $24.95
Signet 1963 Paper 0451163966 $6.99

Set in a mental institution, featuring one of the all-time great protagonists in Randall Patrick McMurphy, who dominates almost every scene, this early '60s fable about conformity, rebellion, and the stifling power of rule-bound institutions will always resonate with teens who want to be hip and well read. **Grades 10–12 (mature). PJ**

Keyes, Daniel. **Flowers for Algernon.** 274 pages.

Bantam 1975 Paper 0553274503 $6.50
Harcourt 1995 Trade 0151001634 $17.00

Charlie, a sweet man with an IQ of 68, lives a contented life as a baker's helper. Through the miracles of modern science fiction, he undergoes surgery that not only reverses his retardation, but develops his mind into that of a genius. Narrated by

Charlie himself, his "progress reports" reveal the gradual crescendo of his intelligence and its heartbreaking disintegration as the experiment ultimately fails. The story is sufficiently suspenseful to keep the most jaded reader turning the pages but is easily accessible to even reluctant readers. **Grades 8–12. PT**

Kim, Helen. ***The Long Season of the Rain.*** 275 pages.

Henry Holt 1996 Trade 0805047581 $15.95

One of the first books in Holt's Edge imprint was one of the best, a classic coming-of-age tale about a young girl's path toward independence. The title refers to the rainy season in Korea, the book's setting. Once the rain arrives, life stops and families seek refugee in their houses. Junehee, the book's narrator, is 11 years old and dreads another season trapped in the house with her sisters, her mother, and grandmother. Her father, although not always at home, is like rain: always present. When the family takes in a young orphan boy, he becomes a catalyst for change for Junehee. She has allowed her father to run her life and watched his disrespect for her mother, but as the book moves along and secrets are revealed, it becomes obvious that Junehee is gaining the courage to step out into the sun. **Grades 7–10. PJ**

Reviews: *Booklist* 11/1/1996, *SLJ* 12/1/1996, *VOYA* 2/1/1997

Kincaid, Jamaica. ***Annie John.*** 148 pages.

Farrar Straus Giroux 1997 Paper 0374525102 $10.00

An amazing novel about the complicated dynamics of a mother-daughter relationship. Although the setting might be exotic (Antigua), the emotional landscape should be familiar to any female reader. Entering her teenage years, Annie finds that the comfortable relationship with her mother starts to fall apart. Soon, the destruction is deliberate as Annie, feeling betrayed and unloved, sets out to drive her mother to distraction. A beautifully written novel about some of the ugly truths that occur when love turns to hate, trust transforms into suspicion, and togetherness begets dysfunction. **Grades 9–12. PJ**

Kindl, Patrice. ***Owl in Love.*** 204 pages.

Puffin 1994 Paper 014037129X $5.99
Houghton Mifflin 1993 Trade 0395661625 $16.00

Before Harry Potter, there was the story of a shape-shifting young girl who can transform herself into an owl. At night, she flies into the trees outside the window of her true love: her high school science teacher. It is there, however, that she observes a boy closer to her own age, whom she soon finds even more intriguing. This isn't *Animorphs*, but rather animated metaphor, through which Kindl deals with coming-of-age issues like identity and acceptance as well as the author of any "straight" young adult novel. A Best Book and Quick Picks selection. **Grades 7–12. PJ <YALSA>**

Reviews: *Booklist* 9/1/1993

King, Laurie. R. ***The Beekeeper's Apprentice.*** 347 pages.

Doubleday 2002 Paper 0553381520 $11.95
St. Martin 1994 Trade 0312104235 $23.95

Sherlock Holmes is enjoying his retirement, keeping bees on his estate in Sussex. He is glad to be free of solving crimes and rid of his bumbling assistant, Watson. Then one day he bumps, quite literally, into his intellectual match: a 15-year-old girl named Mary Russell. Holmes adopts her as his protégée, and she cuts her teeth in the detective business. It's all jolly fun until someone tries to kill Russell and Holmes with a homemade bomb. **Grades 10–12. PJ**

Reviews: *Booklist* 2/1/1994, *SLJ* 7/1/1994

King, Stephen. ***Carrie.*** 199 pages.

Random 2001 Paper 0609810901 $9.50
Pocket 2000 Paper 0671039733 $12.95

Even Stephen King admits that his first full-length publication is "raw," but it remains a necessary addition to the King oeuvre. A sad-sack teenager, Carrie White, victim of vicious school mates and a religiously fanatic mother, discovers one day that she has telekinetic powers, and her revenge on her tormentors is bloody indeed. King's gift for revealing the horror against an environment of mundane life is just beginning to expand itself in *Carrie*, but it's still a good read. **Grades 9–12. PT**

King, Stephen. ***Christine.*** 526 pages.

Signet 1983 Paper 0451160444 $7.99
Viking 1983 Trade 0670220264 $27.95

This is the horror novel for teenage boys obsessed with cars. Arnie Cunningham comes into possession of Christine, initially unaware that the car is possessed. And alive. Nothing will come between Christine and her obsession with Arnie, as a number of characters discover before King finishes with them all. **Grades 9–12. PT**

King, Stephen. ***Different Seasons.*** 527 pages.

NAL 1998 Paper 0451197127 $7.99
Dutton 1993 Paper 0451167538 $7.99

A collection of four novellas, each sharply different from the other, this book is so well written that three of the four stories have been made into excellent and well-received movies. "Rita Hayworth and the Shawshank Redemption" became *The Shawshank Redemption*; "Apt Pupil" was translated into a film of the same name; and "The Body" morphed into *Stand by Me*. Ironically enough, as accomplished as these novellas are, the strongest, "Breathing Lessons," about a woman determined to keep her baby alive against horrific odds, has not made it to Hollywood. Highly recommended, and very useful for the reader who hesitates at the prospect of lengthy books but needs more of a challenge than very short works. **Grades 9—12. PT**

King, Stephen. ***Firestarter.*** 428 pages.

NAL 1991 Paper 0451167805 $7.99

One King novel starring a young girl, *Firestarter*, is particularly well written, and, like *Hearts in Atlantis*, is a telling denunciation of the governmental excesses of the '60s. Charlie McGee's parents, Andy and Vicky, sold themselves as lab animals in 1968 to become subjects in experimental drug tests. Subsequently, their child born the next year had a few unanticipated revisions in her DNA, the most startling being her ability to start fires telekinetically. Like Carrie White before her, she becomes quite dangerous when angered. Of course, the government evil-doers pop back up, murdering Vicky and sending Charlie and Andy on the run. The Shop, the branch of the covert operations conducting those drug tests so long ago, naturally doesn't know what it's dealing with, and its arrogance is going to bring them to burn. Literally. **Grades 9—12. PT**

King, Stephen. ***The Girl Who Loved Tom Gordon.*** 244 pages.

Pocket 2000 Paper 0671042858 $7.99
Scribner 1999 Trade 0684867621 $16.95

Stephen King doesn't usually filter his stories through young girls, but when he does, you'd think he was nine-year-old Trisha McFarland, lost in the woods on a family hiking trip, battling critters, exposure, and fear-induced hallucinations. Or are they really hallucinations? With King, it's never certain, which is part of the fun. Red Sox pitcher Tom Gordon, to whom Trisha listens on her Walkman, is one of the benevolent apparitions, serving as the "good" side of the battle between sanity and madness that King's characters so often must fight. Beautifully written, this *Girl* can satisfy a wide range of readers. **Grades 9—12. PT**

Reviews: *SLJ* 3/1/2000, *VOYA* 8/1/1999

King, Stephen. ***Hearts in Atlantis.*** 523 pages.

Pocket 2000 Paper 0671024248 $7.99
Pocket 2001 Paper 0743436210 $7.99
Scribner 1999 Trade 0684853515 $28.00

This collection of five stories begins with Bobby Brautigan, a child with a yen for a Schwinn, a mother too consumed with her own pain to love him, and a mysterious lodger who brings Bobby into the world of literature while fleeing mysterious men who are possessed of supernatural powers and evil intent. The other four stories explore the unique decade of the '60s with Vietnam as the consistently hovering metaphor. A group of college kids who'd rather play the card game hearts than graduate descends from Saturday night philosophizing into their own brand of inhumanity, and King's comparison of the game of the mind and the game of war not only ties the narratives together, it creates a new filter through which to view the horrors of which only human beings are capable. **Grades 9—12. PT**

King, Stephen. *It.* 1138 pages.

Dutton 1997 Paper 0451169514 $7.99

Whether it was because of its daunting length, its spooky cover, or its terrifying premise (that bad things can, and often do, happen to the innocent), I replace this book annually in my young adult collection. **Grades 9—12. (Annotation by Angela Benedetti)**

King, Stephen. *Night Shift.* 336 pages.

Signet 1976 Paper 0451170113 $7.99

A relatively early collection of short stories, this is a good choice for those intimidated by the length of some of King's novels. Among the main offerings, there's an early, short version of *Salem's Lot*; a wonderfully disgusting story about giant mutant rats ("Graveyard Shift"); a surprisingly effective tale about an ironing machine possessed by the devil ("The Mangler"); a college campus serial killer ("Strawberry Spring") with plenty of shock value; and "The Ledge," which is NOT recommended for those nursing a phobia about heights. Many of these stories have been made into movies, but in most cases the stories themselves are far superior. **Grades 9—12. PT**

King, Stephen. *Salem's Lot.* 631 pages.

Pocket 2000 Paper 067103975X $13.99
Simon & Schuster 1999 Paper 0671039741 $7.99

King's second novel shows a monumental leap in craft from the publication of *Carrie*. Jerusalem's Lot, a tiny town in Maine, is systematically being subsumed by vampires of the Bram Stoker nature: hideously ugly, shape-shifters, evil from the lowest depths of Hell. Even after a quarter century, *Salem's Lot* is still one terrifying read, and might be too frightening for the young unacquainted with Stephen King's penchant for reality horror. King has said that the town itself, filled with latent human evil, scared him more than the undead monsters gleefully sucking it dry. **Grades 9—12. PT**

King, Stephen. ***The Shining.*** 704 pages.

> Pocket 2002 Paper 0743437497 $14.00
> Pocket 2001 Paper 0743424425 $7.99
> Doubleday 1990 Trade 0385121679 $35.00

One of King's most genuinely terrifying, *The Shining* has been made into two films, the original, which he disavowed because it took such liberties with the plot, and the television mini-series, which King himself supervised. Though both have their frightening moments, neither can approach the level of chill bumps produced by this account of the Torrance family and their winter sojourn in the fabled Overlook Hotel. Once the playground of the rich and infamous, the Overlook seems a perfect place for Jack to finish his novel, Wendy to care for him and their son, and Danny to explore and play. Too bad for them all that the place is haunted by the most evil of ghosts; Jack's alcoholism rages rapidly out of control; Wendy is reduced to tears and cunning to save her family; and Danny is the object of the haunts' most vicious desires. The scene with the moving topiary still has the power to make a reader shiver, despite its predating of some of King's seminal horrors. After that chapter, you'll want to sleep with the lights on. **Grades 9—12. PT**

King, Stephen. ***The Stand.*** 823 pages.

> Random 2001 Trade 0517219018 $19.99
> NAL 1981 Paper 0451169530 $8.50
> NAL 1994 Paper 0451160959 $6.99
> Doubleday 1990 Trade 0385199570 $45.00

Though a debate over which of King's works is his supreme achievement will never be resolved, *The Stand* is hard to beat. Originally published with about 400 pages deleted, it has been re-released in its full form, making it the longest of all King's novels. The book is worth the journey. Dickensian in form, the plot follows a plethora of characters who've survived the "superflu" that killed 90 percent of the world's population, and are seeking their way west following directions given to them in dreams. There are two camps in this end-of-the-world thriller: the Good, heading to Denver at the behest of Mother Abigail, an ancient black woman who's not entirely thrilled with her role as leader of her disciples, and the Bad, banding together in Las Vegas (naturally) under the paralyzing influence of Randall Flag, who is, for all intents and purposes, the Devil himself. At stake is the survival of humanity and its collective soul, and King miraculously makes every character, even the most minor, memorable and believable. If you read only one Stephen King in your life, this is the one. **Grades 9—12. PT**

Klass, David. ***You Don't Know Me.*** 262 pages.

> HarperTempest 2002 Paper 0064473783 $6.99
> Frances Foster 2001 Trade 0374387060 $17.00

"You don't know me," chants the narrator, John, over and over in the opening pages of this powerful novel about abusive families, about knowing oneself, about problems at school. Klass's work is by turns able to make the reader laugh out loud with John's insightful wit, and cringe from the brutality from which John uses humor to protect himself. I couldn't put it down, and that's been the reaction of everyone to whom I've given the book to date. **Grades 7–12. (Annotation by Dr. Lois Stover)**

Reviews: *Booklist* 3/1/2001, *SLJ* 3/1/2001, *VOYA* 6/1/2001

Klause, Annette Curtis. ***Blood and Chocolate.*** 264 pages.

Laurel-Leaf 1997 Paper 0440226686 $4.99
Delacorte 1997 Trade 0385323050 $16.95

Vivian is a werewolf. Her pack family has moved again, this time staying outside of Baltimore; soon after bloody murders happen on the nights of full moons. Vivian is distracted though by Aiden, a boy at her school she has fallen madly in love with, although she fears that she can never show him her true self. Back in the pack, Vivian becomes involved in a fierce rivalry and literally fights for her life. This is simply one of the best teen fiction tomes of the 1990s. Klause examines teen angst issues like identity while still providing a generous supply of gross-outs. **Grades 9–12. PJ**

Reviews: *Booklist* 6/1/1997, *SLJ* 08/1/1997

Klause, Annette Curtis. ***The Silver Kiss.*** 198 pages.

Dell 1992 Paper 0440213460 $4.99

Klause's debut novel was a sensation upon publication, mixing a coming-of-age story with a vampire tale long before Buffy ever slayed a vampire on television. The book's main character is Zoë, whose mother is dying from cancer. She is alone and scared with no one to turn to, until she meets Simon. Simon knows a great deal about death, for he is already dead. He is a vampire. More than a horror story, it is a love story, with a few scenes that are erotic for young adult fiction. Simply one of the best young adult novels of all time; certainly a stunning debut. **Grades 8–12. PJ <MOCK><YALSA>**

Knowles, John. ***A Separate Peace.*** 186 pages.

Bantam 1985 Paper 0553280414 $5.99
Scribner 1996 Trade 0684833662 $20.00

Long a standard of American literature curricula in high schools, Knowles' novel of a boy's prep school set against the gathering threat of World War II continues to evoke strong emotional reaction. Gene Forrester narrates, and his perspective seems to be above suspicion until the depths of his jealousy of Finny, the school's golden boy become clear. Finny is also the classic innocent who trusts his best friend so completely that when that trust proves not only unfounded but foolhardy, Finny is destroyed. Friendship sustained by lies and illusion is Knowles' method for examining the emotional as well as physical cost of surrendering to the hatred and paranoia that, on a large enough scale, inevitably add up to warfare. **Grades 9—12. PT**

Koertge, Ron. *The Brimstone Journals.* 113 pages.

Candlewick 2001 Trade 0763613029 $15.99

A dramatic turn for an author more known for creating laughs than controversy. This is Koertge's Columbine book; his attempt to make sense of what happened that fateful day in Colorado. Rather than a straight novel, Koertge calls upon free verse disguised as journal entries. The characters here are—appropriately—mostly types; Koertge wants readers to understand the events at Columbine could happen everywhere. There are 15 main characters in all, but it is Boyd who is the center of the book. Determined to get revenge upon anyone who ever hurt him, Boyd is a time bomb waiting to go off. Each poem or journal entry is another ticking of the clock as Boyd is determined to exact vengeance upon every name on his list. **Grades 9—12. PJ**

Reviews: *Booklist* 4/15/2001, *SLJ* 3/1/2001, *VOYA* 8/1/2001

Koller, Jackie French. *The Falcon.* 181 pages.

Atheneum 1998 Trade 0689812949 $17.00

The diary of 17-year-old Luke Carver reveals the drama of his present and the trauma of his past. On the surface Luke seems to have it all together; he's a popular athlete with a winning personality. But his life is not as simple or shiny, as he is plagued by what seems to be his rash of hard luck, including an auto accident. A fight with his girl friend is the final straw that drives Luke off the deep end, forcing him to confront a disability he has been hiding and an incident in his past he has been avoiding. **Grades 7—10. PJ <TEN>**

Reviews: *Booklist* 4/15/1998, *SLJ* 5/1/1998, *VOYA* 2/1/1999

Koller, Jackie French. *A Place to Call Home.* 204 pages.

Aladdin 1997 Paper 0689813953 $4.99

A novel about a woman who takes her own life by driving into the lake, leaving behind her bi-racial teenage daughter Anna, five-year-old Mandy, and a baby son named Casey. Anna's first task is to keep the family together by hiding her mother's death, knowing that Child Protective Services would surely split them up. Like many a novel of this genre, Anna is forced into an adult role before she is ready. **Grades 7—10. PJ**

Reviews: *Booklist* 10/15/1995, *VOYA* 2/1/1996

Konigsburg, E. L. **Silent to the Bone.** 261 pages.

> Atheneum 2000 Trade 0689836015 $15.99
> Aladdin 2002 Paper 0689836023 $5.99

A "ripped from the headlines" book (the Louise Woodward nanny case) from an author known more for her wit than grit that works on several levels. From the frantic 911 call that jump-starts the book through the silent scenes of one character talking while another merely blinks his eyes, Konigsburg has crafted a tour de force. Branwell doesn't make the 911 call, but whatever happened that day has left him mute, and he is accused of assaulting his own infant sister. The book is told from the perspective of Branwell's best friend, Connor. Like a mystery, clues are slowly revealed as Connor attempts to figure out his friend's guilt, but also the reasons for his silence. A surprisingly edgy book looking at a variety of coming-of-age issues in a unique way. **Grades 6–8. PJ**

> Reviews: *Booklist* 8/1/2000

Koontz, Dean. **Fear Nothing.** 391 pages.

> Bantam 1998 Paper 0553579754 $7.99
> Bantam 1998 Trade 0553106643 $26.95

Afflicted with rare *xerodema pigmentosum*, a disease that causes cancer in those exposed to almost any kind of light, Christopher Snow seems to suffer the torments of a modern day Job. His parents died suspiciously, and while Christopher investigates the cause, he's being threatened by mysterious characters who want him to leave well enough alone. If he refuses, then his best friends—dog Orson, surf buddy Bobby, DJ girlfriend Sasha—may pay the price for his tenacity. The lyrically named Moonlight Bay, California, becomes a town full of creeping dangers, and even the ordinary townsfolk seem to be succumbing to a particularly nasty form of horror. Often funny, certainly suspenseful, *Fear Nothing* is one of Koontz's better books, despite his occasional indulgence in overwriting. He's having a lot of fun with this (note the tag names), and the readers will, too. **Grades 8–12. PT <TEN>**

> Reviews: *Booklist* 12/15/1997, *SLJ* 6/1/1998, *VOYA* 6/1/1998

Koontz, Dean. **Seize the Night.** 401 pages.

> Bantam 1999 Paper 0553840207 $7.99
> Bantam 1999 Paper 0553580191 $7.99
> Bantam 1998 Trade 0553106651 $26.95

Chris Snow is back, along with Bobby, Sasha, and Orson. This time, the dangers of Moonlight Bay include kidnapping, and Orson, the beer-loving dog, is one of the victims, along with the son of Lilly, Christopher's ex-girlfriend. Between sunset and sunrise, Chris, who is still living the vampiric existence of the XP sufferer, tries to recover the stolen people and pets. Danger lurks, as it always does with Koontz, everywhere. There's a time machine; crazed, genetically altered monkeys (back from the earlier novel); and those darn townspeople, revisiting their penchant for morphing into monsters. As always, the reading is fun, quick, and for those who've already Fear(ed) Nothing, comfortable. **Grades 8—12. PT**

Reviews: *Booklist* 12/1/1998, *VOYA* 4/1/1999

Koontz, Dean. **Watchers.** 352 pages.

Berkley 1987 Paper 0425107469 $7.50

Koontz's most straightforward take on the eternal struggle between good and evil brings us two escapees from a government experimental laboratory. With them they bring either monstrous horror or restorative love, depending on the recipient. This is familiar Koontz territory with characters endangered by their own histories and fears, the salvation of love, and the-ever-constant Bad Government run amok. **Grades 8—12. PT**

Korman, Gordon. **Losing Joe's Place.** 240 pages.

Scholastic 1991 Paper 0590427695 $4.50

What sounds now like the plot of a teen movie is actually a pretty funny novel by Gordon Korman, a stand-up comic trapped in the body of a young adult novelist. Jason is in high school, but gets the chance to sublet his brother's apartment for one summer. Along with the apartment comes a fancy car, lots of nice electronic equipment, as well as the opportunity to interact with a bevy of college-aged girls who live in the complex. Obviously wacky complications ensue mixed in with slapstick comedy and sitcom situations that deliver a punch line with perfect timing. **Grades 8—10. PJ**

Reviews: *Booklist* 3/1/1990, *SLJ* 5/1/1990

Koss, Amy. **The Girls.** 121 pages.

Puffin 2002 Paper 0142300330 $4.99
Dial 2000 Trade 0803724942 $16.99

For young teens leaving *The Babysitter's Club* behind comes this simple novel about a group of five girls: Brianna, Renee, Maya, Darcy, and Candace. Like any group, there are numerous dynamics at work, as well as the distinct individual personalities of each member. Short on plot but long on character, *The Girls* examines the ups, downs, and strange curves of teen friendships. Rival factions are formed, lies are told, and feelings are hurt as each girl tries to find her place in the group, and in the world at large. As good a book about developing friendships and positive self-esteem as almost any self-help publication. **Grades 6—8. PJ**

Reviews: *Booklist* 8/1/2000, *SLJ* 6/1/2000

Krisher, Trudy. **Spite Fences.** 288 pages.

> Bantam Doubleday Dell 1996 Paper 0440220165 $5.50
> Doubleday 1995 Trade 0385309783: $18.95

Like *To Kill a Mockingbird*, it is the story of prejudice in a small town in the 1950s where water fountains are still labeled "colored." The narrator of the book, Pert, a young girl whose family is one of the few Catholics, is an outcast because of her religion. Pert's best friend is Maggie, whose mother strives for social status but soon finds her family isolated as well. The isolation is literal after she surrounds their house with a large pine fence. When Maggie ventures back out into her town (called Kinship), she begins to photograph the inequality she sees all around her. She soon learns the simple fact, however, that the worst injustices often take place right at home. Maggie's fall from grace in her mother's eyes and the healing power of friendship form the center of this coming-of-age novel. **Grades 8–12. PJ**

> Reviews: *Booklist* 12/1994, *SLJ* 11/1/994, *VOYA* 10/1/994

Lamb, Wally. **She's Come Undone.** 405 pages.

> Pocket 1998 Paper 0671021001 $7.99
> Pocket 1992 Trade 0671014730 $23.00
> Simon & Schuster 1992 Trade 0671759205 $21.00

Long before this novel was touched with Oprah's golden wand, it retained a rabid, if small, fan base. That it is now wildly popular is nothing more than it deserves. The tale of Dolores Price (and she pays a sad price indeed for the privilege of surviving) is a crowded one, filled with the most dysfunctional of parents, the sleaziest of boyfriends, and often the worst of all possible worlds in general. Despite it all, Dolores is hilarious. She's fat, unattractive, insecure, and an emotional mess, but she's one of the more sympathetic characters on the modern literary scene. It is a testament to Wally Lamb's enormous talent that readers who don't pay attention to the author's name would be certain this must be written by a woman. When people finish this novel, they call their friends to insist they read it, too. Highest recommendation. **Grades 10–12 (mature). PT**

> Reviews: *Booklist* 8/1/1992

Lasky, Kathryn. **Beyond the Divide.** 304 pages.

> Aladdin Paperbacks 1995 Paper 0689801637 $4.99
> Simon & Schuster 1983 Library 0027516709 $17.00

In 1849, 14-year-old Meribah Simon leaves her home in Pennsylvania to accompany her father on a dangerous journey by wagon train to California. This book is aptly written and brings history to life. There is enough adventure and facing of difficulties for teens to keep turning pages. When Meribah is abandoned by the wagon train in the High Sierra with winter coming on, the book becomes a survival-in-the-wilderness story that fans of that genre will relish. **Grades 6–10. (Annotation by Diane Tuccillo)**

Lasky, Kathryn. ***True North.*** 267 pages.

> Point Signature 1998 Paper 0590205242 $4.99
> Blue Sky 1996 Trade 0590205234 $14.95

A tale of friendship and female empowerment set during the Civil War. Lucy is the insider, youngest daughter of a wealthy Boston family; Afrika is the outsider, an escaped slave with no sense of her history or her future. The two get together when Lucy finds Afrika hiding out in her grandfather's house, a stop on the underground railroad. The two girls join together on the next part of the journey to head "truth north" towards Canada so that Afrika can escape and start a new life. **Grades 6–9. PJ**

> Reviews: *Booklist* 11/15/1996, *SLJ* 12/1/1996, *VOYA* 4/1/1997

Lawrence, Iain. ***The Wreckers.*** 196 pages.

> Yearling 1999 Paper 0440415454 $5.50
> Delacorte 1998 Trade 0385325355 $15.95

Compared by more than one reviewer to the "old fashioned" yarns of Robert Louis Stevenson, this mix of historical and adventure fiction is a page-turner. John Spencer and his father are shipwrecked on the coast of Cornwall, England. If that weren't bad enough, it turns out that the accident was no accident; it seems the good burghers of this small coastal town are violent pirates who make their living wrecking ships, looting the treasures and possessions, and then killing the survivors. It is into that world that 14-year-old John is cast, with his father missing and his hopes for survival dim. **Grades 6–9. PJ**

> Reviews: *Booklist* 6/1/1998, *SLJ* 6/1/1998

Le Guin, Ursula K. ***The Farthest Shore.*** 223 pages.

> Aladdin 2001 Paper 0689845340 $6.99
> Aladdin 2001 Paper 0689847823 $4.99

Death is the farthest shore. When an enchanter finds a way to cheat death, magic and creativity drain from the world of Earthsea. The young prince Arren joins the archmage Ged on a quest to restore the balance of life and death. Lyrical writing, unique plots, a strange, yet realistic, fantasy environment, and well-drawn teenage characters are hallmarks of the Earthsea trilogy. This third book, unlike *The Tombs of Atuan*, does not stand alone well; the reader will want to have read the first book, *A Wizard of Earthsea*. **Grades 6–9. KE**

Le Guin, Ursula K. ***The Left Hand of Darkness.*** 345 pages.

Ace 1969 Paper 0441478123 $6.99

Imagine another world, Winter, where sexual desire is seasonal and one's sex can change from season to season. Genly Ai, a young emissary from Earth, is forced to make a dangerous trek across Winter with his native guide, Estraven. The ground-breaking speculation on the nature of sexuality and identity made this a science fiction classic. The lyrical writing and well-developed characters will keep intelligent teen readers turning to Le Guin again and again. **Grades 10—12. KE**

Le Guin, Ursula K. ***Tehanu.*** 226 pages.

Aladdin 2001 Paper 0689845332 $6.99

After many years, Le Guin has returned to her world of Earthsea with new stories for an older audience. Slower moving, introspective, and with carefully realized metaphysics of life, death, and power, this book concerns Ged, now an old man stripped of his wizardly powers, and Tehanu, no longer the young heroine of Roke but an old widow, who are reunited in the autumn of their lives. The catalyst to their stories is a badly burned, abused child who may have a connection to the secret magic and ancient powers of Earthsea. The story continues in *Tales from Earthsea* and *The Other Wind*. Younger fans especially will not appreciate Le Guin's changing of "their" familiar imaginative playground, but older teens and adults fresh to the series may well appreciate the new emphasis on interpersonal relationships. **Grades 6—9. KE**

Le Guin, Ursula K. ***The Tombs of Atuan.*** 163 pages.

Macmillan 1990 Trade 0689316844 $21.00

In this stand-alone sequel to *A Wizard of Earthsea*, Tehanu is chosen as a child to become Arha, the eaten one, and servant and priestess to the dark gods. When a young wizard from the heretic islands of Earthsea is trapped in the catacombs beneath her temple, Arha is forced to reexamine her world. While the young priestess is torn between the humanity the young man is trying to reawaken in her and the power (and fear) of the dark powers and temple officials, the reader is held in suspense. Will she choose Arha? Or Tehanu? Once again, Le Guin marries a depth of characterization and metaphysical speculation with a fascinating story in a strange and wonderful setting. This is the second book in the original Earthsea trilogy. **Grades 6—9. KE**

Le Guin, Ursula K. ***A Wizard of Earthsea.*** 197 pages.

Bantam 1984 Paper 0553262505 $7.50

An older, wealthier student challenges Ged, a poor but ambitious teenager, to a forbidden magical duel. The power Ged summons kills his rival and nearly destroys

Ged. First fleeing, then pursuing the monster he created, Ged takes the reader on a strange journey across his world. Earthsea is a strong presence, and also one of the rare fantasy settings where the hero and his people are dark. **Grades 6—12. KE**

Lee, Harper. ***To Kill a Mockingbird.*** 323 pages.

> Warner 1988 Paper 0446310786 $6.99
> HarperPerennial 1999 Paper 0060933275 $20.00
> HarperPerennial 2002 Paper 0060935464 $11.95

Once in a very blue moon a novel appears that can only be assessed as perfect. Harper Lee's only book is the definition of the word. On the surface, a simple story—small town in Macon County during the Depression is home to a wide range of memorable characters—*Mockingbird* is in fact a complex web of murder, mystery, courtroom drama, love, bigotry, courage, cowardice, hate, confusion, wisdom, sacrifice, and selfishness. In short, it is a microcosm of the human condition. Narrated by Scout, the tomboy daughter of widowed attorney Atticus Finch, the tale centers on her view of a world that includes her older brother, Jem, their friend Dill (rumored to be based on a very young Truman Capote), and small town life where nothing is actually as it appears to be. Over a year's time, events unfold in which Scout learns that the human heart may be divined only through tolerance and compassion, and reputation can be nothing more than invidious camouflage: the "regular guy" is an incestuous rapist and the "ghost" with the grisly history is in fact a hero of uncommon valor. Readers of all levels will not forget Boo Radley or Atticus or Miss Maudie or Dill—all of whom are as compelling as if they lived beyond the fictional confines of this extraordinary novel. **Grades 8—12. PT**

Lee, Marie G. ***Necessary Roughness.*** 228 pages.

> HarperTrophy 1998 Paper 0064471691 $5.99
> HarperCollins 1996 Trade 0060251247 $15.95

Chan Kim is undergoing culture shock: one day he is in California playing soccer, practicing martial arts, and hanging out with his friends who, like him, are Korean; a few days later his family moves to a small town in Minnesota. Chan goes from being an insider to an outsider; from playing sports of skill like soccer to American football, which requires, as the title suggests, necessary roughness. But like many sports novels, the field is a backdrop for Chan's personal battles. In addition to his total isolation at school, things are no better at home because he and his father rage at each other. **Grades 6—10. PJ**

> Reviews: *Booklist* 1/1/1997, *SLJ* 1/1/1997, *VOYA* 6/1/1997

Lee, Tanith. ***Black Unicorn.*** 138 pages.

> TOR 1991 Paper 0812524594 $3.99

Tanaquil is the tinkerer daughter of a powerful enchantress in a bizarre but well-developed fantasy universe. When the teenager's construction of a unicorn comes alive and carries her away from her mother's fortress, her journey of self-discovery to adulthood also takes the reader on a ride through a fascinating setting. The books are short, fast reads with adventure lightly touched with horror, and Tanaquil's voice is strong and appealing throughout. Tanaquil's story continues in *Gold Unicorn* and *Red Unicorn.* **Grades 7—10. KE**

L' Engle, Madeleine. *A Wrinkle in Time.* 212 pages.

> Dell 1973 Paper 0440498058 $6.50
> Dell 1976 Paper 0440998050 $6.50
> Farrar Straus Giroux 1990 Trade 0374386137 $17.00

Winner of the 1962 Newbery Award, *A Wrinkle in Time* remains a book that generation after generation delights in discovering, rereading, and remembering as one of childhood's great pleasures. Sophisticated in scope and simple in execution, here is the story of Meg Murry, who believes herself to be ugly, stupid, and unlovable. Her little brother Charles Wallace is thought to be backward, and popular rumor has it that her father has deserted her beautiful scientist mother for another woman. After all, where is he these days? In actuality, Charles Wallace is a genius, Meg is at the doorstep of flowering womanhood (hinted at by her new friend Calvin O'Keefe), and Mr. Murry has been kidnapped to another planet and held hostage by a dreadful force of pure evil. Children and adults alike can take joy in learning the secrets of the Tesseract and the knowledge that while time travel is a marvelous thing, it is nothing compared to the power of love. The story continues in *Wind in the Door, A Swiftly Tilting Planet,* and *Many Waters.* **Grades 6—12. PT**

Lester, Jules. *Othello.* 176 pages.

> Scholastic 1998 Paper 0590419668 $4.99

Just as many a Shakespearean stage or film version is re-imagined by directors, so too has Lester rethought *Othello.* He rewrites the play as a novel, although still retaining much of the Shakespearean dialogue in this slender book. The book is now set in Elizabethan England; Othello and other characters are immigrants from Africa. Played out now against backdrop of racism, the themes of the play are opened up to new interpretation. **Grades 6—12. PJ**

> Reviews: *Booklist* 2/15/1995, *SLJ* 4/1/1995, *VOYA* 5/1/1995

Levenkron, Steven. *The Best Little Girl in the World.* 196 pages.

> Warner 1979 Paper 0446358657 $6.99

A classic young adult "problem novel" in which readers meet the main character (Francesca), suffer through her issue (anorexia), and then pull for her to recover. It's standard stuff and even slightly dated, but it still works because of the central issue: self-image among young women remains relevant. Feeling fat, Francesca starves herself. Not eating becomes an obsession that takes over, and almost ends her life. It is only through the love of her family and friends that she is able to break free of her eating disorder. It's movie of the week stuff, and it works. **Grades 7–12. PJ**

Levine, Gail Carson. ***Ella Enchanted.*** 232 pages.

> HarperCollins 1997 Library 0060275111 $16.89
> HarperTrophy 1998 Paper 0064407055 $6.50
> HarperCollins 1997 Trade 0060275103 $15.95

In a fun twist on the Cinderella story, Ella is blessed—or cursed—by her fairy godmother with the gift of perfect obedience. How can a girl thwart wicked step-relations and win her handsome prince across a landscape of fantasy adventure if she just can't say, "No"? *Ella Enchanted* is a popular favorite with many teens for its likeable heroine, light-hearted romance, and familiar story given new life. Younger teens are the primary audience, but it's easy to sell to older girls looking for a quick relaxing read. **Grades 6–7. KE**

> Reviews: *Booklist* 4/15/1997, *SLJ* 4/1/1997, *SLJ* 12/1/1997

Levitin, Sonia. ***The Cure.*** 192 pages.

> HarperCollins 2000 Paper 038073298X $5.99
> Harcourt Children's Books 1999 Trade 0152018271 $16.00

An imaginative tale mixing the future (the year 2407) with the past, telling a timeless tale about conformity, fear, racial hatred, and the power of self-expression. The book's main character, Gemm, won't conform; his "cure" is to go back in time and live during the Dark Ages as part of a small Jewish community. As the Black Death is sweeping over the land, the citizens blame the Jews, but the mob soon realizes the financial and political benefit of scapegoating. The scenes in 1348 eerily, and perhaps quite deliberately, echo the images from the 1940s of the Jews in the Warsaw ghettos. An intriguing mix of speculative fiction and historical re-creation about themes of social justice, ethnic identity, and passionate nonconforming that will strike many chords with teen readers. **Grades 8–10. PJ**

Lipsyte, Robert. ***The Brave.*** 159 pages.

> HarperTrophy 1993 Paper 0064470792 $5.99

Alfred Brooks, hero of *The Contender*, reappears as a police sergeant who rescues a young Native American boxer from the streets. Sonny Bear reminds Brooks of himself as a young man: headed in the wrong direction with the wrong friends. He sends Sonny on the path that saves him, getting him to channel his rage (what Sonny calls his "Monster") into the boxing ring. But just when it seems the "beast" in Sonny has become tamed and focused, his mettle is tested outside of the squared circle. A Best Books and Quick Picks selection. **Grades 7–12. PJ**

Lipsyte, Robert. ***The Chief.*** 226 pages.

HarperTrophy 1995 Paper 0064470970 $5.99

This sequel to *The Brave* finds Sonny Bear defeated, but still standing strong. His strength is tested first by the temptation of Hollywood, then by being thrust into a dispute over legalized gambling at his reservation. The narrator of this tale is Martin Witherspoon, who is kind of a cross between two of Lipstye's best-known characters: Bobby Marks and Alfred Brooks. The book's climactic scene is the stuff of Rocky movies: a heroic run, not up the steps of City Hall, but over 300 miles. You can almost hear the music rising in the background as Sonny recaptures what he has lost and gets ready to win the heavyweight title. **Grades 7–12. PJ**

Lipsyte, Robert. ***The Contender.*** 182 pages.

HarperCollins 1967 Library 0060239204 $15.89
HarperTrophy 1987 Paper 0064470393 $5.99

This novel, with *The Outsiders* and *The Pigman*, rests in the trinity that created young adult literature. Lipsyte, a sports writer by trade, shows off those chops with hard-hitting action sequences in and out of the boxing ring in this classic coming-of-age story. Alfred Brooks is trapped in a nowhere life with a dead-end job, a destructive life style, and a group of friends from his Harlem neighborhood who offer more wrong turns. He finds himself one day on the door of an old-style boxing gym and soon under the tutelage of Mr. Donatelli, who is going to teach him how to throw jabs, how to take punches, but mostly how to live. The theme of the book is THE theme of most young adult novels: that the journey matters as much as the destination; it is not about winning, but about becoming a contender. **Grades 7–12. PJ**

Lipsyte, Robert. ***One Fat Summer.*** 152 pages.

HarperTrophy 1991 Paper 0064470733 $5.99

Unlike many teens, Bobby Marks doesn't look forward to summer. For him, it is a sheer torture: trapped without friends in a summerhouse, trapped inside his fat body. Despite it, Bobby tries to get along, even taking a summer job landscaping the estate of Dr. Kahn. That's all plot; what matters here is Bobby's transformation during his one fat summer into a better, more understanding, more self-accepting person than he was before. Timeless and very funny to boot. Bobby's trials, tribulations, and tempting taste treats continue in *Summer Rules* and *The Summerboy*. **Grades 6–10. PJ**

London, Jack. ***The Call of the Wild.*** Page count varies with edition.

Atheneum 1979 Paper 067170494X $4.50

Penguin 1993 Paper 0140186514 $7.95
Puffin 1994 Paper 0140366695 $3.99
Macmillan 1994 Trade 0027594556 $19.95

Toward the end of the 19th Century, the Klondike, that Alaskan center of the Gold Rush, grew hungry for dogs large enough to act as beasts of burden (horses were too unreliable on snow and ice). To satisfy that appetite, a sort of black market was created, with dogs all along the west coast being sold like slaves to miners who had no scruples about how they came by their purchases. One such creature was Buck, who, over the course of this short novel, comes to slowly dispense with the niceties taught him in civilization and to heed only the call of the wild: survival. An entire novel from a dog's point of view may have limited appeal, but older teens might enjoy it as a metaphor examining the thin veneer of the "civilized" behavior man adapts for himself, and which he can, as easily as an animal, dispose of. **Grades 6–12. PT**

London, Jack. ***White Fang.*** Page count varies with edition.

Dover 1991 Paper 048626968X $1.50
Puffin 1994 Paper 0140366679 $3.99
Viking 1999 Paper 0670884804 $18.99
Viking 1999 Trade 0670884790 $25.99

The plot reverses from *The Call of the Wild*; this time the poor dog must endure great abuse before being rescued by human affection. Again, the canine is the star. White Fang, half-dog, half-wolf, struggles to survive against cruel nature and crueler man; the vernacular may be a bit confusing to younger readers, but the story is not geared to interest those older than eighth grade, unless they're rabid London (or dog) fans. **Grades 6–8. PT**

Lovecraft, H. P. ***Call of Cthulhu and Other Weird Stories.*** 304 pages.

Viking Penguin 1999 Paper 0141182342 $12.95

Lovecraft is a touchstone for horror writers: it seems almost every one of them, from Stephen King to Anne Rice, refer to him as influence, even if few readers know his work. This collection allows teen readers a glimpse into the nightmare world of Lovecraft: filled with strange demons and humans on the brinks of madness. Much of his work appeared in pulp magazines, such as *Weird Tales*, and that journal seems the obvious choice for Lovecraft. He is the "missing link" between the birth of the American horror tale with Poe and the dawning of speculative fiction masters, who later inspired the best-selling horror writers like King. One of the Penguin Twentieth-Century Classics. **Grades 10–12. PJ**

Lowry, Lois. ***Gathering Blue.*** 215 pages.

Laurel-Leaf 2002 Paper 0440229499 $6.50

Houghton Mifflin 2000 Trade 0618055819 $15.00

Lois Lowry has created a dystopian society where life is primitive, nasty, brutal, and short. Kira, an orphaned cripple, is given the chance to restore the historical pictures on a robe worn during the annual Ruin Song Gathering. By finding a plant that can restore the lost color—blue—Kira has a chance to reinvent their history—but at a cost. Lowry's speculations on the source of creativity, the role of art, and the power of individuals to change society are grounded in the struggles of teens and children trying to survive in a dangerous and ugly future. Fans of *The Giver*, or of speculative fiction in general, will not be disappointed in *Gathering Blue*. **Grades 6–10. KE**

Reviews: *Booklist* 6/1/2000, *SLJ* 8/1/2000, *VOYA* 10/1/2000

Lowry, Lois. ***The Giver.*** 180 pages.

Bantam 1999 Paper 0553571338 $6.99
Laurel-Leaf 2002 Paper 0440237688 $6.50
Houghton Mifflin 1993 Trade 0395645662 $16.00

Lowry pays homage to Le Guin's "Those Who Walk Away From Omelas" with *The Giver*. Young Jonas is selected to assist his blissful, technologically advanced community's Giver of Memories. As the Receiver, however, he learns the cost of their utopia and refuses to pay the price. Young readers who have never been exposed to the power of speculative fiction will be blown away by Lowry's delicate, but challenging, novella. **Grades 6–10. KE <HIPPLE><MOCK><YALSA>**

Reviews: *Booklist* 4/15/1993, *SLJ* 5/1/1993

Lynch, Chris. ***Freewill.*** 149 pages.

HarperCollins 2001 Library 0060281774 $15.89
HarperTempest 2002 Paper 0064472027 $6.99
HarperCollins 2001 Trade 0060281766 $15.95

A totally original young adult novel that tests readers on every level. Even the broad outline of the plot is challenging: a community faces a rash of teen deaths, at least one a suicide. At the site of each death is a wooden statue. The maker of those figures is Will, who soon becomes known as the "carrier pigeon of death." Add to that strange premise Lynch's choice to tell the tale in second person. From that voice, we learn about Will, a deeply troubled young man who has no real family (a violent murder haunts him) or any connections at school and has, it seems, a growing disconnection with reality. This is as difficult to read as its main character is to understand, and that's a plus. **Grades 9–12 (mature). PJ <PRINTZ>**

Reviews: *Booklist* 5/15/2001, *SLJ* 3/1/2001, *VOYA* 8/1/2001

Lynch, Chris. **Gypsy Davey.** 179 pages.

> HarperCollins 1998 Paper 0064407306 $11.00

Lynch begins his stylistic experimentation with this novel about a brain-damaged 12-year-old boy who just happens to be the "man of the house." The book is told in alternating voices: a third person viewpoint lays out the facts, while Davey's thoughts, slow and jumbled, speak to the feelings caused by this very dysfunctional family. Davey's mother, Lois, is a mess—a high maintenance machine—while his teenage sister, Joanna, seethes with anger at the world around her. These women belong on *Jerry Springer* shouting at each other, not in a small house where their immaturity and selfishness trap Davey in the middle. With a father who seems to have left for good and Joanna's new baby recently arrived, Davey wants to feel safe and secure in the maelstrom of emotion and inappropriate actions swirling around his family. **Grades 7—10. PJ**

Lynch, Chris. **Slot Machine.** 241 pages.

> HarperTrophy 1996 Paper 0064471403 $5.95

Elvin and his buddies head to a summer program required for incoming freshman at Flagship Academy. To Elvin's horror, the camp is geared toward athletics, an area for which he has no interest and even less talent. Overweight and unsure of himself, Elvin is forced to try sport after sport, looking for his "slot" in the jock world. His primary gift is for gab and wise cracks, so he fails miserably and publicly at every attempt. This is an interesting look at fitting in, which mixes sports action and smart remarks to create a coming-of-age story about growing up male in a macho culture and what it means to play the game. Like Lipsyte's *One Fat Summer*, Lynch captures an overweight boy's battle with self-esteem. *VOYA* noted it was "crisp, humorous, sarcastic, sad, sensitive, realistic, and sometimes raunchy, but never dull. An unforgettable read." A Best Books for Young Adults and Quick Picks selection. **Grades 6—9. PJ**

> Reviews: *Booklist* 9/1/1995, *SLJ* 10/1/1995

Magorian, Michelle. **Good Night, Mr. Tom.** 318 pages.

> HarperCollins 1981 Library 0060240792 $16.89
> HarperTrophy 1986 Paper 006440174X $6.99

The main character in this tearjerker set in England during World War II is Willie, a young man who's living a hard life like all Londoners during the war, even more so because the main violence is not falling from the sky, but from the hands of his mother. After being removed from the house and bouncing around, he finally finds a home, but then he is evacuated to the country. There he meets a kindly old man named Mr. Tom. Tom needs something in his life to help him deal with the recent death of both his son and wife. The two bond and those chapters are the center of the book. A teen reader on Amazon wrote: "I cannot remember one moment in the book where I wanted to stop.

The experiences of little William became a part of me and I wanted to encourage this character as he went struggling through his rough life." **Grades 6—9. PJ <YALSA>**

Mahy, Margaret. ***Memory.*** 288 pages.

Aladdin 1999 Paper 0689829116 $8.00

On the fifth anniversary of his sister's death, 19-year-old Jonny Dart is still troubled by guilt and an imperfect memory of the accident that took her life. He goes searching for the only other witness to the fatal event, his sister's best friend. Instead of finding the answers he's looking for, he finds Sophie, a gentle old woman suffering from Alzheimer's disease, who teaches him about remembering and about loss. Mahy has written books with a supernatural theme, but this one stays closer to realism and with great effect. **Grades 6—9. PJ**

Reviews: *Booklist* 4/15/1988, *SLJ* 3/1988

Marsden, John. ***Letters from the Inside.*** 146 pages.

Laurel-Leaf 1996 Paper 0440219515 $4.99
Houghton Mifflin 1994 Trade 0395689856 $16.00

This epistolary novel follows the correspondence of two young women: Tracy and Mandy. Like any relationship, it begins slowly, with each trying to impress the other. But with every letter, the truth about each girl is slowly revealed. Mandy's bright happy life is a sham, for slamming into the middle of it is the dark violence of her brother. Tracy's life is a lie: she is writing not from her wonderful home, as she claims, but from inside a prison cell. Like a mystery, Marsden drops clues along the way so that readers figure out, perhaps only one step ahead of the characters, the real truth about both young women. Excellent and essential, this is a breakthrough book for Marsden that perhaps has even more relevance in the age of e-mail and chatting, where white lies are part of the game. **Grades 7—10. PJ**

Reviews: *Booklist* 10/15/1994, *SLJ* 9/1/1994,

Marsden, John. ***So Much to Tell You.*** 180 pages.

Fawcett 1990 Paper 0449703746 $5.99

Before there was *Speak*, there was this novel (winner of Australia's Book of the Year Award) about a mute young woman who only communicates through writing in her journal. Fourteen-year-old Marina begins life at boarding school upon her release from a mental hospital. That was her second hospital trip; the first was to repair her face, which was disfigured in an incident involving her parents. In the journal, Marina slowly opens up about her experiences in the boarding school, commenting upon the other students, the teachers, and her therapy sessions. She comments only on paper, for speech eludes her. It returns only when she summons the courage to confront her father in a riveting scene that ends this powerful journal-as-novel masterpiece. **Grades 7—10. PJ**

Marsden, John. ***Tomorrow When the War Began.*** 286 pages.

> Laurel-Leaf 1996 Paper 044021985X $4.99
> Houghton Mifflin 1995 Trade 0395706734 $16.00

When Ellie and six of her friends return home from a camping trip deep in the Australian bush, they find that their country has been invaded and everyone in town has been taken prisoner. Now, that's a concept. Cut off from everyone they know, the seven teens face life-and-death decisions as they struggle first to survive, then to fight back. But it won't be one round of battle: while the war began here, the popularity of the series, with its great mix of adventure and adolescent characters acting heroic, led to a succession of sequels. **Grades 7—10. PJ <YALSA>**

> Reviews: *Booklist* 4/15/1995, *SLJ* 6/1/1995

Martin, Valerie. ***Mary Reilly.*** 263 pages.

> Vintage Anchor 2001 Paper 0375725997 $12.00

A modern rendition of *Dr. Jekyll and Mr. Hyde*, Martin's brilliant novel retells the story through the eyes of Mary Reilly, a young housemaid and abuse survivor who worships Dr. Jekyll. All the original details are here, refiltered through the eyes of a character mentioned only once in the original. A tour de force, this novel is a splendid companion piece to Stevenson's book, or it can stand alone as one of the most original pieces of fiction of our time. Clear prose makes it accessible to most readers, while layered and diverse context offers much more to those of accomplished comprehension. **Grades 10—12. PT**

Martinez, Victor. ***Parrot in the Oven.*** 216 pages.

> HarperCollins 1996 Library 0060267062 $16.89
> HarperTrophy 1998 Paper 0064471861 $5.99
> HarperCollins 1996 Trade 0060267046 $15.95

A coming-of-age story set in a California housing project. Manny is trying his best to grow up right, but all around him is desperation. His father spends his time drinking and hanging out at the pool hall; his mother loves him but is too busy working to pay attention to him. In the middle of the crowded barrio, Manny is growing up too fast, all alone. Spanish phrases and words add texture to this multiple-award winner. **Grades 7—12. PJ**

> Reviews: *Booklist* 10/15/1996, *SLJ* 11/1/1996, *VOYA* 4/1/1997

Mason, Bobbie Ann. *In Country.* 247 pages.

HarperPerennial 1985 Paper 0060913509 $13.00

Set in 1984, as Bruce Springsteen's anthem for Vietnam vets "Born in the USA" is blaring out of every car radio, is this coming-of-age story about a young woman still grappling with her father's death in Nam. Sam lives in a small town with her mom and uncle, a Vietnam vet still scarred by the war. She's thinking about college, thinking about a boyfriend, but it is mostly a box of letters written by her father when he was "in country" that captures her attention. Who was he? Why did he die? Why did he kill? The book is about her answering those questions, as well as those about her place in the world. This slender novel features a heart-wrenching final scene that takes place at the Vietnam Memorial in Washington, D.C. **Grades 10—12. PJ**

Mazer, Harry. *The Last Mission.* 182 pages.

Dell 1981 Paper 0440947979 $5.50

In 1944, Jack Raab, a 15-year-old who dreams of being a hero, lies his way into the U.S. Air Force. From their base in England, Jack and his crew fly 24 treacherous bombing missions over occupied Europe. Hitler is near defeat when Jack is shot down behind enemy lines and taken to a German POW camp. Mazer drew upon his experiences as a 17-year-old in the Army Air Corps to pen this award-winning novel, which maintains its relevance decades after its publication. Easily Mazer's best and most honest book. **Grades 7—10. PJ**

Mazer, Norma Fox. *After the Rain.* 291 pages.

Avon Flare 1987 Paper 0380750252 $5.99
Morrow 1987 Trade 0688068677 $16.95

There's not a whole lot of plot in this Newbery Honor Book about the relationship between a teenage girl and her dying grandfather. Rachel, like many teens, is pretty wrapped up in her own life, made worse by her penchant for worry and self-doubt. She thinks more about friends and boyfriends than about her parents and her cranky grandfather. *After the Rain* tells the story of how Rachel is able to reach out to an older adult and, in doing so, learn a great deal about her history, but even more about herself. **Grades 7—10. PJ**

Reviews: *SLJ* 5/1/1987

Mazer, Norma Fox. *Out of Control.* 217 pages.

Avon Flare 1994 Paper 0380713470 $5.95

Something happened to Valerie in a deserted school hallway. She can't piece together details, but she knows it was horrific and she knows a group of boys was involved. The novel examines the aftermath as Valerie tries to heal, and the boys involved grapple with their motives. One of the boys, Rollo, narrates the book, and he is the one most shaken by his involvement. Filled with shame, Rollo attempts to reach out to Valerie, who isn't sure of his or her own intentions. A powerful novel about sexual harassment in schools, the circumstances that create it, and the actions of adults and school administrators, who only make it worse. **Grades 7—10. PJ**

Mazer, Norma Fox. ***When She Was Good.*** 228 pages.

> Scholastic 2000 Paper 0590319906 $4.99
> Arthur A. Levine 1997 Trade 0590135066 $16.95

One of the books that launched the "edgy novel" subgenre in the mid—1990s paints a sad picture of life for one young woman. Em Thurkill's life is a survival story as jarring as those set in the wilderness. She has suffered through her father's alcohol-induced rage coupled with her mother's silent acceptance. Yet even worse is her life with her abusive, mentally ill, and downright cruel older sister. This family is hyperdysfunctional. This novel isn't about coping with issues; it is about living with pain and searching for hope. **Grades 7—10. PJ <HIPPLE>**

> Reviews: *Booklist 9/1/1997, SLJ 9/1/1997*

McCafferty, Megan. ***Sloppy Firsts.*** 288 pages.

> Crown 2001 Paper 0609807900 $10.95

The author was an editor at *Cosmopolitan* and has penned pieces for *Glamour, Cosmo Girl, YM, Details,* and other top fashion and sex-fueled magazines. The influence shows in a very mature young adult novel chronicling the life of 16-year-old Jessica. Distant from her parents, smarting from the sudden departure of her best friend, and coming up empty in romance leaves Jessica sullen and searching for answers. This will appeal to fans of the Rennison novels since the concerns and characters are somewhat similar, as is the uncanny mix of humor with heartache. **Grades 9—12 (mature). PJ**

> Reviews: *VOYA 4/1/2002*

McCaffrey, Anne. ***Black Horses for the King.*** 217 pages.

> Ballantine 1997 Paper 0345408810 $10.95
> Ballantine 1998 Paper 0345422570 $6.99
> Harcourt 1996 Trade 0152273220 $17.00

In an Arthurian romance firmly set in fifth-century Britain, Galwyn Varianus leaves his abusive uncle to take up with the charismatic Artos (Arthur) and his companions. In order to best the Saxons, the young heroes attempt to breed war-horses and master horseshoeing. Masses of period detail, a chivalrous wartime setting, and an engaging young character's viewpoint make this a welcome addition to historical fiction collections that both girls and boys would enjoy. **Grades 7—10. KE**

Reviews: *Booklist* 6/1/1996, *SLJ* 6/1/1996

McCaffrey, Anne. ***Crystal Singer.*** 311 pages.

Ballantine 1985 0345327861 $5.99
Bantam 1980 Paper 0553258559 $7.50

When Killashandra Ree discovers that she can never be the opera star she's dreamed of becoming, she signs with the mysterious Heptite Guild for a dangerous, but potentially wildly profitable, job as a crystal singer on Ballybran. Desperately needed to power the galaxy's faster-than-light communications and travel, the crystals take a deadly toll on the health and sanity of those who mine them. Danger in an exotic setting, a heady sexual romance, and a headstrong protagonist determined to master any challenge and rise to the top make this an appealing book for many young women. Killashandra's adventures continue in the less absorbing sequels, *Killashandra* and *Crystal Line*. **Grades 9—12. KE**

McCaffrey, Anne. ***Dragonsinger.*** 264 pages.

Double Day 1978 Paper 0553141279 $10.00
Bantam 1977 Paper 0553258524 $7.50
Bantam 1983 Paper 0553258540 $7.50

If you were to purchase only one Anne McCaffrey novel, this would be it. The fourth book in the continuing adventures of Menolly of Pern, the first girl ever to be accepted to the prestigious Harper Hall, can easily stand alone, but your young readers will demand the earlier books once they've read *Dragonsinger*. The setting is half the fun and teens with musical ambitions will immediately place Pern's Harper Hall at the top of their "if only I could" list. Menolly is a misfit with special talents who makes good in a challenging and fantastical school setting—a story that will have extra appeal in the wake of the Harry Potter phenomenon. For those who want the entire series, clear the shelves. The original series begins with *Dragonsong*. A complete list is posted on McCaffrey's official Web site: www.annemccaffrey.org/.
Grades 9—12. PJ/KE <YALSA>

McDaniel, Lurlene. ***Don't Die, My Love.*** 256 pages.

Bantam Books 1995 Paper 0553567152 $4.99

The book that the Library of Congress selected for a time capsule project is a paint-by-numbers McDaniel weeper, and this is not a bad thing. Prep football star Luke and pretty, smart Julie are lifelong sweethearts and seemingly blessed with everything most teens could desire, but everything changes when Luke is diagnosed with Hodgkin's disease. The effect of that death sentence upon the two young people, as well as on their family and friends, is the heart of this heartbreaking novel. It is for-mula writing, but it works because McDaniel gets readers caring about the characters and caught up in the spirit of crisis. Even if the ending is inevitable and predictable, that doesn't diminish the writing. In fact, it is a testament to McDaniel's skill that she can tell the same story, more or less, over and over, yet each time she can make readers care and wish for a happy ending that never comes. **Grades 6—8. PJ**

Reviews: *Booklist,* 9/15/1995, *SLJ* 10/1/1995

McDaniel, Lurlene. ***Till Death Do Us Part.*** 214 pages.

Bantam Doubleday Dell 1997 Paper 0553570854 $4.99

The doctor's diagnosis for April Lancaster is not good. April has a brain tumor that cannot be operated on. She's only 18, and her future is uncertain. But when she meets Mark, a 21-year-old with a passion for car racing, she feels she has something to cherish in her life and a reason to battle on. But Mark is also battling a life-threat-ening illness—cystic fibrosis, and this leads April to a painful choice when Mark proposes marriage. Tragic love as only Lurlene McDaniel can provide in what has proven to be one of her most popular novels. **Grades 6—8. PJ**

McDonald, Janet. ***Spellbound.*** 138 pages.

Farrar Straus Giroux 2001 Trade 0374371407 $16.00

Raven, a 15-year-old high school dropout on welfare, lives with her mother and infant son in the projects of Brooklyn, as does her best friend, Aisha. Yet, Raven's sis-ter, Dell, got out of the projects and now has a successful career. Raven and Aisha both dream of escape, and much of the book is dialogue between the two young girls, loaded with humorous asides and high ambition. Raven's one chance, it seems, is to win a spelling bee that is offering a college scholarship as the grand prize. Like a sports novel, the narrative then becomes a tale of a young girl's struggle against incredible odds, not so much to win the big game as to become a better person in the process. Her quest is complicated by the reappearance of the baby's father into her life and the constant dark cloud of racism with its crippling effects upon young peo-ple of color. **Grades 7—10. PJ**

Reviews: *Booklist* 11/1/2001, *SLJ* 09/1/2001, *VOYA* 10/1/2001

McDonald, Joyce. ***Swallowing Stones.*** 245 pages.

Yearling 1999 Paper 0440226724 $4.99

The randomness of life and death is driven home in this remarkable novel about two teenagers brought together because of a tragic accident. At the party for his 17th birthday, Mike celebrates by firing a rifle into the air. The bullet lands, miles away, in a man working on his roof. Mike buries the rifle and tries forgetting the incident.

Fifteen-year-old Jenna, the daughter of the man who was shot, also tries to get on with her life. The narrative crosscuts between the two teens as circumstances draw them closer together to a stunning conclusion. **Grades 7—10. PJ <YALSA>**

Reviews: *Booklist* 10/15/1997

McKillip, Patricia A. ***The Forgotten Beasts of Eld.*** 217 pages.

Magic Carpet 1996 Paper 0152008691 $6.00

Possibly McKillip's best book; her evocative language and unusual imagery combine to achieve the poetic ideal. The mood of beauty, mystery and magic is almost a character in its own right. An ageless enchantress, who has summoned and mastered the most terrible and powerful of magical beasts—including a dragon—discovers that she is a novice in the ways of the heart when she takes on an abandoned child. The child and she begin on a—for her—terrible discovery of her own humanity and the nature of loss, regret, and love. Appropriate for both older and younger teens, though the more mature reader will get more out of the story. **Grades 7—10. KE**

McKillip, Patricia A. ***Ombria in Shadow.*** 304 pages.

Ace Books 2003 Paper 0441010164 $14.00
Ace Books 2002 Trade 044100895X $22.95

When the prince is murdered, his mistress is cast off into the street and his child becomes the puppet of Domina Pearl, the scheming sorceress who murdered him. In a Renaissance Venice-like city where the past is a living shadow that those touched by magic can sometimes inhabit and control, Domina's seemingly invincible power is challenged by those also touched by love and loyalty: the young prince's mysterious cousin, the cast-off mistress, and a fey child who is coming only slowly to understand that she, too, might be human. In the mysterious world of half-shadow and half-real, McKillip draws readers on by tantalizing them with the possibility of understanding its secrets. For older teens who enjoy magical realism and poetic storytelling, the stunning K.Y. Craft book cover guarantees that they will pick it up and examine it. **Grades 8—12. KE**

McKillip, Patricia. ***Riddle-Master: The Complete Trilogy.*** 592 pages.

Ace 1999 Paper 0441005968 $16.00

An omnibus edition composed of *The Riddle Master of Hed, The Heir to Sea and Fire,* and *The Harpist in the Wind.* Although McKillip is justly famous for her poetic imagery and coolly beautiful prose, in these original stories she also proves herself a master of plot and suspense. The hero, a young man named Morgan of Hed, begins to ask, "Who am I?" and touches off a whirlwind of danger and intrigue. His quest to discover the secret of his identity and why this mystery caused the murder of his parents and a threat to his own life and family also becomes a quest to discover the secret history of the marvelously crafted fantasy world in which he lives. This is a fine book to give fantasy readers who enjoy Big Quest Books as well as to those who demand beautiful language, thoughtful characterization, and a page-turning plot. It's also useful to give young men suffering from the misunderstanding that they cannot enjoy adventure stories with female heroines. The first book ends with a cliffhanger, and in the middle book, *Heir to Sea and Fire*, Morgan's lover Raederle picks up the story. **Grades 7–12. KE**

McKillip, Patricia A. ***The Tower at Stony Wood.*** 294 pages.

    Ace 2001 Paper 0441008291 $16.00

McKillip takes an old story and gives it an unusual twist. The king's bride is stolen and replaced by a magical shape-changer who will destroy him, and only his best friend, a brave young knight, can see the truth. Set within a fantastical world reminiscent of medieval Scotland and the Hebrides, the young knight flees the court to save the "true bride" only to find himself caught up in a seemingly endless series of distracting claims on his charity and strength. As is often the case with McKillip's later stories, the suspense of understanding what is actually going on in her magical world and getting to the heart of its secrets drives the plot. Most readers of fantasy should enjoy this one, and the stunning cover art will cause many teens to look it over. **Grades 7–10. KE**

McKinley, Robin. ***Beauty.*** 247 pages.

    HarperCollins 1993 Paper 0064404773 $5.99
    HarperCollins 1978 Trade 0060241497 $15.95

One of the finest retellings of Beauty and the Beast and the unacknowledged inspiration for the popular Disney movie, McKinley's heroine is a rather plain teenager named "Honour," whose nickname "Beauty" was a cruel taunt. The familiar tale is not so much changed as expanded, with deeper characterizations of the Beast, Beauty, her loving family, and their attempts to cope with sudden impoverishment. A fine book to give to both young fantasy readers and older teens who can't resist a well-told fairy tale. **Grades 6–12. KE <YALSA>**

McKinley, Robin. ***The Blue Sword.*** 272 pages.

    Ace 1982 Paper 0441068804 $5.99
    Puffin 2000 Paper 014130975X $5.99
    Greenwillow 1982 Trade 0688009387 $16.95

When Angharad Crewe, or "Harry" to her friends, joins her soldier-brother in his desert outpost station she is kidnapped by Corlath, king of the semi-nomadic Hillfolk. Harry adapts surprisingly well to life on horseback and to the magic of "kelar" that seems to be awakening in her, but her loyalties are challenged by a war that threatens to engulf both her people and Corlath's. McKinley has taken the exotic setting of Rudyard Kipling's *Kim* and turned it on its head: keeping all of the adventure, but with a female protagonist and the natives as the heroes. *The Blue Sword* is an intensely satisfying read, unabashedly romantic, but with a clean, tight narrative line. Readers of both fantasy and adventure are sure to demand more "Damar" novels once they've read this one. **Grades 6—12. KE <YALSA>**

McKinley, Robin. ***The Hero and the Crown.*** 246 pages.

> Berkley 1987 Paper 0441328091 $5.99
> Ace 1997 Paper 0441004997 $12.00

Often mistakenly billed as a "prequel" to *The Blue Sword, The Hero and the Crown* is about the courageous adventures of a fantasy heroine before she becomes the stuff of legend. Aerin is the seemingly talentless and clumsy daughter of the king of Damar, who finds solace and friendship when she nurses his former half-crippled war-horse back to health. Their partnership, and Aerin's enforced isolation from the power structure at court, will lead her down the road to her role as "Aerin-sol Dragon-slayer." Less action driven than *The Blue Sword*, Aerin's drive to create a future for herself, her struggling humanity, and McKinley's own distinctive and pleasing voice will keep readers wanting more. Do your teenage readers a favor, however; encourage them to read *The Blue Sword* first. **Grades 6—10. KE**

McKinley, Robin. ***The Outlaws of Sherwood.*** 282 pages.

> Ace 1989 Paper 0441644511 $6.50
> Firebird 2002 Paper 0698119592 $6.99
> Morrow 1988 Trade 0688071783 $17.00

A persuasive and congenial version of the Robin Hood story that takes a historical and realistic, rather then a magical or legendary, approach. Though neither die-hard Howard Pyle nor die-hard Robin McKinley fans will be completely pleased, this is the best—indeed, the only—modern novelization of the legend for older teens. Despite her desire to remain "historically unembarrassing," McKinley retains most of the traditional accoutrements of the legend while bringing changes to themes of love, loyalty, feminism, and tolerance. Her Robin Hood remains a neat resetting of a classic story within the concerns of the 20th century. **Grades 6—12. KE**

McKinley, Robin. ***Spindle's End.*** 422 pages.

> Ace 2001 Paper 0441008658 $6.50
> Firebird 2002 Paper 0698119509 $6.99
> G.P. Putnam's Sons 2000 Trade 0399234667 $19.99

As the premier teller of fairy tale novels, McKinley takes the Sleeping Beauty story and transplants it into her legendary "ancient" Damar, telling us the story of what the Beauty ("Rosie") was doing all those long years she was hidden from the spiteful curse of the wicked enchantress: apprenticing herself to the village blacksmith. The novel twists on a familiar story; the well-realized and engaging characters and McKinley's distinctive storytelling voice are all present in *Spindle's End*. Readers will find themselves quickly absorbed by McKinley's original setting and hooked by the constant threat overlying the ordinary magic of Rosie's life. Teenage fans of McKinley's lighter books will not be disappointed by this romp, despite the bitter-sweet ending. **Grades 6–12. KE**

Reviews: *Booklist* 4/15/2000, *SLJ* 6/1/2000, *VOYA* 4/1/2000

McNamee, Graham. ***Hate You.*** 119 pages.

Laurel-Leaf 2000 Paper 0440227623 $4.99

A powerful look at families and forgiveness. Told in the first person, this is the story of Alice, a talented young songwriter who would love to sing her own creations, but her abusive father shattered her voice box when she was a young child. After years of hating him from afar, Alice learns that her father is dying, and she must summon the courage to face her violent past, her painful present, and an uncertain future. Alice is angry, funny, and smart—with an emphasis on angry. A rough coming-of-age story about a young girl finding her "voice" in more ways than one. **Grades 7–10. PJ**

Reviews: *Booklist* 2/1/1999, *SLJ* 3/1/1999, *VOYA* 4/1/1999

Meyer, Carolyn. ***White Lilacs.*** 242 pages.

Gulliver 1993 Paper 0152958762 $6.00
Gulliver 1993 Trade 0152006419 $12.00

With the "based on the true story" kicker, Meyer tells a story that seems so unreal and inhumane that it is hard to believe the events took place. Meyer invents a character, Rose Lee, a young African American girl growing up during the 1920s in the Texas town of Dillon. Like most southern towns, the city is segregated, with blacks living in a section called Freedom. The irony is heavy as the white residents elect to evict the residents of Freedom so they can build a "whites-only" park. Rose Lee depicts the events of the final days, which include a Klan march and an attack on her brother. **Grades 7–10. PJ**

Reviews: *Booklist* 11/1/1993, *SLJ* 10/1/1993

Mikaelsen, Ben. ***Petey.*** 280 pages.

Hyperion 2000 Paper 0786813369 $5.99
Hyperion 1998 Trade 0786804262 $15.95

The first part of the book introduces Petey, who is born with cerebral palsy. But since that part of the story takes place in 1905, the doctors misdiagnose his illness. Rather than getting treatment, Petey is locked away in a series of institutions. The story shoots forward when Trevor, a rather self-centered teenage boy, reluctantly befriends the now elderly Petey. The second part of the novel is mostly about Trevor's finding value in helping Petey achieve a quality of life in his final days to make up for all that was taken from him at an early age. The book is quite deliberately sentimental and pulls all the right strings, demonstrating what happens when people, regardless of age or ability, are able to really connect. **Grades 6—9. PJ**

Reviews: *Booklist* 11/1/1998, *SLJ* 11/1/1998, *VOYA* 2/1/1999

Mikaelsen, Ben. ***Touching Spirit Bear.*** 256 pages

HarperCollins 2002 Paper 038080560X $5.95
HarperCollins 2001 Trade 0060291494 $16.89

Ben Cole has been getting into trouble for violence all his life. When he bashes Peter's head against the cement repeatedly and puts him into a coma, Cole is arrested and offered the choice between going to jail or "Circle Justice." He chooses Circle Justice, thinking it will be easy to escape. He is sent to live alone on an island in Alaska. **Grades 6—9. (Annotation by Hope Baugh)**

Reviews: *Booklist* 1/15/2001, *SLJ* 2/1/2001, *VOYA* 6/1/2001

Miklowitz, Gloria. ***Past Forgiving.*** 153 pages.

Simon & Schuster 1995 Trade 0671884425 $16.00

Fifteen-year-old Alexandra is deeply in love with her new boyfriend Cliff, despite his short temper. That's only a flash of a far darker side of this personality, which soon seeks to control every aspect of Alexandra's life. At first, she blames herself as Cliff's abuse escalates, before realizing she needs to get out of the relationship in order to stay alive. Notable as one of the first novels to tackle the subject of dating violence, it is pretty standard movie-of-the-week stuff, never getting deeply into the issues or the characters. Yet, with so few books on the subject, there is enough here to make it a core collection pick, as well as a way to introduce readers to the prolific Miklowitz. **Grades 7—10. PJ**

Reviews: *Booklist* 5/1/1995, *SLJ* 6/1/1995

Mitchell, Margaret. ***Gone with the Wind.*** 959 pages.

Warner Paper 0446365386 $7.99

Perhaps the most famous novel in the history of American publishing, it is surprising today how many younger people have yet to read it. Mitchell's tight, yet descriptive, prose, her unforgettable characters, and her story of thwarted love set against the Civil War and Reconstruction all remain as a yardstick for excellence to anyone wanting to read or write the Great American Novel. While the three-plus-hour movie continues as a superb achievement, time constraints forced the deletion of many characters and scenes, and it is not a complete substitute for the Margaret Mitchell experience. The story of Scarlett O'Hara, Rhett Butler, Ashley Wilkes, and Melanie Wilkes plays out across a massive landscape of time and action, and it is still a glorious read for anyone over the age of 12. If you hear grumbling about finishing so long a novel, remind your readers that "tomorrow IS another day." **Grades 10—12. PT**

Montgomery, Lucy Maud. ***Anne of Green Gables.*** 320 pages.

> Alfred A. Knopf 1995 Library 0679444750 $14.95
> Scholastic 2002 Paper 0439295777 $4.99

The classic adventures of Anne Shirley, red-haired orphan sent to Prince Edward Island as a farm hand, hasn't lost any of its appeal over its long publishing history. As ward of Marilla and Matthew Cuthbert of Green Gables, Anne dives into life full force, always emerging with new friends. She's also always getting into scrapes, and these episodes define the tragicomedy of her existence. Particularly appealing for younger girls, the novel is the first of eight; you might want to include the whole set for Green Gable fans: *Anne of Green Gables, Anne of the Island, Anne of Avonlea, Anne of Windy Poplars, Anne's House of Dreams, Anne of Ingleside, Rainbow Valley,* and *Rilla of Ingleside.* **Grades 6—10. PT**

Moriarty, Jaclyn. ***Feeling Sorry for Celia.*** 288 pages.

> St. Martin's Press 2002 0312287364 $12.95

Moriarty manages to convey exactly who these characters are without breaking voice as they write to each other. Relationships between the players and plot are all flaw-lessly conveyed, and the humorous letters from Elizabeth's imaginary groups, such as the Association of Teenagers, provide crystal clear insight into the self-esteem prob-lems so many young adults face. Although this book will naturally attract more girls than boys, there are some boys who will read and enjoy it, if only because the letters make the text easy to swallow in small doses. **Grades 6—9. (Annotation by Spring Lee Boehler)**

Morris, Gerald. ***The Squire's Tale.*** 212 pages.

> Houghton Mifflin 1998 Trade 0395869595 $15.00

When Terrence, a boy with a mysterious past, meets Sir Gawain of Camelot, he jumps at the chance to become his squire. In the course of their adventures, Terrence comes into his own and discovers the secret of his parentage. There's swordplay and magical danger aplenty, and the plot moves swiftly along. Loosely based on Mallory's *Morte d'Artur,* but with all the boring and inconsistent bits struck out and plenty of light humor, Morris' series of Arthurian adventures is the boys' answer to *Ella*

Enchanted and is sure to be a hit with most middle school teens. Terrence and Gawain's adventures continue in the sequel, *The Squire, His Knight and His Lady*, which retells the legend of Sir Gawain and the Green Knight. **Grades 6—9. KE**

Reviews: *Booklist* 4/15/1998, *SLJ* 7/1/1998

Morrison, Toni. ***Beloved.*** 275 pages.

Random 1998 Paper 0375704140 $19.95
Alfred A. Knopf 1987 Trade 0394535979 $27.50
Random 1998 Trade 037540273X $16.95

There are reasons Toni Morrison won the Nobel Prize for literature, and this book is one of them. Having garnered a Pulitzer as well, *Beloved* is a ghost story with the primary haunt being the memories of slavery living on in 1870s Ohio. Having made her way north after unspeakable brutalities were visited upon her as a slave, Sethe wants little more than peace for her family and relief from the memories of her dead baby, known only as Beloved. When the spirit of a murdered child begins to turn things upside down in Sethe's household, she finds herself encouraging it, half believing it is her Beloved come back to her. With that as a starting point, the novel weaves back and forth in time, complex, horrifying, and realistic. *Beloved* is considered—and rightly so—to be Morrison's greatest book, and for those ready for it, should not be missed. **Grades 10—12 (mature). PT**

Morrison, Toni. ***The Bluest Eye.*** 215 pages.

NAL 1994 Paper 0452273056 $12.95
Plume 2000 Paper 0452282195 $12.95
Alfred A. Knopf 2000 Trade 0375411550 $15.00

Of her first novel, published in 1970, Toni Morrison has noted the lack of sophistication in its structure and language. Fortunately for her readers, Morrison's impossibly high standards do not detract from the accomplishment of *The Bluest Eye*, the book that set up the themes she has followed for the last 30 years: racism, memory, and the weapon that is language (to be wielded for defense or offense as the occasion arises). In 1941, Pecola Breedlove takes stock of her family in Lorain, Ohio, and finds them each and every one revoltingly ugly. She doesn't spare herself from the same condemnation, but her lack of physical beauty doesn't protect her from being raped and impregnated by her own father, patriarch and poster boy for dysfunctional families. Though Pecola manages to recount the miseries inflicted upon herself without falling victim to a victim's voice, she does wish mightily she looked like someone with the "blondest hair and the bluest eye," supposing such transformation would change her very life. It is evidence of Morrison's reputation as perhaps the greatest novelist living today that we see the world through Pecola's non-blue eyes while simultaneously retaining our own vision as bystanders to the often unspeakable events recounted here. **Grades 10—12 (mature). PT**

Mosher, Richard. **Zazoo.** 248 pages.

Clarion 2001 Trade 0618135340 $16.00

One of Amazon.com's Best of 2001, this is a suspense story of a different sort. It is not a thriller; instead the mystery at hand is Zazoo, a 14-year-old orphan girl looking for clues into her past. Zazoo lives in France with her adoptive grandfather, but she knows she was born in Vietnam. She is haunted by vague memories of that war-torn country, just as her grandfather can never escape his actions during World War II. This intergenerational story about two people is driven forward by the dialogue between Zazoo and her grandfather, while history pulls them toward harsh truths that emerge in time of war. **Grades 7–10. PJ**

Reviews: *Booklist* 12/15/2001, *SLJ* 11/1/2001, *VOYA* 10/1/2001

Mowry, Jess. **Babylon Boyz.** 211 pages.

Pocket 1999 Paper 0689825927 $7.99

The title refers to a group of inner-city teens, Dante, Pook, and Wyatt, who are faced with a difficult ethical decision. All of them are outsiders, forever looking for a place to fit. While they bring each other friendship, they can't help each other escape from their violent Oakland neighborhood, which is as much a war zone as it is a community. But when they find a large package of cocaine, it provides them with the means to get the money to escape their fate. Yet, to sell the drugs, they realize, would be to help inflict more misery in the hood. What to do? With graphic descriptions of gang violence and occasional sex scenes, this is a gritty portrait of the lives of some young men of color. **Grades 8–10. PJ**

Mowry, Jess. **Way Past Cool.** 309 pages.

HarperCollins 1993 Paper 0060975458 $13.95

A gang of young African American boys, whose leader is only 13 years old, battles for turf in a rough section of Oakland when a 16-year-old drug dealer instigates a fight with them. But the dealer's unwilling bodyguard emerges as the key player in this tense street drama. This is a gangsta equivalent to *The Outsiders*, complete with street battles, busted families, and dreams of making it alive. **Grades 9–12 (mature). PJ**

Murphy, Rita. **Night Flying.** 129 pages.

Laurel-Leaf 2002 Paper 0440228379 $4.99
Delacorte 2000 Trade 038532748X $14.95

This coming-of-age story captured the Delacorte Press Prize for First Young Adult Novel. Georgie's house is run by her grandmother's strict rules and severe punishments. As Georgie prepares for her 16th birthday, she faces a mix of fear and excitement at the prospect of her first solo flight. In tradition of magic realism, this is the story of a young woman with the power to fly, but lacking the willpower to stand up for herself until her rebellious aunt provides her with support. Despite the heavy metaphor, the book is lyrical in describing Georgie's flight toward independence. **Grades 7–10. PJ**

> Reviews: *Booklist* 12/15/2000, *SLJ* 11/1/2000

Myers, Walter Dean. ***145th Street: Short Stories.*** 151 pages.

> Laurel-Leaf 2001 Paper 0440229162 $5.50
> Delacorte 2000 Trade 0385321376 $15.95

A collection of stories about one neighborhood in Harlem, although the setting is about the only thing these stories have in common. There are a rich variety of teen characters, from hip high school hoop star Jamie to the quiet middle school Cassandra named Angela, to "Big Time Henson," a young man already looking death in the face. Myers is the mix-master, putting stories with comic spin against those that are placed under a shadow of sorrow and a storm of violence. **Grades 7–10. PJ**

> Reviews: *Booklist* 12/15/1999, *SLJ* 4/1/2000

Myers, Walter Dean. ***Fallen Angels.*** 309 pages.

> Scholastic 1991 Paper 0590409433 $4.99
> Scholastic 1988 Trade 0590409425 $16.95

Banned in more than one school because of four-letter-filled language, Myers presents the definitive YA novel about Vietnam. The main character is Perry, who finds himself "in country" rather than at college. In addition to the typical, albeit well done, battle scenes showing the horror of war, Myers has Perry not just firing bullets, but also firing off questions about why he (i.e., the United States) is there. Winner of the Coretta Scott King Award. **Grades 8–12 (mature). PJ <HIPPLE> <MOCK> <YALSA>**

> Reviews: *SLJ* 6/1/1988

Myers, Walter Dean. ***Monster.*** 281 pages.

> HarperCollins 1999 Library 0060280786 $15.89
> HarperTempest 2001 Paper 0064407314 $6.99
> HarperCollins 1999 Trade 0060280778 $15.95

Did he do it? Is he innocent? Teens can go around and around, contemplating the issues and discussing the situations in this interesting and creative novel. The format is the main attraction. As 16-year-old Steve Harmon tries to figure out how he ended up in prison and accused of being an accomplice to a murder, he sorts things out by constructing a screenplay of his experiences in jail and in the courtroom—and the things that led him there. **Grades 7–10. (Annotation by Diane Tuccillo) <PRINTZ>**

Reviews: *Booklist* 5/1/1999, *SLJ* 7/1/1999

Myers, Walter Dean. ***Scorpions.*** 216 pages.

HarperCollins 1988 Library 0060243651 $16.89
HarperTrophy 1996 Paper 0064406237 $5.99

This Newbery Honor Book shows the devastating effects of gangs upon one family.
When 12-year-old Jamal's brother Randy is sent to prison, the members of Randy's
gang look for a new leader. They find one in Jamal, although he wants nothing to do
with the life. The book is tough and gritty, and the tension escalates when Jamal
acquires a gun. It seems like Jamal is going to become just another statistic, unless he
can turn his life around. **Grades 6–9. PJ**

Myers, Walter Dean. ***Slam.*** 266 pages.

Signature 1998 Paper 0590486683 $4.99

Myers revisits basketball in another coming-of-age story. Like Lonnie Jackson, Greg
Harris is a natural on the hardwoods and somewhat of a loss off the court. He dreams of
escaping to the NBA, but the gravity of his circumstances hold him back—trouble brewing at home, at his new primarily white school, and on the streets with his friends.
Like Lipsyte's *The Contender*, this is a story of Harris' learning that making choices in
life is harder than any game he will ever play. **Grades 7–10. PJ <TEN><YALSA>**

Reviews: *Booklist* 11/15/1996, *SLJ* 11/1/1996

Myers, Walter Dean. ***Somewhere in the Darkness.*** 168 pages.

Apple 1997 Paper 0590341863 $4.99

While the story is somewhat light on plot, it is heavy in describing the complex relationship between 14-year-old Jimmy and his convict father. Jimmy lives with his grandmother
and has never known his father, Crab. Crab, who has escaped from prison, convinces
Jimmy to travel with him. The road trip bonds Jimmy and his father, even if Jimmy can
never really accept Crab's criminal life. The book is dialogue heavy as Jimmy and Crab
work out their relationship. One of the few novels dealing with teens with criminal parents, this is one of Myers' most important works. **Grades 7–10. PJ <YALSA>**

Na, An. ***Step from Heaven.*** 156 pages.

Front Street 2001 Trade 1886910588 $15.95

There's a story/joke told about immigrants arriving in the United States at Ellis
Island expecting the streets to be paved with gold. First they find the streets are not
paved with gold; then they find the streets are not paved at all, finally they learn it is

the immigrant's job to pave the street. That's the theme here as Korean-born Young Ju Park and her family learn that life in the United States is not perfect; it is a step from heaven. As she grows up, her parents fear she will neglect her Korean culture. But as she grows into a strong, confident young woman, her father declines: his rage is directed outward at his wife and children and inward through depression and drunkenness. *A Step from Heaven* thus works on many levels: as a coming-of-age story, as a story about rising above a dysfunctional family, and as a story about the immigrant experience, all of it told in the present tense in poetic language, sprinkled with Korean words. **Grades 7—10. PJ <PRINTZ>**

Reviews: *Booklist* 6/1/2001, *SLJ* 5/1/2001, *VOYA* 6/1/2001

Napoli, Donna Jo. **Beast.** 272 pages.

Atheneum 2000 Trade 0689835892 $17.00
Pocket Books 2002 Paper 0689835906 $8.00

At the same time comic pranksters like Jon Sciezka and Lane Smith are cranking fairy tales through a parody machine, authors like Napoli are revisiting these stories to explore and expand the characters behind them. This is a prequel to *Beauty and the Beast* as Napoli traces the story of the "beast" from a dashing young Persian prince to a creature walking on all fours. Filling the tale with Persian and Arabic language, Napoli provides a rich texture to allow readers to really understand the Beast's character and his underlying humanity, from his passion for roses to his search for true love. **Grades 8—10. PJ**

Reviews: *Booklist* 10/15/2000, *SLJ* 9/1/2001

Napoli, Donna Jo. **The Magic Circle.** 118 pages.

Puffin 1995 Paper 0140374396 $4.99
Dutton 1993 Trade 0525451277 $15.99

As any fan of action films knows, the more despicable the villain, the better the film. Without evil, there can be no good. The question then always is, what makes evil? Napoli provides the background story for the witch in the Hansel and Gretel story. The story finds the witch making a deal with the devil to earn the power to heal. But like all Faustian bargains, there's a catch that transforms the healer into a witch who seeks to kill, not cure children. Thus, her fiery end isn't a horrible death, but a release from the spell of evil cast over her. **Grades 6—9. PJ**

Reviews: *Booklist* 1/1/1995, *SLJ* 1/1/1995

Nelson, Theresa. **Earthshine.** 182 pages.

Orchard 1994 Trade 0531068676 $16.95

One of the early AIDS novels and still one of the best. The female protagonist, nicknamed Slim, lives in L.A. with her father, an actor, and his lover. But also living in the house is AIDS, which infects her father. She goes to a support group for children whose parents have AIDS and there she encounters Isaiah. The name fits him as he is a true believer, refusing to accept his mother's death (book was written pre-AZT) and instead he attempts to get Slim to join him in seeking out a "healer" called the Miracle Man. Slim is torn: waiting for a miracle to come through, yet knowing deep down she must come to terms with her father's terminal disease. **Grades 7–10. PJ <YALSA>**

Reviews: *Booklist* 9/1/1994, *SLJ* 9/1/1994

Neufeld, John. ***Lisa, Bright and Dark.*** 125 pages.

Puffin 1999 Paper 0141304340 $5.99
Signet 1969 Paper 0451166841 $5.99
S.G. Phillips 1969 Trade 087599153X $26.95

For 30 years, this novel of a 16-year-old girl's descent into madness has worked its power on readers in much the same way as *I Never Promised You a Rose Garden*. The hook in this one is tragic: Lisa Shilling's parents and teachers refuse to acknowledge the downward spiral her mental health is taking; only her friends offer compassion and attempted help. Still powerful as an indictment of the adult world refusing to involve itself in the very real slings and arrows that teenage flesh is heir to, *Lisa, Bright and Dark* is perhaps—sadly—more relevant now than ever. **Grades 7–10. PT**

Newth, Mette. ***The Dark Light.*** 246 pages.

Farrar, Straus & Giroux 1998 Trade 0374317011 $18.00

Norwegian author Mette Newth gave young adult literature a shot in the arm with this highly unusual tale of a 13-year-old girl who, struck with leprosy in early 19th-century Norway, learns to travel beyond the physical confines of her disease by reading books. Haunting and evocative, *The Dark Light* defies categorization. **Grades 8–10. (Annotation by Jennifer Hubert) <LOST>**

Reviews: *Booklist* 6/15/1998, *SLJ* 6/1/1988, *VOYA* 2/1/1999

Niven, Larry. ***Ringworld.*** 342 pages.

Del Rey 1992 Paper 0345333926 $6.99

Imagine that all the planets in a solar system have been cannibalized to build a giant ring 600,000,000 miles long and 1,000,000 miles wide around its sun: Two humans and two aliens crash on this "ringworld," built, they think, by alien engineers. Solid characterization keeps the reader interested in their adventures as they explore the new world, but the big draw is Niven's thoroughly worked-out engineering marvel and the secret behind its construction. Fans of hard science fiction looking for that "sense of wonder" need look no further. The lackluster (and unnecessary) sequels are *Ringworld Engineers* and *The Ringworld Throne*. **Grades 9—12. KE**

Nix, Garth. *Sabriel.* 292 pages.

> HarperTrophy 1997 Paper 0064471837 $6.99
> HarperCollins 1996 Trade 0060273224 $17.95

When her father, the Abhorsen, contacts teenage Sabriel from beyond death, she leaves her safe girls' school on the reality-based side of the wall, and returns to her magical and deadly homeland. There she must take up her father's role as an anti-necromancer to save him, and her world, from those who would destroy the boundary between life and death. Sabriel has a strong and believable voice as a young woman tested beyond her expectations. Nix's concept of constitutional magic, where chaos and power are bounded by contracts that the hereditary magicians can perceive and work within, is very clever, increasing the sense of plausibility his well-developed world creates. As fantasy edged with horror, fans of both genres will enjoy. **Grades 7—10. KE <YALSA>**

> Reviews: *Booklist* 10/1/1996, *SLJ* 9/1/1996

Nix, Garth. *Shade's Children.* 312 pages.

> HarperTrophy 1998 Paper 0064471969 $6.99
> HarperCollins 1997 Trade 0060273240 $17.95

In a world where all the adults mysteriously disappeared decades ago, the children are raised in dormitories as fodder for the Overlord's games. On the "sad" 13th birthday their brains and bodies are harvested to create monsters. Ella and her friends, however, have escaped and found refuge with Shade, an intelligent computer program who arms them, trains them, and promises to help them retake their world—but intends, in the end to betray them. The strong and well-developed lead characters, particularly teenage Ella and Drum, draw the reader into their story, so that the bittersweet ending really packs a punch. This mixture of action-adventure, science fiction, and horror should have wide appeal among teens both old and young. **Grades 7—10. KE <LOST>**

> Reviews: *Booklist* 10/1/1997, *SLJ* 8/1/1997

Nixon, Joan Lowery. *The Other Side of Dark.* 185 pages.

> Dell 1987 Paper 0440966388 $4.99

One of Nixon's best and most lasting mysteries starts with a great hook. Stacy wakes up in a hospital bed totally disoriented. She has been in a coma for four years as a result of a gunshot wound. She was shot at the same time that her mother was killed.

Once she awakens, there is great press coverage leading to a renewed interest in the case by both the public and the criminal. **Grades 6—9. PJ**

Nixon, Joan Lowery. *The Séance.* 142 pages.

Dell 1981 Paper 0440979374 $4.99

An early Nixon work with another great premise. A group of teenage girls get together for a séance. Even though the young woman acting as the medium is faking, strange things still occur, including the disappearance of one of the girls. Soon that girl is found dead, and then another one is missing. The title alone is a sure winner. **Grades 6—9. PJ**

Nixon, Joan Lowery. *Whispers from the Dead.* 192 pages.

Bantam Doubleday Dell 1991 Paper 0440208092 $4.99

Sarah has the gift: She has the ability to hear voices of the dead. When her parents move into a new house, she discovers, to her horror, that it is the site of a hideous murder, as yet unsolved. The obvious tie-in with pop culture (the TV show *Crossing Over* and the movie *The Sixth Sense*) cause this Nixon mystery to rise above the others, if not in quality, then in teens' interest. **Grades 6—9. PJ**

Nolan, Han. *Born Blue.* 277 pages.

Harcourt 2001 Trade 0152019162 $17.00

Janine, aka Leshaya, is a survivor; it is not like she has any choice in the matter, as life keeps dealing her knock-out blows. Born to a heroin-addicted mother, her childhood is spent in foster homes, passed around from person to person, and few take time to parent her. Her only salvation is music, for when she opens her mouth to sing, then and only then, does Janine feel alive. Yet, she looks all over for love: in food, in drugs, and always, always falling in with the wrong man. Her mother kidnaps her, sells her for drugs, and yet somehow Janine keeps pushing on, sure that this is merely the hard road she must travel in order to find success. **Grades 10—12 (mature). PJ**

Reviews: *Booklist* 9/15/2001, *SLJ* 11/1/2001, *VOYA* 10/1/2001

Nolan, Han. *Dancing on the Edge.* 244 pages.

Puffin 1999 Paper 0141302038 $5.99
Harcourt 1997 Trade 0152016481 $16.00

The 1997 National Book Award-winner for youth literature tells the story of a lonely young girl's search for love and acceptance. Her entrance into the world was not an easy one: she lived but her mother died. As she reaches adolescence, her father goes missing and she suffers a breakdown after burning herself in a strange incident. In this book, which has been compared with novels such as The Bell Jar, Nolan gives readers a fascinating look into the mind of a young woman who dances on the edge of sanity, and back again. **Grades 7—10. PJ**

Reviews: *Booklist* 10/1/1997, *SLJ* 9/1/1997, *VOYA* 2/1/199

Nolan, Han. *If I Should Die Before I Wake.* 225 pages.

Harcourt 1996 Paper 0152380418 $6.00
Harcourt 1994 Trade 015238040X $18.00

Nolan's first novel uses a time-travel conceit to explore a wide variety of issues. In a hospital ICU are two patients: one a rebellious young woman who flirts with neo-Nazi beliefs; the other Chana Bergman, an elderly Holocaust survivor. The younger woman, Hilary, is in a coma and in this state "merges" herself into Chana's memories of the Holocaust. The book then becomes a Holocaust novel as Hilary (as Chana) struggles with life first in the ghetto, and then in the camps. While many faulted the book's conclusion and Hilary's conversion, the premise and the precise detailing of Chana's life create an intriguing read. **Grades 7—10. PJ**

Reviews: *Booklist* 4/1/1994, *SLJ* 4/1/1994

Noon, Jeff. *Vurt.* 324 pages.

St. Martin's 1996 Paper 0312141440 $13.95

The idea of a drugged-out future is nothing new, but Noon spins his tale with 50 years of pop culture behind him and the promise of virtual reality clearly in everyone's entertainment future. Noon also plugs into the ethos of cyberpunk: the book is a mix of William Gibson and Huxley, with a tip of the hat to the thug life found in *A Clockwork Orange*. With those three influences, Noon then writes up a storm about his character Scribble's search for his sister and for the mysterious English Voodoo. Along the way, he and his pals steal, drink, fight, and always, always, get loaded up on Vurt, the surreal stuff that dreams are made of. *Vurt* won the 1994 Arthur C. Clarke Award for Best Science Fiction Novel. **Grades 10—12 (mature). PJ**

O'Brien, Robert. *Z for Zachariah.* 246 pages.

Macmillan 1975 Paper 0020446500 $4.99

It's the end of the world as we know it, and 14-year-old Ann Burden, one of the survivors, feels anything but fine. She is alone and scared; every day is a struggle for physical and emotional survival. When it seems as if she can no longer go out, a stranger arrives and she believes that things are returning to normal—she needs to think again. **Grades 7—10. PJ <YALSA>**

O'Brien, Tim. ***Going after Cacciato.*** 338 pages.

> Broadway Books 1999 Paper 0767904427 $13.00
> Dell 1992 0440329655 $5.99

The film *Saving Private Ryan* depicts the brutal realism of World War II as an entire squad is sent in to find one soldier; the book *Going after Cacciato* uses magical realism to depict the nightmare qualities of Vietnam as an entire squad chases after the elusive Private Cacciato, who is walking from Vietnam to Paris to shake things up at the peace talks. This winner of the National Book Award is not only one of the definitive novels to capture the American Vietnam experience; more than that, it is a small epic about a journey into the dark heart, stranger than any taken by Conrad. **Grades 10–12. PJ**

O'Brien, Tim. ***The Things They Carried.*** 288 pages.

> Penguin Putnam 1991 Paper 014014773X $12.95

A genre-busting book tracing the Vietnam experiences of a group of young men, one of whom is the author Tim O'Brien. But it is not autobiography, it just reads that way because O'Brien makes his characters come alive in this volume of 22 interconnected short pieces. In some ways, this is a family saga, except these young men are not related by name but rather by time, place, and the horror of Vietnam. Through dialogue and deft description, O'Brien places readers "in country" so they can experience the emotional rainstorm of those who went to Vietnam, almost all of whom came back with their lives permanently scarred. **Grades 10–12 (mature). PJ <YALSA>**

O'Dell, Scott. ***Black Star, Bright Dawn.*** 134 pages.

> Fawcett 1990 Paper 0449703401 $6.50
> Houghton Mifflin 1988 Trade 0395477786 $17.00

O'Dell is an author walking the fine line between juvenile books for grades four through six and those for the youngest teenagers. While many of his books are fodder for the historical-fiction required reading, they are some of the finest examples of that genre. With an attention to accurate details, yet still using timeless themes, O'Dell rarely fails to satisfy. Bright Star, a 17-year-old Eskimo girl, is thrust into a leadership role because of her father's injury. She finds herself charged with running the Iditarod, the more than 1,000-mile-long dogsled race across Alaska, thus adding a classic man-versus-nature conflict to go along with the strong female coming-of-age story. **Grades 6–9. PJ**

> Reviews: *SLJ* 5/1/1988

Oke, Janette. ***Dana's Valley.*** 300 pages.

> Bethany House 2001 Paper 0764224514 $11.99

Bethany House 2001 Trade 0764225146 $15.99

Oke is one of the all-time best-selling Christian fiction authors, popular with readers of all ages. This volume, co-authored with her daughter, moves away from her
normal historic setting à la Laura Ingalls Wilder and more into the land of Lurlene
McDaniel. The story concerns Dana, a teenage girl, who is stricken with cancer.
Rather than pulling the family together, the disease shakes the foundations of the
family, including Dana's sister's religious conviction. While the book isn't ultimately successful either as Christian fiction or trauma drama, this might introduce
to Oke some readers who would never wander over to the inspirational fiction
area. **Grades 8–10. PJ**

Orr, Wendy. *Peeling the Onion.* 166 pages.

> Holiday House 1997 Trade 082341289X $16.95
> Laurel-Leaf 1999 Paper 0440227739 $4.99

A book similar to *Izzy Willy Nilly* by Voigt and Crutcher's *Crazy Horse Electric
Game* about a teenager's valiant struggle to overcome a disability brought on by an
accident. Anna's neck is broken, and so is the telling of the tale as Orr uses a diary
format with short slices from Anna's life. The normal issues for teens of fitting in,
getting along with parents, and finding a place in the world are magnified a hundred
times for Anna, whose main goal is simply to walk normally again. This book is also
about Anna's attempts to cope with the almost unmanageable and unimaginable pain
her accident has caused. Yet, she must face the most painful step of all: meeting the
man who caused the accident that changed her life forever and shattered her dreams.
Grades 7–10. PJ <YALSA>

> Reviews: *Booklist* 4/1/1997, *SLJ* 5/1/1997, *SLJ* 12/1/1997

Orwell, George. *1984.* 314 pages.

> Signet Classic 1950 Paper 0451524934 $6.95
> Signet 1983 Paper 0452262933 $12.95
> Harcourt 2001 Trade 0151351015 $20.01

Big Brother seems to be watching almost as closely in reality these days as he was in
Orwell's "futuristic" novel originally published in 1949. Bringing additions to the dictionary (newspeak, thought police, etc.), Orwell created a dystopia where even a rea-
sonable questioning thought could bring the wrath of the Party down on its hapless
citizenry. Winston Smith exists in constant danger for the dreadful crime of retaining
his memory. He knows the Party's press releases concerning its winnings of its constant world wars are so much wishful thinking and that history is literally rewritten
and recreated daily. Joining an underground resistance group called The Brotherhood,
Winston, along with his forbidden love, Julia, sets out to see if a small band can
reclaim the world from the great powers squeezing all humanity out of it. Still a razor-

sharp condemnation against the failures of communism, *1984* remains an excellent introduction to political satire for high school and above. **Grades 8—12. PT**

Orwell, George. ***Animal Farm.*** 140 pages.

> Signet 1996 Paper 0451526341 $6.95
> Alfred A. Knopf 1993 Trade 0679420398 $15.00
> Harcourt 1996 Trade 0151002177 $30.00

"All animals are equal, but some are more equal than others." With that single cele-brated sentence George Orwell summed up the hypocrisies of totalitarian regimes advertising themselves as "people's" governments. When the animals take over the farm in this fantasy/satire, everything seems to be halcyon; too soon, however, the pigs begin taking over, flaunting the rules they themselves made (animals will not smoke, drink, wear clothes, gamble, sleep in beds, etc.). A group of chickens too dumb to stop pointing out the pigs' inconsistencies simply vanish (perhaps to the rural version of a gulag), and before long, the decent, idealistic animals are doing all the backbreaking labor and the pigs are negotiating with the Enemy—human beings. The satire may be broad, but the book has entered the ranks of American classics because it is unique. Nearly any reading level can access the story; the message dif-fers as to one's level of knowledge of history and political savvy. **Grades 7—12. PT**

Palahniuk, Chuck. ***Fight Club.*** 208 pages.

> Henry Holt 1999 Paper 0805062971 $13.00
> Penguin 1999 1565113306 $24.95

An underground classic since its first publication in 1996, *Fight Club* is recognized as the most original and provocative gen-X novel published, and that Brad Pitt movie cer-tainly didn't hurt sales. This is a very, very, very dark novel about a nameless white-collar drone who hates his empty brand-name life. He is a zombie who finally comes to life when he forms an after-hours fight club that would make Vince McMahon proud. The catalyst for his transformation is the charismatic Tyler, who is all id, in more ways than one. A tale that is violent, sexy, and then more violent. Few public libraries would house this in their young adult area, but it's exactly the type of novel that Hesse-read-ing high school hipsters will want to explore. **Grades 10—12 (mature). PJ**

Paterson, Katherine. ***Jacob Have I Loved.*** 216 pages.

> HarperTrophy 1990 Paper 0064403688 $6.50
> HarperTrophy 1990 Paper 0064470598 $6.50

This story of sibling rivalry between twins is one of the most honored books for youth. For all the "problem" novels and gritty fiction that would follow, Paterson tack-les head-on the biggest "problem" of all: the complicated process known as growing up and establishing a unique identity. The Newbery selection committee noted that "the novel's strength of characterization and memorable external and internal action mark this superbly crafted novel." **Grades 7–10. PJ <HIPPLE> <MOCK><YALSA>**

Paterson, Katherine. **Lyddie.** 182 pages.

> Puffin 1995 Paper 0140373896 $5.99
> Lodestar 1978 Trade 0525673385 $15.99

Paterson captures the life of the "Lowell" mill girls perfectly in this historical fiction with timeless themes about making choices and standing up for one's self. Like most of the mill girls, Lyddie has moved from the farm to work in the factory to help support her family, or in this case, to reunite her family. Desperate for money and in need of a job, Lyddie is a teen Norma Rae, wondering if she is willing to risk her personal goals for the larger issues of creating a safe work environment. One of the few novels to deal with the exploitation of young women in the mills, *Lyddie* is first-rate historical fiction and even better as a social justice novel. **Grades 6–9. PJ**

> Reviews: *SLJ* 2/1/1991

Paulsen, Gary. **Beet Fields: Memories of a Sixteenth Summer.** 160 pages.

> Laurel-Leaf 2002 Paper 0440415578 $5.99
> Delacorte 2000 Trade 0385326475 $15.95

In some ways, almost every Gary Paulsen book is a coming-of-age story about the experiences that turn boys into young men. As readers have learned, many of these characters are based on Paulsen's own life. That life is examined again, this time with the bark off. The narrator is unnamed and the start of the book finds him running away from home, escaping his mother's drunken sexual advances. He hits the road, taking a series of jobs, including work as a migrant worker in the beet fields of South Dakota. After a while, he finds a different job, working as a carny, shilling for the geek show. Along the way, he meets up with plenty of adults, few of whom he can trust. What sounds like a boy's adventure story, however, is a tough-minded novel with mature themes and sexual situations. It is ironic that Paulsen would choose as a subtitle the phrase "Sixteenth Summer," which in some ways epitomizes what young adult literature used to be before writers like Hinton, and later Paulsen, began writing tales of learning the facts of life the hard way. **Grades 9–12 (mature). PJ**

> Reviews: *Booklist* 7/1/2000, *SLJ* 9/1/2000, *VOYA* 12/1/2000

Paulsen, Gary. **Hatchet.** 195 pages.

> Houghton Mifflin 1995 Paper 0395732611 $10.20
> Aladdin 1996 Paper 0689808828 $5.99
> Aladdin 1999 Paper 0689826990 $5.99
> Atheneum 1987 Trade 0689840926 $16.95

One of the most loved young adult books of all time and for good reason: it is a hell of a story and well told. After a plane crash, Brian spends 54 days surviving in the Canadian wilderness with nothing more than his wits and a hatchet. Behind the adventure story is Brian's coming-of-age and his acceptance of his parents' recent divorce. Almost every chapter is a cliffhanger, but Brian's rescue no doubt brings mixed emotions for the reader: happy for Brian to be headed home; sad for themselves that there is not more to the story. Related books are the nonfiction title *Guts* and the novels *The River, Brian's Winter,* and *Brian's Return.* **Grades 6—9. PJ <HIPPLE>**

Paulsen, Gary. ***The Island.*** 202 pages.

>   Dell 1988 Paper 0440206324 $5.50
>   Orchard 1988 Trade 0531057496 $17.95

Many a teenager has dreamed of being able to find refuge from trouble at school and at home. Wil has that rare luxury in an island near his parents' house. With voices at home raised more often than not, Wil heads off to his island paradise where he can be alone, write, think, paint, fish, and watch nature as a temporary reprieve from real life. That life takes a nasty turn when a bully challenges Wil. His answer is to escape to the island, although this time he is not planning on coming home ever again. **Grades 6—9. PJ**

>   Reviews: *SLJ* 5/1/1988

Paulsen, Gary. ***The Monument.*** 162 pages.

>   Yearling 1993 Paper 0440407826 $4.50

Gary Paulsen chronicles the events that take place in a small Kansas town when an itinerant artist is commissioned to construct a memorial to the town's war dead. Full of strong statements about the power of art to both instigate and heal, *The Monument* was a BBYA the year it was published, but seems to get lost in the shuffle of Paulsen's enormous body of work. **Grades 6—10. (Annotation by Jennifer Hubert) <LOST>**

Paulsen, Gary. ***Nightjohn.*** 92 pages.

>   Laurel-Leaf 1995 Paper 0440219361 $4.99
>   Doubleday 1993 Trade 0385308388 $15.95

This slim novel explodes any fantasy you may have had about the treatment of slaves. Sarny's matter-of-fact description of slave life and her willingness to risk brutal punishment to learn to read are a powerful indictment of a shameful period in our history. Her story concludes in the sequel, *Sarny: A Life Remembered.* **Grades 7—10. (Annotation by Jill Patterson)**

>   Reviews: *Booklist* 12/15/1992

Paulsen, Gary. *Sisters.* unpaged.

> Harcourt 1993 Paper 0152753249 $6.00

The sisters here are actually not related, but rather two girls who live in the same Texas town even though most of their lives they are miles apart. One girl is named Rosa; she is a 14-year-old illegal alien who makes money, most of which she sends back to Mexico, as a prostitute. She speaks almost no English, her life is one of constant hardship, and her only goal in life is to survive. The other girl is Traci, a mall rat whose goal in life is to make the cheerleading squad and fulfill all her (and her mother's) fantasies. But a fateful meeting changes both of their lives forever. The book is told not only in alternating chapters with different narrators, but a Spanish language edition is also included. A perfect example of why a "thin book" doesn't always mean easy; while the writing is sparse, the themes are challenging as Paulsen wants readers to connect the dots before the characters meet. **Grades 8–10. PJ**

> Reviews: *Booklist* 1/1/1994, *SLJ* 1/1/1994

Paulsen, Gary. *Soldier's Heart: Being the Story of the Enlistment and Due Service of the Boy Charley Goddard in the First Minnesota Volunteers.* 106 pages.

> Laurel-Leaf 2000 Paper 0440228387 $5.50
> Delacorte 1998 Trade 0385324987 $15.95

Paulsen based his book on the real-life experiences of a young enlisted man in this novel, which is sure to remind readers of the *Red Badge of Courage*. Young Charlie wants to do his part for the Union cause, earn a little money, get off the farm, and have an adventure. But his wide eyes are quickly filled with the horrors of war, the details of which Paulsen is generous in providing. Unlike a book such as *Hatchet*, in which an adventure turns an innocent boy into a confident young man, Charlie's fate is much different. He survives the war, but dreams only of suicide to escape the memories and the heaviness he carries in his soldier's heart. Writing on Amazon.com, Patty Campbell noted this "superb, small masterpiece transcends any of his earlier titles in its remarkable, memorable intensity and power." **Grades 7–10. PJ <YALSA>**

> Reviews: *Booklist* 6/1/1998, *SLJ* 9/1/1998

Payne, C. D. *Youth in Revolt: The Journals of Nick Twisp.* 512 pages.

> Doubleday 1996 Paper 0385481969 $16.95

Youth in Revolt is the journals of Nick Twisp, California's most precocious diarist, whose ongoing struggles to make sense out of high school, deal with his divorced parents, and lose his virginity result in his transformation from an unassuming 14-year-old to a modern youth in open revolt. As his family splinters, worlds collide, and the police block all routes out of town, Nick must cope with economic deprivation, homelessness, the gulag of the public schools, a competitive Type-A father, murderous canines, and an inconvenient hair trigger on his erective response—all while vying ardently for the affections of a beauty. **Grades 10—12 (mature). PJ**

Reviews: *Booklist* 7/1/1993

Peck, Richard. ***Long Way from Chicago.*** 148 pages.

Puffin 2000 Paper 0141303522 $5.99
Dial 1998 Trade 0803722907 $15.99

Told in flashback, an old man remembers the summers in a small town in Illinois during the Great Depression. The first story finds the narrator, Joey, and his sister, Mary Alice, heading off by train to meet up with Grandma Dowdel. In each story, Grandma Dowdel is the hero; a larger than life personality who takes on all comers, more like a carny wrestler than a gray-haired grandmother. Each story is filled with humor, homespun wisdom, as well as Peck's attention to the details of small-town life in the depression era. The Horn Book called the book "a small masterpiece of storytelling." **Grades 6—7. PJ**

Reviews: *Booklist* 9/1/1998, *SLJ* 10/1/1998

Peck, Richard. ***Remembering the Good Times.*** 181 pages.

Delacorte 1986 Paper 0440973392 $5.50

The book's jacket copy asks the central question: How well do we know our best friends? Not well enough is the answer in this story of three best friends (Trav, Kate, and Buck) as they go through their high school years. While coming from different backgrounds, the three become instant pals and bond during long nights spent playing games and talking at Kate's house. But as they grow older, the pressures upon Trav to do well in school overwhelm him to the point that he takes his own life. An interesting take on teen suicide in that it isn't the book's "problem"; instead, the book is about friendship, loss, and limits. **Grades 7—10. PJ**

Reviews: *Booklist* 8/1/1997, *SLJ* 1/1/1995

Peck, Richard. ***A Year Down Yonder.*** 130 pages.

Puffin 2002 Paper 0142300705 $5.99
Dial 2000 Trade 0803725183 $16.99

In this quasi-sequel to *A Long Way from Chicago*, Peck brings back Grandma Dowdel, although he writes out Joey. Instead, his sister Mary Alice is the focus of the book, which takes place during the summer of 1937. Rather than just one week, Mary Alice spends an entire year with her feisty granny, who continues with schemes and shenanigans. More wacky complications ensue as Grandma Dowdel continues her wily ways that make her a unique role model. **Grades 6—7. PJ**

Reviews: *Booklist* 10/15/2000, *SLJ* 9/1/2000

Peck, Richard. **Unfinished Portrait of Jessica.** 192 pages.

Bantam 1993 Paper 0440218861 $3.99.

Arguably one of Richard Peck's best works, *Portrait* documents the events in 13-year-old Jessica's life that lead to her first major disillusionment—the slow realization that her adored photographer father is really a selfish philanderer. For a male writer, former schoolteacher Peck excels at breathing life into female characters, and Jessica was one of his finest, most realistic creations. **Grades 6—10. (Annotation by Jennifer Hubert) <LOST>**

Pennebaker, Ruth. **Don't Think Twice.** 262 pages.

Henry Holt 2001 Paper 0805067299 $6.95

Annie is the narrator in this ensemble piece set in a rural Texas home for pregnant teens. It is 1967 and abortion is still illegal, meaning the only option available to most girls, especially those who are poor and rural, is to keep the child. The teenage girls whom Annie encounters and writes about in her journal all have their own stories, from the icy older sorority princess to the 12-year-old pregnant with her father's child. The plot here is the interaction among the girls as they work out their lives, figuring out what the next stop is down this road that many never intended to take. Annie is funny, smart, and sometimes bitter about her fate, but as the novel progresses so does her acceptance of her responsibilities as well as her identity as a strong, courageous young woman. **Grades 8—10. PJ**

Reviews: *Booklist* 5/1/1996, *Booklist* 8/1/1997, *SLJ* 5/1/1996

Peters, Julie Anne. **Define Normal.** 196 pages.

Little, Brown 2000 Trade 0316706310 $16.95

The Odd Couple set in high school in this story about two girls with nothing in common who end up as friends. Antonia is the class brain, a member of the math club, and an A student. Jazz is the "punk" more likely to be found at a loud party than study hall. They also come from different social classes: Antonia, child of the single mother struggling every day while Jazz lives in a big house with a big pool. They are destined probably never to meet until their lives intersect when Antonia signs up to be a peer counselor and finds Jazz as her first match. The early scenes are filled with humor, but as the intimacy grows, so also does the seriousness of the conversations as the two girls discover that despite differences on the outside, inside they share the same hopes, fears, and dreams. What could be a cliché turns out to be a well-crafted novel with real characters growing and changing on the page. **Grades 6—9. PJ**

Reviews: *Booklist* 5/15/2000, *SLJ* 7/1/2000, *VOYA* 6/1/2000

Pfeffer, Susan. **The Year Without Michael.** 164 pages.

Bantam 1988 Paper 0553273736 $4.99

Somewhere between home and the softball field, 16-year-old Jody Chapman's younger brother disappeared, and now the family is falling apart. Her parents hardly speak to each other, her younger sister is angry and bitter, and Jody's friends, always so important to her, are slowly slipping away. It seems that all anyone can do is wait. Wait—for Michael to walk in the door. Wait—to stop missing him. Wait—to stop waiting. When a private detective can't uncover a single clue about Michael's disappearance, Jody's urgent need to find him drives her to make a last desperate attempt to hold her family together. **Grades 6—9. PJ**

Philbrick, Rodman. ***Freak the Mighty.*** 169 pages.

> Scholastic 2001 Paper 0439286069 $4.99
> Scholastic 1993 Trade 059047412X $15.95

Forget the terrible Sharon Stone movie, this is a tremendous novel about friendship and overcoming hard times. Owing more than a little to Steinbeck's *Of Mice and Men*, *Freak* is about the friendship between the very tiny, very crafty Kevin (aka Freak because of his stunted growth as a result of a birth defect) and the large, slow Max. Separate, they both are at the mercy of bullies; together, they are "Freak the Mighty" and afraid of nothing and no one in their neighborhood. But in their past, both have demons they have yet to admit, let alone accept. **Grades 6—9. PJ <HIPPLE>**

> Reviews: *Booklist* 12/15/1993, *SLJ* 12/1/1993

Philbrick, Rodman. ***The Last Book in the Universe.*** 223 pages.

> Scholastic 2002 Paper 0439087597 $4.99
> Blue Sky 2000 Trade 0439087589 $16.95

An entertaining mix of the *Matrix* with *Fahrenheit 451* concerns a future society where most everyone is illiterate, in part because most citizens are pulled into brain-draining home entertainment systems. But Spaz, because of his epilepsy, can see the truth (like Neo, he is the one) and with the help of an older man and a group of other outcast teens, he wants to break the mold. But before he can save the world, he must first save his sister's life, if he can reach her in time. A classic coming-of-age story told as a meaningful journey tale with a futuristic setting creates a fascinating read for younger teens, readers who might just relate to a world where Gameboy is God. **Grades 6—9. PJ**

> Reviews: *Booklist* 11/15/2000, *SLJ* 11/1/2000, *VOYA* 12/1/2000

Pierce, Meredith Ann. ***The Darkangel.*** 223 pages.

> St. Martin 1998 Paper 0812503287 $2.95

When Ariel attempts to sacrifice herself to the dark angel, the winged vampiric "son" of the White Witch, to save her mistress, Eoduin, she finds herself abducted by the most beautiful man she's ever seen. Ariel must now find a way to save not only her mistress and the dark angel's other 12 brides (reduced to near-ghosts), but also the dark angel himself before he takes a 14th bride and the power of the White Witch is cemented forever. Ariel, a believable and likeable young woman, grows throughout the series and provides a solid "everyman" viewpoint through which the reader can enjoy the unfolding magical and dreamlike world Pierce has created. Pierce's original take on a vampire story with its evocative setting and sense of mystery works extremely well in the first two books, *Dark-Angel* and *Gathering of Gargoyles*. So much so that the unsatisfying conclusion, *The Pearl at the Soul of the World*, is still worth reading. **Grades 8—10. KE**

Pierce, Meredith Ann. ***The Woman Who Loved Reindeer.*** 242 pages.

Magic Carpet 2000 Paper 0152017992 $6.00

In the prehistoric far north, in a land that (perhaps) never was, Caribou reluctantly agrees to raise her sister's bastard infant boy. He is a "trangl"—part human, part reindeer, and though Caribou eventually loses her heart to the beautiful boy, he leaves her for his wild heritage. When catastrophe strikes Caribou's people, however, the boy, now a young man, returns, becoming her lover and helping her lead her people through an epic and adventure-filled journey to a new home. Despite the fantasy setting, this novel has the broad appeal of a *Mists of Avalon*. Pierce is extremely skilled in absorbing the reader into her world, making the strangeness seem real. Her strong female heroines and their desire to find love in the hearts of men who may not be capable of loving them are likely to speak to many young women. **Grades 7—10. KE**

Pierce, Tamora. ***Alanna: The First Adventure.*** 241 pages.

Random House 1989 Paper 0679801146 $5.50
Peter Smith 1999 Trade 0844670022 $20.00

When young Alanna switches places with her twin brother, giving him the chance for the cloistered academic training of a wizard she despises, it seems as if her dream of studying at the medieval fantasy kingdom of Tortall's military academy has come true. From page to squire to knight, Alanna must continually prove herself despite her smaller size and strength, while keeping her secret, even as the Kingdom itself and her schoolmates come under magical attack. This first book in the Song of the Lioness Quartet will undoubtedly appeal to young Harry Potter fans as a school story in an exotic magical setting. The story, however, quickly follows Alanna through womanhood and her adventures (and lovers) outside the royal court in the sequels, *In the Hand of the Goddess, The Woman Who Rides Like a Man,* and *Lioness Rampant.* Nonetheless, Alanna has great appeal for young women who enjoy fast-paced adventure stories with a competent, likeable heroine. **Grades 6—10. KE**

Reviews: *SLJ* 4/1/1999

Pierce, Tamora. ***Circle of Magic: Sandry's Book.*** 252 pages.

Point Signature 1999 Paper 0590554085 $4.99
Scholastic 1997 Trade 0590553569 $15.95

Lady Sandrilene fa Toren (Sandry) does not appreciate or understand her magical gifts. She has few friends, no sense of who she is or what she wants out of life, and feels as if she's good for nothing but a politically expedient marriage. Sandry, like Daja, child of nomadic sea-traders; Briar, a street thief; and Trisana, a merchant girl, will be rescued by the mage Niklaren Goldeye and brought to a school of magic. Short, well crafted, and with enough action to keep the pages turning, Sandry's book chronicles her growing self-discipline, self-esteem, and friendships. Each subsequent novel in the *Circle of Magic* series (*Tris's Book, Briar's Book*, and *Daja's Book)* focuses on a different friend's coming to terms with their talents, their relationships, and their place in the world. Both in content and reading level, these novels are admirably suited to young teens. The follow-up series, *The Circle Opens*, is just as good and sure to be in demand by Pierce's fans. **Grades 6—10. KE**

Reviews: *Booklist* 9/1/1997, *SLJ* 9/1/1997, *VOYA* 12/1/1997

Pierce, Tamora. ***First Test.*** 216 pages.

Random House 2000 Paper 0679889175 $4.99
Random House 1999 Trade 0679889140 $16.00

While Alanna succeeded in becoming a woman knight by hiding her identity, young Keldry is the first girl to openly join Tortall's military academy. The likeable young woman responds to an unsympathetic headmaster who is determined to run her out, and to bullying and hazing with courage, determination, and common sense. Keldry's struggles are set within the larger adventures of the Kingdom of Tortall, now under attack by magical terrorists. As the stories and her competence progress, Keldry plays a larger role in the exciting battles to save her home. Finding friendship, fighting injustice, and making a place for herself within the best fantasy school setting since Harry Potter, Keldry is sure to be a hit with Tamora Pierce's legion of young fans—and generate many more. Keldry's story and the *Protector of the Small* series continue in *Page, Squire* and *Lady Knight.* **Grades 6—8. KE**

Reviews: *VOYA* 6/1/2000, *Booklist* 6/15/1999

Pike, Christopher. ***Chain Letter.*** 185 pages.

Avon Flare 1986 Paper 038089968X $4.99

Riffing off of Duncan's *I Know What You Did Last Summer*, Pike takes the same basic plot, and even plot hook, but with much different results. Alison is the first to get the letter signed "Your Caretaker," which tells her that the accidental murder she and her friends committed is not a secret. One by one each member of the group gets the letter. The object isn't physical harm, but something much worse: public humiliation.

One of the best examples of the late 80s/early 90s thriller genre showing that even the most basic mystery plot can be given a whole new, nasty, twist. **Grades 6—9. PJ**

Pike, Christopher. *Last Vampire #1.* 182 pages.

Archway 1994 Paper 0671872648 $5.99

With obvious debt to the Anne Rice books, Pike's mini-series follows a family of vampires in search of blood, vengeance, but mostly for peace. In every book, the creatures of the night interact with human teenagers with horrifically entertaining results. Four sequels (as of this writing). **Grades 6—9. PJ**

Pike, Christopher. *Monster.* 229 pages.

Pocket 2001 Paper 0743428005 $5.99

Mary walked into the party with a loaded shotgun. In the blink of an eye she blew two people away. She wanted to kill more, but was stopped by her best friend, Angela, and the police. The next day, when Angela visits Mary at the jail, she asks why she did it. Mary responds, "Because they were no longer human." Angela thinks she's crazy until she probes deeper into Mary's claims and discovers a horror so unimaginable that she thinks she herself is going crazy. This is all red eyes and raw meat; a delicious romp through the horror of adolescence and the thing that won't die. **Grades 8—10. PJ**

Pike, Christopher. *Remember Me.* 240 pages.

Pocket Books 2002 Paper 0743428013 $5.99

Pike novels always toy with the supernatural, but here he goes all out with the story of Shari Cooper, teen spirit. The book begins with Shari looking down at her corpse on a slab in the morgue. The police label it a suicide, but Shari knows she was murdered. With the power to spy on everyone, as well as enter their dreams, she sets out to find the real killer. That is where she comes face to face with The Shadow: a nightmare and a thing more horrible than death itself. Pike is at his best mixing up his strange brew of revenge, parapsychology, and cold-blooded murder. **Grades 8—10. PJ**

Pinkwater, Daniel. *Five Novels: Alan Mendelsohn the Boy from Mars, Slaves of Spiegel, The Snarkout Boys and the Avocado of Death, The Last Guru, Young Adult Novel.* 656 pages.

Peter Smith 1998 Trade 0844669768 $23.23
Farrar, Straus & Giroux 1997 Paper 0374423296 $11.95

Pinkwater is an acquired taste, but for those who "get it," these five novels are a smorgasbord of wackiness. *Young Adult Novel* is the best of the lot: a send-up of every YA novel cliché put through Pinkwater's gag blender to create something unique. All of these books feature characters at home in any Zindel novel, a collection of eccentric teens who look at life through joke- and jaundice-colored glasses. Look up "quirky" in the dictionary and no doubt Pinkwater's pudgy face is staring out from the page. **Grades 6—8. PJ**

Plath, Sylvia. ***The Bell Jar.*** 229 pages.

> HarperCollins 1996 Trade 0060174900 $20.00
> Alfred A. Knopf 1998 Trade 0375404635 $17.00

Since her suicide in 1963, Sylvia Plath has achieved nearly legendary status as the female version of *The Catcher in the Rye*. While the comparison is apt, it should be noted that *The Bell Jar* is in many ways a more complex novel, and as accomplished as it is, it does not reach the rich and varied levels of her superb poetry. Nonetheless, the thinly disguised autobiography seems to speak particularly to teenage readers, though it is compelling for adults as well. In the 1950s Plath's alter ego, Esther, wins junior editorship at a famous New York magazine (much as Plath spent a memorable summer at *Mademoiselle*). Tall, creative, intriguing, a girl of great attractiveness, Esther nevertheless begins losing her hold on sanity and her relentless suicide fantasies (she carries 19 razor blades in her purse) grow more and more graphic. Trapped beneath the bell jar of madness—one of literature's most original motifs—the girl with everything to gain rapidly becomes an emotional wraith, desperate to lose it all. The fact that Plath ended her own life at 28 at the height of her professional and personal powers makes *The Bell Jar* all the more poignant. **Grades 9—12. PT <YALSA>**

Plum-Ucci, Carol. ***The Body of Christopher Creed.*** 248 pages.

> Volo 2001 Paper 0786816414 $6.99
> Harcourt 2000 Trade 0152023887 $17.00

Christopher Creed is a joke to most everyone at school, a weird kid who makes a convenient target for taunts and an occasional beating. When Creed disappears—leaving behind a baffling note on the school library computer—three of his worst tormentors become the focus of everyone's attention. Torey and his friends try to find Christopher to clear the suspicion that surrounds them, but the shame and remorse from their immature actions still hang heavy. While most mysteries look at guilt in the legal scene (who done it), Torey confronts an inner guilt, wondering why he behaved so badly. In the post-Columbine world, this is another novel that examines the consequences of bullying for all involved. **Grades 7—10. PJ <PRINTZ>**

Reviews: *Booklist* 3/15/2001, *SLJ* 7/1/2000, *VOYA* 8/1/2000

Porter, Connie Rose. ***Imani All Mine.*** 212 pages.

> Houghton Mifflin 2000 Paper 0618056785 $12.00

This adult novel is set in a housing project in Buffalo, New York. Tasha is 14 years old and has just given birth to her first child. She desperately wants to be a good mother, as well as return to school and get good grades, but she finds little support from her mother. There's not a lot of plot here; instead Porter examines the life of a smart, funny, hopeful young woman who finds herself in circumstances she didn't choose, but accepts and then hopes to rise above them. Tasha tells the story in her own voice, heavy on urban dialect, with the soundtrack of life in the projects humming the background. **Grades 10—12 (mature). PJ**

Reviews: *Booklist* 1/1/1999, *SLJ* 1/1/2000, *VOYA* 1/1/1999

Potok, Chaim. ***The Chosen.*** 284 pages.

Fawcett 1987 Paper 0449213447 $6.99
Fawcett 1997 Paper 0449911543 $14.00

Set in Brooklyn in the 1940s, this book follows the accidental friendship between two very different teen boys: Reuven and Danny. While there is the basic stuff of growing up, the real issues here are about the relationships between fathers and sons, and what it means to be a Jew. While the two boys have some adventures as their friendship grows, it is more what they say and think about the world and their places in it that matters the most. **Grades 10—12. PJ <YALSA>**

Powell, Randy. ***Dean Duffy.*** 169 pages.

Aerial 1998 Paper 0374416990 $5.95
Farrar Straus Giroux 1995 Trade 0374317542 $15.00

The athlete-comeback story is always a great young adult tale, and Powell's *Dean Duffy* is a strong example of this subgenre. Dean has a gift for baseball; he can hit, field, run, but mostly throw. The question isn't will he make it one day to "the show" but whether he will even have to waste time in the minors. But an arm injury derails his plans and forces him to re-evaluate life off the field as well. Told in first person, Powell captures the voice of a confused and scared teenage boy in all of his wild mood swings. Dean's cockiness masks his insecurities and fear of failure; now that his identity as "jock" is removed, he is trying to figure out exactly who Dean Duffy really is. **Grades 7—10. PJ**

Reviews: *Booklist* 4/15/1995, *SLJ* 5/1/1995

Powell, Randy. ***Run If You Dare.*** 183 pages.

Farrar Straus Giroux 2001 Trade 0374399816 $16.00

Gardner doesn't seem to have any goals in life. While everyone else in high school is talking about college and careers, he plays it cool. It is something he shares with his father, also not known for his ambition. When his father is laid off, however, even Gardner is surprised by his father's casual acceptance of circumstances and his lack of will to change his life. These events lead to Gardner's decision to commit himself to running, to prove he can stick to something and follow through. Yet, while he grows as a person, he watches his father disappear into depression and apathy. **Grades 7–10. PJ**

Reviews: *Booklist* 8/1/2001, *SLJ* 3/1/2001, *VOYA* 6/1/2001

Powell, Randy. ***Tribute to Another Dead Rock Star.*** 214 pages.

Farrar Straus Giroux 1999 Trade 0374377480 $17.00

This book about the trials and tribulations of Grady Grennen, a skateboard punk whose one claim to fame is being the son of a dead heavy-metal singer, is touching, clever, and masterfully written. In addition, Grady's arguments with his deeply Christian stepmom over his mentally disabled brother are probably the best examinations of morality and conscience in young adult literature. **Grades 7–10. (Annotation by Jennifer Hubert) <LOST>**

Reviews: *Booklist* 3/1/1999, *SLJ* 5/1/1999

Power, Susan. ***Grass Dancer.*** 300 pages.

Berkley 1995 Paper 0425149625 $5.99

The chapters read like a series of interlocking short stories, as *Grass Dancer* follows the fortunes of a group of North Dakota Sioux; the chronology is flexible, with individual stories moving around in time as they give voice to different generations. One of Power's talents is her ability to make such a diverse number of characters so believable: Anna Thunder; her daughter, Crystal; her granddaughter, Charlene; Red Dress, an ancestor of Anna's; Margaret Many Wounds; Harley; and Herod Small War all are distinct and memorable. Beautifully written, but not appropriate for younger or reluctant readers. **Grades 9–12. PT**

Reviews: *Booklist* 1/1/1995, *SLJ* 5/1/1995, *VOYA* 1/1/1995

Pratchett, Terry. ***Amazing Maurice and His Educated Rodents.*** 256 pages.

HarperCollins 2001 Library 006001234X $17.89
HarperCollins 2002 Trade 0060012331 $16.95
HarperCollins 2003 Paper 0060012358 $6.99

Ostensibly set within his popular Discworld environment, one of Pratchett's rare offerings specifically for teens retells the story of the Pied Piper from a unique viewpoint: that of cat and his rat associates running the scam for the Piper. The adventure begins when Maurice, who truly has the morals of an alley cat (but he's working on it), runs afoul of a strange town where a vicious crime lord has set up a competing (and similar) fraud. Both Maurice and the mice have only recently become self-aware; their struggle to work out a code of ethics and find a future for themselves adds depth and poignancy to the horror-tinged action of the story. The dim piper-boy Maurice uses as his front man and the odd local girl who befriends him provide comic relief in this short, intelligent, and tightly plotted novel. While easily accessible to younger teens, Pratchett's novel is sophisticated enough to appeal to older readers as well. **Grades 6—10. KE**

Reviews: *Booklist* 1/1/2002, *SLJ* 12/1/2001, *VOYA* 2/1/2002

Pratchett, Terry. ***The Colour of Magic.*** 205 pages

HarperPrism 2000 Paper 0061020710 $6.99
St. Martin's 1983 Trade 0312150849 $16.98

Discworld, as the opening pages of each novel in the Discworld series explains, exists in a reality-challenged corner of the universe: It's flat, powered by magic, and rides through space on the back of a giant turtle. Rincewind, an inept young wizard with a well-developed talent for running away, is drafted as native tour-guide for the discworld's first tourist, the naive Two-Flower and his murderous sentient luggage. From Unseen University, the college of gluttonous egoists who advance by assassination through the mean streets of Ankh-Morpork to the end of the world, Pratchett takes his readers on a madcap spoof of the fantasy clichés. Unlike the remaining books in the series, this one cannot stand alone without the sequel, *The Light Fantastic.* Nonetheless it's a short, fast-paced, fun introduction to an immensely popular fantasy series, sure to be enjoyed by teens who like *The Hitchhiker's Guide to the Galaxy.* **Grades 9—12. KE**

Pratchett, Terry. ***Reaper Man***. 384 pages.

HarperCollins Publishers 2002 Paper 0061020621 $6.99

One of the most moving, and funny, of the Discworld novels features the anthropomorphic personification of Death, who, after untold millennia of doing a job nobody appreciates, is fired. While Death finds a temp job as farm hand (he does, after all, have his own scythe), the Discworld is threatened by a voracious monster that threatens to destroy the world: a strip mall. From Death, to the sharp old biddy who hires him, to the foolish wizards of Unseen University, Pratchett's characters are deftly drawn. Each of the Discworld novels can stand alone, though the more of them one reads, the greater the cumulative effect of some of the subtle running gags. Pratchett's tight plots and his clear affection for the foibles of human nature (combined with a complete lack of self-righteousness) keep his satires deeply appealing. Older teens who enjoy intelligent humor laced with moments of tragic relief won't want to miss the Discworld books. A list of the 20+ Discworld novels can be found at his official U.S. Web site: www.terrypratchettbooks.com/. **Grades 7—10. KE**

Price, Susan. ***The Sterkarm Handshake.*** 438 pages.

> HarperCollins 2000 Library 0060293926 $17.89
> HarperCollins 2000 Trade 0060289597 $17.95

Andrea Mitchell, an overweight, socially awkward anthropologist, has been hired by the mega-corporation that created the device to travel back in time to 16th-century Scotland where she will work with Sterkarms as an interpreter and company spy. Andrea's professional obligations and personal loyalties soon clash with the Corporation's plans: The past is not really "our" past, but that of a closely parallel Earth, ripe for tourist exploitation and strip-mining by the ethically challenged Corporation pirates. Andrea is warmly welcomed by the tribe since the handsome chief's son, Per, is attracted to her and they begin a passionate affair. The Sterkarms, however, are no noble savages, but terrible neighbors, treacherous and violent, happy to pillage and rape any outsiders not of their tribe. Andrea and Per's attempt to thwart the Corporation and their tragic love affair drive the story forward. Price has created a thoughtful time-travel adventure: The combination of violent action, doomed romance, and complex moral choices should engage the mature teen reader. **Grades 9—12 (mature). KE**

> Reviews: *Booklist* 10/1/2000, *SLJ* 12/1/2000, *VOYA* 12/1/2000

Pullman, Philip. ***The Amber Spyglass: His Dark Materials.*** 518 pages.

> Del Rey 2001 Paper 0345413377 $6.99

In a rough-edged conclusion, Lyra, Will, and their friends from the first two books successfully rebel against the Authority. The pace is uneven, one major plot thread seemingly pointless, and worse, Pullman often descends to having ancillary characters lecture the reader to make his point. Generally speaking, the metaphysics and moral speculation so strongly raised in the first two books are a wash. Happily, the first two parts of the story are so superb that the originality, generally fine prose, suspenseful plot, and scope of inventiveness of part three largely make up for its defects. Less demanding readers will adore the entire story and find the ending both beautiful and deeply tragic. **Grades 6—12. KE <TEN>**

Pullman, Philip. ***Clockwork.*** 112 pages.

> Scholastic 1999 Paper 0590129988 $4.99

When Karl, the clockmaker's apprentice in the imaginary 19th-century German town of Glockenheim, tells Fritz, a young storyteller, that he has failed his journeyman piece, an evil magician from Fritz's next story mysteriously appears and offers Karl his heart's desire. Only evil can come from such a bargain, but true love and an innocent child will put it right. Pullman's horror-tinged fairy tale deftly blends reality and fantasy, the plot tightly spinning out until the happily-ever-after conclusion. Although a very satisfying read for the middle school crowd, older teens may appreciate the understated sophistication of its construction. **Grades 6—7. KE**

Reviews: *Booklist* 9/15/1998, *SLJ* 10/1/1998

Pullman, Philip. ***The Golden Compass.*** 399 pages.

Del Rey 1997 Paper 0345413350 $6.99
Alfred A. Knopf 2002 Paper 037582345X $11.95
Alfred A. Knopf 1996 Trade 0679879242 $20.00

In an Oxford, England, in a universe parallel to our own, the Church is the ultimate temporal power, and one's essential nature is embodied in animal form as one's "demon." As the story opens, Lyra's powerful and handsome explorer father is racing the Church to discover the secret of Dust and the power that mastering it will bring. When the Oblation board captures her best friend, the spunky, half-wild heroine runs afoul of the Board's plot to first steal children, then, through a vicious operation, sever them from their demons. Though the results are horrific, the Church hopes to obtain sexually neuter, docile, and "sinless" people. With her father's magical "truth meter" (the golden compass of the title) in hand, Lyra's quest will take her to the frozen North, where armored polar bears and Lapland witches enliven a stark and beautiful landscape. The mix of horror, suspense, fantastic world building, and solid-characterization is near perfect, while the universal questions Pullman raises about the nature of the human soul and the dangers of ideologically driven power add tremendous depth to the novel. Good readers, both young and old, will devour this challenging, brilliantly written novel. **Grades 6—12. KE <TEN><YALSA>**

Reviews: *Booklist* 3/1/1996, *SLJ* 4/1/1996

Pullman, Philip. ***I Was a Rat.*** 164 pages.

Alfred A. Knopf 2000 Library 0375901760 $17.99
Yearling 2002 Paper 0440416612 $4.99
Alfred A. Knopf 2000 Trade 0375801766 $15.95

When a half-starved pageboy who was once a rat (left over from Cinderella's adventures) wanders into the life of a washerwoman named Joan and her cobbler husband, they take him in, dub him "Roger," and soon look upon him as their son. The rat-boy, however, can't make heads or tails of ordinary human life and after a series of comic misadventures is soon on the run. Alas, even his old home, the sewers, are closed to him now, but a kindly Cinderella eventually engineers a happily-ever-after ending. The nugget of sharp social commentary embedded in the fairy-tale spoof may shoot right past the middle school audience, but Pullman's older fans will appreciate it. **Grades 7—12. KE**

Reviews: *Booklist* 2/1/2000, *SLJ* 3/1/2000, *VOYA* 4/1/2000

Pullman, Philip. ***Ruby in the Smoke.*** 230 pages.

Alfred A. Knopf 1988 Paper 0394895894 $5.50

It's truly difficult to create an active female heroine within the context of Victorian England without sacrificing historical accuracy, but Pullman pulls it off. When 16-year-old Sally begins investigating her father's mysterious death, she runs afoul of London's criminal underworld. Finding unlikely friends (and a lover) from among the bohemian set, the competent young woman goes from adventure to adventure within a fully realized 19th-century world. The socialist commentary (at a time when the impartial cruelty of the industrial revolution was spawning the movement) is particularly apt and never heavy-handed. With each book in the series, a mystery is successfully (and satisfyingly) resolved, while the ground is laid for a deeper mystery that underpins it. Sally's adventures continue, through the murder of her lover, the danger to their child, and the eventual routing of her enemies in the next two books of the Sally Lockhart trilogy: *The Shadow in the North* and *The Tiger in the Well*. Fans of both tightly plotted mysteries and historical fiction will enjoy this series.
Grades 7–12. KE <YALSA>

Reviews: *Booklist* 4/15/1995

Pullman, Philip. ***The Subtle Knife.*** 326 pages.

Del Rey 1998 Paper 0345413369 $6.99
Alfred A. Knopf 2002 Paper 0375823468 $11.95
Alfred A. Knopf 1997 Trade 0679879250 $20.00

The second part of the story, beginning on what may be the Oxford, England, of our universe, introduces us to Will Parry, who will play Adam to Lyra's Eve. Will's attempt to escape his missing father's enemies drives him to murder. Fleeing, the boy finds himself in the creepy alternate world of the subtle knife. Will captures the knife, which can slice doors between worlds, and travels between the universes, eventually meeting up with Lyra, finding out the truth about his father, and joining Lyra in what will become a universe-spanning rebellion. Astute readers will notice that Pullman is setting up a retelling of Milton's *Paradise Lost*, one in which God (the Authority) is the villain and Lucifer (represented by Lyra's father), the hero. The Authority of *The Subtle Knife* is deeply un-Christian, a power-mad dictator determined to crush individuality, sexual joy, and free thought from all sentient life. The same fine qualities that made *The Golden Compass* such an outstanding book are all present here, though the book feels incomplete, ending with Lyra having been kidnapped and Will on the verge of death. **Grades 6–12. KE <TEN>**

Reviews: *Booklist* 7/1/1997, *SLJ* 10/1/1997

Pullman, Philip. ***The Tin Princess.*** 290 pages.

Alfred A. Knopf 1999 Paper 0679876154 $5.50

Pullman returns to the late Victorian world of the Sally Lockhart books to spin a melodramatic and suspenseful story of intrigue and danger in the Ruritanian principality of Razkavia. Several of the younger characters from the series, including Becky (tutor to Adelaide, the former-prostitute turned princess), and Jim, now a detective (and still in love with Adelaide), take center stage. When her husband is assassinated, Adelaide seizes power and it's up to her young friends to uncover the plots and save the day. Though Pullman keeps the reader aware of the injustices of pre-World War I Europe, he never takes the edge off the fun. The story is fast paced, with plot twist piled upon twist. Happily, Pullman also manages to give readers the well-developed character relationships his readers have come to expect. Mature teen readers won't be disappointed. **Grades 6–12. KE**

Reviews: *Booklist* 3/1/1996, *SLJ* 1/1/1995

Puzo, Mario. **The Godfather.** 446 pages.

New American Library 2002 Paper 0451205766 $14.00
Putnam 1969 Trade 0399103422 $24.95

Though it has inspired three of the most acclaimed films in American history, Puzo's novel is still a work beyond compare. The story of Don Corleone and his struggles to control his Mafia empire in the 1940s is well known to any moviegoer, but the brush with which Puzo paints his characters, major and minor, is finer than what appears on-screen. As the Corleone sons and daughter try to make sense of their various "normal" lives set against the backdrop of organized crime, we see that this is as much or more so a picture of the human condition, of a man who loves his family above all, than it is a riveting tale of violence in America. The book still has the power to shock, and it should be noted that it includes sexual scenes inappropriate for younger readers. **Grades 10–12 (mature). PT**

Pynchon, Thomas. **V.** 492 pages.

HarperCollins 1999 Paper 0060930217 $14.00

Thomas Pynchon is unique among modern writers, and his protagonist in *V* is the child of his singularity. Home from the Navy, Benny Profane (and he is profane, to be sure) nurses his ambition to spend as much time in bars as possible and avoid anything even vaguely approaching responsibility. His circle of friends is called The Whole Sick Crew, which gives you an idea that he's not going to benefit from much good influence there. The plot gains speed when Benny meets Stencil, who possesses the energy Benny has studiously been ridding himself of. Stencil is on the path of a mysterious woman known only as V, who has unaccountably vanished. As Benny is drawn into the intrigue, his life begins to alter dramatically. A word to the wise: This is not a book for young adults. The outset finds Benny and his crew singing a song concerning Santa having "barmaids who like to screw" in his bag, and that's just the opening chapter. It grows more raucous with every passing page. **Grades 7—12 (mature). PT**

Qualey, Marsha. ***Close to a Killer.*** 182 pages.

Laurel-Leaf 2000 Paper 0440227631 $4.99

Qualey writes mysteries in the Joan Lowery Nixon vein: nice normal teen girls who find themselves playing Nancy Drew roles, even though the home life of their characters is much more contemporary. Barrie knows a great deal about crime: her mother has served time in prison for murder. With other ex-cons, Barrie's mother opens up a beauty salon called Killer Looks that becomes all the rage. But that is threatened, as well as the rekindling of Barrie's fractured relationship with her mother, when two of the shop's customers are found murdered. It is up to Barrie to prove her mother's innocence, all the while trying to avoid being murdered herself. **Grades 7—10. PJ**

Reviews: *Booklist* 2/1/1999, *SLJ* 3/1/1999, *VOYA* 4/1/1999

Qualey, Marsha. ***Thin Ice.*** 272 pages.

Bantam Doubleday Dell 1999 Paper 0440220378 $4.99

Seventeen-year-old Arden Munro has been raised by her older brother, Scott, ever since the death of their parents 10 years earlier in a plane crash. Now another accident has struck, and her brother's snowmobile is found submerged in a river. While no body is found, it is assumed by all that Scott has meet a watery death. Arden refuses to accept that fact; instead she does investigating on her own and reaches a much different conclusion. While all the sleuthing is at the center of the story, Qualey adds depth to the Arden character to make readers feel not just the thrill of the hunt, but her sadness at the loss of her family. **Grades 6—9. PJ**.

Reviews: *Booklist* 11/1/1997, *SLJ* 11/1/1997

Quarles, Heather. ***A Door Near Here.*** 231 pages.

Laurel-Leaf 2000 Paper 0440227615 $4.99

Katherine's mother, after being fired from her job, retreats into drunken limbo leaving her 15-year-old daughter the responsibility of running the house. Katherine has three younger siblings, each a different set of problems, but none more so than Alisa. Alisa wants to escape the situation at home, which leads her to an unhealthy obsession with the *Chronicles of Narnia* books. In addition to all the emotional turmoil in the house, Katherine also needs to run the day-to-day cooking, cleaning, and caring for the house. For every fantasy teens might have about living on their own without parents, a book like this shows the severity of such a situation. **Grades 7—10. PJ**

Reviews: *Booklist* 9/1/1998, *SLJ* 11/1/1998, *VOYA* 10/1/1998

Rand, Ayn. **Anthem.** 253 pages.

Plume 1999 Paper 0452281253 $13.95

Rand's first novel was published in the U.S. as a pamphlet; it is as much rhetoric as storytelling. But the story that is told resonates with many teens, especially those who have read *The Giver* but are not quite ready for *1984*. The protagonist lives in a collectivist society where all is done for the state and nothing for the individual. Independent actions, including love, are forbidden in this dronelike world. But one man stands up against the state and dares to be his own person. The book is like an anthem: a celebration of ideology, ideals, and spirit—but to the self, not to any state. **Grades 10–12. PJ**

Randle, Kristen D. **Only Alien on the Planet.** 228 pages.

Point Signature 1996 Paper 0590463101 $4.99

While the title might lead readers to think this was a science fiction romp, it is instead an edgy, realistic novel. It is the roadmap for both *Tangerine* (a long hidden act of violence) and *Speak* (a young person who refuses to). Smitty, the nonspeaker, is isolated at his high school. Written off as a weirdo, he has no friends. But when a new girl arrives in town, she is fascinated with the silent student. As the two grow closer and make a connection, Smitty is finally able to confront his past and take the first steps to "joining" the human race again. **Grades 7–10. PJ**

Reviews: *Booklist* 1/15/1995, *SLJ* 3/1/1995, *VOYA* 4/1/1995

Rapp, Adam. **The Buffalo Tree.** 188 pages.

HarperTempest 2002 Paper 0060012269 $6.95
HarperCollins 1998 Paper 006440711X $11.00
Front Street 1997 Trade 1886910197 $15.95

A difficult novel about life in a juvenile detention center. Rapp, pun intended, has created almost a rap novel with a unique cadence, rhythm, and vocabulary, told in the first person by Sura, a 12-year-old sent up for stealing hubcaps. Though the crime is slight, the time is not. Behind bars, Sura encounters a diverse cast of characters, from streetwise fellow residents to sadistic staff. He grows closest to his cellmate Coly, who seems to have come in from a Cadnum novel (his crime is breaking into houses, not to steal, but just for the thrill of it). Once inside the detention center, however, Coly is lost in the system and while Sura watches on, fights to retain his dignity, humanity, and sanity. **Grades 9–12 (mature). PJ**

Reviews: *Booklist* 9/1/1997, *SLJ* 6/1/1997, *VOYA* 8/1/1997

Rawls, Wilson. **Where the Red Fern Grows.** 212 pages.

Yearling 1996 Paper 0440412676 $5.99

Delacorte 1996 Trade 0385323301 $16.95

The red fern in question is the Native American legend of the sacred plant growing over the graves of Billy Colman's dogs, and symbol for coming to peace when coming of age. Billy roams the Ozark Mountains in Oklahoma with his blue tick hound chasing adventure and raccoons. A coon-hunt contest, a "ghost coon," and a tragic battle with a mountain lion all contribute to the fast-moving pace of this beloved children's classic, enjoyable for those aged nine and up. **Grades 6—7. PT**

Rees, Celia. **Witch Child.** 261 pages.

Candlewick 2002 Paper 0763618292 $7.99
Candlewick 2001 Trade 0763614211 $15.99

Using a *Blair-Witch-Project*-like "is it real or not" conceit, this is far from just another telling of the hysteria in Salem. The protagonist Mary is a self-confessed witch who watches her grandmother burned at the stake. She escapes a similar fate by sailing to colonial America. Similar more to *Blood and Chocolate* than to *The Witch of Blackbird Pond*, this novel is about a young woman with special powers who must hide them or face grave consequences from the "normals" that surround her. It is not a Wiccan novel, but there are plenty of that religion's rituals and regalia featured. The cover belongs on an issue of *Seventeen*, not a historical novel, but that makes sense in a way since the real subject of this book isn't persecution of witches in the past, but how those with different beliefs are rejected by society. **Grades 7—10. PJ**

Reviews: *Booklist* 6/1/2001, *SLJ* 8/1/2001, *VOYA* 10/1/2001

Remarque, Erich Maria. **All Quiet on the Western Front.** 292 pages.

Ballantine 1996 Paper 0449911497 $12.95
Fawcett 1987 Paper 0449213943 $6.99
Little, Brown 1983 Trade 0316739928 $24.95

Just as the 1930 film version of Erich Maria Remarque's masterpiece continues as a powerful representation of the novel, so the novel remains both a showcase for language in the hands of a superior craftsman and an uncompromising condemnation of war. Enlisting with his schoolmates in the German Army, Paul Baumer looks upon World War I as an adventure not to be missed. As is so often the case with misplaced youthful enthusiasm, Paul's anticipation of battle turns to horror when he suffers his first bombardment. As the war in the trenches drags on and on, seemingly endless and unwinnable, Paul tries to hold on tight to his sanity by defining the darker nature of humanity that creates war and vowing to oppose it. All he has to do is emerge from the trenches alive. Some books never go out of fashion. *All Quiet on the Western Front* is one of them. **Grades 9—12. PT**

Rennison, Louise. ***Angus, Thongs and Full-Frontal Snogging: Confessions of Georgia Nicolson.*** 256 pages.

> HarperCollins 2003 Paper 0060521848 $6.99
> HarperCollins 2000 Library 006028871X $15.89
> HarperCollins 2000 Trade 0060288140 $15.95

One of the most popular pure young adult novels of all time got great reviews and even better word of mouth from teenage girls who marveled at the honest portrayal of Rennison's 14-year-old heroine. While compared to the smash *Diary of Bridget Jones*, and for good reason, Rennison's voice is still fresh as her English teen girl obsesses about her lovelife (or lack thereof). Georgia's confession comes warts and all; she's not only not perfect, she can be downright nasty, and perhaps related, also very funny. **Grades 7–10. PJ <PRINTZ>**

> Reviews: *Booklist* 7/1/2000, *SLJ* 7/1/2000, *VOYA* 6/1/2000

Rennison, Louise. ***Knocked Out by My Nunga-Nungas: Further, Further Confessions of Georgia Nicolson.*** 192 pages.

> HarperCollins 2002 Library 0066236568 $15.99
> HarperCollins 2002 Trade 0066236959 $15.89

In the third installment, Georgia chronicles her family holiday to Scotland, more complications with her boyfriend (the Sex God), and more confusion, matched with cutting remarks about the whole snogging situation. **Grades 7–10. PJ**

> Reviews: *SLJ* 5/1/2002, *VOYA* 8/1/2002

Rennison, Louise. ***On the Bright Side, I'm Now the Girlfriend of a Sex God: Further Confessions of Georgia Nicolson.*** 256 pages.

> HarperCollins 2002 Paper 0064472264 $6.99
> HarperCollins 2001 Library 0060288132 $15.99
> HarperCollins 2001 Trade 0060288728 $15.89

Georgia's sarcastic commentary on her family, friends, and finally fulfilled lovelife continues in this sequel. The main plot is standard stuff: girl gets boy, boy dumps girl, and girl schemes to get boy back while sitcom circumstances conspire against her. It's attitude, not narrative, that hooks teen girls on reading Georgia's diary, which perhaps mirrors the ones they would like to write. **Grades 7–10. PJ**

> Reviews: *Booklist* 5/15/2001, *SLJ* 5/1/2001, *VOYA* 6/1/2001

Rice, Anne. ***Interview with the Vampire.*** 340 pages.

> Ballantine 1991 Paper 0345337662 $7.99
> Alfred A. Knopf 1993 Trade 0394498216 $27.95

Anne Rice's Vampire Chronicles took the public imagination by storm, beginning with *Interview* in 1974. The story of Louis, the reluctant vampire who recounts his life first as a man then as a member of the undead club to an eager reporter, is filled with Rice's signature lush descriptions, complex characterizations, and the fictional world she created with such conviction that it has become part of the American cultural landscape. Although she disavowed the movie starring Tom Cruise originally, she later admitted she felt Cruise was acceptable as Lestat, her main-attraction vampire. While the film is good, it cannot begin to represent the layers of emotional turmoil in Louis or the conflicting desires of his interviewer. Like Lestat, this is a story that will not die; several sequels have emerged for the teens to sink their teeth into. **Grades 10—12 (mature). PT**

Rinaldi, Ann. **The Last Silk Dress.** 350 pages.

Laurel-Leaf 1988 Paper 0440228611 $5.99

One of Rinaldi's most popular historical novels is set during the Civil War. The main character, 14-year-old Susan, is too young to fight for the Rebels, but desperately wants to support her family and its cause. Her plan is to create a hot-air balloon sewn from dresses to function as a spy plane made of silk dresses sewn together. Her project never really gets off the ground as she is distracted first by love, then by the uncovering of a family secret. An entertaining story that asks readers to consider questions such as loyalty and honor. **Grades 6—9. PJ**

Rinaldi, Ann. **Wolf by the Ears.** 252 pages.

Scholastic 1993 Paper 0590434128 $4.99

Rinaldi retells the story of Thomas Jefferson and his slave/mistress Sally Hemmings through the eyes of Harriet Hemmingway, the daughter of the couple. The book follows Harriet's choice to leave Jefferson's care and attempt to pass in white society. With big issues like slavery and race relations balanced by teen issues such as identity and family, Rinaldi crafts a tale that *VOYA* called "tantalizing . . . history brought to life by a skillful and imaginative author." **Grades 6—9. PJ**

Robbins, Tom. **Another Roadside Attraction.** 337 pages.

Doubleday 1990 Paper 0553349481 $12.95
Bantam 1991 Paper 0553292056 $5.95

Tom Robbins has been accused of many writing sins, but dullness has never been one of them. In his first novel, he split the literary atom, and the resulting explosion is *Another Roadside Attraction*, which may or may not be the corpse of Jesus Christ. In Captain Kendrick's Memorial Hot Dog Wildlife Preserve, anything can—and often does—happen. Clairvoyant Amanda brings back a flea circus as public entertainment, and reintroduces fertility worship as the best choice of religious practice. Nothing is predictable, nothing is sane, and nothing is worth missing in this minefield of a novel. Not for the reader easily offended by the outrageous. **Grades 10—12 (mature). PT**

Rostkowski, Margaret I. ***After the Dancing Days.*** 217 pages.

> HarperTrophy 1988 Paper 0064402487 $5.99
> HarperCollins 1986 Library 006025078X $15.89

Set in the aftermath of World War I, the horror of the conflict is brought home in this heavily honored book. Annie's favorite uncle is killed in the war, while her physician father cares for wounded soldiers in a veterans' hospital. It is there that Annie meets Andrew, a bitter young man disfigured in the war. As Annie enters Andrew's life, she finds her own life transformed as well as some of her notions about the "glory" of war. Award include Notable Children's Books, Best Books, *Booklist's* Youth Editors' Choices, and Golden Kite Award for Fiction (SCBW). **Grades 6—9. PJ**

Rowling, J. K. ***Harry Potter and the Chamber of Secrets.*** 341 pages.

> Scholastic 2000 Paper 0439064872 $6.99
> Scholastic 1999 Trade 0439064864 $19.95

The Chamber of Secrets continues the Harry Potter story, and it is to Rowling's credit that her characters change and grow. With the students, they are literally maturing. With the adults, more is revealed, especially of Hagrid, Headmaster Dumbledore, and favorite teacher Professor McGonagall. Oh, and someone is turning the students to stone, and Harry has to find out who, why, and how to put an end to it. **Grades 6—12. PT <TEN>**

> Reviews: *Booklist* 5/15/1999, *SLJ* 7/1/1999

Rowling, J. K. ***Harry Potter and the Goblet of Fire.*** 734 pages.

> Scholastic 2000 Trade 0439139597 $25.95

Goblet of Fire finds Harry in his fourth year at Hogwarts, an upperclassman, Quidditch champion, and on the brink of discovering the greatest secret yet: girls. Hermione, he and Ron see in amazement, cleans up quite well for a school dance, and the stage is set for possible romance in future volumes. Harry's also got something of a crush on lovely Cho Chan, fellow Quidditch player, whom he would like to get to know a little better if he can avoid all the perils awaiting him on and off the Quidditch field. **Grades 6—12. PT**

> Reviews: *Booklist* 8/1/2000, *SLJ* 8/1/2000

Rowling, J. K. ***Harry Potter and the Prisoner of Azkaban.*** 435 pages.

> Scholastic 1999 Trade 0439136350 $19.95

Harry finally comes face to face with the horror that murdered his parents and almost dispatched him on the same night. In some respects this one is the darkest of all the books. Lord Voldemort and his army of hellish enforcers, The Dementors, are chilling enough creations to adults, much less children. However, Rowling has set the stage for the great evil represented by these beings, and it is an inescapable part of Harry's development from orphan to hero. **Grades 6—12. PT <TEN>**

Reviews: *Booklist* 9/1/1999, *SLJ* 10/1/1999

Rowling, J. K. *Harry Potter and the Sorcerer's Stone.* 309 pages.

Scholastic 1999 Paper 059035342X $6.99
Arthur A. Levine 1998 Trade 0590353403 $19.95

Unless you've been living on the planet Pluto for the past five years, you've either read Harry Potter or know several people who have. A publishing phenomenon of the first order, J. K. Rowling has become her own cottage industry, licensing everything from bookends to coffee cups, not to mention the first of seven planned films. Each of the four books in the series so far published follows one year in the life of Harry Potter as he attends Hogwarts School for Witches and Wizards. There are three books announced for the future, culminating in his graduation from the school and his emergence into the world as a fully educated magician. Harry's adventures begin as he is invited to attend Hogwarts, an idea most displeasing to his hideous family, the Dursleys: aunt, uncle, and repulsive cousin Dudley. A kind of male Cinderella, Harry must live in a tiny closet under the stairs and hasn't had a birthday party in 11 years. Rescued by Hagrid, the fascinating giant and Hogwarts resident beast tender, Harry undergoes a transformation from abused nobody to school celebrity. Harry's dead parents, it seems, are legendary, and he is, too, by virtue of the fact that he survived the murder attempt on his infant life. Just who tried to kill him is hush-hush—not even the name is spoken—but eventually Harry begins to unravel both the secrets of Hogwarts and of his own past. Accompanied on every adventure by Hermione (loosely based on Rowling herself), the booksmart girl who uses her intelligence as an early warning defense system, and Ron Weasley, the red-headed boy who adores Harry, the future wizard acquits himself equally well in the classroom, on the Quidditch field, and against the ever-more mysterious beings that threaten Hogwart's. **Grades 6—12. PT <HIPPLE> <TEN> <YALSA>**

Reviews: *Booklist* 9/15/1998, *SLJ* 10/1/1998

Ryan, Pam Munoz. *Esperanza Rising.* 262 pages.

Scholastic 2000 Trade 0439120411 $15.95

When her father is murdered, 14-year-old Esperanza's picture-perfect life is shattered. Growing up wealthy on a ranch in Mexico, she has never wanted for anything. After the murder, however, her life becomes one of desperation as she and her mother are forced from their land and into a life as migrant workers in California. Ryan is also a poet; she fills the book with Spanish phrases and lyric images. The beauty of the language contrasts sharply with the harshness of Esperanza's new life. Set during the Great Depression, the novel is sometimes a young adult version of *The Grapes of Wrath* with Esperanza in the Tom Joad role of observer of strikes, violence, and injustice. The book is heavy with family and community as a young woman discovers where "true wealth" lies. **Grades 6—9. PJ**

Reviews: *Booklist* 12/1/2000, *SLJ* 10/1/2000, VOYA 12/1/2000

Ryan, Sara. ***Empress of the World.*** 213 pages.

Viking 2001 Trade 0670896888 $15.99

Ryan takes a basic young adult set-up, the summer camp novel, and adds a twist. Nicole, the book's narrator, is a budding anthropologist; thus, the novel is filled with her "field notes" about the people she encounters. Nicole grows close to a small group of friends, but is particularly drawn to Battle, a charismatic young woman. The book builds to Nicole and Battle's sharing their first kiss and what that means to each of them. Nicole is spunky, likable, and smart as she tries to figure out her sexual identity. **Grades 8—10. PJ**

Reviews: *Booklist* 7/1/2001, *SLJ* 7/1/2001, *VOYA* 8/1/2001

Rylant, Cynthia. ***Missing May.*** 89 pages.

Dell 1993 Paper 0440408652 $5.50
Orchard 1992 Trade 0531059960 $14.95

Summer has been passed around from relative to relative during her childhood. She finally finds a home at age six with her Aunt May and Uncle Orb in the hills of West Virginia. But her love for May turns to grief during her 12th year when her beloved aunt dies. Told in first person, Summer's story is one of struggles with the loss of her aunt, her uncle's deep sadness, as well as her growing attraction to a neighborhood boy. This Newbery Award winner is light on action, but heavy on mood and emotion. **Grades 6—7. PJ**

Reviews: *SLJ* 3/1/1992

Sachar, Louis. ***Holes.*** 233 pages.

Farrar Straus Giroux 1999 Trade 0374332657 $17.00

Take one part coming of age, one part adventure, one part survival story, one part historical narrative, and one part prison-escape story and you have the perfect mixture for a book that will keep readers flipping pages right to the end. Sachar's book will appeal to the teen who feels wrongfully accused and to those young adults who just feel that the grown-ups don't have a clue as to what's really going on in the world. **Grades 6—12. (Annotation by Hope Baugh)** <HIPPLE><MOCK><YALSA>

Reviews: *Booklist* 6/1/1998, *SLJ* 9/1/1998

Saint-Exupery, Antoine de. ***The Little Prince.*** 80 pages.

Harcourt 2000 Trade 0152023984 $18.00

Who can resist the charm of *The Little Prince*, alone on his own planet, reaching understanding of the great lessons of life? Absolutely delightful, the book reads easily but tackles some of the basic philosophies of being human. Enchanting and highly recommended for all readers. **Grades 6—12. PT**

Salinger, J. D. ***The Catcher in the Rye.*** 277 pages.

Little, Brown 1991 Paper 0316769487 $5.99
Little, Brown 2001 Paper 0316769177 $13.95

"If you really want to know," says the quintessential teenage anti-hero Holden Caulfield, and he says it often, because like so many adolescents, he's pretty sure adults don't want to know. And he may have a point. Salinger's 1950 seminal work explores Holden's confusion about life, love, sex, family, and most of all, hypocrisy. After being expelled from a number of tony East Coast prep schools, Holden travels home to New York, running a commentary on all the "phonies" he meets along the way. There are two people in the world who command his respect: his little sister, Phoebe, and his dead brother, Allie. Haunted by memories, disgusted by the world, longing for the simplicity of a time when he took Phoebe to see the mummies at the Met, Holden's journey is peppered by images of death and lost love. His eventual breakdown and confinement to a psychiatric hospital (from which he narrates the story of his life) are the inevitable consequences for a boy who sees too clearly the things in life his so-called "role models" choose to ignore. *Catcher* has the greatest resonance with those in the 15- to 20-year age range, but Salinger is a writer of such insight and clarity that those who first read his novel a lifetime ago—especially those with children of Holden's age—might want to revisit it now and again. **Grades 9—12. PT**

Salisbury, Graham. ***Under the Blood Red Sun.*** 246 pages.

Dell 1995 Paper 0440411394 $5.5

As with most everyone, Tomi's life is shattered on the morning of 7 December 1941 when the Japanese attack Pearl Harbor. Tomi is playing baseball that morning with his best friend Billy and watches the plane fly over, running for cover to avoid the bullets shooting from the sky. But his running is really just beginning, as it is for all Japanese Americans. His grandfather and father are soon arrested; his mother loses her job; and his young sister loses her will to live. Salisbury shows a young man caught in the middle of a historic event, pushed from all sides, and wondering if there is a safe way out. Salisbury loads the book with historical detail and excellent scenes of the attack itself, but the real story is the growing paranoia and suspicion between the Japanese and Americans. **Grades 6—8. PJ**

Sanchez, Alex. ***Rainbow Boys.*** 233 pages.

Simon & Schuster 2001 Trade 0689841000 $17.00

This book takes a look at adolescent male homosexuality from three different stand-points: the completely "out" kid, the one whom everyone suspects but who hasn't really come out, and the jock whom nobody suspects. The book is great until the very end where is resolves itself too quickly and nicely. **Grades 9—12. (Annotation by Melanie Atkinson)**

Reviews: *Booklist* 11/15/2001, *SLJ* 10/1/2001, *VOYA* 12/1/2001

Sapphire. ***Push.*** 141 pages.

Random House 1997 Trade 0679446265 $20.00

The title is appropriate: a novel that certainly pushes the envelope about what teens should or shouldn't read. This novel is an index of abuse set in Harlem. The main character, Precious, has a life that is anything but. Raped by her father since age five, she is now pregnant by him for the second time. The first child was born with Down Syndrome. If those were not enough odds against her, she is also poor, barely literate, and feels totally unloved and alone. It seems she has no way out of her living hell, until she enrolls in a literacy class. There she meets a teacher who reaches out and encourages her to push herself above her circumstances. Graphic language, gritty descriptions, a first-person narrative rendered in the dialect of someone barely literate, and difficult themes make this a novel for mature readers who can go below the surface of sensation and find the message of hope and the power of words. **Grades 10—12 (mature). PJ**

Reviews: *Booklist* 5/1/1996

Scoppetton, Sandra. ***Happy Endings Are All Alike.*** 184 pages.

Alyson 1999 155583177X $6.95
Alyson 2000 Paper 1555835112 $10.00

After many years this early young adult novel about a gay romance is back in print as part of the Alyson Classics series. The plot is pretty standard stuff about two high school students who fall in love. They hide their relationship, in particular from their parents, but they are exposed; that is when bad things happen to these two good people. While somewhat dated, the emotions of the characters remain strong. One Amazon reviewer noted, "I read this book when I first thought I might be a lesbian. This book left a deep impact on me and I have never found a book so powerful, sad, and so easily relatable." **Grades 7—12. PJ**

Sebestyen, Ouida. ***The Girl in the Box.*** 166 pages.

Laurel-Leaf 1988 Paper 0440228735 $4.99

An amazing and overlooked survival novel with a frightening premise. Jackie has been kidnapped; she has no idea why or by whom. The novel is her thoughts as she sits alone in the dark, wondering about her future but also going through her past. **Grades 6—9. PJ**

Sebestyen, Ouida. ***Words by Heart.*** 162 pages.

Dell 1997 Paper 044041346X $5.50

Vowing to gain her father's approval and her white classmates' respect by winning a Bible-quoting contest, Lena, an African American girl, is horrified when her success brings violence and death to her home. **Grades 6—9. PJ**

Sheldon, Dyan. ***Confessions of a Teenage Drama Queen.*** 272 pages.

Candlewick 2002 Paper 0763618489 $6.99
Candlewick 1999 Trade 076360822X $16.99

Sheldon's flawed heroine, Mary Elizabeth Cep, hilariously accepts the gauntlet villainously thrown by the scheming Carla Santini, as both vie for the coveted position of Drama Queen of Dellwood High. Funnier than *Angus, Thongs* and *Full Frontal Snogging, Confessions* perfectly encapsulated all the pettiness, manipulation, and sheer fun of female adolescence long before Georgia crossed the Atlantic. **Grades 6—9. (Annotation by Jennifer Hubert)** <LOST>

Reviews: *Booklist* 11/1/1999, *SLJ* 10/1/1999, *VOYA* 2/1/ 2000

Sherwood, Ben. ***The Man Who Ate the 747.*** 260 pages.

Bantam 2002 Paper 0553582801 $6.50
Bantam 2000 Trade 0553801821 $19.95

In Ben Sherwood's universe, a man bringing a woman candy and flowers is passé. If you want to impress a girl, try emulating the lovesick farmer who's chowing down, one bite of fuselage at a time, on a 747 to prove his passion. The premise of this charming novel is constructed on the travels of J. Smith, Keeper of the Records for the Book of Records; Smith wanders the world to record all the wonderfully weird human endeavors that qualify for entrance into his Ripley's-like account. Magical realism at its most delightful, *The Man Who Ate a 747* is a vivid exploration into the ridiculous for all readers. **Grades 10—12. PT**

Reviews: *Booklist* 8/1/2000

Shetterly, Will. **Elsewhere.** 272 pages.

> TOR 1992 Paper 0812520033 $3.99
> Harcourt 1991 Trade 0152007318 $16.95

Bordertown is just that: a border between two worlds. On one side is the real world; on the other is the world of Faire. This threshold is no paradise, however; violence lurks about as gangs of humans, elves, and "halfies" struggle for control. Into this strange land comes Ron Starbuck, a young man on a quest to locate his missing brother. With its odd mix of dark fantasy and light fairy tales, *Elsewhere* is more about a peculiar place than about plot in what some have called the first punk fantasy. **Grades 9—12. PJ**

Shetterly, Will. **Nevernever.** 226 pages.

> TOR 1995 Paper 0812551516 $4.99
> Harcourt 1993 Trade 0152570225 $16.95

In this sequel, Ron returns for more adventures. Along for the ride this time is an oddball assortment of human runaways, elves, and the halfies. The quest this time around is twofold; first for Ron to reverse the spell that has turned him into a were-wolf; second, to protect the heir to the elf kingdom. Loaded with more strange characters and nail-biting action, Shetterly's unique vision is bound to score with the hip and well-read. **Grades 9—12. PJ**

> Reviews: *Booklist* 9/15/1993, *SLJ* 10/1/1993

Shusterman, Neal. **The Dark Side of Nowhere.** 185 pages.

> Starscape 2002 Paper 076534243X $5.99
> TOR 1998 Paper 0812568788 $4.99

Jason Miller is living a perfectly content, predicable, and boring life in his small town of Billington. But when his best friend dies suddenly and mysteriously, Jason realizes that something is amiss. Very, very amiss it turns out, as Jason discovers that his parents, everyone's parents, are really space aliens who are scouts for an impending invasion. Despite the *X-Files*-like plot, Shusterman creates a real character in Jason, and readers will follow his plight. An ALA Best Books and Quick Picks selection. **Grades 6—9. PJ**

> Reviews: *VOYA* 12/1/1997

Shusterman, Neal. **Downsiders.** 244 pages.

> Simon & Schuster 1999 Trade 0689803753 $16.95
> Aladdin 2001 Paper 0689839693 $4.99

Lindsay thought moving to New York would be stressful, but she had no idea. Soon after arriving in the city with her newly divorced mother, she makes the acquaintance of a strange young man named Talon. Talon soon introduces Lindsay to his part of New York: a strange underground city where he and other "downsiders" dwell. Despite coming from very different worlds, the two grow close, until Lindsay's father reappears and threatens not just Talon, but the entire underground lair. Romance, suspense, and science fiction elements all play a part, but like a *Twilight Zone* episode, the real story is about how beings learn to live peacefully with one another. **Grades 6—9. PJ**

Reviews: *SLJ* 7/1/1999, *VOYA* 8/1/1999

Silverberg, Robert (Editor). ***Legends: Short Novels by the Masters of Modern Fantasy.*** 850 pages.

TOR 1999 Paper 0812566637 $6.99
TOR 1998 Trade 0312867875 $27.95

It is like an all-star game as authors like Stephen King, Robert Jordan, Orson Scott Card, Ursula K. Le Guin, Anne McCaffrey, and Raymond E. Feist offer up not just new tales, but stories with a foundation in their best-known worlds. As each of these novelists alone is a favorite of teen readers, this collection of the brightest presenting some of their best work is sure to appeal. **Grades 8—12. PJ**

Reviews: *Booklist* 8/1/1998

Silverberg, Robert. ***Lord Valentine's Castle.*** 449 pages.

HarperPrism 1995 Paper 0061054879 $6.50
Bantam 1995 0553274368 $4.50

Outside the fabled city of Pidruid, Lord Valentine, his past lost, his future uncertain, joins a strange band of four-armed jugglers and motley near-humans in a journey across the magical land of Majipoor. Silverberg's invented landscape with its grotesqueries and vivid characters are revealed through (for Silverberg) transparent prose. Valentine's own destiny provides an undercurrent of suspense to keep readers following the conflicted hero throughout his varied and cinematic adventures. Ostensibly a novel of the far future, the flavor of the novel is pure fantasy; readers who prefer the latter won't be disappointed. **Grades 7—12. KE**

Sinclair, April. ***Coffee Will Make You Black.*** 239 pages.

Avon 1995 Paper 0380724596 $12.00
Hyperion 1993 Trade 1562827960 $19.95

If Holden Caulfield had been a girl, black, and poor, he might have been Stevie Stevenson, whose high school years begin in 1967 when being black was often considered a political statement as much as a physical attribute. Enduring all the usual adolescent angst, Stevie grapples with the hard lesson that being cool isn't always the best choice, and sometimes sexual choices require as much tolerance as skin color.

While the novel hasn't the literary value or the wide appeal found in Salinger, for young African American girls *Coffee* is a book with which to identify. **Grades 10—12. PT**

Reviews: *Booklist* 12/15/1993,

Sinclair, Upton. ***The Jungle.***

Bantam 1981 Paper 0553212451 $5.95

It is said that when President Teddy Roosevelt was reading Sinclair's 1906 novel about the unspeakable conditions in Chicago's meat-packing industry, he threw his breakfast sausages out the window in horror. What is certain is that Upton Sinclair's muckraking prose launched a government investigation that changed the working world. While the book may have limited appeal for younger readers, *The Jungle* is both a literary coup d'état and a historical revelation for those who are ready. After all, how many novelists can say their books were equally admired by as diverse a group as Roosevelt, Edmund Wilson, and George Bernard Shaw? **Grades 10—12. PT**

Sleator, William. ***The Duplicate.*** 154 pages.

Puffin 1999 Paper 0141304316 $4.99

It seems so obvious to David, when he finds the strange "Spee-de-dupe" machine, which only duplicates living things, that his dreams have come true. He can stay home and play video games while his hapless duplicate is stuck with schoolwork and chores. It soon becomes clear that his duplicate has a mind of its own, including replacing, even killing, the original. Some fairly serious science fictional speculation on identity and responsibility is tucked in amongst the fast-paced suspense. David is a very real "everyteen," and young readers will eagerly identify with his dilemma and plunge into his nightmarish adventure. **Grades 6—9. KE**

Sleator, William. ***House of Stairs.*** 166 pages.

Puffin 1991 Paper 0140345809 $5.99

William Sleator's all-time creepiest book has held up splendidly over time: Five "expendable" 16-year-olds wake up in a strange house with no walls, no ceiling, no floors—just stairs going up and out in every direction. On the single landing they find a machine, which, they soon discover, will only provide food and water if they perform certain actions in a specific order—and all five must participate! Very soon it becomes clear to them that they are being conditioned, but their only choice seems to be to obey or die of hunger and thirst. It is intensely disturbing for a book with no gore, sado-eroticism, raw language, or graphic violence. Sleator also sneaks in some thought-provoking ideas about free will and conformity. Easily accessible to younger teens, but sophisticated enough for high school, its readers will remember it for years to come. **Grades 6—9. KE <YALSA>**

Sleator, William. ***Interstellar Pig.*** 197 pages.

> Puffin 1995 Paper 0140375953 $5.99

Three attractive young yuppies move into the beach house next door and transform teenage Barney's boring summer vacation with the clever new board game they teach him, Interstellar Pig, which quickly becomes Barney's obsession. All is not as it seems, however, and the reader matches Barney's growing realization that losing the game could prove fatal, not only to Barney, but to the rest of mankind. Inventive characters and a plot that quickly piles on the tension without ever letting up make this a fantastic read for middle-school teens. *Parasite Pig*, the sequel, is nearly as much fun. **Grades 6—9. KE <MOCK>**

Sleator, William. ***Oddballs.*** 144 pages.

> Penguin Putnam 1995 Paper 0140374388 $5.99

William Sleator confirms his readers' suspicions that yes, he's always been weird, in these 10 autobiographical short stories. His affectionate portrait of an unconventional but loving family (and their hapless neighbors) is deftly drawn. From his unconventional parents to his sister's favorite car game (the Queen of England's bowel movement), the strangeness never lets up. Hand this bizarre and humorous short book to any teen, young or old, who doubts that truth can be stranger than fiction. **Grades 6—9. KE**

> Reviews: *Booklist* 8/1/1993, *VOYA* 12/1/1993,

Sleator, William. ***Others See Us.*** 163 pages.

> Puffin 1995 Paper 0140375147 $5.99

A bizarre accident grants 16-year-old Jared the ability to share the perceptions of those around him. Unfortunately, that means he discovers that his beautiful cousin is a murderous psychopath, and "Granny" shares his psychic ability—and possibly his cousin's moral compass. Although more mature readers might be put off by the piled-up coincidences that seem to drive the plot, younger readers won't care. The unremitting tension and creeping horror as Jason struggles to protect himself and the rest of his family will keep them avidly turning the pages. **Grades 6—9. KE**

Sleator, William. ***Rewind.*** 120 pages.

> Puffin 2001 Paper 0141311010 $4.99
> Dutton 1999 Trade 0525461302 $15.99

Eleven-year-old Peter blows up at his parents, runs out the door, and is struck by a car. Waking up, he finds himself hovering over his own funeral, with a disembodied voice offering him a chance to "rewind" his life and change the past. Although Peter tries to change his somewhat dysfunctional family, the bullies at school, and the teachers who just don't understand him, it is only when he decides to try to change himself does he avoid the fatal incident. The characters are well drawn, the message never overwhelms the tension, and the resolution is ultimately quite satisfying. *Rewind* is an excellent choice for younger teens. **Grades 6—9. KE**

Reviews: *Booklist* 10/15/1999, *SLJ* 8/1/1999

Smith, Cordwainer. ***The Rediscovery of Man: The Complete Short Science Fiction of Cordwainer Smith.*** 671 pages.

New England Science Fiction Association 1993 Trade 0915368560 $25.00

One of the science fictional concepts pioneered by Cordwainer Smith was that the aliens of the future are very likely to be us. In the 33 short stories in this volume the future history of mankind seems as plausible and as poetic as when it was written in the 1930s and '40s. Especially compelling are the stories that feature the Underpeople: animals bioengineered to humanoid shapes in order to serve as our new guilt-free and expendable slaves. This comprehensive collection of Smith's intelligent, often poignant, and deeply imagined short fiction is a must for any library that wants to provide beautifully written speculative fiction. **Grades 9—12. KE**

Reviews: *Booklist* 8/1/1993

Smith, Dodie. ***I Capture the Castle.*** 343 pages.

St. Martin's 1998 Paper 0312201656 $13.95
St. Martin 1998 Trade 0312181108 $23.95

This classic tells the story of 17-year-old Cassandra and her family, who live in poverty in a ramshackle old English castle. Here she strives, over six turbulent months, to hone her writing skills. She fills three notebooks with sharply funny, yet poignant, entries. Her journals candidly chronicle the great changes that take place within the castle's walls, and her own first descent into love. **Grades 10—12. PJ**

Snicket, Lemony. ***The Bad Beginning.*** 162 pages.

HarperCollins 1999 Trade 0064407667 $10.99

Snicket, aka David Handler, is the spiritual and stylistic successor to Roald Dahl. Snicket uses a similar bag of tricks and terrors with few treats as he puts the protagonists of the Series of Unfortunate Events, the three Baudelaire children, through one predicament after the other. The joke, of course, is how bad these events are; these are some unlucky kids, yet they always seem to persevere. There are 13 (get it?) volumes planned, so there are still swords hanging over the lives of these young people. Older kids and younger teens flock to these books, which invert the *Goose-bumps* formula, mixing six parts humor with one part horror. You could also look at it as the *Flowers in the Attic* saga, with its endless series of horror inflicted upon the same kids, played for laughs. **Grades 6—8. PJ**

Reviews: *Booklist* 12/1/1999

Sones, Sonya. ***Stop Pretending.*** 149 pages.

HarperCollins 1999 Library 0060283866 $14.89
HarperTempest 2001 Paper 0064462188 $6.95
HarperCollins 1999 Trade 0060283874 $14.95

From *The Bell Jar* to *Girl, Interrupted*, books about teenage girls and mental illness have a long history. As many teen girls often feel "crazy" as they learn to control a host of new emotions, the appeal of such stories is obvious. The subtitle of this book, *What Happened When My Big Sister Went Crazy*, shows the particular take of this book. The story, told in a series of blank-verse poems, is about an unnamed 13-year-old girl's reaction to her sister's increasingly strange behavior. At first, she feels fear (that she too will go crazy); embarrassment (that her friends will find out); and sadness (at losing her sister, her best friend), but as the book progresses, her feelings grow increasingly complex. Both a Best Books and Quick Picks Selection. **Grades 6—9. PJ**

Reviews: *Booklist* 11/15/1999, *SLJ* 10/1/1999

Sones, Sonya. ***What My Mother Doesn't Know.*** 259 pages.

Simon & Schuster 2001 Trade 0689841140 $17.00

Using the free-verse form, Sones looks at a different kind of crazy that affects teenagers: love crazy. At first Sophie with Dylan, he of the sexy eyes. Then with Chaz, her hot online romance. Finally with Murphy, who isn't hot and isn't sexy; he's just very special. Readers follow Sophie's bouncing heart as she searches for that special someone, although at times, her thoughts are more about lust than love. Along for the ride are two good friends to support her and a mother whose goal is to exasper-ate her. **Grades 6—9. PJ**

Reviews: *Booklist* 11/15/2001, *SLJ* 10/1/2001, *VOYA* 10/1/2001

Soto, Gary. ***Baseball in April and Other Stories.*** 111 pages.

Harcourt 2000 Paper 0152025677 $6.00
Harcourt 2000 Trade 0152025731 $16.00

A collection of 11 stories about growing up by this award-winning poet. Most of the stories are set in California's San Joaquin Valley and concern the experience of Latino youth. The events covered in these stories, such as playing baseball, are small in themselves, but Soto's looking at the larger issues in the lives of young people. In particular, Soto looks at the importance of relationships, with friends and families and neighbors, in the lives of teenagers. In that way, his stories speak to teens from all backgrounds. **Grades 6—9. PJ**

Soto, Gary. ***Buried Onions.*** 149 pages.

> HarperCollins 1999 Paper 0064407713 $11.00
> Harcourt 1996 Trade 0152013334 $17.00

A thin novel in which the main character isn't a person, but a place. Soto, with his eye for detail and talent for images, brings the streets and alleys of Fresno, California, to life. The barrio is a landscape of the walking wounded, people of all ages deeply scarred by violence, drugs, and a lack of a better tomorrow. Walking those streets of fire is 19-year-old Eddie, who wants out. His family isn't interested in Eddie's escape from this cycle of violence, but instead urges him to avenge the murder of his cousin. Teens who like happy endings will want to avoid this book. **Grades 7—10. PJ**

> Reviews: *Booklist* 11/15/1997, *SLJ* 1/1/1998, *VOYA* 10/1/1997

Soto, Gary. ***Jesse.*** 166 pages.

> Point Signature 1996 Paper 0590528378 $4.99
> Harcourt 1994 Trade 015240239X $17.00

In what might seem to be an autobiographic novel, Soto tells the tale of a teen's coming of age in 1968. The setting again is Fresno, and the main character Jesse is a sensitive, searching, artistic young man facing numerous obstacles. He has moved out of his home and into an apartment with his brother in order to escape his alcoholic, abusive father. Both he and his brother know their options are few and their future, with the fields of Vietnam hovering like a dark cloud over them, is not bright. Education is their ticket, but to earn that money, they have to work in the field of California's fruit basket. But Jesse's most important job is becoming a man, which Soto depicts with realism and compassion. **Grades 8—10. PJ**

> Reviews: *Booklist* 10/1/1994, *SLJ* 12/1/1994, *VOYA* 2/1/1995

Soto, Gary. ***Local News.*** 148 pages.

> Scholastic 1994 Paper 059048446X $4.99

In a sort of sequel to *Baseball in April*, Soto present another collection of short stories about everyday life for Latino teens. Nothing earth-shattering in these stories, which are peppered with Spanish words and phrases, but instead, ordinary events in the lives of Latino teens, events that matter the world to them. **Grades 6—9. PJ**

Soto, Gary. ***Petty Crimes.*** 157 pages.

> Harcourt 1998 Trade 0152016589 $17.00

Another collection of stories that seems to walk the border between the light of stories in *Baseball in April* and the darkness found in novels like *Buried Onions*. The setting is the same, but coming of age seems harder: more poverty, more crime, more violence, and more confrontations. If some of Soto's other works are about the power of relationships, this collection focuses a little bit more on dangerous relationships, such as gangs and bullies. The language is filled with powerful images, Spanish phrases, and Soto's authentic voice. **Grades 6–9. PJ**

Reviews: *Booklist* 3/15/1998, *SLJ* 5/1/1998

Sparks, Beatrice. ***Almost Lost: The True Story of an Anonymous Teenager's Life on the Streets.*** 240 pages.

Avon Flare 1996 Paper 038078341X $4.99

The "true story" of Sam, a suicidal, depressed teenage boy who travels the road to hell and back emerged from tapes of Sam's therapy session as he lays his life on the line. It's all here: running away from home, involvement in a gang that becomes just another dysfunctional family for him, life on the streets, and a deluge of self-hatred. Sam is cut off from the world; his only connection is to his own loathing and loneliness. But, as with all the Beatrice Sparks "anonymous" books, the real message isn't the grit but rather the pearl of hope as another young person escapes the hard life through peace, love, and understanding. **Grades 9–12. PJ**

Reviews: *SLJ* 7/1/1996

Sparks, Beatrice. ***Annie's Baby: The Diary of Anonymous, a Pregnant Teenager.*** 245 pages.

Avon Flare 1998 Paper 0380791412 $5.99

The title really says it all. Sparks shapes the story of Annie, pregnant at age 14. There's little action, or even exploitation; instead readers watch as Annie struggles with decisions, first and foremost wondering if she should keep the baby or give it up for adoption. **Grades 7–12. PJ**

Reviews: *SLJ* 7/1/1998, *VOYA* 6/1/1998

Sparks, Beatrice. ***Go Ask Alice.*** 159 pages.

Aladdin 1998 Paper 0689817851 $4.99

As important a book in young adult literature as *The Outsiders* or *The Chocolate War*. As dated in some ways as those *Dragnet* episodes about "hippies" and urban legends about LSD, this "true story" of an addicted teen is, in fact, timeless. The drugs may have changed, from LSD to ecstasy, and the slang makes it read more like historical fiction, but the core of the story rings true. An isolated teen, trying to fit in while also pleasing her parents, turns her life over to drugs. The drugs give her comfort, but then they take control. Despite the obvious propaganda value of this book, teens still read it because the core issues remain relevant. **Grades 7–12. PJ <YALSA>**

Sparks, Beatrice. *It Happened to Nancy.* 241 pages.

Avon 1994 Paper 0380773155 $5.99

Fourteen-year-old Nancy meets eighteen-year-old Collin, and the picture of the young in-love couple seems perfect. Then he rapes her, also destroying her life because she discovers that she is now infected with HIV. The book takes off from there as Nancy finds support from her friends and her family to heal her spirit, even if there is no way (at the time the book was written) to heal her body. The cautionary tale ends, of course, with Nancy's death, followed by a list of resources regarding rape and HIV. **Grades 7–12. PJ**

Reviews: *Booklist* 6/1/1994, *SLJ* 6/1/1994

Sparks, Beatrice. *Jay's Journal.* 192 pages.

Simon & Schuster 1996 Paper 0671735594 $6.50

More urban legend comes to life as Sparks recounts the story of Jay, a teen who goes from dabbling in drugs to becoming society's worst nightmare: the drug-crazed Satanic teen. Jay's first foray into drugs lands him in rehab, where he encounters Pete. Soon he is playing with Ouija boards and, before you know it, making animal sacrifices and becoming a disciple to the Dark Lord. It is over-blown, but unbelievably readable. **Grades 9–12. PJ**

Sparks, Beatrice. *Kim Empty Inside.* 165 pages.

HarperCollins 2002 Paper 0380814609 $5.99

Featuring a slightly older character than normal—Kim is a college freshman—the formula remains the same: finding an outlet for the pain of growing up. Here, when loneliness makes Kim feel empty, she decides to mirror the state of her mind with that of her body and begins the cycle of binging/purging. **Grades 7–12. PJ**

Sparks, Beatrice. *Treacherous Love: The Diary of an Anonymous Teenager.* 164 pages.

Morrow/Avon 2000 Paper 0380808625 $4.99

Another 14-year-old whose life spins out of control. Beginning with the usual stew of social isolation and a dysfunctional family, Jennie is lost and alone. The answer isn't in drugs but, instead, in finding someone to care about her. Enter Mr. Johnstone, a math teacher who takes a special interest in Jennie. A very special interest, which soon takes control of her life. **Grades 7–12. PJ**

Speare, Elizabeth George. ***The Sign of the Beaver***. 135 pages.

> Dell 1985 Paper 0440479002 $5.50
> Houghton Mifflin 1983 Trade 0395338905 $16.00

Elizabeth Speare, twice a winner of the Newbery Award (for *The Witch of Blackbird Pond* and *The Bronze Bow*), scores again with this story of the relationship between 13-year-old Matt and the Native American Attean and Attean's grandfather. Trading survival skills for literacy, Matt learns Indian culture while teaching Attean to read. An ALA Notable Book and IRA Teachers' Choice, *Sign of the Beaver* is another excellent novel from a tried and true master of the young adult genre. **Grades 6–8. PT**

Spinelli, Jerry. ***Maniac Magee.*** 184 pages.

> Little, Brown 2000 Paper 0316809063 $5.95
> Little, Brown 1990 Trade 0316807222 $15.95

Lionel Magee is a legend in his own time. They say he can run faster than anyone, which makes sense because Lionel has spent a lot of time running away. Homeless at age 12, Lionel shows up one day in Two Mills, Pennsylvania, and starts turning heads with his displays of athletic prowess. But his real courage isn't on the field; it is in his directly and boldly confronting the racism that is tearing the town apart. This Newbery Award winner tackles tough issues with humor and grace. A favorite of young teens who can find in Maniac a role model and a hero, whether he is real of not. **Grades 6–10. PJ**

Spinelli, Jerry. ***Stargirl.*** 186 pages.

> Random House 2002 Paper 037582233X $8.95
> Knopf 2000 Library 0679986375 17.99
> Knopf 2000 Trade 0679886370 $15.95

Stargirl captures the heart of narrator Leo Borlock—and she captures the reader's as well—in this book about conformity, popularity, and being true to yourself. When my daughter turned 15 and I asked whom we should invite to her birthday party, she wistfully said, "I wish Stargirl could come." High praise for a literary character who lives well beyond the last page of this novel, which is also about the intensity of first love and the magic of seeing the world through someone else's eyes. **Grades 6–9. (Annotation by Dr. Lois Stover)**

> Reviews: *Booklist* 6/15/2000, *SLJ* 8/1/2000

Staples, Suzanne Fisher. ***Haveli.*** 276 pages.

> Random House 1995 Paper 0679865691 $5.50

In this sequel to *Shabanu: Daughter of the Wind*, readers follow Shabanu as she attempts to live life both as a wife and mother, even if she herself is still a child. One of four wives to her husband, she is trapped in a terrible situation, so she focuses her attention on making sure her daughter does not repeat her life. But when she sees a chance for true happiness and love, she must once again summon the courage and strength to battle a culture posed to crush any woman's desire for independence. **Grades 8—10. PJ**

Reviews: *Booklist* 6/1/1993, *VOYA* 12/1/1993

Staples, Suzanne Fisher. ***Shabanu: Daughter of the Wind.*** 240 pages.

Alfred A. Knopf 1991 Paper 0679810307 $5.99

When Shabanu turns 13 in her homeland of Pakistan, it won't be parties, trips to the mall, and figuring out which boy to like. When Shabanu becomes a teen, her culture requires her to marry a man selected by her father. At first, Shabanu doesn't mind this so much, but when she finds out her match is a much older man who just happens to be rich, she rebels. Rebelling against a father's wishes in Pakistan doesn't mean getting grounded. It means her father can kill her. Shabanu must decide to face her fate or somehow find her own way in the world despite the danger. This is a powerful book, giving a clear picture of the Pakistani culture. Very well-drawn characters, especially that of Shabanu, make this story come alive and bring the issue of women's rights to the forefront. It can also help teens understand that life for teens in other countries can be extremely different from the life to which they are accustomed. **Grades 8—10. (Annotation by Diane Tuccillo) <YALSA>**

Reviews: *Booklist* 1/1/1995, *Booklist* 8/1/1997

Steinbeck, John. ***The Grapes of Wrath.*** 619 pages.

Simon & Schuster 1988 Paper 0671006924 $3.95
Viking 1992 Paper 0140186409 $13.00

Winner of the Pulitzer Prize in 1940, *The Grapes of Wrath* traces the journey of the Joad family from Dust Bowl Oklahoma to what they believe will be salvation in California. Ma Joad and her grown children, Tom and Rose of Sharon, are quickly disillusioned. The lot of the migrant worker is exceedingly difficult, and John Steinbeck's championship of the working poor is never more movingly delivered than in this novel. Most appropriate for high school and above. **Grades 9—12. PT**

Steinbeck, John. ***Of Mice and Men.*** 186 pages.

Viking 1994 Paper 0140188290 $5.00
Penguin 2002 Paper 0142000671 $11.00

Published in 1937, this is the novella that brought Steinbeck international acclaim. The story about the bond between migrant workers George Milton and Lennie Small is poignant and tragic. Two ranch hands who dream of owning their own farm, George is a father figure to Lennie who, though small of intellect, is huge in both body and heart. When Lennie accidentally kills the rancher's daughter-in-law, George must make an impossible decision regarding his dearest friend. Reborn as a three-act play in 1937 and as several movie versions, *Of Mice and Men* has a universal appeal in its theme of goodness disguised by ugliness hiding behind the societal "norm." **Grades 10—12. PT**

Steinbeck, John. ***The Red Pony.*** 100 pages.

> Puffin 1993 Paper 0140177361 $6.95
> Penguin 1994 Paper 0140187391 $10.00

Four related stories make up this novella from 1945. The most famous is "The Gift," in which young Jody Tiflin is given a red pony to care for and to train. Despite Jody's efforts, the poor animal dies, and Jody learns early the mercilessness of Nature. Also included are "The Great Mountains," "The Promise," and "The Leader of the People," in which Jody expands his maturation. An excellent introduction to Steinbeck. **Grades 8—10. PT**

Stephenson, Neal. ***Snow Crash.*** 440 pages.

> Bantam 2000 Paper 0553380958 $13.95

A book that knows its audience; it seems as if it could have been produced by a teen focus group. This early cyberpunk novel set in the not-so-distant future has it all, including a main character named Hiro, who is a hacker, samurai swordsman, and pizza-delivery driver. Hiro uses all of those skills to battle a deadly new drug slash computer virus. He's not just on a rescue mission; he's also on a spiritual quest. This has it all, not to mention Stephenson's smart, sarcastic commentary on a Rollerball-like world where corporations, not governments, rule the world. Influential, entertaining, and exciting. **Grades 10—12. PJ**

> Reviews: *Booklist* 4/1/1992

Stevenson, Robert Louis. ***Dr. Jekyll and Mr. Hyde.*** Page count varies with edition.

> Signet 1997 Paper 0451523938 $3.95

Despite the mob of movies and the Broadway musical, this late work from Robert Louis Stevenson is neither a typical horror story nor appropriate reading for anyone without a high level of sophisticated comprehension. Following in Mary Shelley's footsteps, Stevenson creates a creator, but Dr. Jekyll's monster is, in fact, himself. A spiritual and intellectual journey through the maze of human dichotomy, *Dr. Jekyll and Mr. Hyde* is rendered through multiple points of view, in dense prose, and with far fewer plot points than the films would lead you to believe. A short work, it casts a gigantic shadow across much of the 20th-century literature that was to follow it. The eternal question of why man's good nature is required to battle with its own dark side is one of the fundamental philosophical queries in human history, and with *Jekyll and Hyde* it has never been more powerfully or more uniquely explored. **Grades 7—12. PT**

Stine, R. L. ***Nightmare Hour.*** 148 pages.

> HarperCollins 1999 Trade 0060286881 $14.95
> HarperAvon 2000 Paper 0064408426 $4.99

One of Stine's few stand-alone and hardcover books is a collection of 10 scary stories. In addition to the stories, there are illustrations and Stine's own introductions telling readers about his writing process. Like most Stine books, the stories find young teens face to face with something quite horrible. There are gross-outs, ghost stories, and a few softer tales that make this collection a great introduction to Stine. As usual, Stine keeps the pace moving with short, punchy sentences; realistic, if often abbreviated, dialogue; and plenty of cliffhangers. **Grades 6—7. PJ**

> Reviews: *Booklist* 10/15/1999, *SLJ* 12/1/1999

Stoehr, Shelley. ***Weird on the Outside.*** 192 pages.

> Bantam Doubleday Dell 1996 Paper 0440220106 $3.99

Shelley Stoehr's detailed account of a wayward teenage stripper was one of the first truly "gritty" young adult novels of the 90s. Without romanticizing her protagonist's actions or moralizing about their consequences, Stoehr presented an honest, unflinching look at the underbelly of the adolescent experience. **Grades 8—10. (Annotation by Jennifer Hubert) <LOST>**

> Reviews: *SLJ* 2/1/1995, *VOYA* 2/1/1995

Strasser, Todd. ***Give a Boy a Gun.*** 146 pages.

> Simon Pulse 2002 Paper 0689848935 $4.99
> Simon & Schuster 2000 Trade 0689811128 $16.00

A controversial book trying to make sense out of the shooting at Columbine High School. Told from the point of view of several different narrators and heavily footnoted with facts about teens and guns, Strasser confronts school violence head-on. Two high school misfits (Gary and Brendan) decide to take vengeance on all those who have taunted and teased them throughout the year, in particular macho jocko Sam Flach. The two boys gather guns and make bombs, then storm the school. The drama and trauma inside the school asks more questions than can be answered, in part, because there are no easy solutions to the high school high-testosterone environment that creates both victims and bullies. **Grades 7—12. PJ**

> Reviews: *Booklist* 10/1/2000, *SLJ* 9/1/2000, *VOYA* 10/1/2000

Strasser, Todd. ***How I Changed My Life.*** 186 pages.

> Aladdin 1996 Paper 068980895X $4.99

In alternating first-person narratives, two teenagers describe their decisions to transform themselves. Bo is a shy, slightly overweight teenage girl. She loves theater, but is far too self-conscious to step out front; instead she acts as the stage manager. Entering stage center is Kyle, a high school football hunk who needs to keep busy while nursing an injury. Standing between them is Kyle's current heartthrob, Chloe, who is everything that Bo is not. Good teen movie fodder. **Grades 7–10. PJ**

> Reviews: *Booklist* 5/1/1995, *SLJ* 5/1/1995, *VOYA* 10/1/1995

Strasser, Todd. ***How I Spent My Last Night on Earth***. 169 pages.

> Aladdin 2000 Paper 0689822871 $4.99
> Simon & Schuster 1998 Trade 0689811136 $16.00

Allegra Hanover is the class brain: perfect SATs, Honor Society president, and National Merit Scholar. She's always driven to get good grades with no time for distractions, such as love. She's focused on her future. But if there is no future, if the end of the world—thanks to an asteroid hurling itself toward Earth—is really upon her, then what does she really want out of life? The answer is to be with Andros Bliss, the surfer dude, the "anti" of everything she believes in. Strasser's work doing movie tie-ins serves him well as he keeps the pace moving, throws in lots of easily identifiable high school types, and ties the whole thing together with lots of comic dialogue. **Grades 7–10. PJ**

> Reviews: *Booklist* 11/1/1998, *SLJ* 11/1/1998, *VOYA* 08/1/1999

Stratton, Allan. ***Leslie's Journal.*** 196 pages.

> Annick 2000 Paper 1550376640 $8.95
> Annick 2000 Trade 1550376659 $19.95

School Library Journal called this novel in diary form about dating violence the "*Go Ask Alice* of this millennium." In her journal, Leslie records her inner feelings, confident that her teacher will abide by her promise never to read the content of the journals. But when a substitute teacher peeks inside, she is horrified at what she learns about Leslie's life. Leslie's days and nights revolve around her boyfriend Jason. Desperate for attention and affection, she is drawn to Jason and sticks with him, even after he rapes her. She stays with him because it is better than being alone, but Jason begins to control her every move. When she tries to leave, he threatens her and she fears for her life. A harrowing look at teen love gone horribly wrong. **Grades 9–12 (mature). PJ**

> Reviews: *Booklist* 3/15/2001, *SLJ* 4/1/2001, *VOYA* 2/1/2001

Sweeney, Joyce. **Players.** 222 pages.

> Winslow 2001 Paper 158837016X $5.95
> Winslow 2000 Trade 1890817546 $16.95

A slam-bang sports novel with a tint of suspense. Corey is the captain and star player of his high school basketball team. But when a new player (Noah) joins the team, not only is Corey's place on the team threatened, but also the team's entire season is in jeopardy because of a series of strange accidents and incidents. For Corey, the worst occurs when his best friend is kicked off the team for having a gun in his locker. Like most sports novels, what matters most isn't the play, but the players and how these young men interact with each other and with adversity. **Grades 6—9. PJ**

> Reviews: *SLJ* 9/1/2000, *VOYA* 12/1/2000

Tan, Amy. **The Joy Luck Club.** 288 pages.

> Random House 1991 Paper 067972768X $12.95
> Putnam 1989 Trade 0399134204 $24.95

That famous 1960s expression "generation gap" is never so well illustrated as by these stories about four Chinese mothers and their Americanized daughters. It's 1949 San Francisco, and a group of immigrant women begin an informal alliance to play mahjong, eat a little dim sum, and talk. And so is born the Joy Luck Club. Each of the four has suffered more than should be asked of any woman, but they never succumb to self-pity; indeed, they draw strength from one another as their bonds of friendship deepen. Segue to 1989, and the narratives are now the web upon which the women's grown daughters try to unravel their mothers' secrets while coming to terms with the clash of opposing familial cultures. As the daughters begin to know their mothers from different perspectives, their own troubles begin to pale in comparison, and they discover reconciliation with and newfound respect for a generation of women who endured what their daughters could only guess at. Very accessible, of particular interest to anyone interested in considering family history and emotional ties. **Grades 10—12. PT**

Tashjian, Janet. **The Gospel According to Larry.** 227 pages.

> Henry Holt 2001 Trade 0805063781 $16.95

This book shows the lengths one can go to re-invent oneself and how even the most well meaning of actions can have their consequences. I feel most teens will be able to relate to many of the many emotions that "Larry" goes through throughout the story. **Grades 7—10. (Annotation by Melanie Atkinson)**

> Reviews: *Booklist* 11/1/2001, *SLJ* 10/1/2001, *VOYA* 12/1/2001

Taylor Mildred D. **_Roll of Thunder Hear My Cry._** 276 pages.

> Puffin 1997 Paper 0140384510 $6.99
> Phyllis Fogelman 2000 Trade 0803726473 $17.99

The Newbery-winning novel about the Logan family inspired three sequels as well as a prequel. The Logans are a poor black family struggling through poverty and racism in Depression-era Mississippi. The stories are told from Cassie's eyes, the Logan's only daughter, who watches as her family struggles for dignity and courage under intolerable conditions. Sequels and prequels are _Road to Memphis, Let the Circle Be Unbroken, The Land,_ and _The Well._ **Grades 6–12. PJ <MOCK>**

Temple, Frances. **_Grab Hands and Run._** 165 pages.

> HarperTrophy 1995 Paper 0064405486 $5.99

A political activist tells his family in El Salvador, "If they come for me, grab hands and run." The book tells the story of 12-year-old Felipe's journey from Central America to Canada. While this is a story of a journey, the true tale is about the strength of families under pressure. **Grades 6–9. PJ**

> Reviews: _SLJ_ 11/1/1996

Temple, Frances. **_Ramsay Scallop._** 310 pages.

> HarperTrophy 1995 Paper 0064406016 $6.99

Life as a young women in the Middle Ages is the theme of this award-winning novel. Eleanor, all of 14, is to be married to Lord Thomas, who has returned injured from the Crusades. The village priest sends the two of them on a pilgrimage to Spain. During the trip, the two young people learn more about each other, while the reader, because of Temple's attention to detail, learns about life in the 13th century. **Grades 6–9. PJ**

Tepper, Sheri S. **_Beauty._** 412 pages.

> Bantam 1992 Paper 0553295276 $6.99
> Doubleday 1991 Paper 0385419406 $19.00

Drawing on the wellspring of tales such as "Sleeping Beauty," _Beauty_ is a moving novel of love and loss, hope and despair, magic and nature. Set against a backdrop both enchanted and frightening, the story begins with a wicked aunt's curse that will afflict a young woman named Beauty on her 16th birthday. Though Beauty is able to sidestep tragedy, she soon finds she has embarked on an adventure of vast conse-quences. **Grades 10–12. PJ**

Terris, Susan. **_Nell's Quilt._** 162 pages.

> Sunburst 1996 Paper 0374454973 $5.95

In Massachusetts in the late 1800s, Nell is forced by her parents to marry a man for whom she holds no affection. She attempts to delay the marriage by working on a quilt and slowly starving herself. **Grades 6—9. PJ**

Thesman, Jean. **The Other Ones.** 181 pages.

> Viking 1999 Trade 0670885940 $15.99
> Puffin 2001 Paper 0141312467 $5.99

Fifteen-year-old Bridget wavers back and forth between embracing her fate as a family witch and her desire to just be "normal." Jean Thesman's dreamy, yet challenging, literary writing makes this young adult novel more *Jane Eyre* than *Sabrina*. **Grades 6—9. (Annotation by Jennifer Hubert) <LOST>**

> Reviews: *Booklist* 5/1/1999, *SLJ* 6/1/1999, *VOYA* 8/1/1999

Thomas, Joyce Carol. **Marked by Fire.** 164 pages.

Avon Tempest 1999 Paper 038081434X $7.95

A young African American girl has grown up under a vast Oklahoma sky shaded with pecan trees and dotted by endless rows of cotton. She has the gift of song, a storyteller's talent, the love of her parents, and the affection and pride of her community. Then the troubles begin: a tornado hits and drives Abby's family apart, a deranged neighbor targets her for a campaign of vengeful terror, and a physical assault all but breaks her will. **Grades 6—9. PJ**

Thomas, Rob. **Doing Time: Notes from the Undergrad.** 184 pages.

> Aladdin 1999 Paper 0689824149 $4.99

Here are 10 interconnected stories told in the voices of 10 different high school students doing community service in order to graduate. Some of the stories are funny, others sad, but all of them are honest in language, tone, and the fact that not all endings are happy and not every life can be changed. **Grades 8—10. PJ**

> Reviews: *Booklist* 10/1/1997, *SLJ* 11/1/1997, *VOYA* 12/1/1997

Thomas, Rob. **Rats Saw God.** 219 pages.

> Aladdin 1996 Paper 0689807775 $4.99
> Simon & Schuster 1996 Trade 0689802072 $17.00

Rats Saw God tells the story of Steve York, a National Merit finalist who is also a habitual dope smoker ("stoner"). He is failing senior English and has a rash of run-ins with school authorities. His guidance counselor, Mr. DeMouy, gives him the opportunity to avoid summer school by writing 100 pages about any subject. After several false starts, the writing project (which consumes half of the novel) takes off as a diary. Steve writes about his early high school years, mainly spent in Houston, Texas, living with his father. Steve always refers to his father as "the astronaut." It is a relationship that is strained, at best. He is floating on the outside of the school when he decides to form his own club for other outsiders. Around the same time, he falls deeply in love with a young woman named Dub, and the club falls under the guidance of an English teacher, Mr. Waters. Their betrayal of him serves as the catalyst transforming Steve from future college scholarship material to full-time stoner in what might be the best young adult novel ever. **Grades 8—10. PJ <MOCK>**

Reviews: *Booklist 6/1/1996, SLJ 6/1/1996*

Thomas, Rob. ***Slave Day.*** 188 pages.

Aladdin 1998 Paper 068982193X $4.99

The student council of a large Texas high school traditionally sponsors a "slave day," when students raise money by purchasing the services of teachers and fellow students. Outraged by the event, high school junior Keene Davenport decides to make a statement. Told in several first-person narratives, Thomas provides a variety of perspectives on both slave day and Keene's protest. **Grades 8—10. PJ**

Reviews: *SLJ 4/1/1997*

Tolkien, J. R. R. ***The Fellowship of the Ring.*** 479 pages.

Ballantine 1982 Paper 0345339703 $6.99
Houghton Mifflin 1994 Paper 0618002227 $12.00

Frodo Baggins inherits the magical ring from his Uncle Bilbo, who has grown old and weary of the ring bearer's burden, and wants to retire to an even quieter place than Hobbiton, where he is now famous, to finish writing the story of his adventures. As Bilbo reluctantly gives up the ring and goes on his way, Frodo is faced with a quest that would daunt even the strongest—to journey to the place where the ring was created, in the heart of the evil lord Sauron's kingdom, and throw it into the fiery depths of Mount Doom. Because this is such a momentous undertaking, an unlikely fellowship, including Gandalf, several hobbits, elves, dwarves, and warriors, joins Frodo, knowing that great dangers, and possibly death, await them. As they journey towards the forbidding mountain, members of the fellowship fall in battle against evil forces trying to regain possession of the ring, the band becomes separated, and Gandalf is lost. **Grades 6—12. (Annotation by Patricia Foster)**

Tolkien, J. R. R. ***The Hobbit.*** 310 pages.

Del Rey 1986 Paper 0345339681 $6.99
Ballantine 1990 Paper 0345368584 $12.95
Houghton Mifflin 1966 Trade 0395071224 $16.00

This is the beginning of Tolkien's classic fantasy epic about a magical ring of power. Bilbo Baggins, one of a race of small men known as hobbits, is very comfortable and contented in his snug little house built in the side of a hill in Hobbiton. He would like nothing better than to spend his remaining days there, but he is drawn into an adventure that includes Gandalf the wizard, 13 dwarves seeking to return to their underground home in the Lonely Mountains, the great dragon Smaug, an odd, little, nasty, treacherous creature called the Gollum, and assorted orcs, trolls, giant spiders, and wolves. This story stands alone, but ideally readers will be drawn into the adventure and want to continue on to the *Lord of the Rings* trilogy. *The Hobbit* was first published in 1937, and countless readers are still enjoying it as the first stepping stone into the world of epic fantasy. **Grades 6–12. (Annotation by Patricia Foster)**

Tolkien, J. R. R. ***The Return of the King.*** 544 pages.

> Penguin 2002 1565116690 $19.95
> Houghton Mifflin 2001 Paper 0618129111 $12.00
> Houghton Mifflin 1988 Trade 039548930X $22.00
> Ballantine 1993 Paper 0345339738 $6.99

In the finale to the *Lord of the Rings*, Frodo, with the help of his hobbit companion Sam, reaches Mount Doom, and the final climactic struggle for the ring of power takes place, with Aragorn calling up an army of the dead to defeat Sauron and save Middle-Earth. Tolkien's epic is rich and complex, drawing on his years of study of Anglo-Saxon mythology. Practically all modern-day fantasy stems from this first masterpiece of fantasy literature. Although the plot includes very few strong female figures, I would still recommend this book to anyone with an interest in fantasy, fairytales, and folklore. With a vast cast of characters, there is something to interest any reader and to give a firm grounding in the heroic fantasy genre—from sturdy little loyal hobbits to valiant heroic noblemen, ferocious uncompromising dwarves to mystical ethereal elves, the benevolent wizard Gandalf to the sneaky double-natured Gollum, vicious giant spiders to gigantic tree-people, and, of course, a fiery dragon and the evil orc armies of Sauron. Who could ask for more? Enjoy! **Grades 7–12. (Annotation by Patricia Foster)**

Tolkien, J. R. R. ***The Two Towers.*** 352 pages.

> Ballantine 1986 Paper 0345339711 $6.99
> Houghton Mifflin 1994 Paper 0618002235 $12.00
> Houghton Mifflin 2001 Paper 0618129081 $12.00
> Houghton Mifflin 1988 Trade 0395489334 $22.00

In *The Two Towers*, only two of the hobbits, Frodo and Sam, continue traveling toward Mount Doom, guided by the treacherous Gollum, as the weight of the ring becomes an almost intolerable and wearisome burden to Frodo. Gandalf returns to fight again, and other members of the band, led by Aragorn, a mysterious man also known as Strider, join forces with the immortal tree-people, the Ents, to battle Sauron's evil army of orcs. **Grades 7–12. (Annotation by Patricia Foster)**

Toole, John Kennedy. ***A Confederacy of Dunces.*** 338 pages.

> Grove 1987 Paper 0802130208 $14.00
> Louisiana State University Press 2000 Trade 0807126063 $24.95

This Pulitzer Prize winner is a great funny read for older teens. The book follows the madcap adventures of Ignatius J. Reilly, the "Don Quixote of the French Quarter whose windmills are the daily grinds of modern living." **Grades 10–12. PJ**

Townsend, Sue. ***The Secret Diary of Adrian Mole.*** 293 pages.

> Avon Flare 1984 Paper 0380868768 $5.99
> Avon 1997 Paper 0380730448 $12.95

Before Bridget Jones or Georgina Nicolson, there was Adrian Mole. This diary-as-novel features Adrian, a 13-year-old growing up in England and full of doubts, dreams, and a deadly sense of humor. He's the center of his universe, deftly dealing with decisions about girls, school, parents, and mates. Though heavy on British slang and now-dated references to U.K. pop culture, what matters most is the honest and hu-morous observations of Adrian. Both Adrian Mole books are available in one volume. **Grades 8–10. PJ**

Trueman, Terry. ***Stuck in Neutral.*** 114 pages.

> HarperCollins 2000 Library 0060285184 $14.89
> HarperCollins 2000 Trade 0060285192 $14.95
> HarperTempest 2001 Paper 0064472132 $6.95

A very engaging, fast read told from the point of view of a guy in a wheelchair who cannot communicate at all with the people around him. He thinks his dad might be thinking of killing him "to end his pain," and there is nothing he can do about it. **Grades 6–9. (Annotation by Hope Baugh) <PRINTZ>**

> Reviews: *Booklist* 7/1/2000, *SLJ* 7/1/2000

Turner, Megan Whalen. ***Thief.*** 219 pages.

> Puffin 1998 Paper 0140388346 $5.99
> Greenwillow 1996 Trade 0688146279 $16.95

Gen, a young thief in ancient times, has been imprisoned for life. He is granted a chance to earn his freedom by the king if he can steal a legendary stone hidden in a mysterious temple. Like a character in a video game, Gen has to overcome many obstacles on his quest. **Grades 6—9. PJ**

Reviews: *Booklist* 1/1/1997, *SLJ* 10/1/1996

Twain, Mark. ***The Adventures of Huckleberry Finn***. Page count varies with edition.

Signet 1997 Paper 0451526503 $4.95
Bantam 1981 Paper 0553210793 $4.95
Modern Library 1948 Trade 0679424709 $16.95

Be advised: Huck Finn is no Tom Sawyer. While the latter is a classic children's story, the former is one of the most serious works in American literature, despite its folksy language and the apparent naiveté of its narrator. The story of Huck and his escape from "sivilization" is well-known; Huck and runaway slave Jim build a raft and plan to arrive in the Northern states via the Mississippi; during a terrible storm one night, their course is shifted, and too late they find themselves traveling down river, deeper into slave territory. Their adventures are the means by which Twain can deliver his often bitter condemnation of everything from hypocrisy to human cruelty; Twain is funny, often hilarious, but the intent of this novel is not. By the time Huck and Jim are rescued and returned to safety, Huck is already thinking about how to "light out for the territories," as he—like us upon completion of the book—are good and sick of "civilized" life. Because Twain uses authentic dialect, the infamous "N" word is peppered throughout the dialogue. In recent years this has given rise to shouts of racism from some quarters; what has never been mentioned in that ongoing debate is the fact that Huck makes the most difficult moral decision in all of American literature, and one few would emulate: rather than turn Jim in to the authorities, he chooses what he is certain will be his fate for so great a crime—to be delivered upon his death into Hell. This kind of satire is not for the faint of heart. **Grades 6—12. PT**

Tyree, Omar. ***Flyy Girl***. 416 pages.

Simon & Schuster Trade Paperbacks 1997 Paper 0684835665 $14.00
Simon & Schuster Trade Paperbacks 2001 Paper 0743218574 $6.99

Set in Philadelphia in the 1980s, this is an urban coming-of-age story about Tracy, who is growing up very fast. With lots of tension at home, her peers are her support system, in particular her best friend Mercedes. Tracy is a true material girl: consumed with fashion, but also engaged in several sexual relationships during her teen years. Gritty, sometimes vulgar, but also painfully honest and often heartbreaking, this tale is popular for those very reasons and seems to disprove the assumption that teens won't read "fat" books. While seemingly controversial because of the heavy sexual content, Tyree's message is actually quite conservative and moral: bad things happen to bad people, and they end up in jail, dead, or becoming crack whores. **Grades 10—12. PJ**

Vail, Rachel. ***Do-Over.*** 143 pages.

> Avon Flare 1994 Paper 0380721805 $3.99
> Orchard 1992 Trade 0531054608 $15.95

Junior high and lows are the center of this witty and perspective novel by Vail. Whitman is in eighth grade, but school isn't his main concern, not when there are friends, enemies, and a potential romance on the horizon. His world is set spinning when his parents split up, and what little identity he's formed is challenged. Vail tells the hell that is eighth grade the same way Whitman tries to live his life: with honesty, humor, and smarts. **Grades 6–9. PJ**

> Reviews: *Booklist* 8/1/1992, *SLJ* 9/1/1992

Vail, Rachel. ***Wonder.*** 122 pages.

> Puffin 1993 Paper 0140361677 $4.99
> Orchard 1991 Trade 0531059642 $15.95

Fitting in didn't used to seem to matter so much to Jessica, until she entered seventh grade. Getting teased didn't used to hurt as much, and making friends didn't seem so hard back in elementary school. Jessica's trying to do the right thing, be the right person, but sometimes trying isn't enough. Reminiscent of Paula Danziger in the mix of humor and heart, Vail finds laughs and lumps in the throats describing Jessica slipping on the banana peel that is seventh grade. **Grades 6–9. PJ**

> Reviews: *Booklist* 9/1/1991, *SLJ* 8/1/1991

Vande Velde, Vivian. ***Companions of the Night Magic.*** 212 pages.

> Carpet 2002 Paper 0152166696 $5.95
> Jane Yolen Books 1995 Trade 0152002219 $17.00

One lonely night at the laundromat, Kerry helps a sexy young man escape from the gang of lunatics threatening to murder him. Unfortunately for Kerry, the loonies were perfectly sane: Her seductive new friend really is a vampire, and he's as willing to prey on her and her family as he is to make her a part of his dark underworld. This is romantic horror at its best. The moral complexity goes hand in hand with the page-turning suspense. Older teens will find it alluring. **Grades 7–10. KE**

> Reviews: *Booklist* 4/1/1995, *SLJ* 5/1/1995, *VOYA* 10/1/1995

Vande Velde, Vivian. ***Magic Can Be Murder.*** 190 pages.

> Puffin 2002 Paper 0142302104 $5.99
> Harcourt 2000 Trade 0152026657 $17.00

When kind-hearted Nola's magic powers cause her to witness a murder, she tries to do the right thing, but can't directly reveal what she discovered. In Vande Velde's generic medieval setting, if the locals discover that Nola and her mother are witches, they'll probably be killed. To add to her troubles, while she's magically disguised as a lovely house servant, Nola finds herself falling in love with the chief investigator. Keeping her story straight, her disguise in place, and trying to help the investigator solve the murder keep Nola very busy, right up to the somewhat too convenient conclusion. Still, the comedy of errors and the life-or-death tension of Nola's plight make this humorous mystery an enjoyable read for younger teens. **Grades 7—10. KE**

Reviews: *Booklist* 12/15/2000, *SLJ* 11/1/2000, *VOYA* 12/1/2000

Vande Velde, Vivian. ***Never Trust a Dead Man.*** 194 pages.

Laurel-Leaf 2001 Paper 044022828X $4.99
Harcourt 1999 Trade 0152018999 $17.00

In a macabre mix of suspense and humor, teenage Selwyn is walled up alive in his medieval village's burial caves with the decomposing body of Farold, his one-time rival and supposed victim. A good-hearted (or is she?) witch appears in the caves and offers to return the spirit of the murdered young man to life so that Selwyn can prove his innocence. Reincarnated first as a bat, then a canary, then a duck, the unfortunate Farold plays George Burns to Selwyn's naïve Gracie Allen. Vande Velde has created an utterly original murder mystery that younger teens are sure to enjoy. **Grades 7—10. KE**

Reviews: *Booklist* 4/1/1999, *SLJ* 5/1/1999, *VOYA* 8/1/1999

Vande Velde, Vivian. ***Tales from the Brothers Grimm.*** 128 pages.

Dell 1997 Paper 0440413001 $3.99
Harcourt 1995 Trade 0152002200 $17.00

Vande Velde delivers what her title promises by reinventing familiar fairy tales with tongue-in-cheek absurdities. From a Little Red Riding Hood who's a complete pest to the truly bake-worthy brats of Hansel and Gretel, Vande Velde's energy and inventiveness will keep the reader chuckling. Several of the stories (particularly the fine "Straw into Gold"), leaven their humor with a touch of tragedy, creating a lovely poignant counterpoint to the slapstick comedy. *Tales* is the perfect collection for a younger audience or for reluctant readers looking for something short and funny. **Grades 6—9. KE**

Reviews: *SLJ* 1/1/1996

Verne, Jules. ***Around the World in Eighty Days.*** 304 pages; varies with edition.

Puffin 1995 Paper 014036711X $4.99
Viking 1996 Paper 0670867934 $19.99
Morrow 1988 Trade 0688075088 $24.95

Published in 1872, here is the yarn of Phileas Fogg, who packs a few pair of socks, his valet Passepartout ("go by everything"), 20,000 pounds of supplies (apparently that's Verne's favorite number), and hops a hot air balloon to circumvent the globe in 80 days, all simply to win a bet. Hot on his trail is Fix, a private detective who's mistaken Fogg for a bank robber, and their cat-and-mouse chase covers three continents and a variety of traveling vehicles (aforementioned balloon, trains, an elephant, and even a sail-sledge). Constant action and imaginative adventures fill every page, culminating in Fogg's rescue of a Hindu widow, Aouda, from ritual immolation. Once home, his bet won, and his innocence established, Fogg lives happily ever after with his bride Aouda. Excellent for those looking for action, action, and more action. **Grades 7–12. PT**

Verne, Jules. **Journey to the Center of the Earth.** 290 pages; varies with edition.

> Bantam 1991 0553213970 $3.95
> Puffin 1994 Paper 0140367152 $4.99

Second in his series of *Voyages Estraordinaires* (1863–1910), *Journey* chronicles the explorations of Otto Lidenbrock, a geology professor who, upon discovering a centuries-old manuscript detailing a passage to Earth's core, sets out to find it. With his nephew, Axel, and a guide, Lidenbrock spends a number of months exploring fabulous secrets of ancient civilizations and monstrous creatures thriving in a subterranean world. Verne wrote for an audience of adults and children, and he neither bores the one nor patronizes the other. **Grades 7–12. PT**

Verne, Jules. **Twenty Thousand Leagues Under the Sea.** Page count varies with edition.

> Oxford 1998 Paper 0192828398 $10.95
> Troll 1990 Paper 0816718806 $5.95
> Morrow 2000 Trade 0688105351 $21.95

Translated from the French, this most popular of Jules Verne's sea-going science fiction first appeared in 1869. Narrated by Professor Aronnax, the novel follows his adventures as he investigates what appears to be a series of attacks on international shipping by some sort of sea monster. The monster turns out to be the *Nautilus*, a steel-plated submarine (who ever heard of such a thing?!), helmed by Captain Nemo, poster captain for the misanthropic. Nemo hates land and the men who live upon it and is one of the most vivid characters in world literature. From Atlantis to the North Pole, the *Nautilus* finds adventure everywhere. Just the thing for those looking for a little watery excitement. **Grades 7–12. PT**

Vinge, Joan D. **Psion.** 420 pages.

> Warner 1996 Paper 0446603546 $5.99

Cat is a young telepath growing up on the mean streets of an alien world. Captured at last by the police, the teenager is given the chance to trade his stiff prison sentence for a stint in an experimental government project. Hated for his powers and alien appearance but seen as a useable tool, the young man must struggle to be true to himself and still survive. Themes of prejudice, identity, and coming of age make this somewhat predictable sci-fi adventure appealing to teens. The sequel, following his kidnapping by a powerful quasi-legal corporate family, has none of *Psion's* minor flaws. By *Catspaw*, Cat is an entirely believable young man struggling with a talent that is part curse, part gift. Don't purchase one without the other—or better yet, find a copy of the omnibus volume *Alien Blood*. A final novel, *Dreamfall*, is an unassuming continuation of Cat's adventures as he seeks out his part-alien heritage. **Grades 7–10. KE**

Vinge, Joan D. ***The Snow Queen.*** 480 pages.

> Warner Books 2001 Paper 0446676640 $13.95
> Warner Books 1989 Paper 0445205296 $6.99

On the alien world of Tiamat, the beautiful and seemingly immortal Arienrhod rules as the Queen of Winter from the baroque city of Carbuncle. Soon, however, the Stargate that links Carbuncle to the rest of the galaxy will close, the offworlders and their technology will be banished, and Arienrhod's life will end. Arienrhod believes, however, that she will be the first Snow Queen to survive; she has secretly created a clone, Moon, and planted her among the tribal Summer People. When the anxious despot summons Moon to Carbuncle, Moon's life is nearly destroyed and her lover, Sparks, is corrupted. Moon and Sparks' story of love and redemption humanizes the plot twists and machinations of this epic adventure. The two young lovers provide a completely believable viewpoint through which the reader untangles the mysteries of Tiamat. Two sequels, a connecting novel *World's End* and the equally fine *Summer Queen*, make this a series similar in scope and complexity to Frank Herbert's *Dune*. Mature readers who enjoy top-notch science fiction won't want to miss this one. **Grades 10–12. KE**

Voigt, Cynthia. ***Elske.*** 245 pages.

> Aladdin 2001 Paper 0689844441 $10.00
> Atheneum 1999 Trade 0689824726 $18.00

Captive of a violent Viking-like tribe, 12-year-old Elske is saved from ritual gang rape and sacrifice on the burning pyre of the dead chief when her grandmother secretly takes her place. Smuggled to the civilized south, Elske attempts to build a new life for herself among the growing bourgeoisie. She is soon embroiled in the violent political conflicts, however, when she becomes companion to the young noblewoman Beriel, rightful heir to a disputed throne. Elske's violent and fascinating life and the scope and vividness of her world keep readers hooked. As in Voigt's other novels of an imaginary but realistic kingdom, Elske's characters are well drawn and the violence of medieval life is handled with thoughtfulness and care. **Grades 7–10. KE <TEN>**

Reviews: *Booklist* 9/1/1999, *SLJ* 10/1/1999, *VOYA* 10/1/1999

Voigt, Cynthia. ***Homecoming.*** 312 pages.

Pocket 2002 Paper 0689851324 $5.99
Atheneum 1981 Trade 0689308337 $18.00

A young adult classic that hits hard upon teen dreams and fears. When their mother abandons Dicey and her three siblings, it falls upon the 13-year-old to save her broken family. Afraid to go to the authorities, knowing it will only result in foster homes, Dicey leads her siblings on a perilous journey to their aunt's house. The journey isn't just about miles, but about the courage, determination, and intelligence that Dicey must show as she assumes an awesome responsibility. Once they arrive, they are disappointed to learn their aunt has died and their cousin is running the household, without much success. Dicey soon realizes she has yet to find a home, and decides to embark on another journey in search of someone to care for her and her siblings. The Tillerman family saga continues in the Newbery-winning *Dicey's Song* and concludes with *Seventeen against the Dealer.* **Grades 7–10. PJ**

Voigt, Cynthia. ***Izzy Willy-Nilly.*** 258 pages.

Atheneum 1986 Trade 0689312024 $18.00

A series of small choices and white lies lead popular, happy, and destined-for-success Isabelle down a road to tragedy. Despite the clichéd plot device of the drunk-driving accident setting events in motion, Izzy is a real character faced with an unreal and unexpected personal challenge of living life as a disabled person. Once readers get past the terrible cover and confusing title, they will be hooked on Izzy's struggles, setbacks, and successes. **Grades 7–10. PJ <MOCK>**

Reviews: *SLJ* 4/1/1986

Voigt, Cynthia. ***Jackaroo.*** 291 pages.

Atheneum 1985 Trade 0689311230 $20.00
Point Signature 1995 Paper 0590485954 $4.99

Jackaroo is clearly set in a past that never was, but the story reads more like historical fiction than fantasy. Like many of the peasantry, Gwyn is inspired by the legendary tales of the Jackaroo, a folk hero who robs from the rich the taxes they've squeezed from the poor, and grants summary justice to those whose station places them above the law. When Gwyn discovers the secret behind the legend, she is prompted to take up the mask and sword of the hero herself. Voigt's speculation about the nature of heroism and how we create our own legends lends depth to her spunky heroine's fast-paced adventures. **Grades 7–10. KE**

Voigt, Cynthia. **On Fortune's Wheel.** 276 pages.

Aladdin 1999 Paper 0689829574 $5.50

Voigt returns to the quasi-medieval world of Jackaroo two generations later in this romantic adventure. Birle, the innkeeper's daughter, abandons a secure future to run off with Orien, a young lordling caught stealing her father's boat. The wheel of fortune turns for them both as their love is threatened by misunderstanding, poverty, slavery, and fear. Like *Jackaroo*, Voigt's thoughtful story will be enjoyed by teens who want intelligent romance and well-written historical fiction—even if the history never was. **Grades 7–10. KE**

Voigt, Cynthia. **The Runner.** 181 pages.

Scholastic 1994 Paper 0590483803 $4.99

One could almost suspect that this was ghost-written by Chris Crutcher as it has all the elements of his works: a young athlete facing challenges at home, at school, and on the playing field. Set during the 1960s with the chopper blades of Vietnam rumbling in the background, Bullet's future is uncertain as he tries to decide if he should join the army. Like a Crutcher hero, Bullet has his own code, which is challenged by changing circumstances. **Grades 7–10. PJ <YALSA>**

Voigt, Cynthia. **Solitary Blue.** 189 pages.

Atheneum 1983 Trade 0689310080 $18.00
Scholastic 1993 Paper 0590471570 $4.99

Voigt created a novel from a minor character introduced in *Dicey's Song*, although she is working with similar themes. In this novel, Jeff Greene takes center stage, a place he does not occupy in the life of his own family. His mother split when he was young and his smart, successful father is distant. When his mother returns, Jeff, much like the Tillerman children, believes that a "happy family" is still possible, only to learn that a dream that doesn't come true isn't a lie; it is something worse. **Grades 7–10. PJ**

Voigt, Cynthia. **When She Hollers.** 177 pages.

Scholastic 2003 Paper 0590467158 $5.99

Tish's voice is raw and powerful as Voigt masterfully takes us through the one day when Tish decides she has had enough. As readers, we are with her when she picks up the knife, confronts her abuser, and lets him—and the world—know he has pushed her too far and he won't ever hurt her again. **Grades 7–12. (Annotation Dr. Lois Stover)**

Reviews: *Booklist* 11/15/1994, *SLJ* 11/1/1994, *VOYA* 12/1/1994

Voigt, Cynthia. ***The Wings of a Falcon.*** 467 pages.

Scholastic, 1995 Paper 0590467131 $4.99

Connected to *Jackaroo* and *On Fortune's Wheel* by the lush faux-historical setting, this third book of the kingdom maintains the thoughtful tone but punches it up with fast-paced, almost non-stop heroic adventure. Oriel goes from slave to heir to a barbarian warlord, is caught and enslaved again by a predatory tribe of "Wulfers," wins an earldom in mortal combat, and arranges a surprising peace in the face of rebellion and betrayal. Oriel and his world are well developed and the reader can appreciate the cost of war, social change, and Oriel's own mixed ambitions. By far the most accessible of Voigt's adventure stories; *The Wings of a Falcon* should appeal to most teenage boys. **Grades 7–10. KE**

Von Ziegesar, Cecily. ***Gossip Girl: A Novel.*** 208 pages.

Little, Brown Children's Books 2002 Paper 0316910333 $8.95

The late 90s equivalent to *Less Than Zero* following a crew of hard-partying, rich New York private-school teens. The book follows a group of three characters who shop, swear, and talk their way through one school year. Sex seems to be every person's preoccupation, with gossiping coming in a close second. This is *Sex and the City* for the teen set. **Grades 9–12. PJ**

Reviews: *SLJ* 6/1/2002, *VOYA* 6/1/2002

Vonnegut, Kurt. ***Cat's Cradle.*** 233 pages.

Delta 1998 Paper 038533348X $12.95

From Ilium, New York, to a nameless banana republic, the travels of the characters in *Cat's Cradle* are representative of Vonnegut at his most irrepressible. Is there a government experiment gone awry? You bet. Are there strange religions, absurd philosophies, and weird characters abounding? Absolutely. Of course, there's also ice nine, an apocalyptic weapon that will destroy the earth by instantly freezing everything it touches. For readers new to Vonnegut, this is a great place to begin. While not as revolutionary now as it was at its inception, *Cat's Cradle* is still a thoughtful—and hilarious—ride through the mind of Vonnegut. **Grades 10–12. PT**

Vonnegut, Kurt. ***Slaughterhouse Five.*** 205 pages.

Dell 1991 Paper 0440180295 $7.50
Bantam 1999 Paper 0385333846 $11.95
Bantam 1994 Trade 0385312083 $23.95

Perhaps Vonnegut's signature work, *Slaughterhouse Five* is—just as its creator—difficult to categorize. Both very funny and very saddening, the novel pulls out all stops with a recipe of satire, historical allusion, and science fiction. Billy Pilgrim, a World War

II veteran, becomes "unstuck" in time, and as a result bounces back and forth from wartime Dresden to the present to some vague dimension where the aliens are hanging out. Lots of characters from Vonnegutville add to the fun, with perhaps the most interesting being Kilgore Trout, a writer of science fiction who is sorely lacking in professional respect. Juxtaposing the sublime with the ridiculous, Vonnegut creates a nightmarish world in which we can never escape our pasts, or UFO's either! **Grades 10–12. PT**

Walker, Alice. ***The Color Purple.*** 290 pages.

> Pocket 1996 Paper 0671727796 $7.50
> Washington Square 1998 Paper 0671019074 $14.00
> Harcourt 1992 Trade 0151191549 $24.00

It is hard to keep track if this book about growing up black, poor, and repressed has won more awards or been banned in more cities. Walker's masterpiece about the black experience in America focuses on female empowerment, sexuality, and the power of friendships and family. Celie's journey to womanhood, overcoming endless obstacles, is as inspirational as any ever put to paper. **Grades 9–12 (mature). PJ**

Wallace Rich. ***Playing Without the Ball.*** 213 pages.

> Laurel-Leaf 2002 Paper 0440229723 $5.50
> Alfred A. Knopf 2000 Trade 0679886729 $15.95
> Alfred A. Knopf 2000 Library 0679986723 $17.99

Wallace is working in Crutcher-land here: a tough luck teen whose parents have left him and who is making his way alone. Although cut off from his high school team, the young man eats, sleeps, and breathes basketball, and has more than a passing interest in sex. **Grades 8–10. PJ**

> Reviews: *Booklist* 9/1/2000, *SLJ* 10/1/2000

Wallace, Rich. ***Wrestling Sturbridge.*** 133 pages.

> Alfred A. Knopf 1997 Paper 0679885552 $4.99

Somewhere in the background John Mellencamp is singing "Small Town" as the soundtrack for this novel about a young man stuck in a small town with the only future awaiting him a dead-end job in a factory. Ben's only shot is to win a wrestling scholarship; the problem is that his best friend wrestles at the same weight class and he's better. A new girl arrives in town to liven up his senior year, but this isn't *Rocky* with trumpets blaring at the end. A Best Books and Quick Picks winner. **Grades 8–10. PJ**

> Reviews: *Booklist* 9/1/1996, *SLJ* 10/1/1996

Walter, Virginia. ***Making Up Megaboy***. 62 pages.

> DK 1998 Trade 0789424886 $16.95

While it looks "simple" because of the almost picture-book format, Walter's explosive tale of violence in urban America is anything but easy. On his 13th birthday, with his father's gun, Robbie Jones shot Jae Koh, who had, for eight months, operated the Main Street Liquor Store. Eighteen people in all give their points of view concerning the killing, but no one, including Robbie, has a clear idea of his motivation for murder. In some ways, this seems like a prelude to *Monster* with lots of facts and opinions, but no conclusions. **Grades 7–12. PJ**

Reviews: *Booklist* 2/15/1998, *SLJ* 4/1/1998, *VOYA* 8/1/1998

Watt, Alan. ***Diamond Dogs.*** 243 pages.

Warner 9/1/2001 Paper 0446677841 $13.95
Little, Brown 9/1/2000 Trade 0316925810 $23.95

Another "adult" story featuring a strong and honest first-person teen voice. The story starts with a high school senior/football star doing a little binge drinking, which leads to a hit-and-run accident. Our hero stuffs the body in the trunk of his car, only to find it missing the next morning because of the intervention of his father, the town sheriff. That is just the beginning of a coming-of-age novel that, like the teen protagonist, ricochets between moods. Some parts of the novel are LOL funny, but mostly Watt is looking at the dark side of teen years. Like a Crutcher novel, there are secrets and betrayals, but right up front is the struggle between a stubborn son and an angry father. **Grades 10–12 (mature). PJ**

Reviews: *Booklist* 7/1/2000

Weaver, Will. ***Farm Team.*** 283 pages.

HarperCollins 1999 Paper 0064471187 $5.95

One reviewer hit the mark describing the novel as *Field of Dreams* played against the backdrop of Lake Wobegon. The novel introduces simple country boy Billy Baggs, who lives for baseball, but a series of events, including his father's arrest, place obstacles in the path of fulfilling his promise. Billy's story continues in the essential *Hard Ball* and *Striking Out.* **Grades 6–9. PJ**

Review: *Booklist* 9/1/1995

Wells H. G. ***The Time Machine.*** 160 pages; varies with edition.

Ace 2001 Paper 0441009190 $5.99
Modern Library 2002 Paper 0375759239 $5.95

Widely regarded as the father of the time travel genre, H. G. Wells published his first novel in 1895 and was rapidly catapulted to world fame. Though in the many movie adaptations the narrator is often called Wells, the novel's protagonist is nameless, known only as the Time Traveler. Inventing a fantastic machine of ivory, brass, and crystal, he sets out to the year 802,700 and finds a world both totally alien and eerily familiar. A million years into the future, the world is divided neatly into two: the Eloi, beautiful, basically helpless creatures who live above ground, and the Morlocks, beastly creatures surviving on depravity and cannibalism. The Eloi are certainly a thinly disguised Victorian upper class, with the Morlocks as their societal counter-part. **Grades 6—12. PT**

Werlin, Nancy. ***The Killer's Cousin.*** 229 pages.

Delacorte 1998 Trade 0385325606 $15.95
Laurel-Leaf 2000 Paper 0440227518 $4.99

A page-turning psychological thriller in the Lois Duncan mode tells the story of a young man who has been acquitted of the murder of his girlfriend and tries to start a new life. Demons from his past, both real and imagined, complicate his life in this teen favorite, which was a Best Book and Quick Picks selection. It also won the Edgar Award for best YA mystery. **Grades 7—10. PJ**

Reviews: *Booklist* 9/1/1998, *SLJ* 11/1/1998

Wersba, Barbara. ***Whistle Me Home.*** 108 pages.

Henry Holt 1997 Trade 0805048502 $15.95

This heartbreaker was a departure from the quirky, clever stories Barbara Wersba penned throughout the 80s. Here, tomboy Noli falls for sensitive T. J. and is utterly destroyed when she discovers he is gay. A proud predecessor and perfect companion novel to the also outstanding Printz Honor book *Hard Love*, by Ellen Wittlinger. **Grades 7—10. (Annotation by Jennifer Hubert)**

Reviews: *Booklist* 4/1/1997, *VOYA* 8/1/1997

Whelan, Gloria. ***Homeless Bird.*** 216 pages.

HarperCollins 2000 Library 0060284528 $16.89
HarperCollins 2000 Trade 0060284544 $15.95
HarperTrophy 2001 Paper 0064408191 $5.95

One of the few young adult titles set in India, this is a novel about a young girl's coming of age in a culture where the odds seemed stacked against her. While the plot is almost soap opera, a young girl married to a young boy with TB so that her dowry may be used to buy medical treatment, the social issues raised in the book are any-thing but light entertainment. The novel won the National Book Award for young adult literature. **Grades 6—9. PJ**

Reviews: *Booklist* 3/1/2000, *SLJ* 2/1/2000

Whitcher, Susan. *The Fool Reversed.* 192 pages.

Farrar Straus Giroux 2000 Trade 0374324468 $16.00

A gritty novel concerning a young girl's infatuation for an older man. Instead of mentoring the young girl, the older man sexually exploits and manipulates her. **Grades 9–12 (mature). PJ**

Reviews: *SLJ* 3/1/2000, *VOYA* 6/1/2000

White, Ellen. *The President's Daughter.* 256 pages.

Scholastic 1994 Paper 0590477994 $3.25

A teen cult favorite, this is the first of three books about the spunky character Meghan Powers, your typical teenage girl whose mother just happens to be the President of the United States. Mixing political intrigue with both a sense of humor and typical teen girl coming-of-age issues, these titles (*Long Live the Queen* and *White House Autumn*) should always find an audience. **Grades 6–9. PJ**

White, Robb. *Deathwatch.* 228 pages.

Dell 1973 Paper 0440917409 $5.50

College student Ben decides to guide Madec on a bighorn-sheep-hunting trip into the Nevada desert, despite the fact that Madec seems cold and cruel. When Madec shoots before he is sure the thing moving on a ridge is actually a sheep, he finds he has made a big mistake. He has killed an old prospector, and when Ben refuses his bribe to keep quiet, Madec takes all the food, water, clothing, and ammunition in the jeep and leaves Ben in the desert to die. Just in case Ben manages to make it the 60 miles back to town, Madec alters the evidence and makes it look like Ben killed the old man. This is one of the best page-turners ever written for teens; it flies off the shelf, and best of all, even the most reluctant reader will finish this exceptionally high-interest adventure story. **Grades 7–12. (Annotation by Diane Tuccillo) <YALSA>**

White, T. H. *The Once and Future King.* 677 pages.

Ace 1987 Paper 0441627404 $7.99
Putnam 1958 Trade 0399105972 $25.95
Ace 1996 Paper 0441003834 $16.95

Originally published in the 1930s as a trilogy, T. H. White's masterpiece became a single volume in 1958 and has held its grip on the King Arthur catalogue ever since. This is not the fairy tale Camelot: Lancelot is physically ugly, Guinevere's hair begins showing streaks of white, and Arthur is often confused, if not outright bewildered. The novel begins with Merlin's tutoring of the young "Wart," and some of the book's funniest moments occur during these passages. As Arthur comes into possession of the crown, however, the story becomes darker and darker, an inescapable sense of doom lingering on every page. Though made into a classic musical, a film, and even a Disney cartoon version, *The Once and Future King* is not for children. Even high school students will find it difficult to comprehend if their reading level is not well advanced. **Grades 9–12. PT**

Wiesel, Elie. ***Night.*** 128 pages.

Bantam Books 1982 Paper 0553272535 $5.99

An autobiographical novel that many teens discover through school, but others seek out on their own. The Nobel prize winner writes much about the Holocaust, but this slender novel about the experience of a teenage boy who survived the death camps is perhaps the most powerful. The most painful parts of the novel are not the horrors of Auschwitz, but the questions about God, humanity, and history that Wiesel poses. **Grades 10–12. PJ**

Willey, Margaret. ***Saving Lenny.*** 164 pages.

Bantam 1991 Trade 0553058509 $13.95

A small but powerful story about two high school seniors who fall in love and move in together, living in an isolated cabin. But the story takes a darker turn when the young woman discovers and begins to deal with her boyfriend's chronic depression, as well as her inability to break free from him. **Grades 7–10. PJ**

Williams, Lori Aurelia. ***Shayla's Double Brown Baby Blues.*** 300 pages.

Simon & Schuster 2001 Trade 0689824696 $17.00

A semi-sequel to Williams' debut novel told with a powerful, lyric, and yet heart-breakingly honest teen voice. This book focuses on the African American teenager Shayla, who feels that she's been replaced now that her father's new wife has given birth to a baby. Her best friend Kambia has found happiness, while her new friend Lamm seems mainly to find his happiness in a bottle. Things change as Kambia becomes the victim of a stalker, and Lamm slowly opens up to the demons that are eating away at him. A novel loaded with emotion, which is lightened by humor, and a strong message about the healing power of unconditional love. **Grades 8–10. PJ**.

Reviews: *Booklist* 7/1/2001, *SLJ* 8/1/2001, *VOYA* 10/1/2001

Williams, Lori Aurelia. ***When Kambia Elaine Flew in from Planet Neptune.*** 200 pages.

Aladdin 2001 Paper 0689845936 $10.00
Simon & Schuster 2000 Trade 0689824688 $17.00

An amazing first novel about a poor, young African American girl with plenty of pain in her own life, who uncovers something even worse happening in her neighbor's house. Twelve-year-old Shayla wants to be a writer, and she fills her notebooks with the fireworks going off in her house, primarily between her mother and older sister. But the girl next door, Kambia Elaine, is like no one Shayla has ever met, and she is intrigued by the wild stories Kambia Elaine tells. Like many new young adult novelists, Williams is as much concerned with style as story, and the prose could pass for poetry. **Grades 7—12. PJ**

Reviews: *Booklist* 2/15/2000, *SLJ* 4/1/2000

Williams-Garcia, Rita. ***Blue Tights.*** 180 pages.

Puffin 1996 Paper 0140380450 $5.99

A talented but unsure African American teenager is crushed when she is cut from the ballet recital. She is down, but not defeated, as she joins an African dance troupe that gives her a new sense of her self and of belonging. **Grades 7—10. PJ**

Williams-Garcia, Rita. ***Every Time a Rainbow Dies.*** 166 pages.

HarperCollins 2001 Library 0060292024 $15.89
HarperCollins 2001 Trade 0688162452 $15.95
HarperTempest 2002 Paper 0064473031 $6.95

An immigrant Jamaican teenage boy witnesses a rape from his window. He helps the victim, only to find himself then strangely drawn to wanting to know and protect her. This is one of those gritty teen novels that shows that there are lots of books for teenagers that are not meant for middle school or junior high school students. **Grades 9—12 (mature). PJ**

Reviews: *Booklist* 12/15/2000, *SLJ* 2/1/2001, *VOYA* 6/1/2001

Williams-Garcia, Rita. ***Fast Talk on a Slow Track.*** 183 pages.

Puffin 1998 Paper 0141302313 $5.99

Denzel Watson is a fast talker with a system, and it's made him valedictorian. But when he goes to a summer program at Princeton, he takes a fall. How can he tell his proud family that he won't be able to cut it in the Ivy League? Instead he spends the summer selling candy door-to-door and figuring out his life. **Grades 7—10. PJ**

Williams-Garcia, Rita. ***Like Sisters on the Homefront.*** 165 pages.

Puffin 1998 Paper 0140385614 $5.99
Lodestar 1995 Trade 0525674659 $15.99

A 14-year-old African American girl is pregnant for the second time. The first time she kept the baby, but this time her mother forces her to have an abortion and then sends her away from the projects in New York with a one-way ticket to family in

Georgia, where she encounters her religious relatives and more than a little culture shock. **Grades 7–10. PJ <TEN>**

Willis, Connie. **_The Doomsday Book._** 578 pages.

Bantam 1993 Paper 0553562738 $7.50

Willis' well-researched story of a headstrong young girl who time travels back to the time of the Black Death will leave readers feeling as if they had gone there with her. Every detail is crisply drawn, and the plot provides enough riveting power to sustain its incredible length. Science fiction buffs will appreciate the believable portrayal of a not-so-distant future when time travel is common enough to be a university program. There's a little something for almost every reader in this book, and the critics agree; it won both the Hugo and Nebula. **Grades 9–12. (Annotation by Spring Lee Boehler)**

Wittlinger, Ellen. **_Hard Love._** 224 pages.

Aladdin Paperbacks 2001 Paper 068984154X $8.00
Simon & Schuster 1999 Trade 0689821344 $16.95

After starting to publish a zine in which he writes his secret feelings about his lonely life and his parents' divorce, 16-year-old John meets Marisol, a zine queen and all-around enigma, who is just about everything he was looking for in a girl. This title won EVERY award in its path, including the Lambda Literary Award. **Grades 9–12. PJ <PRINTZ>**

Reviews: _Booklist_ 10/1/1999, _SLJ_ 7/1/1999, _VOYA_ 8/1/1999

Wittlinger, Ellen. **_The Long Night of Leo and Bree._** 111 pages.

Simon & Schuster 2002 Trade 0689835647 $15.00

Told in alternating first-person narratives, this gritty novel deals with issues such as revenge, redemption, and guilt. On the anniversary of his sister's violent murder at the hands of her abusive boyfriend, a tormented young man seeks refuge from his mother only to cross paths with a wealthy girl who has demons of her own. **Grades 7–12. PJ**

Reviews: _Booklist_ 1/1/2002, _SLJ_ 3/1/2002, _VOYA_ 2/1/2002

Wittlinger Ellen. **_What's in a Name._** 146 pages.

Aladdin 2001 Paper 0689845324 $4.99
Simon & Schuster 2000 Trade 068982551X $16.00

A series of interconnected first-person accounts from teenagers in a suburban high school "debating" a plan to change the name of their town. The search for identity in

these stories has little to do with geography and everything to do with teens exploring the question of "Who am I?" **Grades 7—10. PJ**

Reviews: *Booklist* 1/1/2000, *SLJ* 2/1/2000

Wolff, Virginia Euwer. ***Bat 6.*** 230 pages.

Scholastic Signature 2000 Paper 0590898000 $4.99
Scholastic 1998 Trade 0590897993 $16.95

This ambitious tale featuring 21 short, first-person narratives about coming of age in
the face of prejudice is set against the backdrop of an annual softball game between
two small Oregon towns. **Grades 6—9. PJ**

Reviews: *Booklist* 5/1/1998, *SLJ* 5/1/1998

Wolff, Virginia Euwer. ***Make Lemonade.*** 200 pages.

Scholastic 1994 Paper 059048141X $4.99
Henry Holt 1993 Trade 0805022287 $17.95

In 66 chapters—or are they blank verse poems?—Wolff explores the crippling effects
of urban poverty. Fourteen-year-old LaVaughn baby-sits for a teenage mother of two
to raise money to escape her circumstances only to find that making hard choices is
her first real obstacle. According to some, this just might be the best YA book ever
published. The themes here are those found in most good young adult fiction: struggles with identity, acceptance, and independence. Just as *The Outsiders* reflected
the rough-and-tumble world of adolescent boys on the brink of manhood yet still
longing for family protection, *Make Lemonade* shows another kind of family structure that two teens need to thrust them into adult life. **Grades 7—12. PJ <HIPPLE>
<YALSA>**

Reviews: *Booklist* 6/1/1993, *SLJ* 7/1/1993

Wolff, Virginia Euwer. ***True Believer.*** 282 pages.

Atheneum 2001 Trade 0689828276 $17.00
Simon & Schuster 2002 Paper 0689852886 $7.99

This National Book Award winner is the sequel to *Make Lemonade*, following
LaVaughn into the next phase of her life, including first love. Once again, there is as
much power in Wolff's unique lyrical style as there is in the story of a young black
girl's coming of age. **Grades 7—12. PJ**

Reviews: *Booklist* 2/1/2001, *SLJ* 5/1/2001, *VOYA*, 4/1/2001

Womack, Jack. ***Random Acts of Senseless Violence.*** 255 pages.

Grove 10/1/1995 Paper 0802134246 $13.50

A provocative title for a cyberpunk masterpiece about what might happen just before the end of the world. A 12-year-old girl records in her journal daily life in gang-torn Manhattan in some not-so-distant future. **Grades 10—12 (mature). PJ**

Woodson, Jacqueline. *I Hadn't Meant to Tell You This.* 115 pages.

> Laurel-Leaf 1995 Paper 0440219604 $4.99

In lyrical prose Woodson tells a story of friendship across racial lines that confronts issues from abuse to class snobbery. Beautifully written, this is a haunting story because there are no easy answers. **Grades 7—12. (Annotation by Dr. Lois Stover)**

> Reviews: *SLJ* 1/1/1995

Woodson, Jacqueline. *If You Come Softly.* 181 pages.

> Puffin 2000 Paper 0698118626 $5.99
> G. P. Putnam's Sons 1998 Trade 0399231129 $15.99

In alternating chapters, Woodson tells the story of an interracial couple. Jeremiah, who is African American, and Ellie, who is white, meet and fall in love at their private high school. The book tells their story from their first awkward meeting to a tragic ending. **Grades 7—10. PJ <YALSA>**

> Reviews: *Booklist* 10/1/1998, *SLJ* 12/1/1998

Woodson, Jacqueline. *Lena.* 115 pages.

> Laurel-Leaf 2000 Paper 0440226694 $4.99
> Delacorte 1999 Trade 0385323085 $15.95

In this sequel to *I Hadn't Meant to Tell You This,* Woodson continues the story of the characters Lena and her younger sister, Dion, who have escaped from their sexually abusive father only to face an uncertain future. **Grades 7—10. PJ**

> Reviews: *Booklist* 2/1/1999, *SLJ* 5/1/1999

Woodson, Jacqueline. *Miracle's Boys.* 133 pages.

> Puffin 2001 Paper 0698119169 $5.99
> G. P. Putnam's Sons 2000 Trade 0399231137 $15.99

Ty'ree, Charlie, and Lafayette are three brothers who are raising themselves after they lost their father to an accident and their mother to diabetes. Each brother chooses a different path to handle his grief as they attempt to grow up on their own. **Grades 7—10. PJ**

> Reviews: *Booklist* 2/15/2000, *SLJ* 5/1/2000

Wrede, Patricia C. **Dealing with Dragons.** 212 pages.

Harcourt 1990 Trade 0152229000 $17.00
Scholastic 1992 Paper 0590457225 $4.99

Princess Cimmorene is fed up: she cannot cook, garden, or fence without her royal parents insisting that her hobbies are unladylike, and the perfect princes they offer up to her are a complete bore. Cimmorene's solution is to turn fairytale convention on its head by offering herself to the local dragon as housekeeper, cook, and status item. She promises to show any importunate knights the door. The characters are deftly drawn, while the action keeps up the pace, and the humor stays light. Fans of *Ella Enchanted* will be charmed by this fantasy. Happily, the fun continues in the sequels, *Searching for Dragons, Calling on Dragons,* and *Talking to Dragons.* **Grades 6—12. KE <YALSA>**

Reviews: *SLJ* 12/01/1990

Wrede, Patricia C. **Magician's Ward.** 288 pages.

Starscape 2002 Paper 0765342480 $5.99
TOR 1997 Trade 0312853696 $22.95

Inspired by the wonderful (but temporarily out of print) "Sorcery and Cecelia," Kim, a street thief turned magician's apprentice, is making her bow to high society. The charming conceit of *Magician's Ward* is that of a Georgette Heyer's Regency: a place where magic and adventure (Kim and her magician mentor Mairelon must break up a Fagin-like crime ring) exist side-by-side with wicked dukes, cotillions, and rout parties. Kim's adventures as a street thief can be found in *Mairelon the Magician,* but aren't nearly as much fun. **Grades 7—12. KE**

Reviews: *Booklist* 11/1/1997, *VOYA* 4/1/1998

Wrede, Patricia C. **Snow White and Rose Red.** 273 pages.

TOR 12/1/1993 Paper 0812534972 $4.99

Teens who enjoyed Wrede's *Enchanted Forest Chronicles* will appreciate this slightly more serious retelling of the lesser-known "Snow White." Two beautiful sisters in the Elizabethan England of John Dee live quietly on the border of a haunted wood until magic invades their life in the form of a fairy prince transformed into a wild bear. The detailed characterization of the relationship between the two sisters and the strong sense of place ground this tale of mystery and romance. For older teens willing to try an unusual romance or those who want original fantasy, this entry in Wilding's excellent Fairy Tale series is hard to beat. **Grades 10—12. KE**

Wright, Richard. **Native Son.** 359 pages.

HarperPerennial 1989 Paper 0060809779 $7.95

HarperCollins 1998 Paper 0060929804 $13.00
Simon & Schuster 1987 Paper 0671009125 $3.95

An uncompromising indictment of racism in America, this stark novel introduces us to Bigger Thomas, product of the ghetto and prisoner of the "invisible" class system in America. Growing up black in the Chicago of the 1930s, Bigger was born into a cultural prison from which there is no escape; when he kills a white woman, the prison moves from metaphorical to actual, and his panic and hopelessness are limned in Wright's simple, but striking, prose. No one can help Bigger—not his family, friends, judicial system, law enforcement, or even himself. Caught in a cage of class repression, Wright's protagonist should be an awakening for all colors of middle class Americans too comfortable with the serendipitous circumstances of their birth. **Grades 10–12 (mature). PT**

Yolen, Jane. ***Armageddon Summer.*** 266 pages.

Harcourt 1999 Paper 0152022686 $5.99
Harcourt 1998 Trade 0152017674 $17.00

Co-written with Bruce Colville, who is best noted for his science fiction stories for young teens, this is a very serious story about love and the end of the world. Two teenagers gather with "The 144 Believers" atop Mount Weeupcut in Massachusetts to camp out, pray, and await for Armageddon, scheduled for just a few weeks away. The two narrate the story, alternating chapters. Mixing in documents, sermons, and e-mails, Yolen and Colville create a nail-biting suspense story as a background for larger issues of love, faith, and acceptance. **Grades 7–10. PJ**

Reviews: *Booklist* 8/1/1998, *SLJ* 10/1/1998, *VOYA* 10/1/1998

Yolen, Jane. ***Briar Rose.*** 190 pages.

Starscape 2002 Paper 0765342308 $5.99
TOR 1992 Trade 0312851359 $17.95

Terry Windling's groundbreaking series *Fairy Tales* reworked by modern masters of fantasy reached new levels with this version of the Sleeping Beauty. The only magic here is that of the human heart to resurrect hope and understanding from brutal reality: Rebecca Berlin seeks the truth behind her beloved grandmother's last words, "I am Briar Rose." Thus begins her trek through the horrors of World War II. Part personal Holocaust narrative, part lyrical myth, Jane Yolen's subtle retelling has a depth and complexity that the mature teen will appreciate. **Grades 6–12. KE <YALSA>**

Reviews: *Booklist* 9/15/1992

Yolen, Jane. ***The Devil's Arithmetic.*** 170 pages.

Puffin 1990 Paper 0140345353 $5.99

Yolen takes a basic fantasy set-up of time travel to put her novel about never forgetting the past into motion. Hannah, like most teens, is bored at family events, including the celebration of Passover. When she grudgingly takes part in the ceremony, she finds herself opening the door not for Elijah to enter, but for herself to be thrust back into the Holocaust. There she assumes a new identity, but also brings with her the knowledge of the death camps. She tries to warn everyone, but to no avail. With vivid descriptions of life in the camps, Yolen creates historical horror with a heavy moral lesson. **Grades 6—9. PJ**

Yolen, Jane. ***Dragon's Blood.*** 243 pages.

Harcourt 1996 Paper 0152008667 $6.00

On the impoverished planet Austar IV, Jakkin works as an indentured servant in Master Sarkkhan's dragon nursery. When he steals an overlooked hatchling, Jakkin believes he may finally have a chance to escape a life of drudgery—if only he has what it takes to survive on his own and to train his dragon to become a fighting champion in Austar IV's Pits. The moral quandaries Jakkin faces are understated, the plot consistently suspenseful, and the relationship that develops between the lonely boy and his pet dragon endearing. Younger teens will find it hard to put down and eagerly demand the sequels. Unfortunately, neither *Heart's Blood* nor *A Sending of Dragons* is as compelling for that age group, sacrificing the straightforward action and cool dragons for politics, rebellion, Jakkin's coming-of-age, and a somewhat ambiguous series conclusion. **Grades 6—9. KE**

Yolen, Jane. ***Here There Be Dragons.*** 149 pages.

Harcourt 1993 Trade 0152098887 $16.95
Harcourt 1998 Paper: 0152017054 $10.00

This gorgeously illustrated, oversized book with its stunning cover screams, "Pick me up and take a look." Teens who do won't be disappointed. David Wilgus' soft, detailed pencil drawings complement each entry. Yolen has provided a mix of vignettes, short stories, and poetry that range in style from science fiction ("Cockfight," the story that spawned her popular "Pit Dragon" series) to fantasy, humor, and folk history. The quality of the entries varies, as does the sophistication and reading level, but dragons are perennial favorites; there's something here for nearly every reader. The same ingredients go in to making *Here There Be Angels, Here There Be Ghosts, Here There Be Unicorns,* and *Here There Be Witches,* highly attractive additions to any library collection. **Grades 6—9. KE**

Reviews: *SLJ* 12/1/1993

Zahn, Timothy. ***Heir to Empire.*** 432 pages.

Bantam Books 1992 Paper 0553296124 $6.99

Taking up shortly after the end of Star Wars, Episode VI: *The Return of the Jedi*, Zahn deftly re-creates the Star Wars universe for fans, more cleverly, with better dialogue, and yet utterly true to the movies' best moments. The quest to rebuild a republic in the face of corruption, sabotage and the armed resistance from the remaining Imperial forces led by Grand Admiral Thrawn and a renegade Jedi showcases Zahn's skill at writing both political intrigue and fast-paced action. The character development is limited but solid: All the old favorites are recognizably themselves, and new villains and supporting cast are ably fleshed out. The story continues in book two, *Dark Force Rising*, and winds up satisfyingly in book three, *The Last Command*. Until George Lucas creates Star Wars movies 7–9, Timothy Zahn's novels remain one of the best substitutes for fans, in addition to being enjoyable and well-written science fiction adventure in their own right. **Grades 9–12. KE**

Reviews: *SLJ* 2/1/1992

Zindel, Paul. **The Doom Stone.** 173 pages.

Hyperion 1996 Paper 0786811579 $4.95
HarperCollins 1995 Trade 0060247266 $15.95

Goths and gross-out lovers will adore this story of creatures running amuck and blood-letting around Stonehenge. **Grades 6–9. PJ**

Reviews: *Booklist* 12/15/1995, *SLJ* 12/1/1995

Zindel, Paul. **The Pigman.** 182 pages.

HarperCollins 1968 Library 006026828X $17.89
Bantam 1983 Paper 0553263218 $5.99

Ignore the hype; it really is that damn good. The story of two teen outcasts, a lonely old man, and the pain of growing up. **Grades 7–12. PJ <HIPPLE>**

Zindel, Paul. **Rats.** 204 pages.

Hyperion 1999 Library 078682820X $16.89
Hyperion 1999 Trade 0786803398 $15.99
Hyperion 2000 Paper 0786812257 $4.99

A scary cover of menacing rodents and a flesh-eating, gross-out first scene sets the dark tone to another man-versus-nature horror feast. In this one, rats from Staten Island invade Manhattan, munching away until a teenage girl comes to the rescue. **Grades 6–9. PJ**

Reviews: *SLJ* 10/1/1999, *VOYA* 2/1/2000

CHAPTER 3

GRAPHIC FORMATS

Arnoldi, Katherine. ***The Amazing "True" Story of a Teenage Single Mom.***
unpaged.

Hyperion 1998 Trade 0786864206 $15.50

Arnoldi uses words and pictures to tell a familiar story in an unconventional way,
thus once again proving that graphic formats are not just about superheroes. Instead,
they can be used to capture the heroic daily struggles of regular people overcoming
hardship. **Grades 9–12. PJ**

Reviews: *Booklist* 11/15/1998, *SLJ* 1/1/1999, *VOYA* 2/1/1999

Augustyn, Brian (Editor). ***Superman Batman: Alternate Histories.*** unpaged.

DC Comics 1996 Paper 1563892723 $14.95

Collected from the *Elseworld* annual comic books, various writers and artists place
the familiar characters in unfamiliar settings. For example, Superman sides with the
British during the Revolutionary War, or Batman sails the high seas as a pirate. The
artwork and writing style varies with each stand-alone episode. Teens who enjoy
superhero comics will appreciate this one. **Grades 7–12. KE**

Barry, Lynda. ***Freddie Stories.*** 123 pages.

Sasquatch 1999 Paper 1570611068 $12.95

Before there were "mature" graphic novels, there were mature comic strips, like
Lynda Barry's weekly cartoon, *Ernie Pook's Comeek*. This collection of comics features sisters Marlys and Maybonne and their spunky little brother Freddie as they
try to make their way through a world of confusing, confounding, and sometime
confrontational adults. The strips feature Freddie, an outcast teen reeking of angst,
who just wants to be loved. **Grades 10–12 (mature). PJ**

Reviews: *Booklist* 2/1/1999, *SLJ* 11/1/1999

Beatty, Scott. ***Batman: The Ultimate Guide to the Dark Knight.*** 128 pages.

Dorling Kindersley 2001 Trade 078947865X $19.95

For those who want to know it all, DK has put together the ultimate guide. With the usual DK mix of two-parts illustrations to one-part text, this volume (like others in the Ultimate series) looks at all things Batman. There is not just the standard history of Bruce Wayne, but also, thanks to access granted from DC Comics, an exploded archive. There are over 700 illustrations, most in color, about bat villains and allies, contents of the bat cave and the utility belt, not to mention a plethora of pictures unearthing objects in the bat cave. From equipment to costumes, through the various origin stories, Robin avatars (she's been a girl twice), and cast of characters, this book touches on it all. **Grades: 6—12. KE/PJ**

Reviews: *Booklist* 1/1/2002

Bendis, Brian Michael. ***Ultimate Spider-Man.*** 128 pages.

Marvel 2001 Paper 078510786X $14.95

With the huge success of the Spider-Man movie in the summer of 2002 and sequels no doubt in the planning stages, this title puts a contemporary spin on the webbed one, focusing on his early years. **Grades: 6—12. PJ**

Bissette, Steve. ***Age of Monsters.*** 248 pages.

Dark Horse Comics 1998 Paper 1569712778 $17.99

When young Noriko's father awakens Godzilla, her life will change, eventually centering on studying and supporting the benevolent monster, and leading her to a role in the super-scientist team "G-Force." *Age of Monsters* remains true to the 1950 monster movies that spawned it, including the mostly black-and-white artwork, while retelling and reimagining Godzilla and his world for a modern audience. **Grades: 6—12. KE**

Brennan, Michael. ***Electric Girl: Vol. 1.*** 168 pages.

Mighty Gremlin 2000 Paper 0970355505 $9.95

With stylized black-and-white artwork reminiscent of underground comics (albeit with a cleaner line), *Electric Girl* lives up to its promise to be something unusual. Collected here are the first four comic book adventures of Virginia, a girl who can conduct electricity through her fingertips; her dog Blammo; and an irrepressible gremlin buddy, Oogleeoog. It's real life, charmingly drawn, with a twist. A great book to hand teenage girls looking for more (if lighter) Francesca Lia Block, and to those who imagine that graphic novels are limited to science fiction, weird fantasy, and costumed heroes. **Grades: 6—10. KE**

Reviews: *Booklist* 5/1/2002, *SLJ* 5/1/2002

Busiek, Kurt. ***Astro City: Life in the Big City.*** 192 pages.

Wildstorm 1999 Paper 156389551X $19.95

The first in the series of graphic novels that kick-start the superhero genre. In a world where costumed superheroes are an accepted fact of life, what must their lives—and that of ordinary human beings—be like? From the relentless pressure on the "Superman"-type to always be on the job, saving lives, through the experiences of a young woman from a haunted Eastern European ghetto, to the perspective of a small-time crook, Astro city and the superheroes there provide a backdrop to the very human stories Busiek tells. This graphic novel provides a new and very appeal-ing take on the superhero genre, likely to please older and younger teen fans alike. **Grades: 7—12. KE/PJ**

Busiek, Kurt. ***Marvels.*** 192 pages.

Marvel 1994 Paper 0785100490 $19.95

What if Spider-Man, the Hulk, the Fantastic Four, Captain America, and their kind really lived among us? How would your average Joe react to a world of superheroes? From asking this simple question comes not so much a re-imagining of the Marvel Universe, but a different perspective. The hero of this story is Phil Sheldon: a mid-dle-aged man who works as a photographer, mainly taking pictures of men in capes. **Grades 7—12. PJ**

Busiek, Kurt. ***Spider-Man: Goblin Moon.*** 288 pages.

Berkley 2000 Paper 0425174034 $6.99
Penguin Putnam 1999 Trade 0399145125

Combine a hugely popular superhero with one of the most talented graphic novelists to create a no-holds-barred battle between the hero and a super villain; that is the recipe for a core-collection pick. **Grades 8—10. PJ**

Busiek, Kurt. ***Supreme Justice: The Avengers.*** 304 pages.

Marvel 2001 Paper 785107738 $17.95

Marvel's big three: Captain America, Thor, and Iron Man are joined by the Scarlet Witch, the Vision, and Warbird, as well as a few interns, in this re-imaging of the Avengers by one of comics' hot young hands. While the story—good versus the very, very, evil—remains the same, the takes of the characters are fresh. **Grades 7—12. PJ**

Byrne, John. ***Superman: The Man of Steel.*** 128 pages.

DC Comics 1991 Paper 0930289285 $7.50

One of the first reworkings of the Superman story after the success of DC's *Batman*, the Dark Knight, this graphic novel showcases John Byrne's distinctive artwork. The clean lines and stylized faces remain, and the colors still work on the off-white newsprint of the collected edition. All the familiar elements of the Superman story are in place (including a cameo appearance by Batman) but expanded by the "human" story: Clark Kent's relationship with parents, friends, and girlfriends. A novelty in its time, The Man of Steel is still a pleasant read and sure to be popular with younger teenage fans new to the genre. **Grades: 7—12. KE**

Byrne, John. **Superman and Batman: Generations.** 208 pages.

DC Comics 2000 Paper 1563896052 $17.95

Originally published as a four-issue series, Generations re-imagines Batman and Super-man. If both were "born" into the world of superheroes in 1939, what happens as the years tick by? Wouldn't someone notice that Bruce Wayne and Clark Kent are ageless? The premise is that the guise of Batman and Superman is passed down through genera-tions, with new individuals assuming the secret superhero identities. **Grades: 7—12. PJ**

Carlton, Bronwyn. **Books of Faerie.** 144 pages.

Vertigo 1998 Paper 1563894017 $14.95

A spin-off from the Timothy Hunter stories (The Books of Magic series), this stand-alone graphic novel tells how an orphaned human child becomes Queen Titania of Faerie, and one day, Timothy's mother. The edgy, slightly twisted artwork and layout are similar to that of the Sandman series and aptly fit the slightly warped Renaissance world of the story and the cruel beauty of the Courts of Faerie. The bittersweet story will appeal to fantasy readers who like a touch of horror. **Grades: 9—12. KE**

Choi, Brandon. **Gen 13 A-B-C.** 192 pages.

Image Comics 1997 Paper 1887279660 $6.95

Although the newsprint paper and page-reduction of the reprint doesn't do justice to Campbell and Garner's brilliant artwork, this is an excellent introduction to a pop-ular teen superhero comic. The depth of visual characterization, clean lines, and lay-out make a nice counter to the almost stereotypical huge-breasted fighting women in tights who make up half the Gen-13 team. The group of genetically enhanced teenagers work as part of a secret government agency, but very quickly begin to seek their freedom. Nice by-play (and a rare lesbian "superhero") among the teens make this a solid addition to any superhero collection. While fan boys drool, girls will probably appreciate the strong female heroines. **Grades 10—12. KE**

Clowes, Daniel. **Ghost World.** 80 pages.

Fantagraphics 2001 Paper 1560974273 $9.95

Becky and Enid, best friends, are two teen girls on the verge of womanhood—and separate lives. A series of connected stories about their daily lives gradually reveals their characters and their growing maturity. In this sweetly sad coming-of-age story for girls, Clowes uses limited color and a clean, 1960s black-and-white design to link his visual story with his dialogue. Mature teens will appreciate Clowes' story skills. **Grades: 10—12. KE**

Daniels, Les. ***Batman: The Complete History.*** 206 pages.

> Chronicle 1999 Trade 0811824705 $29.95
> Harry N. Abrams 1993 Paper 0810925664 $24.95

Daniels traces Batman's evolution from his comic book beginnings to the Adam West TV show, then to the emergence of Frank Miller's *Dark Knight* graphic novels, and to the movie franchise. Illustrated throughout with rare comic-book art, sketches, movie stills, and Batman merchandise, this tribute to the Caped Crusader unmasks Batman in all his complexity. **Grades 6—12. PJ**

Daniels, Les. ***DC Comics: Sixty Years of the World's Favorite Comic Book Heroes.*** 256 pages.

> Little, Brown 1995 Trade 0821220764 $40.00

The complete story of America's favorite heroes and their talented, dedicated creators. In over 100 short essays, author Les Daniels examines the company's history, traces the genealogy of the major characters, and interviews dozens of artists and writers. Add onto that over 600 illustrations, and this is the total DC package. **Grades 6—12. PJ**

Daniels, Les. ***Marvel: Five Fabulous Decades of the World's Greatest Comics.*** 288 pages.

> Harry N. Abrams 1993 Paper 0810925664 $24.95

Same idea, different company. **Grades 7—12. PJ**

Daniels, Les. ***Superman, the Complete History: The Life and Times of the Man of Steel.*** 192 pages.

> Chronicle 1998 Trade 0811821625 $29.95

Superman, the icon of all comic book superheroes, debuted in 1938's Action Comics #1. Daniels traces the history of the character from an orphan alien comics hero to a complex multimedia icon. The book is not only loaded with drawings, but it also includes several comics reported in total and photos of Superman stuff. **Grades 6—12. PJ**

> Reviews: *SLJ* 10/1/1999

A CORE COLLECTION FOR YOUNG ADULTS

Daniels, Les. ***Wonder Woman: The Complete History.*** 206 pages.

> Chronicle 2000 Trade 0811829138 $29.95

The most famous female superhero gets her turn as Daniels covers her 50+ years of history. As in the other volumes, there is plenty of artwork, photos, and the like. Most interesting here is Daniels' linking themes in the Wonder Woman comics with larger trends in women's role in society. **Grades 6–12. PJ**

DeFalco, Tom. ***Spider-Man: The Ultimate Guide.*** 168 pages.

> Dorling Kindersley 2001 Trade 078947946X $19.99

DeFalco, a former Marvel editor and author of some of the best-selling Spider-Man comics, presents everything anyone wanted to know about the webbed one. The book contains over 600 full-color images and a detailed text that offers a comprehensive guide to all of the major characters and stories. **Grades 6–12. PJ**

Eisner, Will. ***Contract with God.*** 196 pages.

> Kitchen Sink 1996 Paper 0878160183 $11.95
> Kitchen Sink 1999 Trade 0878160175 $24.95

The book that started it all. Eisner, creator of the Spirit comics, developed these four stories, not about superheroes, but about growing up poor. Unable to sell them to any comic publisher, he coined the phrase graphic novel and the rest is history. **Grades 8–12. PJ**

Ellis Warren. ***Stormwatch: Lightning Strikes.*** 144 pages.

> DC Comics 2000 Paper 1563896508 $14.95

Jenny Sparks, the electrically powered "Spirit of the 20th Century" is the highlight of these collected stories of violent superheroes in a dystopic alternate world, like—but unlike—our own. Mixing political satire and a tongue-in-cheek critique of over-the-top superheroes, *Lightning Strikes* is a good introduction to Jenny Sparks and her teammates. It is, however, the middle volume in a series of four comic book collections: *Force of Nature, Change or Die,* and *A Finer World,* and while it can stand alone, your teenage fans may want to read the entire collection. **Grades: 7–12. KE**

Escher, M. C. ***Magic of M. C. Escher.*** 196 pages.

> Harry N. Abrams 2000 Trade 0810967200 $39.95

M.C. Escher was a 20th-century Dutch artist whose strange drawings and etchings are as much graphic riddles as they are art. Images such as the endless staircases and the cannibalistic lizards are well known, but this volume collects hundreds of Escher's works, which are augmented with quotes from the artist. Popular with lovers of speculative fiction, an Escher book is essential to any collection serving teens. **Grades: 7—12. PJ**

Reviews: *Booklist* 12/15/2000, *SLJ* 3/1/2001

Feelings, Tom. ***Middle Passage: White Ships Black Cargo.*** unpaged.

Dial 1995 Trade 0803718047 $50.00
Dial 1998 Trade 0803719655 $250.00

It is a wordless picture book, but not for young children. Teens will be moved by Feelings' artwork depicting the journey made by slaves from Africa to the United States. The images are correctly horrific: full of violence, death, and mayhem. **Grades 7—12. PJ**

Reviews: *Booklist* 8/1/1997, *Booklist* 10/15/1995, *SLJ* 2/1/1996

Fleischman, Paul. ***Cannibal in the Mirror.*** 64 pages.

Twenty-First Century 2000 Library 0761309683 $24.90

Fleischman makes his readers work, and this provocative book of photographs is just as demanding as his prose poems. Fleischman has selected a series of photographs of contemporary teens doing teen things: playing basketball, dancing, and so on, and looking the way that 21st-century teens tend to: pierced, tattooed, etc. He pairs the contemporary photograph with an illustration from the past, linking the two with a quote to force readers to think about how the more things change, the more they stay the same. A book that really defies classification lands here for its use of pictures (the quotes are nice, but not necessary) to tell the story. **Grades 7—12. PJ**

Reviews: *Booklist* 4/15/2000, *SLJ* 4/1/2000, *VOYA* 10/1/2000

Fleming, Robert (Editor). ***The Big Book of Urban Legends.*** 223 pages.

DC Comics 1994 Paper 1563891654 $14.95

Creepy, disgusting, terrifying, and almost never true, these classic urban legends have been adapted to graphic novel format by a variety of illustrators. Most of the stories are well suited to the visual medium and are rendered in black-and-white in a variety of styles. Just the thing for teens with a taste for the macabre. **Grades 6—12. KE <LOST>**

Reviews: *Booklist* 3/1/1995, *Booklist* 8/1/1997

Gaiman, Neil. ***Death: The High Cost of Living.*** 103 pages.

    DC Comics 1994 Paper 1563891336 $12.95

The title refers to the day in which the angel of death must take human form. It is 1983 in New York, and death is personified in a 16-year-old girl. A Sandman spin-off with a life, er, death of its own. **Grades 10—12. PJ**

Gaiman, Neil. ***The Sandman: Preludes and Nocturnes.*** 233 pages.

    Vertigo 1991 Paper 1563890119 $19.95
    Warner 1991 Paper 0446393630 $14.99
    Vertigo 1995 Trade 1563892278 $29.95

The harsh, rough lines of the illustrations in this graphic novel are a near match to Gaiman's transformation of the pulp-action hero the "Sandman" into a creature of pure fantasy. The new Sandman is none other than "Dream," one of the endless spiritual monsters humanity has created for itself: Death, Desire, and Despair are his siblings. Trapped by spiritualists, freed a century later in a series of connected (and creepy) stories, Dream seeks to regain his kingdom and former power. "The Sound of Her Wings," the final short story, introduces the sweet Goth heroine, Death. This graphic novel is more loosely written and less well-drawn than later offerings, but as the introduction to a stunning and world-class series, it will be demanded by fans of intense graphic novels and elegant horror. **Grades 10—12. KE**

Groening, Matt. ***The Big Book of Bart Simpson.*** 128 pages.

    HarperPerennial 2002 Paper 0060084693 $12.95

The underachieving brat with the heart of gold has his own comic book series. His slapstick adventures (with just a touch of satiric bite) will appeal to young comic book fans and serious devotees of the TV show. Earlier Bart books include *Bart Simpson's Guide to Life: A Wee Handbook for the Perplexed*, and *Bartman: The Best of the Best.* **Grades 6—12. KE**

Groening, Matt. ***The Huge Book of Hell.*** 157 pages.

    Penguin 1997 Paper 0140263101 $17.95

Groening is the 20th century's answer to Ambrose Bierce (albeit more commercially successful). Here his biting, deeply ironic, and heartfelt "Life in Hell" comic strips are collected in one big book. For teens who glory in looking on the dark side with wit and cynicism, the "hell" of school, love, religion, and the rest of life are explored with tiny one-eared rabbits and little fez-wearing men. Mature teens will devour this one and go hunting for more. **Grades 10—12. KE**

Groening, Matt. **School Is Hell.** 48 pages.

Random 1987 Paper 0394750918 $8.95

Before the Simpsons, Groening inked the Hell trilogy. This volume on school being hell may be one of the funniest books ever written about the subject of school. Groening's take is like a stick in the eye: sharp and pointed, and every kid feels the need to run with it. **Grades 9–12. PJ**

Groening, Matt. **The Simpsons: A Complete Guide to Our Favorite Family.** 249 pages.

HarperCollins 1998 Trade 0060193484 $25.00

Part of the fun for those who watch the TV show *The Simpsons* is the inside jokes and if-you-blink-you-missed-it quips, like the phrases Bart has to write on the blackboard during the opening credits. Arranged by season and nailed down for the oblivious, even a casual fan of the show will enjoy the humor. In addition to the fun, there's the kind of history and background detail for each episode (seasons one through eight) that more serious fans will want to catch. The ninth and tenth seasons of the show are covered in *The Simpsons: A Complete Guide to Our Favorite Family . . . Continued.* **Grades 6–12. KE**

Groening, Matt. **Simpsons Comics à-Go-Go.** 127 pages.

HarperCollins 2000 Paper 006095566X $11.95

The long-running animated epitome of "dysfunctional family" is also available in several graphic novels collected from the popular comic books. Despite the crude drawings, the comic book, like the show, mixes oddball humor, biting social commentary, and goofy slapstick with surprising charm. Although the appeal of the TV show cuts across nearly all age lines, the graphic novels will have more success with younger teens and hard-core Simpsons fans. There are several such collections, including (in publication order) *Simpsons Comics Spectacular, Simpsons Comics Simps-O-Rama, Simpsons Comics Strike Back, Simpsons Comics Wingding, Simpsons Comics on Parade, Simpson's Big Bonanza, Simpsons Comics à Go-Go, Simpsons Comics Royale,* and *Simpsons Comics Unchained.* **Grades 6–12. KE**

Reviews: *Booklist* 3/15/2001

Hagenauer, George. **The Big Book of Little Criminals: 63 True Tales of the World's Most Incompetent Jailbirds.** 192 pages.

Paradox 1996 Paper 1563892170 $14.95

From small-time crooks to the mob, criminal losers throughout history are showcased in this black-and-white graphic novel. The criminal histories are largely accurate and the various artists illustrate the stories capably. Despite the subtitle, *63*

True Tales of the World's Most Incompetent Jailbirds, not all the crooks are stupid fools. Older teens will appreciate the solid treatment of a fascinating topic. **Grades 8–12. KE**

Hamanaka, Sheila. ***The Journey***. 39 pages.

> Orchard 1995 Paper 0531070603 $8.95
> Orchard 1990 Trade 0531058492 $19.95

The journey of Japanese Americans is the subject of this unique book, which depicts a large mural created by the author/artist. While there are many stories told here, the centerpiece is those panels concerning the tragic experience of Japanese Americans robbed of their land and liberty during World War II. **Grades 6–9. PJ**

> Reviews: *SLJ* 5/1/1990

Hirsch, Karen D. (Editor). ***Mind Riot: Coming of Age in Comix.*** 127 pages.

> Aladdin Paperbacks 1997 Library 0689806221 $9.99

According to the editor, a mind riot is "a state that ice climbers describe when, in panic, the brain momentarily short-circuits." And that is a hell of a metaphor for adolescence. Hirsch gathers a bunch of alternative cartoonists (who draw commix; not comics) to tell their tales about growing up in words and pictures. The confusion of the teen years is shown through laughter and tears as the artists confront issues of identity, sexuality, strained family relationships, and finding a place in the world. **Grades 9–12. PJ**

> Reviews: *SLJ* 8/1/1997

Jacobs, Frank. **Mad—*Cover-to-Cover: 48 Years, 6 Months, and 3 Days of* Mad *Magazine Covers.*** 224 pages.

> Watson-Guptill 2000 Paper 0823016846 $24.95

From its not-so-humble roots as an alternative to gore comics, *Mad* has launched a humor orgy since 1952. Collected here are covers from the first 400 issues, most featuring Alfred E. Neuman. Jacobs adds commentary, plus there are sketches and photos. **Grades 6–12. PJ**

Jemas, Bill. ***Ultimate Spider-Man: Power and Responsibility.*** 192 pages.

> Marvel 2001 Paper 078510786X 14.95

Ultimate Spider-Man received extensive press coverage and was the highest selling comics launch of the year 2000. It is the reinterpretation of Spider-Man's origin, telling the story of how a tortured teen, Peter Parker, was imbued with startling powers, thanks to a bite from a radioactive spider. Like all the *ultimate* books, the goal is to provide readers new to the storyline with one-stop shopping to learn the origins, powers, and personality of an engaging superhero. With the huge success of the movie, this one won't stick to the shelves. **Grades 7–12. PJ**

Jenkins, Paul. ***The Inhumans.*** 264 pages.

> Marvel 2000 Paper 0785107533 $24.95

The inhumans are a race of super-powered beings who are at war with government soldiers. What sounds simple isn't, as it is not always clear who the "bad guy" is. One intriguing element of this graphic novel is the character of Black Bolt, the king of the inhumans, whose voice is so powerful that he dare not speak lest he destroy the planet. Thus, the book's most powerful character is totally silent, not even internal thoughts are revealed. **Grades 7–12. PJ**

Keeps, David. **National Enquirer*: Thirty Years of Unforgettable Images.*** 256 pages.

> Hyperion 2002 Paper 0786888059 $21.95
> Talk Miramax 2001 Trade 0786868481 $45.00

Glaring from across the check-out aisle at the supermarket, the *National Enquirer* is the true paper of record in a celebrity culture. While the words matter and lead the lawsuits, the tabloid is as much about images. Here, in one volume, is a collection of those faces: famous and infamous, and more often than not, if they landed in the pages of the *Enquirer*, the nexus where those two labels converge. There are photos of dead celebrities in their coffins, and plenty of those who one would think would surely die of embarrassment, having been caught in the sometimes unforgivable act of being human. An entertaining and colorful romp through the periodical that sells more than most any other, yet no one admits to reading. **Grades 9–12. PJ**

Kudo, Kazuya. ***Mai the Psychic Girl.*** unpaged.

> Viz Communication 1995 Paper 1569310661 $19.95
> Viz Communication 1996 Paper 156931070X $19.95

An interesting work of anime that shows a more grown-up side. There is a (brief) nude scene, and blood flies as a result of the action that one teen Amazon reviewer said makes the book appropriate for "older Sailor Moon fans." The book follows Mai, a young Japanese girl with psychic power, who finds herself caught up in a world of intrigue, and it takes more punching than predicting in order to escape from it alive. **Grades 7–12. PJ**

Larson, Gary. ***The Far Side.*** unpaged.

> Andrews & McMeel 1982 Paper 0836212002 $7.95

Animals plus humor equals young-teen-reading gold. This and all the titles are essential for any collection serving teens. **Grades 6—12. PJ**

Larson, Gary. ***There's a Hair in My Dirt.*** unpaged.

HarperPerennial 1999 Paper 0060932740 $10.95
HarperCollins 1998 Trade 006019104X $15.95

The nonsense of the title gives way to Larson's first post-*Far Side* work, a children's picture book for all ages. The familiar Larson elements are abundant in this tale of a young worm's "angst" at his subterranean life. The worm's father decides it is time to teach his son the facts of worm life; in doing so Larson's story tells the tale of what it looks like below earth. One part environmental science mixed with two parts evocative silliness creates a book that teaches about every creature's role in making the earth work, while at the same time teasing the funny bone. **Grades 6—12. PJ**

Reviews: *SLJ* 12/1/1998

Lee, Stan. ***How to Draw Comics the Marvel Way.*** 160 pages.

Simon & Schuster 1984 Paper 0671530771 $16.00

Using artwork from Marvel comics as primary examples, this how-to book graphically illustrates the mechanics and magic of comic art. **Grades 6—12. PJ**

Loeb, Jeph. ***Batman: The Long Halloween.*** 368 pages.

DC Comics 1999 Paper 1563894696 $19.95

The Batman adventures in this graphic novel pull equally from film noir, detective fiction, and Frank Miller's classic *Batman Year One* to create an enjoyable and compelling read. Early in his crime-solving career, Batman is faced with a seemingly untouchable mob boss and a serial killer who strikes only on holidays. The artwork, though nicely moody and dramatically lit, is transparent, driving the story visually without drawing attention to itself. As a classic whodunit, the graphic novel format allows great freedom in placing all the clues visually before the reader, while the sex and violence commonly associated with the genre are stylized or off-stage, where they will not distract from the clever Hitchcock-ian puzzle. **Grades 7—12. KE**

Loeb, Jeph (Editor). ***Superman: No Limits.*** 203 pages.

DC Comics 2000 Paper 1563896990 $14.95

In what appears to be the closing year of the second millennium (1999) several top illustrators team up to continue the Superman story just after his marriage to Lois Lane and "death." Whitmore's colors, the clean layouts, and (for the most part) depth of visual characterization keep the several artists' styles coherent, providing for a seamless story. The team of writers maintains a nice balance between action and personal development as Superman faces familiar villains such as Lex Luthor, threats to his new marriage, and new challenges in the form of a galaxy-destroying menace and sultry "encantadora." One of the rare black heroes, Steel, makes an extended cameo: He and his family are appealingly rendered. A solid addition to any superhero collection and likely to be enjoyed by all readers. **Grades 7—12. KE**

Macaulay, David. ***Motel of the Mysteries.*** 96 pages.

Houghton Mifflin 1979 Paper 0395284252 $13.00

So, if the world ended in 1985, what would archaeologists find if they dug up the remains sometime in the year 4000? That's the jumping-off point for this dig at archaeology. The main character in the book is Howard Carson, who seeks to find relevance in every object from the past. For example, he finds within his dig site (a motel room, hence the title) a skeleton facing a TV, which leads him to believe that the TV is some sort of altar. As always, the artwork is striking and quite sarcastic. **Grades 6—8. PJ**

McCloud, Scott. ***Reinventing Comics.*** 256 pages.

HarperPerennial 2000 Paper 0060953500 $22.95

McCloud uses the graphic format not so much as a sequel but as a continuation and call to arms, tracing the recent history of the art form and calling for "a new revolution of comics." In particular, he sees the Internet as the cure for all of the comic industry's ills. Aimed more at inspiring and analyzing than providing mere information, this is a must for teens who treat comics seriously. **Grades 7—12. PJ**

McCloud, Scott. ***Understanding Comics.*** 224 pages.

HarperCollins 1994 Paper 006097625X $22.95

McCloud uses comic book style to trace the history of sequential art. While he reaches back to the writings on the cave, the real focus is on the innovators, such as Will Eisner and Art Spiegelman. Yet McCloud examines more than the who and when by focusing on both the how and why. He wants readers to understand how comic books work by examining the elements of comic style, picking apart the relationship between art and text. **Grades 7—12. PJ**

Reviews: *Booklist* 8/1/1997

Mignola, Mike. ***Hellboy: The Chained Coffin.*** 176 pages.

Dark Horse Comics 1998 Paper 1569713499 $17.95

"Hellboy" is a kind of Frankenstein monster: a huge red creature almost eight feet tall who is as strong as 10 men. He has a tail, an artificial stone arm, and an origin linked somehow to Nazi experiments at the end of the war. Cut to the present, where a supernatural serial killer is at work and it is up to Hellboy (yes, the good guy is named Hellboy) to stop the carnage. A secret agency that is a cross between the X-Files and Interpol, solving paranormal crimes the world over, employs Hellboy as their last chance. Good writing and art make this twisted tale a hell of a ride. **Grades 10–12 (mature). PJ**

Miller, Frank. ***Batman: The Dark Knight Returns.*** 197 pages.

DC Comics 2002 Trade 156389341X $24.95

The book that changed it all. Miller didn't revisit the Batman character; he re-invented it. Thoughts of the deadpan, yet goofy, Adam West character from the Batman TV show were erased and replaced with a brooding superhero. This is a tale of a middle-aged Bruce Wayne returning one last time to fight crime as Batman, although everything around him is so corrupt, he wonders why he should even bother. That type of self-doubt and even cynicism is not the stuff of Saturday morning superheroes and clearly show the line drawn between kids' comic books and teen graphic novels. This isn't about action; this is about one man's reaction to trying to remain true, just, and heroic while the world around him decays. **Grades 9–12. PJ**

Miller, Frank. ***Batman: Year One.*** 104 pages.

DC Comics 1997 Paper 0930289331 $9.95

After re-inventing Batman, Miller needed to revisit the character's creation. The story is told from the perspectives of Police Officer (one day, Commissioner) Gordon and Batman. Batman wasn't so much part of the solution, but as a lone wolf vigilante, part of the problem. Gordon and Batman realize they must join forces to fight evil, each respecting the other's talents. While not a deal with the devil, this is a darker view of crime fighting. The book also introduces the Cat Woman character as a vengeful ex-prostitute. This is not "kiddy" stuff, but a mature look at the man behind the mask, warts and all. **Grades 7–12. PJ**

Miller, Frank. ***Daredevil Visionaries.*** unpaged.

Marvel 2001 Paper 0785107681 $24.95

Frank Miller reinvented "the man without fear," giving this blind superhero a dark edge in what is now considered one of the best books of the series. Mazzucchelli's gritty artwork ably supports Miller's story of despair and redemption. With his secret identity blown, Daredevil's enemies set about to destroy his career, his friendships, and eventually his life. Left for dead, he is rescued and nursed back to health by a nun working in the slum of Hell's Kitchen. How Matt returns from the dregs to find meaning and purpose is interwoven with the dramatic visual action we've come to expect from Frank Miller. Nearly every fan of action comics will want to read this one. **Grades 9–12. KE**

Moench, Doug. ***The Big Book of the Unexplained.*** 192 pages.

DC Comics 1997 Paper 1563892545 $14.95

Various comic book artists illustrate dozens of black-and-white stories of paranormal mysteries. From crop circles to La Chupacabra, anyone curious about the world of the weird will get a nice overview in a fun-to-read format. Although the uncritical presentation will seriously annoy most skeptics, there is little space for detailed coverage and an extensive bibliography can be used for further research, should anyone care. As with the other Factoid Books, the strength of *The Big Book of the Unexplained* is breadth, rather than depth, of coverage. **Grades 8–12. KE**

Moore, Alan. ***Batman: The Killing Joke.*** unpaged.

DC Comics 1996 Paper 0930289455 $5.95

The Joker is the star of this very dark, very disturbing graphic novel that peers into the twisted mind of Batman's number one nemesis. Joker's crime is a violent and shocking attack on Commissioner Gordon's daughter, for which Batman vows he must pay. The novel isn't just about the chase, but more about the lengths that a crazed killer will go, and then go even one step beyond what anyone, except perhaps Alan Moore, could imagine. **Grades 7–12. PJ**

Moore, Alan. ***From Hell.*** unpaged.

Top Shelf 2000 Paper 0958578346 $35.00

The provocative title strikes the right macabre mood in this graphic novel concerning Jack the Ripper. Moore dives deep into the pool of Whitechapel lore, mixing myth, fact, and speculation to create a horror tale rich in texture and terror. **Grades 9–12. PJ**

Reviews: *Booklist* 6/1/2000

Moore, Alan. ***The League of Extraordinary Gentlemen, 1898 (Vol. 1).*** 176 pages.

DC Comics 2001 Trade 1563896656 $24.95
DC Comics 2002 Paper 1563898586 $14.95

What a concept: create a band of superheroes out of great late-Victorian literature. Moore's English posse is composed of Dr. Jekyll; Captain Nemo; the invisible man, Hawley Griffen; and Allan Quartermain, the adventurer of *King Solomon's Mines.* While they don't don tights and cowls, they do still fight crime, stand up for justice, and inspire awe. Both prose and pictures are rich in period detail as Moore examines another end-of-century frenzy. This trip back in time is a dark ride. **Grades 6–12. PJ**

Moore, Alan. ***Promethea (Collected Ed., Book 1).*** 176 pages.

DC Comics 2001 Paper 1563896672 $14.95

Beautifully drawn and colored, with a realistic approach, clean lines, and a nice art-deco framework, this graphic novel uses the myth of Hypatia (popularized by Kingsley) and the notion that a world of gods and demons may be tapped by those with creative powers. Set in a universe where "superheroes," future technology, and magical powers are the norm, a young college student investigates the many iterations of the avenging goddess-figure Promethea in art and literature only to find herself targeted by powerful enemies. She must become the newest avatar of Promethea and master herself and the myth if she or her loved ones are to survive. Teenage girls who enjoy the popular neo-pagan series and devotees of mythical fantasy with strong female characters will be quickly hooked by Promethea's adventures. The adventure of the mythopoeic figure and her human avatar are continued in *Promethea, Collected ed., Book 2.* **Grades 8—12. KE**

Moore, Alan. ***Saga of the Swamp Thing.*** 176 pages.

DC Comics 1998 Paper 0930289226 $19.95

Steve Bissette's edgy, yet delicate illustrations, which hearken back to old horror comic classics, complement Moore's lyric prose in this recreation of the Swamp Thing "superhero" character. Alec Holland was once human, killed in a bizarre chemical accident; the residue of his consciousness animates a green monster. Grotesquery, beauty, and an ecological sensibility make this an unusually fine horror story, and an excellent choice to give to teenage fans of Stephen King. **Grades 8—12. KE**

Moore, Alan. ***Top Ten: Book One.*** 208 pages.

America's Best Comics 2001 Paper 1563896680 $14.95

Edgy, realistic artwork, held together by clean colorization, aptly brings to life this unusual superhero graphic novel. In a world where super-powered individuals are the norm, some join the police force. It's a twisted, funny, and page-turning take on the police procedural. Personal stories of individual cops' trials, daily lives, and emotional misfortunes are woven into stories of violent serial killers, murder mystery, and gang warfare. From the "Chief" (a Doberman pinscher in a bionic human suit) to the investigation of Baldur's recurring homicide (thanks to Loki), the strange and the familiar are combined with surprising success. Fans of both superhero and alternative comics would want to give this a look. **Grades 8—12. KE**

Moore, Alan. ***The Watchmen.*** unpaged.

DC Comics 1995 Paper 0930289234 $19.95

This graphic novel is one of the best pieces of literature I have read. Moore's characters are real people with real problems. Breaking away from the traditional svelte and muscular hero, Moore's characters inhabit true-to-life bodies, including the middle-aged, pot-bellied Night Owl. Moore also cleverly weaves in a story within a story through a comic book a young man is reading, which is a clever parallel to the main plot. Great for the reluctant reader because of its format, but edgy enough to intrigue the rapacious teen mind. Comes with a caution label for violence and nudity (one naked blue dude and a few butt shots of regular people), but certainly accessible to most older teens. **Grades 7–12. (Annotation by Spring Lea Boehler)**

Moore, Terry. *Complete Strangers in Paradise, Vol. 1.* 296 pages.

> Abstract Studio 1989 Trade 1892597063 $49.95
> Abstract Studio 1994 Paper 1892597004 $8.95

This graphic novel is so skillfully drawn, the balance of line, color and expression so nearly perfect, it's hard to realize that you're reading a soap opera. Sweet, sad and often funny and with a terrific heart, Volume 1 introduces three friends: Francine, Katchoo, and David. Their interpersonal woes, tangled sex-lives, and financial troubles are combined with life-and-death threats from the secrets in Katchoo's and David's pasts. Fans of alternative comics and girls who like "real stories" will fall for this one because they'll come to love the characters, rather than the sometimes melodramatic plots. Once hooked, it's likely they'll want to read the rest of the story, compiled in (thus far) 10 volumes. **Grades 10–12. KE**

Moore, Terry. *Strangers in Paradise: High School.* 80 pages.

> Abstract Studio 1999 Paper 1892597071 $8.95

Two beautifully drawn yet utterly realistic teenage girls (rather than the huge-breasted wasp-waisted darlings of standard comic book fare) form an unlikely friendship: Francine is a child of suburbia, Katchoo, the sexually abused biker chick. From the hell that high school can be for many teens, the two come together only to part. *High School* can stand alone or be enjoyed as part of the background story to Terry Moore's ongoing saga. **Grades 10–12. KE**

Morrison, Grant. *Arkham Asylum.* 120 pages.

> Warner 1997 Paper 0930289560 $14.95

Arkham Asylum for the criminally insane is where all the creepy costumed villains from the DC Comics universe end up. McKean's moody artwork, part painted, part drawn, and part constructed, is perfect illustration for Morrison's edgy stories about a house of freakish madmen. Fans of the Batman superhero comics as well as those with a taste for horror comics will enjoy this graphic novel. **Grades 9–12 (mature). KE**

Morrison, Grant. *JLA: New World Order.* 96 pages.

DC Comics 1997 Paper 156389369X $5.95

Morrison reunites DC Comic's magnificent seven: Superman, Batman, Wonder Woman, Aquaman, the Flash, Green Lantern, and Martian Manhunter. But the forces of good face a most different villain, one whose public face is just as popular as their own. Perhaps the one super power all the JLA share is their ability to sense the true motives of their adversaries. **Grades 6—12. PJ**

Otomo, Katsuhiro. *Akira #1.* unpaged.

Dark Horse Comics 2001 Paper 1569714983 $24.95

This cinematic and bravura science fiction graphic novel is beautifully drawn by creator Otomo. In the first episode, we are introduced to post-holocaust Japan and the idea of Akira: a secret and potentially world-destroying monster. The starting cast consists of Kaneda, his motorbike gang, the Colonel and his project to create and control powerful psychics, and an Underground team, which opposes his schemes. Justly a world-famous manga classic, if you can have only one "japanima-tion" book, buy this one. The epic concludes in books 2–6. **Grades 9—12. KE**

Prohias, Antonio. *Spy vs. Spy: The Complete Casebook.* 304 pages.

Watson-Guptill 2001 Paper 0823050211 $24.95

The year 2001 marked the 40th anniversary of *Mad* magazine's yin/yang, black/white spy duo. Slapstick mime on the printed page, the feature has run in vir-tually every issue since the beginning, with nearly 1,000 installments. This tome chronicles the creation and history of the spies and features all 247 of the strips written and illustrated by creator Antonio Prohias. There are also a few essays, some unpublished drawings, and other archival matter. **Grades 6—12. PJ**

Reviews: *Booklist* 10/1/2001

Rennie, Gordon. *Starship Troopers.* 152 pages.

Dark Horse Comics 1998 Paper 1569713146 $14.95

The only good thing to come out of the abysmally stupid movie *Starship Troopers* was Warren Ellis' graphic novel prequel. Only a third of the book covers the movie itself (and manages to avoid many of its more asinine moments). The majority concerns mankind's first meeting with the alien species that threaten to exterminate it and a moving vignette of one young soldier's attempt to save the town of Port Joe Smith. The artwork is crisp and vivid and suits the taut story-line. Teens who enjoy military action adventure won't put this one down. **Grades 9—12. KE**

Rolling Stone Editors. ***Rolling Stone: The Complete Covers.*** 273 pages.

Harry N. Abrams 2001 Trade 0810982064 $19.98

Thirty years of the biggest names of rock captured in cover images from the pens of artists and the lenses of photographers. This browsing volume with over 700 covers depicts the changes of the music, as well as the changes in the faces of some of rock's biggest names over the years. **Grades 8–12. PJ**

Rolling Stone Editors. ***Rolling Stone Images of Rock and Roll.*** unpaged.

Little, Brown 1995 Trade 0316754684 $50.00

A collection of the magazine's best photos, shot by some of the world's most famous photographers. **Grades 10–12. PJ**

Rose, Joel. ***The Big Book of Thugs.*** 192 pages.

Paradox 1996 Paper 1563892855 $14.95

There are 57 varieties of thugs explored in another stellar collection of graphic storytelling. **Grades 8–12. PJ**

Ross, Alex. ***Earth X.*** 472 pages.

Marvel 2000 Paper 078510755X $24.95

A humanoid robot is summoned by an alien "Watcher" to oversee Earth's preparation for a "grand destiny" as the incubator for a powerful race of galactic beings. The first step, in which every human develops superpowers, throws every community into chaos. The struggles of both the original superheroes and ordinary people in a rapidly disintegrating planet appear likely to be futile. A nice extrapolation of familiar characters into aging desuetude, philosophical debate, and a "what's really going on?" mystery keep the reader engaged. The blocky, jagged illustrations of the main storyline are juxtaposed with finely penciled interludes, nicely mirroring the juxtaposition of action and contemplation. This graphic novel is likely to appeal to teens. **Grades 7–12. KE**

Ross, Alex. ***Wonder Woman: Spirit of Truth.*** 64 pages.

DC Comics 2001 Paper 1563898616 $9.95

An apt title for this graphic novel that is as much about Wonder Woman's "real life" as it is her super heroic acts. As in many contemporary graphic novels, the main character is at a crossroads, questioning her past acts and contemplating a different future. A nice look "behind the mask" of a longtime comic book icon. **Grades 7–12. PJ**

Samura, Hiroaki. ***Blade of the Immortal: Heart of Darkness.*** 240 pages.

Dark Horse Comics 2001 Paper 1569715319 $16.95

Blade, as portrayed on the screen by Wesley Snipes, is a mix of Shaft, Buffy, and Bruce Lee, with a little bit of attitude thrown in. This collection shows Blade at his best and his enemies at their worst. **Grades 10–12. PJ**

Sanderson, Peter. ***Ultimate X-Men.*** 176 pages.

Dorling Kindersley 2000 Trade 0789466937 $19.99

Everything X-men, from the first comic in 1963 up to the 2000 blockbuster movie. This heavily illustrated volume takes readers through the entire history of the X-Men, all the characters, and all the villains. Using both previously published materials, as well as illustrations from the Marvel archive, this is a book that lives up to its title. **Grades 6–12. PJ**

Savans, Ilan. ***Latino USA: A Cartoon History.*** 192 pages.

Basic Books 2000 Trade 0465082211 $19.95

Another example of when a graphic novel is not a novel but, instead, uses the graphic format to educate, inform, and, yes, entertain readers. Four different narrators, including a masked professional wrestler, tell the story of Latino history. The range of topics includes Columbus, *West Side Story*, Castro, Guevara, the Bay of Pigs, the Cuban Missile Crisis, Neruda, Garcia Marquez, the Mariel Boatlift, and Selena. **Grades 6–12. PJ**

Scieszka, Jon. ***Baloney.*** 32 pages.

Viking 2001 Trade 0670892483 $15.99

When aliens go to school, they bring with them a whole host of problems. Filled with language from another planet and drawings that are out of this world, this is another picture book that works on lots of levels, but mostly pulls at the funny bone. **Grades 6–12. PJ**

Reviews: *Booklist* 5/15/2001, *SLJ* 5/1/2001

Scieszka, Jon. ***Math Curse.*** unpaged.

Viking 1995 Trade 0670861944 $16.99

A young girl is stricken with math mania: everywhere she looks she sees addition, subtraction, and functions. Scieszka and Lane Smith get wacky with numbers in this award-winning picture book that is perfect for young adults as well. *USA Today* said:

"As close to genius as one gets in a picture book." **Grades 6–12. PJ <TEN>**

Reviews: *Booklist* 11/1/1995, *SLJ* 5/1/1995

Scieszka, Jon. ***Squids Will Be Squids: Fresh Morals, Beastly Fable.*** unpaged.

Viking 1998 Trade 067088135X $17.99

After beating up on fairy tales for a while, Lane Smith and Scieszka turn their attention to Aesop in this comical send-up of fables. Using everyday examples, these remakes teach the important life lessons, such as "he who smelt it, dealt it." The only moral here seems to be getting to the punch line. Rather than using quiet animals to spin his fables, Scieszka opts for odder vehicles to deliver his humor, such as squids, skunks, and a musk ox. The only thing packed onto the page tighter than puns are Smith's unique illustrations, which give the entire package high teen appeal. **Grades 6–12. PJ**

Reviews: *Booklist* 9/15/1998, *SLJ* 10/1/1998

Scieszka, Jon. ***The Stinky Cheese Man and Other Fairly Stupid Tales/10th Ann.*** unpaged.

Viking 2002 Trade 0670035696 $16.99

Scieszka's wit and Lane Smith's wacky drawings skewer fairy tales. Playing not only with form, but also format, the jokes pile one on top of the other in one of the funniest, and most honored, picture books in the past decade. **Grades 6–12. PJ**

Reviews: *Booklist* 9/1/1992, *SLJ* 9/1/1992

Sendak, Maurice. ***Where the Wild Things Are.*** unpaged.

HarperCollins 1998 Trade 0060282231 $16.95
HarperCollins 1998 Library 0060254939 $17.89
HarperCollins 1998 Paper 0064431789 $7.99

Sendak is an artist who selected children's books as his media; the artwork in this volume stunned everyone when it appeared in the 1960s with its delightful detail and stunning use of color. That this title belongs, in multiple copies, in every elementary school library and public library children's room is a given, but a copy belongs where teenagers can easily revisit it. With its theme concerning the power of imagination, not to mention some pretty scary stuff, this is a robust read for any age. **Grades 6–12. PJ**

Seuss, Dr. ***The Cat in the Hat.*** 48 pages.

Random House 1999 Trade 0679892672 $12.99

Maybe the whole thing is a metaphor for adolescence? Sally and her brother are left home one day when their mother has to run out. The Cat drops by, brings his bag of tricks, and wreaks havoc. Still shows up on "best book" surveys for teens of all ages, not just because it harkens back to the "simple days" of childhood, but also because that Cat is one party animal. **Grades 6—12. PJ**

Seuss, Dr. ***Oh, the Places You'll Go.*** 48 pages.

> Random House 1990 Library 0679905278 $17.99
> Random House 1990 Trade 0679805273 $17.00

As good a book for young adults ever written; it says in 48 pages what teen novels hash about for 300. The pajama-clad hero faces challenges, setbacks, and joyful successes in his journey, wonderfully told and bursting with detailed two-page spreads. A high school graduation staple and with good reason: it is as good a message about growing up and moving on as any, and with pictures! **Grades 6—12. PJ**

> Reviews: *SLJ* 3/1/1990

Sifakis, Carl. ***The Big Book of Hoaxes.*** 212 pages.

> DC Comics 1996 Paper 1563892529 $14.95

For true believers of the *Weekly World News* comes another factoid book, this time handling the history of hoaxes, including crop circles. **Grades 10—12. PJ**

Silverstein, Shel. ***Falling Up.*** 171 pages.

> HarperCollins 1996 Library 0060248033 $17.89
> HarperCollins 1996 Trade 0060248025 $17.95

Silverstein's third book of poems and drawings features silly rhymes, sillier drawings, and more than a passing tip of Shel's hat in hand (and tongue in cheek) to scatological humor. **Grades 4—7. PJ**

Reviews: *Booklist* 1996, *SLJ* 7/1/1996

Silverstein, Shel. ***The Giving Tree.*** unpaged.

> HarperCollins 1964 Library 0060256664 $17.89
> HarperCollins 1964 Trade 0060256656 $15.95

A book that a lot of adults really hate, which alone seems like a recommendation for many teens to embrace it. A simple story with simple line drawings tells the tale of a tree that grants a young man every wish. The book's first line is straightforward: "Once there was a tree . . . and she loved a little boy," but what the ending means is up to the reader. The picture book as moral Rorschach test. **Grades 6—12. PJ**

Silverstein, Shel. ***A Light in the Attic.*** 167 pages.

> HarperCollins 1981 Library 0060256745 $17.89
> HarperCollins 1981 Trade 0060256737 $17.95

A runaway bestseller staying on *The New York Times* list for 182 weeks offers up poems, ballads, and limericks, each accompanied by a line drawing that is often as funny as the words themselves. **Grades 6–8. PJ**

Silverstein, Shel. ***Where the Sidewalk Ends.*** 166 pages.

> HarperCollins 1974 Library 0060256680 $18.89
> HarperCollins 1974 Trade 0060256672 $17.99

In 1974, Robert Cormier was disturbing the universe of young adult literature with *The Chocolate War* by not offering happy endings or false promises: He wanted teen readers to think. The very same year just a few shelves away, Shel Silverstein was disturbing the children's literature universe by not offering poetry full of images of nature or pretty pictures. He wants kids to laugh. Silverstein's spin on kids' verse goes heavier on the naughty than the nice, and his humor is not so much nonsensical as irreverent. This is funny stuff that is indeed for all ages, but mostly for teens who need a good laugh. **Grades 6–8. PJ**

Smith, Jeff. ***Bone: Out from Boneville.*** 142 pages.

> Cartoon Books 1996 Paper 0963660942 $12.95
> Cartoon Books 1995 Trade 0963660993 $19.95

One clear pattern can be found on teen reading-interest surveys. When asked to name favorite fiction genres, those of adventure, humor, and fantasy always are at the top of the list. *Bone* is a wonderful example of all three genres in the comic format. The premise is simple enough: the three Bone cousins are exiled from their home and start out on separate journeys across the desert. At every turn, they encounter various other characters who present them with interesting and amusing interactions. **Grades 6–12. PJ**

> Reviews: *Booklist* 8/1/1995

Smith, Kevin. ***Daredevil Visionaries, Vol. 5.*** 192 pages.

> Marvel 1999 Paper 0785107371 $19.95

Joe Quesada's stunning art nouveau decoration and detailed, clean, and beautiful mood artwork draw the reader instantly into the story of a man whose deepest religious faith is challenged. Daredevil must choose between murdering a child who might be the anti-Christ, or watching everyone he loves, perhaps even his own soul, be destroyed. The creator of *Dogma* and other popular teen movies has crafted a superhero story that pushes the boundaries of the genre and should appeal to young and old fans alike. Kevin Smith's tale is currently the best of the Daredevil: Visionaries books. **Grades 7—12. KE**

Spiegelman, Art (Editor). ***Little Lit: Folklore and Fairy Tale Funnies.*** 64 pages.

HarperCollins 2001 Cloth 0060286245 $19.95

A wide and weird collection of authors, from picture-book stalwart Maurice Sendak to NPR essayist David Sederas, presents short stories told in the graphic format. The book also boosts a new work by *Where's Waldo?* guru Martin Handford and an old work by *Harold and the Purple Crayon* creator Crocket Johnson revisited. An Amazon.com's Best of 2001 selection. **Grades 6—8. PJ**

Reviews: *Booklist* 2001, *SLJ* 2000

Spiegelman, Art (Editor). ***Little Lit: Strange Stories for Strange Kids.*** 64 pages.

HarperCollins 2001 Trade 0060286261 $19.95

Just as Scieszka and Lane Smith turned picture books on their head with their parodies of classic fairy tales, Spiegelman gathers a wide variety of artists and illustrators to upset the apple cart using comic book style. A collection of both new and retold classic tales, the book actually has more in common, in terms of both art and attitude, with the 50s pulp horror comics. There are well-known names from books for kids (David Macaulay) and graphic novels (Daniel Cowles), which makes sense given the age range to which this collection would appeal. This is, as *SLJ* noted, "a cool book" that fits into the neglected niche of books that are gut-bustingly funny. **Grades 6—12. PJ**

Reviews: *Booklist* 12/15/2001, SLJ 3/1/2002

Spiegelman, Art. ***Maus: A Survivor's Tale.***

(vol. 1) Pantheon Books 1986 Paper 0394241258 $14.00
(vol. 2) Pantheon Books 1992 Paper 0679729771 $14.00

Another comic book about heroic acts, although in this one rather than wearing a cape, the main character wears a number burned into the skin on his arm. Instead of a fictional superhero performing superhuman feats of strength, the main character here is real (the author's father) and the feats of strength and courage dwarf that of any crime fighter. Maus tells his father's true story of the Holocaust as metaphor: the Jews are the mice and the Germans are the cats. In the first volume, Vladek Spiegelman goes from being a newlywed starting out his life to a starving, tortured man on his way to a concentration camp. He survives, but within the second volume, readers discover the very same virtues that got him through the dread later become vices in his relationships with his family. The first volume presents the horror of history; the second looks at the long shadow of that history and its effect upon those who lived through the ordeal. **Grades 8—12. PJ <YALSA>**

Starlin, Jim. ***Batman: A Death in the Family.*** unpaged.

DC Comics 1996 Paper 0930289447 $12.95

While neither the artwork (printed, unfortunately, on newsprint) nor the script rise above the commonplace of superhero fare, this graphic novel is something of a milestone in the world of comics: A major comic book character, the second Robin (Jason Todd), was permanently killed off as a result of a reader poll taken as the book was being written. **Grades 6—9. KE**

Takahashi, Rumiko. ***Ranma 1/2, Vol. 1.*** unpaged.

Viz Communication 1993 Paper 092927993X $16.95

The most popular comic book artist in the world (because she's a superstar in Asia!) manga artist and storyteller Takahashi creates the slapstick story of a boy, Ranma, who turns into a girl every time he gets splashed with cold water (hot water reverses the effect). From Japan's communal bathhouses (a particular riot) to problems of mistaken identity (Ranma has suitors who adore him as a girl), the book is engaging teen sitcom fare. Takahashi's illustrations use an expressive, almost impressionistic, anime style. As anime like *Dragonball* and *Sailor Moon* expand into U.S. pop culture, books like *Ranma 1/2* are likely to prove popular with a wide array of teens. **Grades 8—12. KE**

Takaya, Yoshiki. ***Bio-Booster Armor Guyver: Arma.*** unpaged.

Viz Communication 1998 Paper 1569312427 $15.95

Bio-Booster Armor Guyver: Esca. unpaged.

Viz Communication 1996 Paper 1569311366 $15.95

Guyver, an alien life form, adapts to the body of a high school student, Sho. Sho gains superpowers and a suit of armor, but also the wrath of the evil Chaos organization, which seeks to take over the universe in what is considered by many to be one of the best and most popular manga series available. **Grades 8—12. PJ**

Talbot, Bryan. ***The Tale of One Bad Rat.*** unpaged.

Dark Horse Comics 1995 Paper 1569710775 $14.95

The idea of a graphic novel as merely entertainment or as a format that appeals only to those who want action is dispelled in this slim volume. This book tells the story of Helen Potter, sexually abused by her father for years, who runs away from home, heading for the home of her favorite childhood author, Beatrix Potter. The book starts with Helen begging on the streets of London before she heads north to find Hill Top Farm, Beatrix's home. The mix of heavy message with this form is powerful. **Grades 10–12. PJ**

Reviews: *Booklist* 9/15/1995

Taylor, Clark. ***The House That Crack Built.*** unpaged.

Chronicle 1992 Paper 0811801233 $6.95
Chronicle 1992 Trade 0811801330 $12.95

Taylor uses the familiar nursery rhyme cadence to track crack cocaine from the South American drug cartel to the pain caused as drugs devastate users and the youngest, unsuspecting victims. Coupled with powerful drawings that echo the pain of the text, this is anything but a picture book for children; it is, instead, a tale for teens about choices and consequences. **Grades 6–12. PJ**

Reviews: *Booklist* 4/15/1992

Van Allsburg, Chris. ***The Wretched Stone.*** unpaged.

Houghton Mifflin 1991 Trade 0395533074 $17.95

It could be argued that all of two-time Caldecott-winner Van Allsburg's books belong in a core collection for teens. Many teens probably enjoyed them as children, but coming back to them, they'll find deeper meaning and laughs. The metaphor of the "wretched stone" as television is obvious, but the artwork is lush, the text lyrical, and the entire package, like that stone, gives off a peculiar light that might change the way readers think about things. **Grades 6–12. PJ**

Reviews: *Booklist* 10/1/1991, *SLJ* 11/1/1991

Vankin, Jonathan. ***The Big Book of Bad.*** 192 pages.

Paradox 1998 Paper 1563893592 $14.95

Another big book that once again focuses on the warped, weird, and slightly wild side of life, looking at evil through history. It is disturbing, entertaining, and more than occasionally hilarious. **Grades 8–12. PJ**

Vankin, Jonathan. ***The Big Book of Scandal.*** 192 pages.

Paradox 1997 Paper 1563893584 $14.95

Vankin does a great job of concisely and completely dealing with long-forgotten scandals without too much crossover into his previous books (*Conspiracies, Cover Ups and Crimes,* and *60 Greatest Conspiracies*) and he does not pick easy targets. The scandals here come from Hollywood and Wall Street and all points in between, involving mostly the famous getting singed for their exposed sins. **Grades 8–12. PJ**

Verheiden, Mark. ***Aliens: Outbreak.*** unpaged.

Dark Horse Comics 1996 Paper 1569711747 $17.95

Decent, if unspectacular, artwork takes second place to a tight plot in this graphic novel sequel to the popular movie *Aliens II*. Of the three survivors, Wilks (the good soldier, Hicks in the film) has ended up in prison while Newt (the little girl) is stranded in a mental institution. When the government releases Wilks to run an expedition to the alien planet and bring them back a specimen, Wilks rescues the teenage Newt and the fun begins. From lunatic cultists who worship the aliens as gods, to assassins competing with the government to obtain what they believe will become the ultimate terror weapon, conspiracies and plot-twists abound. Fans of the film will enjoy being reunited with their favorite heroes and villains, and older teen fans of SF thrillers will want to check this out as well. **Grades 9–12. KE**.

Waid, Mark (Editor). ***Justice League: A New Beginning.*** 181 pages.

DC Comics 1989 Paper 0930289404 $12.95

A collection of the first seven issues of the Justice League relaunch from 1987. While some big-name superheroes are lacking, this volume is important to restarting the series following the events of *Crisis on Infinite Earths* story cycle, which reordered the DC Comics universe. **Grades 7–12. PJ**

Waid, Mark. ***Kingdom Come.*** 232 pages.

DC Comics 1998 Paper 1563893304 $14.95

This volume, which imagines an earth that is unprotected by Superman, often shows up on best lists. There's little sunlight in this dark ride where Batman, Superman, Wonder Woman, and the rest of the DC Comics stable are forced to take sides in a final battle of good versus evil. **Grades 7–12. PJ**

Ware, Chris. ***Jimmy Corrigan.*** 380 pages.

Pantheon 2000 Trade 0375404538 $29.95

Originally run as a series of newspaper comic strips and later compiled and polished into novel form, Jimmy Corrigan is the detailed character study of an isolated, miserable man. The slight plot—36-year-old Jimmy's pitiful reunion with his deadbeat dad—is framed by parallel stories of his father and grandfather, whose lives mirror the anomie, rejection, and failed hopes that define Jimmy's existence. The artwork, layout, and book design are exquisite, and line and color applied flawlessly. Each panel is a small decorative picture and the book's layout a marvel of William Morris style and clean ornamentation. The very beauty of the storytelling medium throws the utter pointlessness of Jimmy's life into stark relief. Of interest to teens who find comfort in the knowledge that other's lives can be more depressing than their own, to literature classes exploring post-modern storytelling, and to art and graphic-design students fascinated by creators who can push the boundaries of the "comic book" medium. **Grades 10–12. KE**

Review: *Booklist* 11/15/2000

Watterson, Bill. ***The Authoritative Calvin and Hobbes.*** 253 pages.

Andrews & McMeel 1990 Paper 0836218221 $14.95

Though long gone from the Sunday papers, Watterson's comics still make teen readers laugh as they follow the adventures of a boy and his not-so-imaginary friend. Buy this one and all the rest. **Grades 6–10. PJ**

Wick, Walter. ***Walter Wick's Optical Tricks.*** 43 pages.

Cartwheel 1998 Trade 0590222279 $13.95

From the creator of huge children's-favorite *I Spy* series comes this slightly more challenging title. Featuring colorful photographs of objectives and shapes with tricks of light, shadows, and mirrors, this isn't so much a book as it is a fun puzzle and fascinating problem-solving exercise. **Grades 6–12. PJ**

Reviews: *Booklist* 8/1/1998, *SLJ* 9/1/1998

Winick, Judd. ***The Adventures of Barry Ween: Boy Genius.*** unpaged.

Oni 1999 Paper 1929998007 $8.95

Genius hardly describes this 10-year-old with an IQ hovering around 350 who has to play dumb around his parents and peers. It is a great set-up to a seriously funny graphic novel, which one Amazon reviewer described as "South Park meets Dexter's Lab." First in the series. **Grades 10–12. PJ**

Winick, Judd. ***Pedro and Me.*** 187 pages.

Henry Holt 2000 Paper 0805064036 $15.00

Cartoonist Judd Winick was once a member of the MTV show *The Real World*. On the show, he roomed with Pedro Zamora. In this biography, Winick uses the cartoon form to tell the story of his friend who, after years as an AIDS activist, finally succumbed to the disease. **Grades 10–12. PJ**

Reviews: *Booklist* 9/15/2000, *SLJ* 10/1/2000

Wolfman, Mary. ***Crisis on Infinite Earths.*** 368 pages.

DC Comics 2001 Paper 1563897504 $29.95

In the mid-1980s, the DC comic company updated and consolidated the entire "universe" of stories from World War II "ghost tanks" through umpteen "super-hero" incarnations and nearly every major or minor superhero comic book character. The tour de force storyline that pulled this off is ably illustrated by the standard comic-book style of George Perez. This is a fine graphic novel for younger teens and those discovering the DC universe of comic book heroes. **Grades 7–12. KE**

SOURCES AND TIPS

GUIDE TO 100+ "BEST" LISTS

We didn't want to totally reinvent the wheel. While there is no single core collection list published for young adults, there are lots and lots and lots of lists out there. We looked at all of these lists to gather titles. A book that showed up repeatedly on these lists is certainly more than likely to be included here. Reputation counts.

LIST	SOURCE
Amazon's Editors' Choice 2001: Teens.	www.amazon.com/exec/obidos/tg/browse/
Amazon's Teen Classics.	www.amazon.com/exec/obidos/tg/feature/
Amazon's Teen generated lists and reviews.	www.amazon.com
Amazon's Bestsellers 2001: Teens.	www.amazon.com/exec/obidos/tg/feature/
Ammon, Bette, and Gale Sherman. *More Rip-Roaring Reads For Reluctant Teen Readers.*	Teacher Ideas, 1998, 1563085712.
Arlington County (Va.) Public Library's Teen Territory Book Reviews.	www.co.arlington.va.us/lib/ teen/readem.htm
Berkley (Calif.) Public Library's Teen Services Booklists.	www.infopeople.org/bpl/ teen/Booklist.html
Best Books for Young Teen Readers, Grades 7 to 10.	Bowker, 2000, 0835242641.
Bodart, Joni. *The World's Best Thin Books (rev. ed.).*	Scarecrow, 2000, 1578860075.

LIST	SOURCE
Bodart, Joni. *Radical Reads: 101 YA Novels on the Edge.*	Scarecrow, 2002, 0810842874.
Booklist. Editor's Choice 1997.	*Booklist* v. 94, no. 9/10 (Jan. 1–15, 1998): 726–40.
Booklist. Editor's Choice 1998.	*Booklist* v. 95, no. 9/10 (Jan. 1–15, 1999): 774–89.
Booklist. Editor's Choice 1999.	*Booklist* v. 96, no. 9/10 (Jan. 1–15, 2000): 810–29.
Booklist. Editor's Choice 2000.	*Booklist* v. 97, no, 9/10 (Jan. 1–15, 2001): 850–68.
Booklist. Editor's Choice 2001.	*Booklist* v. 98, no. 9/10 (Jan. 1–15, 2002): 850–68.
Booklist's Adult Books for Teens by and about African Americans.	*Booklist* v. 96, no. 12 (Feb. 15, 2000): 1096–67.
Booklist's Adult Christian Fiction for Young Adults: The Best from the Past Three Years.	*Booklist* v. 98, no. 3 (Oct. 1, 2001): 335.
Booklist's Overlooked Books of the 1990s.	*Booklist* v. 97, no. 21 (July 2001): 1998–99.
Booklist's Someday My Printz Will Come.	*Booklist* v. 96, no. 19/20 (June 1–15, 2000): 1874–75.
Booklist's Top 10 Gay and Lesbian Books for Youth.	*Booklist* v. 97, no 19/20 (June 1–15, 2001): 1863.
Booklist's Top 10 Historical Fiction for Youth.	*Booklist* v. 97, no. 15 (Apr. 1, 2001): 1486.
Booklist's Top 10 Youth Romances for Youth.	*Booklist* v. 98, no. 2 (Sept. 15, 2001): 225.
Booklist's Top Ten 10 Fantasy Books for Youth.	*Booklist* v. 97, no. 16 (Apr. 15, 2001): 1561.
Boston Public Library's Teen Lounge.	www.bpl.org/teens/teenreading.htm
Braus, Nancy. *Everyone's Kids'Books: A Guide to Multicultural, Socially Conscious Books for Children.*	Everyone's Books, 2000, 0970381603.
Brooklyn (N.Y.) Public Library Classics (Grades 6–8).	www.brooklynpubliclibrary.org/*Booklist*/classics%20elementary%202.htm

LIST	SOURCE
Brozo, William. *To Be a Boy, to Be a Reader: Engaging Teen and Preteen Boys in Active Literacy.*	International Reading Association, 2002, 0872071758.
Calcutt, Andrew, and Richard Shephard. *Cult Fiction : A Reader's Guide.*	McGraw Hill–NTC, 1999, 0809225069.
Campbell, Patty. "Best New Short Story Collections."	*Journal of Youth Services in Libraries* v. 14, no. 1 (Fall 2000): 14–15.
Carmel Clay (Ind.) Public Library's Teen Advisory Board Suggestions.	E-mail to Patrick Jones (April 2002).
Carnegie Library of Pittsburgh (Pa.) Teen Reading Lists.	www.clpgh.org/ein/ya/yalists.html
Carter, Betty. *Best Books For Young Adults* (2nd ed.).	ALA Editions, 2000, 083893501X.
Chicago Public Library's Teen Edition Reading Lists.	www.chipublib.org/008subject/ 003cya/teened/readlist.html
Cleveland Heights (Ohio) Public Library's You Have Got To Read This!	www.clickthis.ws/gottaread.shtml
Columbus (Ohio) Metro Library's Teen book reviews.	www.cml.lib.oh.us/cmlteens/reviews.cfm
Coquitlam (B.C.) Public Library's Just for Teens.	library.coquitlam.bc.ca/teens/ Booklists.htm
Crowe, Chris. "Young Adult Literature."	*English Journal* v. 90, no. 9 (March 2001): 125–30.
Crowe, Chris. "An Antidote for Testosterone Poisoning: YA Books Girls—and Boys—Should Read."	*English Journal* v. 91, no. 3 (Jan. 2002): 135–37.
Crowe, Chris. "Finding Common Ground: Multicultural YA Literature."	*English Journal* v. 88, no. 2 (Nov. 1998): 124–26.
Darby, Mary Ann. *Hearing All the Voices: Multicultural Books for Adolescents.*	Scarecrow Press, 2002, 0810840588.
Donelson, Kenneth, and Alleen Pace Nilsen. *Literature for Today's Young Adults* (6th ed.).	Longman, 2000, 032103788X.

LIST	SOURCE
Donelson, Kenneth. "Honoring the Best YA Books of the Year: 1964–1995."	*English Journal* v. 86, no. 3 (Mar. 1997): 41–47.
Fairfax County (Va.) Public Library's Selected Titles by Teens.	www.co.fairfax.va.us/library/READING/YA/selected.htm
Gallick, Joyce. "Do They Read for Pleasure? Recreational Reading Habits of College Students."	*Journal of Adolescent & Adult Literacy* v. 42, no. 6 (Mar. 1999): 480–88.
Middle and Junior High School Library Catalog (8th ed.).	H. W. Wilson, 2000, 0824209966.
Senior High School Library Catalog (16th ed.).	H. W. Wilson, 2002, 0824210085.
Haverhill (Mass.) Public Library's Teen Cybercenter's 10 Favorite Teen Books.	www.teencybercenter.org/lists/topten.htm
Hennepin County (Minn.) Public Library's Best Book I Read Survey.	Conducted by Patrick Jones and Hennepin County Library staff, October 2001.
Hennepin County (Minn.) Public Library's Read On: Teen Reviews.	www.hclib.org/teens/ReaderReviews/Reviews.cfm
Hennepin County (Minn.) Public Library's Recommended Books for Teen Readers.	www.hclib.org/teens/teen_readers01.html
Herald, Di. *Teen Genreflecting.*	Libraries Unlimited, 1997, 0585172595.
Houston Public Library's Reading Interest Survey.	Conducted by Patrick Jones, October 1999.
Hubert, Jennifer. "Reading Rants: Out of the Ordinary Teen Booklists."	tln.lib.mi.us/~amutch/jen/index.html
Hunt, Gladys. *Honey for a Teen's Heart.*	Zondervan, 2002, 0310242606.
Internet Public Library. Teen Division. "Your Suggestions."	www.ipl.org/teen/teenread/suggestions.html
Ivey, Gay. "Just Plain Reading: A Survey of What Makes Students Want to Read in Middle School Classrooms."	*Reading Research Quarterly* v. 36, no. 4 (Oct/Dec 2001): 350–77.

LIST	SOURCE
King County (Wash.) Public Library's Teen Zone Book Lists.	www.kcls.org/newya/goodrds.html# Booklists
Lesesne, Teri S. "From Darkness to Light: Tales of Hope for YA Readers."	*Voices from the Middle* vol. 8, no. 3 (Mar. 2001): 71–75.
Lesesne, Teri S. "A Passion for Poetry."	*Teacher Librarian* v. 27, no. 5 (June 2000): 61–62.
Lesesne, Teri. S. "What Books Should All Those Working with Teens Know?"	*Voices from the Middle* v. 9, no. 3 (Mar. 2002): 47–52.
Lesesne, Teri. S. "Winners in My Book."	*Voices from the Middle* v. 9, no. 2 (Dec. 2001): 57–59.
Lesesne, Teri. S. "Nonfiction Matters, Too: Books about People, Places, and Things."	*Journal of Children's Literature* v. 27, no. 2 (Fall 2001): 79–84.
Lesesne, Teri S. "The Long and the Short of It All: Nonfiction Books with Flair."	*Voices from the Middle* v. 9, no 4 (May 2002): 52–54.
Los Angeles (Calif.) Public Library's Young Adult Booklists.	www.lapl.org/teenscape/readlist/ readlist.html
Manczuk, Suzanne. "On the Numbers: Outstanding Nonfiction of 1999."	*Book Report* v. 19, no. 2 (Sept./Oct. 2000): 26–28.
Matulka, Denise. *Picture This: Picture Books for Young Adults: A Curriculum-Related Annotated Bibliography.*	Greenwood,1997, 01313301824.
Minneapolis (Minn.) Public Library's Favorite Young Adult Book Survey Results.	E-mail to Patrick Jones.
Modern Library's 100 Best Nonfiction.	www.randomhouse.com/modernlibrary/ 100best/index.html
Modern Library's 100 Best Novels.	www.randomhouse.com/modernlibrary/ 100best/novels.html
Multnomah County (Ore.) Public Library's Outernet for Teens Booklists.	www.multnomah.lib.or.us/lib/outer/ books.html

LIST	SOURCE
National Council of Teachers of English. *Kaleidoscope: A Multicultural Booklist for Grades K–8* (3rd ed.).	NCTE Press, 2001, 0814125409.
National Council Teachers of English. *Books for You: An Annotated List for Senior High Students* (14th ed.).	NCTE Press, 2001, 081403723.
National Education Association (NEA)'s Poll on Reading Habits of Adolescents.	www.nea.org/readingmatters/readpoll.html
New York (N.Y.) Public Library's *Books for the Teenage (1996–2002)*.	New York Public Library.
Odean, Kathleen. *Great Books for Boys: More Than 600 Books for Boys 2 to 14*.	Peter Smith, 2000, 0844671509.
Odean, Kathleen. *Great Books for Girls: More Than 600 Books for Girls of All Ages*.	Peter Smith, 2000, 0844671517.
"Picture Books for Young Adult Readers."	*ALAN Review* v. 28, no. 3 (Spring/Summer 2001): 24–26.
Rohde, Marjorie. "Booklists for Young Adults on the Web."	www.seemore.mi.org/Booklists/
Salt Lake (Utah) County Public Library's Teen Books: Lists and Links.	www.slco.lib.ut.us/teenbk.htm
Santa Clara (Calif.) Public Library's Bibliography Central.	www-lib.co.santa-clara.ca.us/teen/biblcent.html
Seattle (Wash.) Public Library's Booklists for Teens.	www.spl.org/youngadult/Booklists.html
St. Paul (Minn.) Public Library's "Cyber Scroll: Teen Book Review Site."	www.stpaul.lib.mn.us/bkrevpgs/introyrev.cfm
Sullivan, Ed. "Beyond Anne Frank: Recent Holocaust Literature for Young People."	*New Advocate* v. 15, no. 1 (Winter 2002): 49–55.
Sullivan, Ed. "Information, Please: Books to Inform and Entertain."	*Voices from the Middle* v. 9, no. 2 (Dec. 2001): 83–84.

LIST	SOURCE
Sullivan, Ed. *The Holocaust in Literature for Youth.*	Scarecrow, 1999, 0810836076.
Sullivan, Ed. *Reaching Reluctant Young Adult Readers: A Practical Handbook for Librarians and Teachers.*	Scarecrow, 2002, 081084349.
Teen Hoopla's Teen Book Reviews.	www.ala.org/teenhoopla/reviews/index.html
Teen Hoopla's Best Twenty Books.	www.ala.org/teenhoopla/notrwvote.htm
Teen Reads.com Pre-College Canon.	www.teenreads.com/features/011023–precollege.asp
Teen Reads.com Teen Reads Review Page.	www.teenreads.com/reviews/index.asp
Tucson-Pima (Ariz.) Public Library's Teen Zone Reading Lists.	www.tppl.org/teenzone/
Vandergrift, Kay. Vandergrift's *100: List of Young Adult Authors and Titles.*	www.scils.rutgers.edu/⌐kvander/YoungAdult/100list.html
VOYA: "Will Boys Be Boys? Are You Sure?"	*Voice of Youth Advocates* v. 23, no. 2 (June 2000): 88–92.
VOYA's Best Adult Nonfiction for High School Libraries, 1998.	*Voice of Youth Advocates* v. 21, no. 4 (Oct. 1998): 251–56.
VOYA's Best Adult Nonfiction for High School Libraries, 1999.	*Voice of Youth Advocates* v. 22, no. 4 (Oct. 1999): 232–36.
VOYA's Best Adult Nonfiction for High School Libraries, 1997.	*Voice of Youth Advocates* v. 20, no. 5 (Dec. 1997): 299–302+
VOYA's Best Science Fiction, Fantasy & Horror, 1996.	*Voice of Youth Advocates* v. 20, no. 1 (Apr. 1997): 9–13.
VOYA's Best Science Fiction, Fantasy & Horror, 1997.	*Voice of Youth Advocates* v. 21, no. 1 (Apr. 1998): 8–10.
VOYA's Best Science Fiction, Fantasy & Horror, 1998.	*Voice of Youth Advocates* v. 22, no. 1 (Apr. 1999): 12–16.
VOYA's Best Science Fiction, Fantasy, & Horror, 1999.	*Voice of Youth Advocates* v. 23, no. 1 (Apr. 2000): 10–14.
VOYA's Best Science Fiction, Fantasy, & Horror, 2001.	*Voice of Youth Advocates* v. 24, no. 1 (Apr. 2001): 10–15.

LIST	SOURCE
VOYA's Best Science Fiction, Fantasy, & Horror, 2002.	*Voice of Youth Advocates* v. 25, no. 1 (Apr. 2002): 12–16.
VOYA's Books in the Middle: Outstanding Books of 1995.	*Voice of Youth Advocates* v. 19 (June 1996): 85–88.
VOYA's Books in the Middle: Outstanding Books of 1996.	*Voice of Youth Advocates* v. 20 (June 1997): 83–87.
VOYA's Books in the Middle: Outstanding Titles of 1997.	*Voice of Youth Advocates* v. 20, no. 6 (Feb. 1998): 363–66+
VOYA's Books in the Middle: Outstanding Titles of 1998.	*Voice of Youth Advocates* v. 21, no. 6 (Feb. 1999): 410–13+
VOYA's Books in the Middle: Outstanding Titles of 1999.	*Voice of Youth Advocates* v. 22, no. 6 (Feb. 2000): 380–83.
VOYA's Clueless? Adult Mysteries with Young Adult Appeal, 1997.	*Voice of Youth Advocates* v. 20, no. 5 (Dec. 1997): 294–98.
VOYA's Clueless? Adult Mysteries with Young Adult Appeal, 1998.	*Voice of Youth Advocates* v. 21, no. 5 (Dec. 1998): 331–34.
VOYA's Clueless? Adult Mysteries with Young Adult Appeal, 1999.	*Voice of Youth Advocates* v. 22, no. 5 (Dec. 1999): 304–7.
VOYA's Clueless? Adult Mysteries with Young Adult Appeal, 2000.	*Voice of Youth Advocates* v. 23, no. 5 (Dec. 2000): 318–21.
VOYA's Clueless? Adult Mysteries with Young Adult Appeal, 2001.	*Voice of Youth Advocates* v. 24, no. 5 (Dec. 2001): 332–35.
VOYA's Nonfiction Honor List, 1998.	*Voice of Youth Advocates* v. 22, no. 3 (Aug. 1999): 161–65.
VOYA's Recommended Graphic Novels for Libraries.	*Voice of Youth Advocates* v. 23, no. 5 (Dec. 2000): 322–24.
VOYA's Romancing the YA Reader.	*Voice of Youth Advocates* v. 21, no. 6 (Feb. 1999): 414–19.
VOYA's Teens Top Ten Books, 2001.	*Voice of Youth Advocates* v. 24, no. 5 (Dec. 2001): 329.
VOYA's The Perfect Tens: The Top Forty Books Reviewed in *Voice of Youth Advocates*, 1996–2000.	*Voice of Youth Advocates* v. 24, no. 2 (June 2001): 94–99.

LIST	SOURCE
VOYA's Top Shelf Fiction for Middle School Readers, 2001.	*Voice of Youth Advocates* v. 24, no. 6 (Feb. 2002): 406–10.
VOYA's Top Shelf Fiction for Middle School Readers, 2000.	*Voice of Youth Advocates* v. 23, no. 6 (Feb. 2001): 396–400.
VOYA's You Go Girl! A Road Map to Girl Power.	*Voice of Youth Advocates* v. 22, no. 2 (Jun. 1999): 92–96+
VOYA's Poetry Picks, 1998.	*Voice of Youth Advocates* v. 22, no. 1 (Apr. 1999): 17–18.
VOYA's Poetry Picks, 1999.	*Voice of Youth Advocates* v. 23, no. 1 (Apr. 2000): 15.
VOYA's Poetry Picks, 2000.	*Voice of Youth Advocates* v. 24, no. 1 (Apr. 2001): 20.
VOYA's Poetry Picks, 2001.	*Voice of Youth Advocates* v. 25, no. 1 (Apr. 2002): 26.
Weiner, Stephen. *The 101 Best Graphic Novels.*	NBM, 2001,156163283X.
Worthy, Jo. "What Johnny Likes to Read Is Hard to Find in School."	*Reading Research Quarterly* v. 34, no. 1 (Jan./Mar. 1999): 12–27.
YALSA's Alex Awards.	www.ala.org/yalsa/Booklists/alex/
YALSA's Best Books for Young Adults.	www.ala.org/yalsa/Booklists/bbya/
YALSA's Best of the Best Revisited.	www.ala.org/yalsa/Booklists/bestof best2000.html
YALSA's Michael L. Printz Award.	www.ala.org/yalsa/Booklists/printz/
YALSA's Outstanding Books for the College Bound.	www.ala.org/yalsa/Booklists/obcb/ index.html
YALSA's Popular Paperbacks.	www.ala.org/yalsa/Booklists/ poppaper/
YALSA's Quick Picks for Reluctant Young Adult Readers.	www.ala.org/yalsa/Booklists/quickpicks/
YALSA's Smartgirl.com survey results.	www.ala.org//teenread/trw_surveyre sults.pdf
Young Adults' Choices for 1997.	*Journal of Adolescent & Adult Literacy* v. 41, no. 3 (Nov. 1997): 209–16.
Young Adults' Choices for 1998.	*Journal of Adolescent & Adult Literacy* v. 42, no. 3 (Nov. 1998): 229–35.

LIST	SOURCE
Young Adults' Choices for 1999.	*Journal of Adolescent & Adult Literacy* v. 43, no. 3 (Nov. 1999): 257–63.
Young Adults' Choices for 2000.	*Journal of Adolescent & Adult Literacy* v. 44, no. 3 (Nov. 2000): 281–88.
Young Adults' Choices for 2001.	*Journal of Adolescent & Adult Literacy* v. 45, no. 3 (Nov. 2000): 267–76.

TOP 10 TIPS

You have built it, so now what? While promoting the collection is outside of the scope of this book, it is obvious that, given what we know about the huge number of entertainment options available to teenagers, merely buying these books and putting them on the shelves is not enough. You've got to do something to connect young adults and libraries.

One thing is to maintain the collection. A book might be static, representing a snapshot in place and time. A real collection, even a core one, is dynamic. An active collection needs development. Here are the ten critical steps to ensure that new core titles are added.

1. **Buy** the Printz winners and the honor books.
2. Consider all of the books that are selected for Best Books and Quick Picks; **buy** those that make both of these lists.
3. Consider all the books reviewed in VOYA that receive 4 or 5 in either popularity or quality; **buy** those that are perfect tens.
4. **Buy** any book that is listed as the year's best teen seller on Amazon.
5. **Buy** any book that is listed as the year's best by Amazon's editors (this includes the influential icons Patty Campbell and Jennifer Hubert Swan).
6. Consider any book listed in the various VOYA "best lists" and the other YALSA lists, like the Alex Awards or popular paperbacks; **buy** books on those subjects or by those authors with a strong track record.
7. Look at circulation reports: **buy** another copy of anything that is getting heavy, heavy use, and look at lost books reports: **buy** and replace core titles often.
8. Look at YALSA-BK and follow the discussions of titles. Learn which YALSA-BK reviewers seem to know their stuff and follow their lead. Make local connections with young adult or school librarians, English teachers, bookstore staff, and anyone who is interested in advancing the cause of adolescent literacy. Ask the question: "what are your teens reading?" and **buy** the answer.

9. Look closely at the monthly catalogs of vendors such as Book Wholesalers to find the paperback reprint edition of titles that are, as of this writing, only available in hardback.

10. Ask teens over and over and over again: "Is that what you want?" Survey, open up your Web page to teen reviews, do book discussion groups, conduct exit interviews, conduct an annual favorite book poll, and listen. Ask the question: what are your teens reading and **buy** the answer.

CHOICES FROM LEADING YA LIBRARIANS AND AUTHORS

We invited over one hundred young adult librarians and young adult literature experts to share their ideas of what a young adult core collection would
include. We had over 35 responses, which are listed below. You will find
annotations from these librarians throughout the text. Almost all of the titles
represented in these lists are included in our core collection. The exception
would be books no longer in print; titles that seemed to us to be really more
juvenile titles than books of interest to most young adults; or, in a few cases,
the title didn't really stand up to our criteria for selection. While everyone
approached the "assignment" with a little different take, the results show consensus on a few titles, but also reflect the wide diversity of reading interest
among teenagers. Perhaps Dr. Robert Small and Dr. Donald Kenney from
Virginia Tech University put it best when they wrote in an e-mail to the
author:

> Choosing a few books that should be made readily available for
> teenage readers to explore and read is not an easy task. It required
> leaving out far more wonderful books than the list could contain.
> Educators and librarians are all too familiar with recommended
> lists and the usual criticisms that follow the publication of a list,
> particularly the criticism that the list lacks balance. Yet that sense
> of balance that we have been sensitized to use in compiling recom-
> mended books doesn't always fall into place. The bottom line was,
> What do teenagers like to read? But we were acutely aware that the
> term "teenagers" lumps together a large number of very different
> people. We looked for books that, consistently over many years,
> have spoken to many teenagers, such as *Where the Red Fern
> Grows*. We also looked for books from authors who have written
> for teenage readers and who have a sustained popularity with
> teenagers like Will Hobbs and Chris Crutcher. In the latter case, we
> tried to select one book that could represent all the others, such as
> *Ironman* by Crutcher. Finally, we considered some recent books

that we believe have a good chance of appealing to teenage readers, such as *Skellig*.

Each list begins with the affiliation of the author. While some did rank or classify the titles, we have opted here for a strict alphabetical listing by author. In many cases, the person provided us with an annotation for the title, which we have passed along in the core collection section.

AMY ALESSIO, TEEN COORDINATOR, SCHAUMBURG (ILL.) TOWNSHIP DISTRICT LIBRARY

Avi *The True Confessions of Charlotte Doyle*

Bauer Joan *Hope Was Here*

Card, Orson Scott *Ender's Game*

Cooney, Caroline *Flight #116 Is Down*

Crutcher, Chris *Staying Fat for Sarah Byrnes*

Curtis, Christopher Paul *The Watsons Go to Birmingham—1963*

Doyle, Arthur Conan *The Complete Sherlock Holmes*

Duncan, Lois *A Gift of Magic*

Fleischmann, Paul *Whirligig*

Hinton, S. E. *The Outsiders*

Montgomery, Lucy Maud *Anne of the Island*

Myers, Walter Dean *Fallen Angels*

Paulsen, Gary *The Haymeadow*

Plum-Ucci, Carol *The Body of Christopher Creed*

Rinaldi, Ann *Time Enough for Drums, In My Father's House*

Rowling, J. K. *Harry Potter and the Sorcerer's Stone*

Wodehouse, P. G. *Mike and Psmith*

Wolff, Virginia Euwer *Make Lemonade*

Wrede, Patricia C. *Dealing with Dragons*

MELANIE ATKINSON, YOUTH SERVICES LIBRARIAN, STEELE MEMORIAL LIBRARY, ELMIRA, NEW YORK

Anderson, Laurie Halse *Speak*

Anonymous *Go Ask Alice*
[Sparks, Beatrice]

Jukes, Mavis *The Guy Book*

Nelson, Peter *Left for Dead: The USS Indianapolis and a Young Man's Search for Justice for the USS Indianapolis*

Paul, Anthea *Girlosophy: A Soul Survival Kit*

Rennison, Louise *Angus, Thongs and Full-Frontal Snogging: Confessions of Georgia Nicolson*

Sanchez, Alex *Rainbow Boys*

Silverstein, Shel *Missing Piece*

Spinelli, Jerry *Stargirl*

Strasser, Todd *Give a Boy a Gun*

Tashjian, Janet *The Gospel According to Larry*

HOPE BAUGH, YOUNG ADULT
SERVICES MANAGER, CARMEL (IND.)
CLAY PUBLIC LIBRARY

Bauer, Joan *Hope Was Here*

Block, Francesca Lia *Echo*

Clinton, Cathryn *The Calling*

Crutcher, Chris *Whale Talk*

de Lint, Charles *Trader*

King, Stephen *On Writing: A Memoir of the Craft*

Mickaelson, Ben *Touching Spirit Bear*

Neruda, Pablo *Full Woman, Fleshly Apple, Hot Moon: Selected Poems of Pable Neruda*

Porcellino, John *Perfect Example*

Price, Susan *The Sterkarm Handshake*

Raskin, Ellen *The Westing Game*

Singer, Marilyn *I Believe in Water: Twelve Brushes with Religion*

Spinelli, Jerry *Stargirl*

Trueman, Terry *Stuck in Neutral*

Yolen, Jane *Favorite Folktales from Around the World*

ANGELA BENEDETTI, YOUNG ADULT
LIBRARIAN, KING COUNTY LIBRARY,
RENTON, WASHINGTON

Bradley, Marion Zimmer *The Mists of Avalon*

Card, Orson Scott *Ender's Game*

Chbosky, Stephen *The Perks of Being a Wallflower*

Cormier, Robert *After the First Death*

Creech, Sharon *Walk Two Moons*

King, Stephen *It*

Klause, Annette Curtis *Blood and Chocolate*

Magorian, Michelle *Good Night, Mr. Tom*

Mahy, Margaret *The Changeover*

Moore, Alan *Watchmen*

Pullman, Phillip *The Golden Compass*

Sachar, Louis *Holes*

Turner, Megan Whalen *The Thief*

Werlin, Nancy *The Killer's Cousin*

White, Ellen Emerson *The Road Home*

Willis, Connie *The Doomsday Book*

Wittlinger, Ellen *Hard Love*

SPRING LEA BOEHLER, YOUTH LIBRARIAN,
PHILIP S. MILLER LIBRARY,
DOUGLAS COUNTY,
CASTLE ROCK, COLORADO

Barnes, John *Orbital Resonance*

Card, Orson Scott *Ender's Game*

Duncan, Lois *Down a Dark Hall*

Flinn, Alex *Breathing Underwater*

Lowry, Lois *The Giver*

McCaffrey, Anne *Dragonsong*

Moore, Alan *Watchmen*

Moriarty, Jaclyn *Feeling Sorry for Celia*

Pelzer, David J. *A Child Called It*

Sachar, Louis *Holes*

Sheffield, Charles *Higher Education*

Willis, Connie *Doomsday Book*

JENNIFER BROMANN, LIBRARY
MEDIA SPECIALIST, LINCOLN-WAY
CENTRAL HIGH SCHOOL,
NEW LENOX, ILLINOIS

Block, Francesca Lia 339 *Baby Be-Bop*

Blume, Judy *Forever*

Brashares, Ann *The Sisterhood of the Traveling Pants*

Chbosky, Stephen *The Perks of Being a Wallflower*

Cooney, Caroline B. *The Face on the Milk Carton*

Cormier, Robert *Tenderness*
Duncan, Lois *I Know What You Did Last Summer*
Klause, Annette Curtis *Blood and Chocolate*
Marsden, John *Letters from the Inside*
Plum-Ucci, Carol *The Body of Christopher Creed*
Salinger, J. D. *The Catcher in the Rye*
Spinelli, Jerry *Stargirl*
Thomas, Rob *Rats Saw God*
Tyree, Omar *Flyy Girl*

PATTY CAMPBELL, EDITOR, SCARECROW STUDIES IN YOUNG ADULT LITERATURE SERIES, AND AMAZON.COM REVIEWER

Bauer, Joan *Rules of the Road*
Block, Francesca Lia *Weetzie Bat*
Bloor, Edward *Tangerine*
Cormier, Robert *After the First Death*
Cormier, Robert *The Chocolate War*
Cormier, Robert *Hatchet*
Cormier, Robert *I Am the Cheese*
Cormier, Robert *Tenderness*
Cushman, Karen *Catherine, Called Birdy*
Hesse, Karen *Out of the Dust*
Hinton, S. E. *The Outsiders*
Lowry, Lois *The Giver*
Myers, Walter Dean *Fallen Angels*
Myers, Walter Dean *Monster*
Pullman, Phillip *The Golden Compass*
Sachar, Louis *Holes*
Salinger, J. D. *The Catcher in the Rye*
Wolff, Virginia Euwer *Make Lemonade*

MICHAEL CART, AUTHOR OF *FROM ROMANCE TO REALISM: 50 YEARS OF GROWTH AND CHANGE IN YOUNG ADULT LITERATURE*

Block, Francesca Lia *Weetzie Bat*
Brooks, Bruce *What Hearts*

Chambers, Aidan *Postcards from No Man's Land*

Chbosky, Stephen *The Perks of Being a Wallflower*

Cole, Brock *The Facts Speak for Themselves*

Cormier, Robert *The Chocolate War*

Fleischman, Paul *Whirligig*

Frank, E. R. *America*

Garden, Nancy *Annie on My Mind*

Kerr, M. E. *Night Kites*

Lipsyte, Robert *The Contender*

Myers, Walter Dean *Monster*

Pullman, Philip *His Dark Materials* Trilogy

Sachar, Louis *Holes*

Salinger, J. D. *The Catcher in the Rye*

Scieszka, Jon *The Stinky Cheese Man*

Sones, Sonya *Stop Pretending*

Wolff, Virginia Euwer *Make Lemonade*

JAMES E. COOK, YOUNG ADULT SPECIALIST, DAYTON (OHIO) METRO LIBRARY

Avi *Wolf Rider*

Block, Francesca Lia *Baby Be-Bop*

Blume, Judy *Forever*

Cadnum, Michael *Calling Home*

Cormier, Robert *After the First Death*

Crutcher, Chris *Running Loose*

Fleischman, Paul *Whirligig*

Garden, Nancy *Annie on My Mind*

Holt, Kimberly Willis *When Zachary Beaver Came to Town*

Koertge, Ron *Arizona Kid*

Lowry, Lois *The Giver*

Myers, Walter Dean *Monster*

Paulsen, Gary *Hatchet*

Voigt, Cynthia *A Solitary Blue*

SARAH CORNISH, YOUNG ADULT LIBRARIAN, WARREN (N.J.) TOWNSHIP LIBRARY

Bauer, Joan *Hope Was Here*

Block, Francesca Lia *Dangerous Angels*
Blume, Judy *Forever*
Brooks, Bruce *Midnight Hour Encores*
Card, Orson Scott *Ender's Game*
Chbosky, Stephen *The Perks of Being a Wallflower*
Crutcher, Chris *Staying Fat for Sarah Byrnes*
Dessen, Sarah *Keeping the Moon*
Fleischman, Paul *Whirligig*
Marsden, John *Tomorrow, When the War Began*
McKinley, Robin *Beauty: A Retelling of Beauty and the Beast*
Paterson, Katherine *Jacob Have I Loved*
Thomas, Rob *Rats Saw God*
White, Ellen Emerson *The Road Home*

CINDY DOBREZ, LIBRARIAN, HARBOR LIGHTS SCHOOL, HOLLAND, MICHIGAN

Bauer, Joan *Rules of the Road*
Berry, Liz *China Garden*
Cormier, Robert *I Am the Cheese*
Crutcher, Chris *Stotan!*
Garden, Nancy *Annie On My Mind*
Mosher, Richard *Zazoo*
Nye, Naomi Shihab *What Have You Lost?*
Paulsen, Gary *Hatchet*
Pullman, Philip *His Dark Materials* Trilogy
Rowling, J. K. Harry Potter series
Thomas, Rob *Rats Saw God*

SANDIE FARRELL, FREE LIBRARY OF PHILADELPHIA (PENN.)

Bloor, Edward *Tangerine*
Brooks, Polly *Beyond the Myth: The Story of Joan of Arc*
Cofer, Judith Ortiz *An Island Like You*
Cormier, Robert *After the First Death*
Cormier, Robert *The Chocolate War*
Crutcher, Chris *Ironman*
Deuker, Cal *On the Devil's Court*

Duncan, Lois *Killing Mr. Griffin*

Garden, Nancy *Annie on My Mind*

Hinton, S. E. *That Was Then, This Is Now*

Klause, Annette Curtis *Silver Kiss*

Myers, Walter Dean *Monster*

Nix, Garth *Sabriel*

Paulsen, Gary *Hatchet*

Pike, Christopher *Remember Me*

Spiegelman, Art *Maus: A Survivor's Tale*

Woodson, Jacqueline *If You Come Softly*

PATRICIA FOSTER, SENIOR LIBRARIAN, YA SYSTEM SPECIALIST, SALT LAKE COUNTY LIBRARY SYSTEM, SALT LAKE CITY, UTAH

Adams, Douglas *Hitchhiker's Guide to the Galaxy*

Almond, David *Skellig*

Anderson, Laurie Halse *Speak*

Baum, Frank *Wizard of Oz*

Berry, Liz *China Garden*

Carroll, Lewis *Alice's Adventures in Wonderland*

Crutcher, Chris *Whale Talk*

Dickens, Charles *Charles Dickens' Christmas Ghost Stories*

Klause, Annette Curtis *Blood and Chocolate*

Nix, Garth *Sabriel*

Piven, Joshua *Worst-Case Scenario Survival Handbook*

Pockell, Leslie *100 Best Poems of All Time*

Sleator, William *Interstellar Pig*

Thomas, Rob *Rats Saw God*

Tolkein, J. R. R. *The Hobbit*

Tolkien, J. R. R. *Lord of the Rings* Trilogy

BETSY FRASER, YOUNG ADULT LIBRARIAN, CALGARY (ALBERTA) PUBLIC LIBRARY

Bauer, Joan *Rules of the Road*

Cole, Brock *The Goats*

Cooney, Caroline B. *The Face on the Milk Carton*

Cormier, Robert *The Chocolate War*

Crutcher, Chris *Staying Fat for Sara Byrnes*

Cushman, Karen *Catherine, Called Birdy*

Hesse, Karen *Out of the Dust*

Levine, Gail Carson *Ella Enchanted*

Lowry, Lois *The Giver*

Nix, Garth *Sabriel*

Paulsen, Gary *Hatchet*

Pierce, Tamora *Alanna: The First Adventure*

Pullman, Philip *The Golden Compass*

Sachar, Louis *Holes*

Sleater, William *House of Stairs*

Taylor, Mildred *The Land*

Thomas, Rob *Rats Saw God*

Wolff, Virginia Euwer *Make Lemonade*

BRUCE GREELEY, YOUNG ADULT LIBRARIAN,
KING COUNTY LIBRARY,
SEATTLE, WASHINGTON

Adams, Douglas *Hitchikers Guide to the Galaxy*

Clarke, Arthur C. *Childhood's End*

Curtis, Christopher Paul *Bud, Not Buddy*

Heller, Joseph *Catch–22*

Hesse, Herman *Steppenwolf*

Kerouac, Jack *On the Road*

Kesey, Ken *One Flew over the Cuckoo's Nest*

Lewis, C. S. *Out of the Silent Planet*

Paulsen, Gary *Beet Fields*

Robbins, Tom *Another Roadside Attraction*

Rowling, J. K. Harry Potter Series

Sachar, Louis *Holes*

Shea, Robert *The Illuminatus* Trilogy

Spinell, Jerry *Stargirl*

Thomas, Rob *Rats Saw God*

Tolkien, J. R. R. *Lord of the Rings*

ANDREW HUNTER, COLLECTION DEVELOPMENT
LIBRARIAN/YOUTH MATERIALS, SELECTOR,
DALLAS (TEX.) PUBLIC LIBRARY

Abelove, Joan *Go and Come Back*

Avi *Devil's Race*

Bennett, Jay *Coverup*

Berry, James *Ajeemah and His Son*

Block, Francesca Lia *Weetzie Bat*

Bunting, Eve *A Sudden Silence*

Carter, Alden *Sheila's Dying*

Crutcher, Chris *Staying Fat for Sarah Byrnes*

Davis, Terry *If Rock and Roll Were a Machine*

Feelings, Tom *The Middle Passage: White Ships/Black Cargo*

Fussell, Samuel Wilson *Muscle: Confessions of an Unlikely Bodybuilder*

Kingston, Maxine Hong *The Woman Warrior: Memoirs of a Girlhood among Ghosts*

O'Barr, J. *The Crow*

Quirk, Joe *The Ultimate Rush*

Sapphire *Push: A Novel*

Soto, Gary *Jesse*

Winick, Judd *Pedro and Me*

Zindel, Paul *The Pigman*

PATRICK JONES, CONSULTANT,
CONNECTINGYA.COM,
RICHFIELD, MINNESOTA

Anonymous *Go Ask Alice*
[Sparks, Beatrice]

Bell, Ruth *Changing Bodies, Changing Lives*

Cooney, Caroline B. *Driver's Ed*

Cormier, Robert *We All Fall Down*

Crutcher, Chris *Chinese Handcuffs*

Foley, Mick *Have a Nice Day*

Hinton, S. E. *The Outsiders*

Klause, Annette Curtis *The Silver Kiss*

Llewellyn, Grace *The Teenage Liberation Handbook*

Moore, Alan *Watchmen*

Myers, Walter Dean *Monster*

Pirsig, Robert M. *Zen and the Art of Motorcycle Maintenance*

Shakur, Tupac *The Rose That Grew from Concrete*

Stine, R. L. *The Surprise Party*

Stoehr, Shelly *Crosses*

Thomas, Rob *Rats Saw God*

Tolkien, J. R. R. *The Hobbit*

Wesser, Theodore *The Car Thief*

DAVID LANE, PUBLIC LEARNING AND TRAINING COORDINATOR, HENNEPIN COUNTY LIBRARY, MINNETONKA, MINNESOTA

Almond, Daniel *Skellig*

Boock, Paula *Dare Truth or Promise*

Brashares, Ann *The Sisterhood of the Traveling Pants*

Card, Orson Scott *Ender's Game*

Chbosky, Stephen *The Perks of Being a Wallflower*

Crutcher, Chris *Staying Fat for Sarah Byrnes*

Hautman, Peter *Mr. Was*

Lynch, Chris *Whitechurch*

Pinkwater, Daniel *Five Novels*

Thomas, Rob *Rats Saw God*

Walker, Alice *The Color Purple*

Williams, Lori Aurelia *When Kambia Elaine Flew in from Neptune*

Wittlinger, Ellen *Hard Love*

TERRI LeSANSE, CO-EDITOR OF *VOICES IN THE MIDDLE,* AND PROFESSOR AT SAM HOUSTON STATE UNIVERSITY IN HUNTSVILLE, TEXAS

Anderson, Laurie Halse *Speak*

Cart, Michael *Love and Sex: Ten Stories of Truth*

Cormier, Robert *Fade*

Crutcher, Chris *Ironman*

Duffy, Carol Ann *I Wouldn't Thank You for a Valentine*

Klause, Annette Curtis *Blood and Chocolate*

Korman, Gordon *Don't Care High*

Nixon, Joan Lowery *Whispers from the Dead*

Paulsen, Gary *Hatchet*

Rennison, Louise *Angus, Thongs, and Full-Frontal Snogging: Confessions of Georgia Nicolson*

Thomas, Rob *Rats Saw God*

Zindel, Paul *Rats*

WALTER M. MAYES, LIBRARY MEDIA SPECIALIST AT THE GIRLS' MIDDLE SCHOOL, MOUNTAIN VIEW, CALIFORNIA, AND CO-AUTHOR OF *VALERIE AND WALTER'S BEST BOOKS FOR CHILDREN*

Block, Francesca Lia *Baby Be-Bop*

Brooks, Bruce *Midnight Hour Encores*

Crutcher, Chris *Staying Fat for Sarah Byrnes*

Fleischman, Paul *Seek*

Guest, Judith *Ordinary People*

Kaufman, Bel *Up the Down Staircase*

Lasky, Kathryn *Memoirs of a Bookbat*

Lee, Harper *To Kill a Mockingbird*

Lowry, Lois *The Giver*

Lubar, David *Hidden Talents*

Myers, Walter Dean *Monster*

Napoli, Donna Jo *The Magic Circle*

Pullman, Phillip *The Golden Compass*

Rylant, Cynthia *Soda Jerk*

Winick, Judd *Pedro and Me*

Zindel, Paul *The Pigman*

IAN MCKINNEY, YOUNG ADULT LIBRARIAN, TIPPECANOE COUNTY PUBLIC LIBRARY, LAFAYETTE, INDIANA

Anderson, Laurie Halse *Speak*

Cherryh, C. J. *Downbelow Station*

Clavell, James *Shogun*

Crutcher, Chris *Staying Fat for Sarah Byrnes*

Davis, Jenny *Sex Education*

Duncan, Dave *The Gilded Chain*

Gibson, William *Neuromancer*

Herbert, Frank *Dune*

Klause, Annette Curtis *Blood and Chocolate*

Lowenstein, Sally *Evan's Voice*

Marsden, John *Tomorrow, When the War Began*

Martin, George R. R. *A Game of Thrones*

Peck, Richard *The Last Safe Place on Earth*

Salinger, J. D. *The Catcher in the Rye*
Stewart, Mary *The Crystal Cave*
Stone, Irving *The Agony and the Ecstasy*
Wittlinger, Ellen *Hard Love*
Zelazny, Roger *Nine Princes in Amber*

RICHIE PARTINGTON,
RICHIESPICKS.COM

Anderson, M. T. *Feed*
Anderson, Laurie Halse *Speak*
Crutcher, Chris *Whale Talk*
Farmer, Nancy *The House of the Scorpion*
Helprin, Mark *Winter's Tale*
Hogan, William *The Quartzsite Trip*
Jordan, Sherryl *Secret Sacrament*
Kasher, Steven *The Civil Rights Movement: A Photographic History, 1954–68*
Klass, David *You Don't Know Me*
McCaughrean, Geraldine *The Kite Rider*
Nye, Naomi Shihab *19 Varieties of Gazelle: Poems of the Middle East*
Pullman, Philip *The Golden Compass*
Rowling, J. K. *Harry Potter and the Sorcerer's Stone*
Sachar, Louis *Holes*
Taylor, Mildred *The Land*
Van Doren, Charles *A History of Knowledge: Past, Present, and Future*
Voigt, Cynthia *The Runner*
Wittlinger, Ellen *Hard Love*

JILL PATTERSON, MANAGER,
LA HABRA BRANCH LIBRARY,
ORANGE COUNTY PUBLIC LIBRARY,
LOS ANGELES, CALIFORNIA

Bauer, Joan *Rules of the Road*
Crutcher, Chris *Athletic Shorts*
Cushman, Karen *The Ballad of Lucy Whipple*
Ehrenreich, Barbara *Nickel and Dimed*
Fleischman, Paul *Mind's Eye*
Glenn, Mel *Split Image*
Goldman, E. M. *Getting Lincoln's Goat*
Gould, Steven *Jumper*

McKinley, Robin *Beauty*

Mikaelsen, Ben *Sparrow Hawk Red*

Naylor, Phyllis Reynolds *Alice on the Outside*

Paulsen, Gary *Nightjohn*

Randle, Kristen *The Only Alien on the Planet*

Schlosser, Eric *Fast Food Nation*

Vande Velde, Vivian *Dragon's Bait*

KIM PATTON, YOUNG ADULT SPECIALIST, LAWRENCE (KANS.) PUBLIC LIBRARY

Anderson, Laurie Halse *Speak*

Block, Francesca Lia *Weetzie Bat*

Frank, Anne *Diary of Anne Frank*

Gaiman, Neil *Neverwhere*

Haley, Alex *Roots*

Hinton, S. E. *The Outsiders*

King, Stephen *The Talisman*

Lee, Harper *To Kill a Mockingbird*

McKinley, Robin *Beauty*

Mowry, Jess *Way Past Cool*

O'Dell, Scott *Sing Down the Moon*

Pullman, Phillip *The Golden Compass*

Salinger, J. D. *The Catcher in the Rye*

Taylor, Mildred *Roll of Thunder Hear My Cry*

DAWN RUTHERFORD, YOUNG ADULT LIBRARIAN, KING COUNTY LIBRARY, SEATTLE, WASHINGTON

Adams, Douglas *The Hitchhiker's Guide to the Galaxy*

Block, Francesca Lia *Dangerous Angels*

Bradbury, Ray *The Illustrated Man*

Card, Orson Scott *Ender's Game*

Christie, Agatha *And Then There Were None*

Clowes, Dan *Ghost World*

Crutcher, Chris *Staying Fat for Sarah Byrnes*

Farmer, Nancy *The Ear, the Eye, and the Arm*

Goldman, William *The Princess Bride*

Gut Opdyke, Irene *In My Hands: Memories of a Holocaust Rescuer*

Nix, Garth *Shade's Children*

Pullman, Phillip *The Golden Compass*

Spiegelman, Art *Maus: A Survivor's Tale*

Stephenson, Neal *Snow Crash*

Townsend, Sue *The Secret Diary of Adrian Mole, Aged 13 and 3/4*

White, T. H. *The Once and Future King*

Winick, Judd *Pedro and Me*

ROCHELLE SIDES-RENDA, YA LIBRARIAN, BIRMINGHAM (ALA.) PUBLIC LIBRARY

Anonymous *Go Ask Alice*

[Sparks, Beatrice]

Avi *Nothing but the Truth*

Bauer, Joan *Squashed*

Brooks, Bruce *Dolores*

Card, Orson Scott *Ender's Game*

Corner, June *Teen Sunshine Reflections: Words for the Heart and Soul*

Duncan, Lois *Daughters of Eve*

Duncan, Lois *Gallows Hill*

Hayes, Daniel *Trouble with Lemons*

Hentoff, Nat *The Day They Came to Arrest the Book*

Hrdlitschka, Shelley *Dancing Naked*

Klause, Annette Curtis *Blood and Chocolate*

McKinley, Robin *The Hero and the Crown*

Strasser, Todd *The Wave*

KARYN SIPOS, YA LIBRARIAN/ YALSA PRESIDENT, FORT VANCOUVER (WASH.) REGIONAL LIBRARY

Adams, Douglas *The Hitchhiker's Guide to the Galaxy*

Anderson, Laurie Halse *Speak*

Angelou, Maya *I Know Why the Caged Bird Sings*

Anonymous *Go Ask Alice*

[Sparks, Beatrice]

Card, Orson Scott *Ender's Game*

Cormier, Robert *Chocolate War*

Crutcher, Chris *Staying Fat for Sarah Byrnes*

Garden, Nancy *Annie on My Mind*

Golding, William *Lord of the Flies*

Goldman, William *Princess Bride*

King, Beatrice *Beekeeper's Apprentice*

Lee, Harper *To Kill a Mockingbird*

Myers, Walter Dean *Fallen Angels*

O'Brien, Tim *Things They Carried*

Sachar, Louis *Holes*

Spiegelman, Art *Maus: A Survivor's Tale*

Tolkien, J. R. R. *The Hobbit*

ROBERT SMALL AND DON KENNEY, VIRGINIA TECH UNIVERSITY, BLACKBURN, VIRGINIA

Almond, David *Skellig*

Ashbanner, Brent *Into a Strange Land*

Blume, Judy *Are You There, God? It's Me, Margaret*

Cormier, Robert *Chocolate War*

Crutcher, Chris *Ironman*

Curtis, Christopher Paul *The Watsons Go to Birmingham—1963*

Dunning, Stephen *Reflections on a Gift of Watermelon Pickle*

Frank, Anne *The Diary of Anne Frank*

Greene, Bette *Summer of My German Soldier*

Hinton, S. E. *The Outsiders*

Hobbs, Will *Kokopell's Flute*

Paterson, Katherine *Bridge to Terabithia*

Peck, Robert Newton *A Day No Pigs Would Die*

Philbrick, Rodman *Freak the Mighty*

Salinger, J. D. *The Catcher in the Rye*

Spinelli, Jerry *Maniac Magee*

Taylor, Mildred D. *Roll of Thunder, Hear My Cry*

Woodson, Jacqueline *From the Notebooks of Melanin Sun*

ALICE F. STERN, HEAD LIBRARIAN, WINSOR SCHOOL, BOSTON, MASSACHUETTS

Anderson, Laurie Halse *Speak*

Bauer, Joan *Rules of the Road*

Cormier, Robert *The Chocolate War*

Duncan, Lois *Killing Mr. Griffin*

Finney, Jack *Time and Again*
Garden, Nancy *Annie on My Mind*
Hinton, S. E. *The Outsiders*
Lowry, Lois *The Giver*
Magorian, Michelle *Goodnight, Mr. Tom*
Myers, Walter Dean *Fallen Angels*
Pullman, Phillip *Ruby in the Smoke*
Rowling, J. K. *Harry Potter and the Sorcerer's Stone*
Woodson, Jacqueline *If You Come Softly*

LOIS STOVER, CHAIR, EDUCATIONAL STUDIES, ST. MARY'S COLLEGE OF MARYLAND, ST. MARY'S CITY, MARYLAND

Adoff, Arnold *Slow Dance Heart Break Blues*
Cormier, Robert *The Chocolate War*
Crutcher, Chris *Stotan!*
Gallo, Don *Ultimate Sports*
Hesser, Terry Spencer *Kissing Doorknobs*
Hinton, S. E. *The Outsiders*
Klass, David *You Don't Know Me*
L'Engle, Madeline *A Wrinkle in Time*
Murphy, Jim *The Great Fire*
Naylor, Phyllis Reynolds *Alice in Rapture Sort of*
Naylor, Phyllis Reynolds *The Year of the Gopher*
Spinelli, Jerry *Stargirl*
Voigt, Cynthia *When She Hollers*
Westall, Robert *Gulf*
Woodson, Jacqueline *I Hadn't Meant to Tell You This*

ED SULLIVAN, LIBRARIAN AND AUTHOR OF *REACHING RELUCTANT YOUNG ADULT READERS: A PRACTICAL HANDBOOK FOR LIBRARIANS AND TEACHERS* (SCARECROW PRESS)

Anderson, Laurie Halse *Speak*
Armstrong, Jennifer *Shipwreck at the Bottom of the World*
Armstrong, Joyce Carroll *Poetry after Lunch: Poems to Read Aloud*
Ash, Russell *Top Ten of Everything*
Bauer, Joan *The Rules of the Road*
Block, Francesca Lia *Weetzie Bat*

Cormier, Robert *The Chocolate War*

Elffers, Joost *Play with Your Food*

Gantos, Jack *A Hole in My Life*

Klause, Annette Curtis *Blood and Chocolate*

Myers, Walter Dean *Fallen Angels*

Sachar, Louis *Holes*

SARA SWENSON, HIGH SCHOOL LIBRARIAN, EDINA, MINNESOTA

Azerrad, Michael *Our Band Could Be Your Life: Scenes from the American Indie Underground, 1981–1991*

Bauer, Joan *Hope Was Here*

Bauer, Marion Dane *Am I Blue?: Coming Out from the Silence*

Crutcher, Chris *Staying Fat for Sarah Byrnes*

Goldschneider, Gary *The Secret Language of Birthdays: Personology Profiles for Each Day of the Year*

Goldschneider, Gary *The Secret Language of Relationships: Your Complete Personology Guide to Any Relationship with Anyone*

Hornby, Nick *High Fidelity*

Landvik, Lorna *Patty Jane's House of Curl*

Landvik, Lorna *Your Flame on Oasis Lake*

Lee, Harper *To Kill a Mocking Bird*

Liftin, Hilary *The Story of Two Friends Separated (for a Year) by an Ocean*

O'Brien, Tim *If I Die in a Combat Zone, Box Me Up and Ship Me Home*

O'Brien, Tim *The Things They Carried*

Pullam, Phillip *The Amber Spyglass*

Salinger, J. D. *The Catcher in the Rye*

Sanford, John *Prey Series*

Thomas, Rob *Doing Time*

DIANE TUCCILLO, SENIOR LIBRARIAN/ YOUNG ADULT COORDINATOR, CITY OF MESA (ARIZ.) LIBRARY

Appleman-Jurman, Alicia *Alicia: My Story*

Brashares, Ann *The Sisterhood of the Traveling Pants*

Clements, Bruce *Tom Loves Anna Loves Tom*

Cormier, Robert *We All Fall Down*

Deaver, Julie Reece *Say Goodnight, Gracie*

Dickinson, Peter *Eva*

Glenn, Mel *Class Dismissed: High School Poems*

Hahn, Mary Downing *Look for Me by Moonlight*

Hobbs, Will *Downriver*

Klass, David *You Don't Know Me*

Lasky, Kathryn *Beyond the Divide*

Lee, Harper *To Kill a Mockingbird*

McCoy, Kathy *The Teenage Body Book*

Myers, Walter Dean *Monster*

Pullman, Philip *The Golden Compass*

Staples, Suzanne Fisher *Shabanu: Daughter of the Wind*

White, Robb *Deathwatch*

Yolen, Jane *Dragon's Blood*

RENÉE VAILLANCOURT, AUTHOR OF
MANAGING YOUNG ADULT SERVICES:
A SELF-HELP MANUAL (NEAL-SCHUMAN, 2002)

Anonymous *Go Ask Alice*

[Sparks, Beatrice]

Block, Francesca Lia *Weetzie Bat*

Card, Orson Scott *Ender's Game*

Cole, Brock *The Goats*

Cooney, Caroline B. *The Face on the Milk Carton*

Cormier, Robert *Tenderness*

Crutcher, Chris *Staying Fat for Sarah Byrnes*

Cushman, Karen *Catherine, Called Birdy*

Fleischman, Paul *Seedfolks*

Hinton, S. E. *The Outsiders*

Kerr, M. E. *Night Kites*

Lowry, Lois *The Giver*

Paulsen, Gary *Hatchet*

Plath, Sylvia *The Bell Jar*

Rowling, J. K. *Harry Potter and the Sorcerer's Stone*

Spiegelman, Art *Maus: A Survivor's Tale*

Thomas, Rob *Rats Saw God*

Zindel, Paul *The Pigman*

JAMIE WATSON, YA LIBRARIAN,
ENOCH PRATT FREE LIBRARY,
BALTIMORE, MARYLAND

Block, Francesca Lia *Weetzie Bat*

Blume, Judy *Forever*

Brunvand, Jan Harold *The Big Book of Urban Legends*

Bukowski, Charles *Burning in Water, Drowning in Flame*

Card, Orson Scott *Ender's Game*

Clowes, Daniel *Ghost World*

King, Stephen *The Shining*

King, Stephen *The Stand*

Krakauer, Jon *Into the Wild*

Pullman, Philip *His Dark Materials* Trilogy

Shakur, Sanyika *Monster: The Autobiography of an L.A. Gang Member*

Wolff, Virginia Euwer *Make Lemonade*

Wolff, Virginia Euwer *True Believer*

ANNA ZANARINI, YOUTH SERVICES LIBRARIAN
SALT LAKE COUNTY LIBRARY SYSTEM,
SALT LAKE CITY, UTAH

Anderson, Laurie Halse *Speak*

Anonymous *Go Ask Alice*

[Sparks, Beatrice]

Bauer, Joan *Rules of the Road*

Card, Orson Scott *Ender's Game*

Cooney, Carolyn B. *The Face on the Milk Carton*

Cormier, Robert *The Chocolate War*

Crutcher, Chris *Staying Fat for Sarah Byrnes*

Cushman, Karen *Catherine, Called Birdy*

Duncan, Lois *I Know What You Did Last Summer*

Hinton, S. E. *The Outsiders*

Lowry, Lois *The Giver*

McKinley, Robin *Beauty*

Paulsen, Gary *Hatchet*

Pullman, Phillip *The Golden Compass*

Rowling, J. K. *Harry Potter and the Sorcerer's Stone*

Sachar, Louis *Holes*

Thomas, Rob *Rats Saw God*

White, Robb *Deathwatch*

Wolff, Virginia Euwer *True Believer*

A CONSENSUS

These books appeared on at least five lists from the preceding source.

Adams, Douglas *The Hitchhiker's Guide to the Galaxy*

Anderson, Laurie Halse *Speak*

Anonymous [Sparks, Beatrice] *Go Ask Alice*

Bauer, Joan *Rules of the Road*

Block, Francesca Lia *Weetzie Bat*

Blume, Judy *Forever*

Card, Orson Scott *Ender's Game*

Chbosky, Stephen *The Perks of Being a Wallflower*

Cooney, Caroline B. *The Face on the Milk Carton*

Cormier, Robert *After the First Death*

Cormier, Robert *The Chocolate War*

Crutcher, Chris *Staying Fat for Sarah Byrnes*

Cushman, Karen *Catherine, Called Birdy*

Garden, Nancy *Annie on My Mind*

Hinton, S. E. *The Outsiders*

Klause, Annette Curtis *Blood And Chocolate*

Lee, Harper *To Kill A Mockingbird*

Lowry, Lois *The Giver*

McKinley, Robin *Beauty*

Myers, Walter Dean *Fallen Angels*

Myers, Walter Dean *Monster*

Paulsen, Gary *Hatchet*

Pullman, Philip *His Dark Materials trilogy*

Rowling, J. K. *Harry Potter series*

Sacher, Louis *Roles*

Salinger, J. D. *The Catcher in the Rye*

Spiegelman, Art *Maus: A Survivor's Tale*
Spinelli, Jerry *Stargirl*
Thomas, Rob *Rats Saw God*
Wolff, Virginia Euwer *Make Lemonade*

CHOOSING FROM THE MAJOR YA GENRES

Creating the Science Fiction, Fantasy, and Graphic Novels Collection

A primary characteristic of genre fiction, one that renders it particularly appealing to young readers, is that it does not neglect *story*. Setting, character development, authorial voice, mood, imagery, thematic development, and philosophical speculation may (indeed often are) present, but they cannot, as in literary or mainstream fiction, supplant the plot. If there isn't a page-turning story, the audience (and the market) will go elsewhere. Nearly all of the science fiction and fantasy chosen for this core collection are corking good reads. Nonetheless, genre fiction also comes with a built-in barrier: the conventions and expectations of the form. Science fiction has a great many, from FTL (faster-than-light) travel and technical babble to alien civilizations. Fantasy is more flexible in what the readers expect and what the readers need already know in order to "get" the story; it's more accessible, and enjoys a wider readership. We've tried to note which titles have that "cross-over" appeal, and we've included a mixture of stories for both the novice and the sophisticated fan. For a more detailed discussion of the "genre ghetto" of science fiction and fantasy, Ursula Le Guin's "On Despising Genres" on her Web page at *http://www.ursulakleguin. com/OnDespising Genres.html* is a first-rate resource.

Science fiction and fantasy novels are unique, however, in that they cross age boundaries more than any other form of fiction. The same sophisticated teenager who devoured *The Lord of the Rings* or *The Mists of Avalon* will show up at your desk wanting "another book like *Ella Enchanted*." Quite a few of the core science fiction and fantasy titles bear some notation to the effect that teens from seventh grade through high school have enjoyed them. One caveat, however: teen readers have never been anything but young. Some books (and science fiction and fantasy novels are no exception) simply require some life—and reading—experience to appreciate, and our annotations reflect this.

In addition, science fiction and fantasy run to series fiction. The sort we're most familiar with is the long-running adventures of a particular cast of characters or a particular setting, like Sweet Valley High or Piers Anthony's Xanth novels; in which each book gives readers the same thing—only different. Barring the jaded tastes of adults who've educated themselves to crave novelty, there's nothing intrinsically flawed with this approach. Repetition and variation are hoary artistic traditions. For the librarian building a core collection for teens, any combination of titles from these series will work for her young customers. It's the *other sort* of series that will get her into trouble. While there do exist writers who carefully build their science fiction and fantasy series so that each novel stands alone, they're terribly rare. (Lois McMaster Bujold is one; she treats her Vorkosigan series as an artistic whole, so that while there are emergent themes, each novel can be read independently and in nearly any order.) Much, much more likely is the science fiction or fantasy series that is actually a *serialized* story. No librarian in her right mind would purchase just *The Two Towers*, but teen patrons have been known to find books 2, 3, and 4 of a seven-book story on their library shelves. Imagine opening a book and finding just the middle third, and you'll understand their consternation. In the core collection, you'll find several series of this type—excellent novels, spellbinding stories, true—but if your budget won't run to all three (or seven, or fourteen), don't purchase any. Or buy only Book 1, but expect to have an increase in your request for interlibrary loan services, if your teen readers like it!

The problems librarians can have with serialized fiction reach their nadir with graphic novels. Repeat the mantra with me: it's not a genre, it's a format! The genres contained within the format include literary fiction (from the now-famous Holocaust memoir *Maus* to the post-modern meditation *Jimmy Corrigan*), soap-operatic romance (*Strangers in Paradise*), teen angst (*The Tale of One Bad Rat, Ghost World*), science fiction, horror, and fantasy, all with nary a costumed superhero in sight. Imagine using one single approach for your video or book collection—regardless of content—and you'll perceive the problem. Under the rubric "graphic novel" this core collection includes every type of illustrated story, true graphic novels—which are usually, but not always serialized—as well as nonfiction and comic strip collections.

But just as your video or audio collection can pose challenges unique to their formats, so can graphic novels. The same series considerations outlined above arise with the epic science fiction adventure *Akira*. Buying only a part of the six-volume story is as cruel as purchasing half the chapters of Isaac Asimov's *Foundation*. On the other hand, each of the edgy *Barry Ween, Boy Genius* adventures (or individual *Far Side* comic book collections) can stand alone.

There are two particular challenges for librarians collecting manga, as Japanese comics are known: the content, and the covers. Like many of the manga brought to the United States, the bindings are execrable and the book *will* fall apart after two or three checkouts. When planning your purchases, therefore, prepare to get the approximately one-quarter more expensive library bound versions or pay to have it rebound right from the start. Many companies that service libraries, such as Book Wholesalers, have our core collection titles, and if they do not already come in library or "beewee" binding, they can be so bound for you on request. The content can also prove challenging, literally. If you venture beyond the core collection titles, purchase with care: Ryoichi Ikegami, the justly world-renowned artist of *Mai, the Psychic Girl*, has also illustrated the interesting and equally well-drawn *Crying*

Freeman, much of which would also qualify as soft-core porn. If you aren't familiar with the medium, surf the Web for reviews and preview before you purchase. For a more detailed discussion on the nature and history of Japanese comics, read *Manga! Manga! The World of Japanese Comics* by Frederik L. Schodt (Kodansha International, 1996). KE

Creating the Young Adult Fiction and Nonfiction Collection

The purpose of any collection is to fulfill the wants and needs of a library's users. While every librarian may have different viewpoints on how to go about this mission, the customer is (or should always be) the bottom line. The challenge in serving young adults, of course, is that those wants and needs are huge, varied, and changing. Developing any collection for young adults is like trying to hit a moving target. The titles selected here from the genre known as young adult literature represent books that do the best job of hitting that moving target. They have passed the test of time, represent important authors or trends, and most have the "right stuff" in terms of the quality of writing and the accessibility of the book. Can a book be great if no one reads it? Can a book be great if no one wants to read it again, having forgotten it five minutes after finishing it? The titles I've selected serve both the masters of quality and popularity.

In nonfiction, the target is different. While there are certainly some timeless nonfiction books, there are even more timeless nonfiction subjects: parapsychology, self-help, Holocaust, etc. The nonfiction books here also serve two masters: they are good books that teens will want to read and read again, but they also represent the subject. While, the hip hop books listed here may go out of print, the interest in the subject won't disappear for some time. While books featuring teen writers or voices of teens might wither, those types of titles will not. The subject matter will bring teens to most of these books; the quality of the titles will bring them back to the library for more books.

While there are popular adult authors like Stephen King listed here, we've avoided the rest of the bestseller list: Steel, Clark, Grisham, et al. Those authors have young adult appeal and have their place, but fall beyond the scope of this work. We only want the best of the best for teen readers. Similar, there are plenty of juvenile novels here, for example, the works of authors like Roald Dahl or Gloria Naylor (Alice books), that walk a fine line. Our assumption is that teens are aspirational; for the most part, they wish to read books with characters a year or two older than they are.

If there is a common theme that runs through most of the "pure" young adult fiction and nonfiction listed here it is simply that it focuses on the job of being a teenager. The term "coming of age" appears again and again in the annotations for both fiction and nonfiction. These are books that by speaking to the most basic needs evoke emotional responses among teen readers through the year: core needs create a core collection. PJ

Creating the Classics and Adult Popular Fiction Collection

"If you like to read," I have told my students every year, "then you will never be lonely, and you will never be bored." Many of them (particularly in my class of reluctant readers) were not about to take my pontificating at face value, but almost all of them were willing to take on faith that I might be able to prove it to them. The primary responsibility of teaching, whether in the classroom, the living room, or the playroom, is the transmission of culture, and without literature that transmission is impossible. Here is my personal philosophy: Books are my life. Because they are and have been since I learned to read, my greatest joy has been sharing my exploration of them with others. Language is accessible to everyone, period. Anyone can learn a basic facility with reading if led with gentle reason. Too many people emerge from schools today hating to read because they never discovered that reading is a profoundly personal endeavor. To suppose that finishing a book is a Sisyphean kind of task meant only to garner a passing grade in an English class is to short-circuit the rest of life. I've often thought librarians were the luckiest of souls: ideally, yours is the task of coaxing your patrons into bibliophilic lands unknown. In a culture increasingly dependent on technology, schools and libraries may be the last bastion of the "gentle madness" that is the pursuit of books.

At the conclusion of *Paradise Lost,* Milton observes of Adam and Eve: "and all the world was before them." When a human being is given the gift of literacy, the world is, indeed, all before him. There is no place he cannot travel, no person he cannot meet, no thought he cannot debate; no boundaries rise against him. A successful writer who was once queried as to where he got his information for his novels that were so enormous in scope and character replied, "I get all my ideas from the *New York Times.*" He didn't travel, you see, any farther than the subscription list, and yet he knew the world as if his passport were bulging with customs stamps.

Reading should not be a test of endurance. It should be the key to the prison door, the passage to freedom, the stairway to intellectual heaven. Perhaps this all sounds dreadfully idealistic. I can only say that years after I left the classroom, I'm still receiving correspondence from former students, often in the form of this command: "Have you read . . .? Well, go and get it! I insist!"

Of course, I always do. PT

INDEXES

AUTHOR INDEX

Title	Author	Page
Where the Wild Things Are	Sendack, Maurice	313
Where Wizards Stay Up Late	Hafner, Katie	2
Whirligig	Fleischman, Paul	150
Whispers from the Dead	Nixon, Joan Lowery	218
Whistle Me Home	Wersba, Barbara	281
White Boy Shuffle	Beatty, Paul	104
White Fang	London, Jack	196
White Horse	Grant, Cynthia D.	156
White Lilacs	Meyer, Carolyn	208
White Romance	Hamilton, Virginia	161
Who Do You Think You Are?	Shaw, Tucker	9
Who Killed Mr. Chippendale?	Glenn, Mel	68
Who Killed My Daughter?	Duncan, Lois	30
Wild Nights	Matthews, Anne	37
Wild Seed	Butler, Octavia E.	115
Wildest Ride	Menzer, Joe	58
Wings of a Falcon	Voigt, Cynthia	278
Wise Child	Furlong, Monica	151
Witch Child	Rees, Celia	242
Within Reach: My Everest Story	Pfetzer, Mark	59
Witness	Hesse, Karen	165
Wizard of Earthsea	Le Guin, Ursula K.	191
Wolf by the Ears	Rinaldi, Ann	244
Wolf Rider: A Tale of Terror	Avi	102
Wolf Woman	Jordan, Sherryl	177
Woman in the Mists	Mowat, Farley	82
Women of Hope	Hansen, Joyce Carol	79
Woman Who Loved Reindeer	Pierce, Meredith Ann	229
Wonder	Vail, Rachel	272
Wonder Woman: The Complete History	Daniels, Les	298
Wonder Woman: Spirit of Truth	Ross, Alex	311
Woodsong	Paulsen, Gary	59
Words by Heart	Sebestyen, Ouida	250
Words of Martin Luther King, Jr.	King, Coretta Scott	19
World According to Garp	Irving, John	172
Worst Case Scenario Survival Handbook	Piven, Joshua	28
Wreckers	Lawrence, Iain	190
Wrestling Sturbridge	Wallace, Rich	279
Wretched Stone	Van Allsburg, Chris	318
Wrinkle in Time	L'Engle, Madeleine	193
Wuthering Heights	Brontë, Emily	111
Year Down Yonder	Peck, Richard	226
Year Without Michael	Pfeffer, Susan	227
YELL-Oh Girls	Nam, Vickie	64
Yoga for Teens	Luby, Thia	42
You Don't Know Me	Klass, David	184
You Hear Me: Poems and Writing Boys	Franco, Betsy	62
You Remind Me of You	Corrigan, Eireann	44
Young Person's Guide to Philosophy	Weate, Jeremy	4
Youth in Revolt	Payne, C. D.	226
Z for Zachariah	O' Brien, Robert	219
Zazoo	Mosher, Richard	202
Zen and the Art of Motorcycle Maintenance	Pirsig, Robert M.	10
Zine Scene	Block, Francesca Lia	3

ABOUT THE AUTHORS

Patrick Jones

Patrick Jones runs *Connectingya.com*, a firm dedicated to consulting, training, and coaching for providing powerful youth services including library card campaigns and web projects. He authored for the Young Adult Library Services Association the publication *New Directions in Library Services to Young Adults* (ALA Edition, 2002). In January 2002, he published for Neal-Schuman the books *Running A Library Card Campaign Connecting Young Adults and Libraries: A How To Do It Manual, Do It Right: Customer Service for Young Adults in School and Public Libraries* (co-written with school librarian Joel Shoemaker). Two editions of *Connecting Young Adults and Libraries: A How To Do It Manual,* the first in 1992, the second in 1998, have been successful Neal-Schuman releases as well. Jones also published in 1998 the first volume in the Scarecrow Press Young Adult series called *What's So Scary About R.L. Stine.* For more information, contact him at patrick@connectingya.com.

Patricia Taylor

Patricia Taylor has been an editor, writer, and teacher most of her life. Twenty years in a high school classroom have given way to her present incarnation as full time writer and educational consultant. Beginning in 2003, she will be conducting seminars across the country on teaching the reluctant reader for the Bureau of Educational Research. In 1990, she was selected as a Top Ten Teacher in the State of Texas by the University of Texas and in 1995 was named Humanities Teacher of the Year by the Texas Endowment for the Humanities. For more information, contact Patricia via e-mail at ptaylor2@mail.airmail.net.

Kirsten Edwards

Kirsten Edwards is a librarian for young adults at the King County Library System in Duvall, Washington, and a member of the Washington Library Association. In 2001, she published her first book *Teen Library Events: A Month-by-Month Guide* for Greenwood Press. She is an avid reader of speculative fiction, a frequent contributor to the YALSA-BK listserv, and is currently finishing her first novel. For more information, contact her at carbonelle@juno.com.